# FIREWORKS AT DUSK

# OLIVIER BERNIER

# FIREWORKS AT DUSK

## PARIS IN THE THIRTIES

## LITTLE, BROWN AND COMPANY

Boston   New York   Toronto   London

FIRST EDITION

The author is grateful for permission to quote from the following:

*For the President: Correspondence between Franklin D. Roosevelt and William C. Bullitt* by Orville H. Bullitt. Copyright © 1972 by Orville H. Bullitt. Reprinted by permission of Houghton Mifflin Co. All rights reserved.

All material by Janet Flanner originally published by or in *The New Yorker,* including that reproduced in *Paris Was Yesterday* (Harcourt Brace Jovanovich), by permission of Natalia Danesi Murray.

LIBRARY OF CONGRESS CATALOGING-IN-PUBLICATION DATA

Bernier, Olivier.
    Fireworks at dusk: Paris in the Thirties / Olivier Bernier.
      p.  cm.
    Includes bibliographical references.
    ISBN: 0-316-09275-4
    1. Paris (France — Intellectual life — 20th century.
    2. Celebrities — France — Paris — History — 20th century.  3. Arts and society — France — Paris — History — 20th century.  4. Civilization, Modern — French influences.  I. Title.
    DC715.B328  1993
    944'.360815 — dc20           92-26653

10  9  8  7  6  5  4  3  2

MV-NY

Design by Barbara Werden

Published simultaneously in Canada by Little, Brown & Company (Canada) Limited

PRINTED IN THE UNITED STATES OF AMERICA

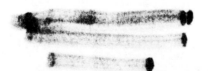

FOR FREDRICA S. FRIEDMAN
*whose insight, constant concern, and wise suggestions
have made an essential contribution
to this book.*


*The author wishes to express, yet again, his gratitude
to the New York Public Library and to its
unfailingly competent and helpful librarians.*

# CONTENTS

# FIREWORKS AT DUSK

# PROLOGUE

VIRTUE, the French agreed in January 1930, had been rewarded: once again, their country was the leading power in Europe. Its economy prospered and the franc, backed by vast gold reserves, was the most solid currency anywhere. Peace, thanks to the successful efforts of Aristide Briand, the perennial foreign minister, was assured. Even the budget provided a sizable surplus. There was indeed reason to rejoice.

As for Paris, it was more glamorous than ever. Society, transformed by the war and the great whirl of the twenties, was mad for pleasure. It was the era of the costume ball, but also of the nightclub. Even that relatively new phenomenon, the automobile, offered a reason for lavish display: every summer, in the Bois de Boulogne, the *concours d'élégance automobile* gathered the best-dressed women and the most dashing autos (many of them with custom coachwork) in a series of great, open-air parties.

More remarkably, perhaps, society and the arts seemed to be communicating again. The comte and comtesse Etienne de Beaumont, the vicomte and vicomtesse Charles de Noailles, among others, brought together great names, great fortunes, and some of the leading talents. The Noailles subsidized Luis Buñuel's first films; the Beaumonts were friends of Picasso and sponsored first-rate concerts; Jean Cocteau provided an ever-scintillating bridge between the different Parisian worlds; and it was clear to all that Paris, always brilliant, was once again the center of the world.

Indeed, it now offered a thrilling blend of tradition and novelty. At the Beaumonts' eighteenth-century house on the Left Bank, for instance, the balls took place in an enfilade of salons where the white and gold *boiseries* had been in place for nearly two hundred years and where precious antiques abounded. As for the guests, many of them bore the noblest names in France; ancestral diamonds and historic jewels sparkled; many guests still owned great country castles and imposing mansions in town. At the same time, the dresses came from the most fashionable couture houses; the themes of the costume balls were bold, innovative, often daring; Picasso himself, on occasion, designed part of the decor; and gossip reigned supreme in these heady meetings of society and the arts.

Of course, great parties do not necessarily go together with first-rate artistic achievement; but there was more. Although they might not go to balls, Joan Miró, Max Ernst, Yves Tanguy, were all painting masterpieces, as indeed were Picasso, Georges Braques, Henri Matisse, Fernand Léger, and a substantial number of others. Constantin Brancusi was carving, with infinite care, those eloquent forms that, featureless, were more meaningful than the most detailed work. Now, as ever, Paris was where you must come if you wanted to see the new painting, and so fledgling artists and enlightened collectors flocked to the city.

Nor was it just the visual arts. The theater thrived, and Jean Giraudoux, the wittiest, boldest playwright of the age, could be counted on to enliven the season every other year. The Opéra was having one of its great moments; divas and instrumentalists sang and played and made the city a great musical capital. As for literature, aside from a most promising group of younger novelists, among whom, opposing stars, Louis-Ferdinand Céline and André Malraux shone most dazzlingly, there was the great arbiter: André Gide, the man who made reputations and defined taste. Never since, seldom before, has a single man been so important in setting the tone of an era. Gide decided what was worthwhile and what was not, what true morality demanded, which feelings could be indulged. He traveled, and the world made sense; he read, and everyone else followed his preference.

Naturally, there was also the other Paris, the Paris of those who just wanted to have a good time, sitting in a café, eating wonderful food, and, most especially, going to one of the music halls for which the city was famous. Great stars brought in the crowds — Josephine Baker, black, sexy, and wonderfully funny; Maurice Chevalier, who made a career of talking his songs; Mistinguett, whose voice was flat, whose dancing was uninspired, but whose earthy appeal, comic and yet sexy, was such that mobs waited for her every night outside the theater. There were also legions of "girls" (often American) whose costumes — ostrich-plume helmets and skirts — made up in dazzle what they lacked in coverage. And finally, for those so inclined, the city's brothels specialized in the exotic: Persian rooms, African rooms, Chinese rooms, medieval rooms, added a touch of remoteness, a hint of the unexpected to the more usual pleasures offered by their employees. There was, in fact, something for everyone: the tall white plumes of the horse chestnuts in bloom, the view of Notre Dame, or the very latest fashion in everything. Dunand, Frank, and half a dozen others designed stark, geometric interiors where the simplicity of line went with the use of the most sumptuous materials — precious woods, ivory, lacquer, sharkskin, shagreen, parchment. And their new look naturally provided the perfect background for that continued proof that French taste reigned supreme, the latest fashion by the boldest designer. All over the world and nowhere more than in the United States, women wore what Paris told them to wear. Chanel, Mainbocher, Molyneux, Vionnet, Worth, and a dozen other houses defined elegance — but none as vividly or inventively as Schiaparelli. Waistlines (rising) and hemlines (dropping), dresses for a morning walk, a formal afternoon, one of the many chic days at the races, or an intimate dance: the couturiers offered it all. There were famous hatmakers, too, whose work completed that of the couture. And the great jewelers, Cartier, van Cleef, Boucheron, made their new, geometric Art Deco gems a necessity: baguette diamonds, square or round rubies, or sapphires (the darker the better) were set in abstract compositions that reminded everyone that the new elegance was supremely modern, supremely tough.

Still, you did not have to be a millionaire to come to Paris. You could, of course, spend a fortune if you chose; but you could also live on almost nothing. There were cheap rooms to be had (without running water) and cheap meals and even cheap theater seats; and so young people came from all over Europe and the Americas, fascinated by the city's reputation, at home once they got there. Paris, for countless American students living on tiny scholarships, was still the latest version of heaven, a place where they could learn and have fun at the same time; and although they did not make the social columns, they added a liveliness, an eagerness that could be felt everywhere they went.

PARIS SHONE; but even so, there were some dark shadows. The war had killed off very nearly a whole generation of young men, so something vital was missing. The daily photographs of government ministers showed it clearly; so many — from Adolphe Chéron, the perennial finance minister, to President Doumergue; from André Tardieu, the brilliant conservative leader, to that greatly admired war minister, André Maginot — seemed to be old men. Across the border Germany, disarmed but resentful, had a population double that of France; it was not likely to accept its subordination forever; and, economically, the growing crisis that had followed the Wall Street crash was bound, eventually, to reach France as well. Even the two wartime allies, the United States and Great Britain, now seemed barely friendly, the first turning firmly away from Europe, the other apparently in love with Germany. Clearly, the future would not be easy.

The French knew it, though, and had, they thought, provided for all future difficulties. Not only had Briand, the almost perennial foreign minister, effected a reconciliation with Germany, there was the chain of treaties that bound her neighbors, Romania, Czechoslovakia, Poland, to France. To the French army and population, theirs could be added; and in case, by some dreadful stroke of fate, it all went wrong, there was the new line of fortresses devised by Maginot that was being built and would soon make the French border impregnable. Vast sums were even then being spent on these massive buried defenses, but no one begrudged them. Never again would France face years of slaughter.

Even that most sensitive index, the franc, showed nothing but continued success. After its collapse in the early twenties, it had been stabilized in 1925 and was now the soundest currency in the world. There would be no more inflation.

Problems, therefore, were not just foreseen but actually solved in advance. As for prosperity, it could only keep growing. France had produced more in 1929 than ever before in its history. Unaffected, so far, by the Wall Street crash, largely relying on its own resources, it could look forward to continued growth. Indeed, the rest of Europe looked on with increasing jealousy. And yet, there was, inchoate and undefined, a feeling of unease: in some way, France did not understand the modern world or feel comfortable in it. The shape of the new Europe, in which that ally, Imperial Russia, had been replaced by the menacing and enigmatic Soviet Union, seemed somehow wrong. The new technologies, aviation, the tank, the spread of motorized traffic, all speeded up life; and many of the French did not like it.

That was all in 1930. Five years later, this peculiar, alien world had caught up with France. Political instability and an attempted coup, drastic economic decline coupled, as usual, with massive unemployment, the rise across the Rhine of a revanchist Nazi Germany, all combined to make the French realize that, bad as things were, they were likely to get far worse.

By 1935, in fact, it was becoming clear that there really was no such thing as France. Instead, the disunited French, class against class, party against party, one half of the nation loathing the other, seemed well on their way to civil war. Impotent governments, whose meager notions of economics would have seemed old-fashioned even in 1914, utterly failed to cope with the Depression, and kept collapsing in consequence. The working class, partly unemployed, partly exploited, felt burning (and deserved) hatred for these governments and for the great industrialists. Fascists and Communists fought in the streets. War in a few years was becoming increasingly probable, while the alliance with the Central European countries looked more and more like a liability.

Even worse, no one could understand why all this was happening, or what had caused this vast and prolonged crisis. There had been economic downturns before, but now the Depression, feeding on itself, grew worse year by year until it looked as if virtually everyone would be out of a job. As it was, the streets were filling with the unemployed and homeless; and, of course, the less they consumed, the weaker the demand, and the more anemic the economy. Men of intelligence and goodwill were utterly puzzled: everything they tried turned out to be useless or, on occasion, actually harmful; and so the component parts of the nation shrank in upon themselves. Workers distrusted peasants, the middle class feared everyone and despised the governments, which, in any event, kept falling. Only Paris society, apparently unperturbed, continued to have fun. Some of the most brilliant balls of the decade were given in 1935.

For the rest of the French, the world appeared to have gone mad. People were hungry in the midst of vast agricultural surpluses; a nation in desperate need of modernizing seemed unable to find outlets for its industrial production. Even the budget defied reason: successive finance ministers zealously cut expenditures, but the deficit kept ballooning.

Statesmen whose best efforts were utter failures, theoreticians whose theories kept being disproved, economists who saw with horror the economy behave in ways they had been taught were impossible, all looked about them in anguish, while the people, whom they were supposed to lead, blamed all impartially. Alienation was the keynote: alienation from the state, alienation from one another, alienation from the traditional parties and solutions. The French were living in a world they did not understand, could not improve, and most fervently disliked.

Alienation, in fact, was the one feeling that was shared by everyone alike — foreign journalists now found the once vivacious French sullen and hostile — but that common response hardly led to greater unity. Instead, hatred became the keynote: hatred within the country for those who disagreed with you, hatred in international relations as Mussolini invaded Abyssinia and Hitler rearmed. In 1930 the French felt that their immense effort of 1914–1918, the sacrifice of all those young lives, had not been in vain; at least, the country was more united, richer, happier than ever before. Five years later, it seemed clear that the effort and sacrifice had been useless. It did not make for pleasant thoughts.

If the French, in their vast majority, failed to understand, failed to adapt, there was one group at least whose members could, in their own way, make sense of it all. People felt alienated, and artists expressed fear and rage in their work. When, in 1937, Picasso painted *Guernica,* he gave the world an eloquent, moving, and definitive statement on the horrors of war and fascism; but even before that, artists like Ernst and Miró had begun to depict a mad, terrifying world in which misshapen creatures dominated, where vast, empty landscapes appeared to reflect some nameless, definitive disaster. To look at the art of the thirties is to understand the anguish of the decade.

Even Giraudoux, that civilized and sophisticated writer, the enemy of all bombast, gave the clearest of warnings. The play he wrote in 1935 was performed with immense success; but its message could not have been grimmer. *La Guerre de Troie n'aura pas lieu* (The Trojan War Will Not Happen) was a frequently funny reconstruction of the moments that led to the Greek capture of Troy and its subsequent annihilation. Its message was perfectly clear: although most of the men in power tried to avoid the war, there was no stopping it. Certainly, no one in France wanted to fight; the massacres of 1914–1918 were still much too fresh; but conflict was beginning to seem as unavoidable, as uncontrollable, as the Depression. Frequently, as they saw the play, the audiences laughed because the Greeks and the Trojans were as witty as Giraudoux himself. The characters who spoke so well were sensible, too: they realized that actual war would be catastrophic, but try as they might, they could not stop it. And so, although the spectators laughed throughout the evening, when they left they looked serious.

In this world gone bad, where men of goodwill apparently made no difference, there was very little left to do except enjoy the moment; and that is just what much of Paris decided to do. One brilliant season succeeded another. Books by Gide, Malraux, Céline, plays by Cocteau and Giraudoux, paintings of extraordinary quality by Picasso, Matisse, Braque, Léger, Miró, Ernst, came pouring out; fashion changed faster and became more luxurious than at any time in memory — Schiaparelli had at least four collections a year and used the most sumptuous fabrics; parties multiplied and scintillated. As the situation grew ever more alarming, Paris society became ever more determined to amuse itself, artists produced works of extraordinary merit in greater numbers, and French culture in all its varied and often opposed segments reaffirmed a primacy greater than at any time since the Age of Reason.

At the same time, however, the economy collapsed, together with France's system of alliances. When Germany was producing six hundred war planes a year, France made a bare dozen; factories aged, machinery became antiquated, so that the newer techniques, although they were known, could not be applied. As for the allies, England turned cold and almost hostile, Central Europe looked more and more to Germany, and it was obvious to all that France was in no position to help Czechoslovakia, Poland, Yugoslavia, and Romania or, indeed, to be helped by them.

Year by year, as Hitler and Mussolini's bombast became more menacing, war came visibly, unavoidably, closer, and although the governments of the decade kept claiming that, should the fight really begin, France must win, no one really believed them. The Great War had not only taught the French that no one could win a modern war: it made them deeply reluctant ever again to endure that kind of slaughter. Besides, every one understood that the next time would be worse than the last: to the horrors of the trenches and poison gas, aerial bombing would now be added. The Parisians expected their city to be destroyed within the very first days of the new war; and what was the point of winning if all you had left was a ruined land?

In 1939, the war came. In 1940, France collapsed before the Nazi onslaught: it had taken just ten years for the leading country in Europe to become a helpless victim. Of course, people had seen it coming; the rage for modernity that characterized the beginning of the decade soon gave way to a headlong retreat into the past and a terrified hope that the future would never come.

Still, there was no avoiding the fact that across the borders new and horrifying regimes were creating a new politics and a kind of anticulture. The French knew that worse was to come, that their civilization could not last as it was. Time was short; the crisis was permanent; all the more reason to make the most of the moment. As it contemplated its own impending demise, one of the world's great cultures seemed, in a last burst of light, to flare brighter than ever, as if it had to give its very best before it disappeared. The day might be ending but it would end spectacularly: fireworks at dusk.

CHAPTER

# ONE

## THE CRISIS THAT WENT AWAY

PARIS in early March 1936 was a busy place. There was a whole series of balls; the new spring fashions required analysis and comments; a great exhibition of contemporary Spanish art opened at the Jeu de Paume, while across the Tuileries gardens the Orangerie offered a widely praised Corot show. There were new American films to be seen, Rachmaninoff gave a concert for charity, and the racing season was well under way. "Yesterday at Auteuil," *Le Figaro* reported, "the attendance was brilliant and numerous . . . and one especially noticed the luxury of the furs."[1]

Even if the forthcoming elections — they were to be held in late April — caused some apprehensions among the usually conservative members of *le Tout-Paris,* that amalgam of society, politics, and the arts, there was no reason why the great whirl should stop. As soon as the weather improved, the most elegant women in Paris would show off their new spring wardrobes. More plays, more films, more balls, were scheduled. Colette was publishing her memoirs, a great event since they were known to tell all about her relationship with that very odd character, her first husband.

Picasso that spring was showing everywhere: his sculpture at Zervos, his paintings at Paul Rosenberg's, and his latest drawings at the Galerie Renou et Colle, and those with eyes to see were startled to note that this often difficult artist was now celebrating the joys of motherhood with pale pinks and ochres. Indeed, it was hard to keep up with it all.

Most people, of course, were not part of this glamorous Paris life; but they were busy too, some desperately looking for a job, others trying to eke out livings on incomes reduced by government fiat, still others preparing for the great upheaval to come. All those who backed the anti-Fascist alliance of left-wing parties, the *Front populaire,* were hard at work preparing for the electoral campaign. And the government itself thought of little else: the result of yet another of the *parti Radical*'s * devious maneuvers. It owed its very existence to the coming elections. Its supposed leader, Albert Sarraut, was an amiable mediocrity with two great advantages: he was the brother of Maurice Sarraut, who owned an influential newspaper, *La Dépêche de Toulouse;* and he had never offended anyone. His presence at the head of the government allowed the Radicals to slide neatly away from their previous support of the Right and ensured that the party would do well in April.

Thus, when on the afternoon of March 7, Hitler's troops entered the hitherto demilitarized Rhineland, no one at all was prepared for it. The government, which had every reason to expect the move, found itself unable even to agree on what the French position should be, something that startled some of the ministers. After all, Germany had violated not just the Treaty of Versailles, which it had been forced to sign, but that of Locarno, in which it had been an eager participant, and France's position was therefore unassailable. As for the press, its reconversion was swift and complete: the great event made the headlines for a few days, but very quickly slid to the inside pages. As soon as it became clear that France would not send in its army, everyone breathed a sigh of relief. Some problems, apparently, were better not faced.

Soon, in any event, the legislative elections were the topic of the day. There were to be two rounds of voting. In the first, only those candidates who won more than 50 percent of the votes were elected; in the second round, which took place in all constituencies where this had not happened, the two leading contenders were pitted against each other. By

*The Radicals, in spite of their name, were a centrist party whose alliances took them to whichever side of the political spectrum was likely to ensure their presence in the government.

May 5, the results were clear: the Popular Front had won a tremendous victory, and that alone was enough to make people forget all about that unpleasant event barely two months earlier. The remilitarization of the Rhineland, it seemed, did not matter after all.

Seldom has a great event passed so fast into temporary oblivion. The earlier crises of French history — the great days of the Revolution, Napoleon's defeat at Waterloo, the beginning of the First World War — were greeted, in their time, as major events; but the move that led first to Munich, then to the fall of France, was happily forgotten within less than a month. Clearly, the French had better things to think about.

THE YEAR 1936 for Pablo Picasso was turning out remarkably well, and those drawings at Renou et Colle showed it clearly. Earlier in the thirties, there had been the terrifying portraits of Olga. The painter and his wife had widely differing tastes and ambitions, but she had been one of his great loves and the separation was slow (it was not final until 1935) and extremely painful, so much so that, for the only time in his life, he found himself unable to paint. But then there was the gentle and affectionate Marie-Thérèse Walter; she offered the painter what he had rarely had, a quiet comfort, and thrilled him by giving birth, early in 1936, to their daughter, Maya. It was no wonder that so many of those new drawings showed a mother tenderly cradling a child in her arms.

As so often happened throughout Picasso's long career, he was able to juggle styles and painted, within the same few months, in manners that appeared wildly different. There was nothing arbitrary about this: each manner expressed a mood, a state of being. Thus, at Rosenberg's, canvases painted in brilliant, cheerful colors, red, purple, green, yellow, showed rounded figures outlined by heavy black strokes, and the subjects were young women sitting, reading, drawing, looking in a mirror. Here, the forms were as soft, harmonious, gentle, as the palette was bright; the canvases seemed suffused with light, the interiors safe and welcoming. Much the same was true of the drawings at Renou et Colle: Marie-Thérèse, cradling her newborn child in her arms, is the very image of all that is joyful, gentle, and kind.

It would have been most unlike Picasso to ignore reality or its violence, though. It is always a mistake to interpret any great artist's work too literally; as it transcends the mundane, it draws on many sources and hints at many possibilities. Whether the violence to be seen in Picasso's other paintings and drawings referred to the disturbed times, to the impulsions of his own unconscious or to that of the Zeitgeist does not matter; whatever the reason, some of his works were full of aggression and pain. Typically, he used a Spanish theme to express all this. His 1934 trip to Spain had reawakened his earlier interest in bullfighting; but as he showed it now, there was nothing glorious about it. The colors are still bright, but the figures are those of wounded, slashed, agonized animals, reduced to shrieking, angular forms that invade one another. Here, most eloquently, is suffering compressed in a small space.

The three exhibitions, with their conflicting styles, were an immense success. Of course, a Picasso opening was automatically a great Parisian event. Only the artist himself, with his usual contempt for convention and public opinion, was absent from the crowds that pressed into the galleries; but he could be relied on to see that his dealers, when they were allowed to sell his work, received the highest possible price for it.

Women were always important in Picasso's life. When Olga made him miserable, he painted that anguish; when Marie-Thérèse brought him happiness, he produced lyrically beautiful work; but many other things mattered to him as well. He had always believed in the existence of an artistic and intellectual community, a little group of talented and creative people: his early friendship with Guillaume Apollinaire was proof of that. Now another friendship was begun with another poet, Paul Eluard, and it mattered immensely.

Like Picasso, Eluard had just undergone a traumatic divorce; his Russian wife, Gala, had left him for Dalí and went on to become famous in the annals of greed. Far more important, however, he was the greatest of the Surrealist poets, a man whose deeply original yet lyrical and accessible verse meant a great deal to his new painter friend. As it was, Picasso had always been interested in Surrealism. He was too powerful a figure himself ever to belong to a school, but he had watched with interest and sympathy as writers and artists broke the bonds of convention and relied instead on the unconscious. The very violence of the movement — its members were given to disrupting the gentilities of the bourgeoisie and enjoyed creating a scandal — appealed to Picasso. The Surrealists' return to the unevolved within us, their taste for the cultures of so-called primitive civilizations such as the Eskimo and the black African, all that was very much a part of his own world; but with Eluard, there was also a close personal friendship.

If the painter loved poetry, the poet also loved art. Eluard was one of the great collectors of the age, and all on very little money. Max Ernst,

Miró, Dalí, were among his friends; he understood Picasso's work better, almost, than anyone; and so, the two men had much to talk about. As usual, when moved, Picasso drew: the first of the Eluard portraits is inscribed *ce soir, le 8 janvier xxxvi*. Soon there were portraits of Nusch, Eluard's beautiful new wife.

Naturally, the poet reciprocated. In May he dedicated a short but splendid poem to Picasso:

> *Bonne journée j'ai revu qui je n'oublie pas*
> *Qui je n'oublierai jamais*
> *Et des femmes fugaces dont les yeux*
> *Me faisaient une haie d'honneur . . .*
> *Bonne journée journée qui commença mélancolique*
> *Noire sous les arbres verts*
> *Mais qui soudain trempée d'aurore*
> *M'entra dans le coeur par surprise.*[2]
>
> (A great day I saw again one I do not forget / One I will never forget / And fleeting women whose eyes / Gave me an honor guard . . . / A great day a day that began, melancholy, / Black under the green trees / But that suddenly suffused with dawn / Found its way by surprise into my heart.)

That was true homage; but Eluard went further. That spring, he said that he was happy to live in this troubled century because he had met Picasso;[3] he accompanied the painter's retrospective to Barcelona (Picasso stayed at home) and made a speech on the radio in which he said, among other things: "I speak of that which helps me to live, of that which is good. . . . Picasso wants the truth."[4]

The retrospective was an immense success. Outside the microcosm of Parisian fashion, Picasso was, everywhere, coming to be seen as the greatest master of his age, something that cannot have displeased him but that, as usual, he refused to acknowledge. At the end of March, he secretly left Paris for the south of France; and when he returned, he began to work on prints to illustrate a new edition of Buffon's *Histoire naturelle*.

Picasso, whether there in person or not, was always one of the great attractions of Paris. Only a few collectors (and fewer dealers) were allowed actually to see him, but his work fascinated all those who cared about art; and, even more than Matisse, he was the most famous painter alive. Then as now, however, discriminating collectors and gallerygoers were relatively few. Most of the people who came to France or lived there firmly ignored galleries and museums alike. Almost universally, though, they cared about fashion, and in the thirties, it came from Paris, and Paris only.

Italy, now ruled by Mussolini, had nothing new to contribute. In Germany, the Nazis' attempts at creating a National Socialist fashion were a bad joke; London knew how to dress men, but its couturiers notoriously left much to be desired; and New York followed Paris. It was thus typical that *The New Yorker,* that sophisticated and still often disdainful magazine, should regularly publish a column on the latest Paris fashion. Early in February 1936, for instance, it brought its readers up to date: "Things you should know about: Robert Piguet's printed evening dresses of wool chiffon and his ruffled evening scarves . . . the evening slippers worn at Bruyère's opening of gold kid with toes that turn up at the tips. Paris shoe designers have been talking about them for a long time. Why haven't they appeared before?"[5] And by the end of the month, there was this frenzied note: "Today, we find ourselves in such a maelstrom of tunics, boleros, ruffled hems and Empire bosoms that we move about with a hand shading our eyes, hoping to find something reasonable."[6]

Perhaps *The New Yorker,* addressing as it did readers so geographically distant from the center of fashion, let itself slip more easily into hyperbole; but in Paris also, couture was a most serious business. To those who called it mere wasteful frivolity, there was a ready-made answer: thousands of cutters, sewers, embroiderers, glovemakers, shoemakers, hatters, and furriers were employed at their trades when, elsewhere in the country, the Depression had caused widespread joblessness. Wearing the latest dress, the newest hat, was not just becoming, it was positively charitable. That the workers in question were grossly underpaid, that they had neither medical insurance nor, after they retired, pensions, apparently did not matter.

There was another attraction to fashion: at a time when the world was coming apart, it offered reassurance on many levels. It distracted and amused those who could afford couture dresses and even those who merely read about them; it made France seem as if nothing much had changed, as if it still led the world, even if its factories were obsolete or closing. When the political system was collapsing, when it was becoming clear that France had lost her military supremacy, it was one field in which the French still came first. It offered, in a word, the illusion of normality.

As a result, it was a major topic, not only among the Tout-Paris but throughout the country and the press. *Le Figaro Illustré,* for instance, covered all the more important trends of modern life (there was an issue on flying, that new and daring way of traveling) and emphasized the arts, but it also offered regular accounts of the latest designs. In January 1936 it described in loving detail a Lanvin dress for a very young woman — a *robe de jeune fille* — made of "pink matte crepe, with a pink and gold belt, adorned at the neck and sleeves with a ruching lit up by a gold embroidery,"[7] while pointing out that the influence of the costumes worn in Giraudoux's play was clearly discernible in an Alix creation, "a narrow midnight blue crepe dress on which two scarves are draped [at the shoulders and waist]."[8]

Perhaps the relative calm of these texts owed something to the winter weather. When it came to spring, though, there was no restraining the chronicler: she offered a veritable ode to the new fabrics. "The materials for spring are light," she wrote. "Is that not their first duty? Of course, there is lightness and lightness, and that of today's woolens and silks seems worth our attention inasmuch as it foretells tomorrow's fashion: dresses which are draped, wrapped, tied, moving, and flying, which may require a vast yardage without becoming heavy. The fashion for the spring of 1936," she concluded with an almost audible sigh, "will witness the triumph of femininity," going on to marvel at "the amazing diversity of the spring hats."[9]

This was not a rare note. The same paper thereafter continued to describe fashion in the same lyrical tone. This time it was Vionnet's spring collection: "All the alliances of subtle colors, green and blue, orange and gray, violet and purple, rose and beige, are used in becoming incrustations on the bodices of dressy afternoon costumes, and the airy voiles of the dancing dresses reproduce with a unique dazzle the mixed hues of the flowers of our gardens. There are many scattered petals, spread-out motifs, and huge melting forms artistically enhanced by the vibrant note of a satin belt crossed on itself and tied under the breasts."[10]

All these splendid costumes predated the German advance into the Rhineland; but even when that was an accomplished fact, life went on exactly as before. The event itself did, for a while, cause a certain disturbance. For a short while — a very short while — the Parisians thought the French government might actually do the sensible thing, the courageous thing, and send its army to push the Nazis out.

"In search of news, everybody in Paris consumes the evening paper with dinner, has nightmares afterwards and wakes up to gobble another front page for breakfast," Janet Flanner (writing as "Genêt") noted in *The*

*New Yorker.* "The only special sight in Paris which could be honestly reported as unusual has been the dense, anxious crowds gathered around the newspaper kiosks, morning, noon and night, waiting for the three incoming regular editions. Three times a day all kiosks are raided; young men shout, the old kiosk women squeal, *sous* are tossed in a barrage, papers wave like white flags."[11] That, however, did not last long. Within a few days, the old women stopped squealing and the Parisians went back to their usual amusements. It was, after all, as lively a season as any in memory.

There were galas everywhere. Some were meant to launch a film: *Samson* was a justly forgotten adaptation of an equally forgettable play by Henry Bernstein, but there was also Chaplin's *Modern Times.* Others emphasized great cultural events. Janet Flanner, always up on the latest, reported in May:

> The Opéra's galas started with Richard Strauss coming from Vienna to conduct *Le Chevalier à la Rose* in French and will include Furtwängler leading *Die Meistersinger* with a German cast; Bruno Walter conducting *Don Giovanni* with the American-born Dusolina Giannini and an Italian cast; and German singers in Beethoven's *Fidelio.* Melchior, of the Metropolitan, will sing here with the Opéra's Mme Germaine Lubin, both in German in *Tristan and Isolde.* . . . We must also mention the Opéra's premiere of the ballet *Harnasie* by Karol Szymanovsky, which made a gala evening, with the Polish colony and the diplomatic corps all out in grand tra-la-la.[12]

These, at least, were cultural events; but the more frivolous amusements of the season continued undisturbed. At the Opéra, there was the ball given to honor the Ecole Polytechnique, one of the French elite graduate schools, attended, *L'Illustration* noted, by "a brilliant crowd where you could see dazzling uniforms and exquisite dresses. At eleven, the President and Mme Albert Lebrun arrived."[13] That was followed by the Navy Ball, then by the Air Force Ball; the armed forces, in fact, seemed more intent on dancing than on preparing to resist German aggression. A little later, there was a *Nuit Romantique* at the Moulin de la Galette, where you were supposed to come in nineteenth-century costume, but many people showed up in exotic attire and there was even a daring young woman who came wearing a tuxedo (with, however, a skirt instead of trousers). And as usual there were spectacular benefits that undoubtedly raised funds for a variety of good causes but in fact seemed specially designed to amuse the Tout-Paris.

Thus, if you belonged to the right circles, you could have gone to the Bal du Grand Prix, which raised money for the improvement of horse breeding. It took place at the Opéra, which was specially closed for the occasion, and was organized by the princesse Murat. "The success was thorough and thorough was the discrimination which presided over the invitations and protected the true elegance of this fete, which marked the end of the Paris season," a society memorialist noted.[14]

There were other events attended only by the select few: the reception of a new member of the Académie française was traditionally among these, and it was never truer than for the entry of Claude Farrère into that body in early May. A mediocre novelist and worse travel writer, Farrère owed his election to his right-wing views, and there was a large section of Paris society eager to applaud the occasion.

That was glamorous enough; but even then it did not approach the two great private balls given that year — both for charity, naturally, even if the charities in question were rather obscure — the Bal Velázquez and the Bal des Valses. Both were eagerly awaited; both caused anguish among those who were not sure they would be invited (but what a thrill when that big envelope appeared!), and tooth-gnashing among those who were, in spite of much intriguing, left out.

The first of these great occasions, the Bal Velázquez, required all participants to dress as if they belonged in one of the master's paintings; the costumes were designed by Worth. For a night, Philip IV and his court sprang back to life, and even if the Infantas were a little too numerous, that perhaps made up for the shortage of dwarfs. But the Bal des Valses was even more brilliant. Given by the prince and princesse (Baba to her friends) de Faucigny-Lucinge, it was generally agreed to have been nothing short of triumphant. "In a vast private house on the avenue Marceau," *L'Illustration* reported, "so brilliantly decorated that luxury becomes actual elegance, the princesse de Faucigny-Lucinge received the Tout-Paris at the ball organized to benefit 'So That the Mind Lives On' [a charity that helped foreign intellectuals]. Those present went, in a series of contrasts, from the grand salon, where Gainsborough's portraits smile on the walls, to the dining room, where the crystal drops of modern sconces cascade down. It was all a charming and unexpected setting for the romantic spectacle given by the entrance of twenty specially costumed couples."[15] For those not fortunate enough to be present, however, the costumes worn by some of the dancers might have looked very like contempt for the poor. In a country racked by the Depression, where bankruptcies multiplied and many lived lives of extreme difficulty, the theme chosen to open the ball was a Waltz of the Millions, danced by a couple dressed in banknotes and gold coins. That the couple in question — the baron and baronne de Perregaux — should have been descended from eighteenth-century Geneva bankers was perhaps appropriate.

There were, however, other occasions for the Tout-Paris to meet under slightly less ostentatious circumstances. On the afternoon of March 7, the very day the German troops marched into the Rhineland, for instance, there was a "particularly brilliant meeting of the Friends of French Books at the house of the duchesse de Broglie during which the duc de Lévis-Mirepoix gave a lecture on 'French fairies in Andersen's country.'"[16] Sometimes, of course, the pretext was music: on the fifteenth came the last of a series of bimonthly concerts given by Mme Henry Gouin in her music room and attended by such luminaries of society as the duchesse d'Ayen, the duc and duchesse de Maillé, the duc de Gramont, the duc de Guiche, and the comte Etienne de Beaumont, whose own concerts were famous.

Of course, you could hear music without being invited to so recherché a gathering. In March alone, you had the choice of Rachmaninoff, Adolf Busch, Rudolf Serkin, and Fritz Kreisler, a stellar constellation, which, however, surprised no one; Paris in 1936 was still one of the world's great musical centers, so much so that one of the important new operas of the decade, Enesco's *Oedipe,* had its premiere there. And there were the visual arts.

The Corot exhibition, for instance, proved to be the revelation of an artist who had been considered slightly second-rate until then, in part because there were so many fakes around; now he was seen to be a very great master. "There is no other example of an art so simple yet so complete, so close to nature, classical and innovative at the same time, audacious because it is true and so subtly right," *L'Illustration*'s art critic noted.[17] In fact, now that Corot's work could be seen properly, without fakes, and in quantities sufficient to give a fair idea of his achievement, the artist's delicate poetry and subtle color seduced everyone. His silvery greens lightened by the flash of a river, the slowly drifting clouds across a pale blue sky, with, below, a bank of lacy trees, all that defined an entrancing and magic world.

Naturally, in a city that prided itself with reason on being a great literary center, books were important as well. There was a new novel by François Mauriac, *Les Anges Noirs,* in which that often acid writer offered his usual brew of hating families, torn consciences, and social observation; but the focus that March was on Colette's new book. "*Mes Apprentissages* are the Parisian reader's latest 'must,'" Janet Flanner recorded. "[They] are easy to peruse, are hard on her husband Willy, and, for vocabulary and evocation, are one of her best performances."[18] André Gide, that taste setter, was away from Paris, but he read the book and agreed, noting in his journal: "Here, there is more than talent, a sort of very particularly feminine genius and the greatest intelligence. What choice, what arrangement, what happy proportions, in a story so apparently spontaneous! What perfect tact, what courteous discretion and what openness. . . . Not a word whose effect fails, written . . . as if in play but with a thorough and subtle art."[19] Colette must have been pleased; Gide's journal, far from being private, was regularly published in the *Nouvelle Revue Française*.

*Mes Apprentissages,* in fact, is a delicious and often titillating series of confidences. As a very young woman, Colette had married M. Willy, a professional litterateur and man-about-town who rapidly discovered his young wife had the talent he lacked. The result was a series of books, the Claudines, in which the naive, provincial heroine discovered the complexities of life and the even more stimulating pleasures of sex. Through Willy, Colette was introduced to a variety of milieus — literary, journalistic, theatrical — and even to the fringes of society. Her evocation of that long-gone prewar world combined spice and nostalgia in just the right amounts; and there was always the author's wicked sense of humor. Here, for instance is how she describes life with her constantly unfaithful husband at a point when the Claudines were already a huge success.

> My husband had then realized what I could produce, and it was he . . . who saw to it that I had a solid writing table, a lamp with a green shade, all the comforts of a scribe. To reach my narrow domain, I had to walk across the living room. . . . One day, I found M. Willy there with an unknown lady very close to him. With the ease that comes from habit, and a sense of humor which, as an irreplaceable employee, I felt free to indulge, I stopped for just a moment and whispered to M. Willy, in an urgent tone: "Quick, quick, the next one has been waiting for fifteen minutes!"[20]

The success enjoyed by Colette when *Mes Apprentissages* came out was thoroughly deserved; the book was fresh, funny, and beautifully written, but it also owed something to the period it described. The twenties had thoroughly rejected the Belle Epoque, the era between 1900 and the war;

by the mid-thirties, it began to glow in memory as a period of solid prosperity, of calm and unmenacing politics; and Colette's stories had the added attraction of bringing part of that world back to life. Thus, it seemed particularly appropriate when the writer, who, as a woman, could not belong to the Académie française, was received on April 4 into the more open-minded Académie de Belgique.

This yearning for a different — past or imaginary — world also goes a long way to explain the success of another, much more difficult book. Julien Green, although his work is unquestionably first-rate, preferred a carefully contrived distance to Colette's easy humor. His characters and their complicated feelings seemed to live in a realm remote from ordinary life; here, the semiconscious is what matters. This was true of his new novel, *Minuit,* which was, *Le Figaro* explained, "really the outline of a dream where all actions answer to a logic of the absurd, where keys turn by themselves within the locks, where doors open on rooms without floors that turn into abysses," before going on to call it a masterpiece.[21] *Le Figaro* was right about that: in the strange family whose doings are chronicled by Green, the main character lives only at night, and it is hard to tell just who is who; betrayer and betrayed are as one; the generations merge until finally we feel we are reading less about separate characters than, perhaps, about the different elements of one person's unconscious.

There were other ways to use the past for reassurance as well. The battle of Verdun had been fought just twenty years before, and its anniversary was celebrated by official ceremonies and a spate of mediocre but highly praised books. Here, too, the lesson was obvious: the Germans, in 1916, had failed to take Verdun. If someday there was another war, they would fare no better. It was unfortunately typical that even this slightly artificial outburst of patriotism should celebrate so passive an achievement: the Germans, it is true, had been stopped, but they, at least, had been on the offensive.

Other achievements were being celebrated as well. France, everyone agreed, remained the center of civilization, a notion that could not be sufficiently emphasized. The Germans might be rearming, but the French carried high the torch of culture; and thus great attention was paid to a new play by Jules Supervielle, a playwright and author given to the kind of forced fantasy that does not age well. His *Bolivar,* a historical (but grossly inaccurate) play about the South American hero, was immensely successful, and so was the incidental music by Darius Milhaud, which combined Latin rhythms and a touch of jazz.

No doubt articles celebrating French technology were even more reassuring. Much was made, for instance, of the new decor of the *Lieuten-ant de Vaisseau Paris,* the world's largest seaplane. Here might and culture could be happily combined: there was a main salon with red lacquered walls and a great sculpted plaque depicting flight, eight cabins with two beds each, and even proper bathrooms. Considering that the *Hindenburg* had just been making its much-advertised Atlantic crossings, this news seemed especially satisfying; and, of course, no one knew that the plane was so poorly designed that it would capsize within the year.

A plane was impressive; but so were the monuments being built in Paris. In February the public got its first look at the plans for the vast new buildings to rise between the Trocadéro and the Seine. Then there was Auguste Perret's latest masterpiece, the new Garde-meuble. This build-ing, in which all the furniture belonging to the state was to be stored — everything from eighteenth-century masterpieces to thousands of little gilt party chairs — was nothing if not sober. Built on three sides of a rectangular courtyard closed by a semicircular colonnade, it used both prestressed concrete and stone on the facade. All was strict, geometrical, and more than a little dour, with plain, unadorned windows and a heavy cornice; but, although rather bleak, it was widely considered a triumph of modern architecture.

There was more. Cézanne in his lifetime had been firmly ignored by his compatriots who waited until he had long been dead before they con-descended to discover his work. As a result, there were virtually no Cé-zannes in French museums, so when a major exhibition of the artist opened in June, it attracted great crowds, as did the Greek sculpture gal-leries of the Louvre, newly renovated and electrically lit during the eve-ning opening hours.

This, it was felt, was bold and successful; but then, was not decor a French specialty? Any doubt about that was promptly dispelled by a look at the more glossy magazines that published month after month the most elegant new interiors. Molyneux, the great couturier, was naturally at the very forefront of this group of enlightened patrons. Art Deco, which had appeared in the early twenties and been confirmed at the 1925 Exhibition of Decorative Arts, was still the reigning style. It relied on sleek geometric forms, often bare walls, and a kind of austerity belied by the luxury of its materials.

Thus, in Molyneux's dining room, which had been designed by Drian, the walls were covered with transparent glass painted, in black, with groups of flying birds. There were huge parrots, ibises, egrets, all austere but sumptuous against a very pale beige ground, with broad diagonal black stripes further enhancing the feeling of movement; and the dining table, naturally, was made of a vast sheet of clear glass.

Glass was also used as the key element in Molyneux's study, but there it was silvered and set in a pattern of squares on which the map of the world was engraved; and flights of white and gray planes reflected the light, while the furniture, massive and strictly geometric, would not look out of place in a modern environment today.

These painted images were all the rage. José-María Sert was doing frescoes for Robert de Rothschild, Maurice de Wendel, a member of one of the great industrial families, and the comte de Rougemont. And, of course, there were many fashionable decorators. Louis Sue, for instance, was an architect who designed structures, interiors, and furniture. For one of Paris's great ladies, the Honorable Mrs. Reginald Fellowes (in spite of her name she was the French daughter of the duc Decazes, and very rich), Sue designed a library with pale beige walls (obviously the fashionable color) and rosewood shelves. Opposite the entrance door, two truncated marble columns were topped by eighteenth-century busts, while the floor, inlaid with woods of different colors, was adorned with the signs of the zodiac. Here, however, the furniture was not new: Mrs. Fellowes, understandably, decided to keep her Régence armchairs.

Sue knew how to blend the new and the traditional; but another designer, Jean-Michel Frank, was uncompromisingly modern. As a result, the comte Pecci-Blunt's library was as spectacular as it was bold: the semi-circular room had pale pink plaster walls against which stood shelves of crystal mounted in gilded bronze, the whole supported by faux straw uprights. The light came through blades of crystal above the shelves, and the vast, rounded armchairs were made of natural pearwood and covered in leather.

Elegance was the keynote everywhere. In early April, when it had become entirely clear that neither France nor Great Britain was prepared to expel the German army from the Rhineland, the Paris season shone more brightly than ever. Luckily for the fashion chroniclers, the racing season at Auteuil was now in full spate; and there was much to be seen. "The silhouette is in perpetual transformation," *L'Illustration* noted. "The most recent, with its square shoulders, looks rather martial . . . but it is the hats that display the most picturesque fantasy. Tiny, worn sideways with a devil-may-care look, they take on the most unexpected shapes."[22] Perhaps, given the government's pusillanimity, the ladies' shoulders were the right place for a martial look.

It seemed, though, that no matter how hard people tried to concentrate on other periods and entertaining subjects, reality was unavoidable. On April 11, for instance, *L'Illustration,* an immensely popular weekly, published an article with photos on a new technique that would make it possible to take down, in less than a day, all the stained-glass windows from France's Gothic cathedrals in case of war. Severe bombings, the magazine warned, would follow the declaration of war and no doubt cause grave damage.

This was not something people wanted to hear. Janet Flanner, who understood Paris and was always aware of what people thought, saw it clearly. "The French think Hitler is a medieval maniac," she wrote in early April;

> they think his Germany now is not twentieth-century civilized Western Europe but tenth-century tribal and northern hinterland. . . . Were France permanently free from the fear of her invasion, the rest of Europe might cease bolstering her up into the posture of a first-rate power. Free for peace and to take her own shape, France could sink back into literature, fine conversation, the making of superb wines, the producing of a sensibly restricted number of babies, could protest against taxes devoted to building armaments, could see to the purifying and strengthening of her democratic practice of government before liberal institutions disappear off the face of the globe. . . . In other words, France could relax with a sigh into being a second-rate power or a first-rate state of civilization.[23]

As usual, Flanner was right: exhausted by the war, France was no longer capable of being a great power. The tragedy was that neither her people nor her government was willing to face the fact, and that given the rise of Hitler, it was dangerous, perhaps fatal, to be a second-rate power.

CHOOSING and applying a policy, in fact, was becoming an increasingly rare activity. Racked by the Depression, enmeshed in a highly disagreeable world, most political men preferred to administer without leading. By 1936 it was clear that none of the economic and financial measures passed in the last four years had worked; European politics posed a series of apparently insoluble problems; and the country itself was more sharply divided than at any time within memory.

That put the Radicals in a most difficult position. Although it insisted it belonged to the left of center, the Radical party's main purpose was to be in the government. Once, at the turn of the century, it had stood for a number of daring innovations, like the separation of church and state; but having helped to carry though the changes it had advocated, it then utterly failed to set itself new goals. It remained unquestionably attached to the Republic, though, and was on occasion willing to support a little mild reform. Its problem was that at the moment it was split right down the middle.

The right wing of the party was led by Edouard Herriot, who had been a disastrous Premier in the twenties and again briefly in 1932. A huge man, with broad shoulders, a majestic paunch, and crisply curling black hair, Herriot, who had also been mayor of Lyon for some thirty years, was brilliantly intelligent. His vast erudition and his gift for striking formulas made him an effective public speaker and a spellbinding conversationalist. His knowledge of food and wine, those favorite topics of the French, was encyclopedic; and he was thoroughly honest. That, unfortunately, was not enough to make him a statesman. At a time when, for obvious reasons, economic problems came first, he understood nothing about economics. A tolerant man himself, he failed to see how intolerant the Right had become. He did, however, care a great deal about his position within the Radical party; having, on several occasions, been its undisputed leader, he was willing, if needs be, to step down temporarily, but only as a maneuver that would eventually allow him to recapture his position.

In early January, however, he was opposed by one of his former protégés — as, indeed, he had been for the four previous years. Edouard Daladier, who was twelve years younger than Herriot, was also eager to lead the party. Since Herriot, some appearances to the contrary notwithstanding, was thoroughly conservative, Daladier decided to lead the Radicals' left wing. This normally entailed the most moderate sort of liberalism; but, in a desperate effort to stave off electoral defeat, the party in early January positioned itself further left than usual: it had just become a part of the Popular Front and was thus allied with the Socialists, the Communists, and several other anti-Fascist groups.

This was due far less to conviction than to the clear understanding that the Radicals' role in the current legislature was likely to be severely punished by the voters. After an electoral triumph in 1932, the Radicals had not only failed to carry out any of the reforms they had promised during the campaign (first and foremost a policy designed to relieve distress and create jobs), they had also, as a result of the Stavisky affair (see Chapter Five), joined a series of conservative governments, the most reactionary of which, led by Pierre Laval, was still in power.

Because France was a parliamentary democracy whose governments depended on retaining a majority in the Chamber of Deputies and in the Senate, the Radicals were usually in a most convenient position: as a center party, their votes could give the majority to either side of the political spectrum. Since February 1934 they had supported the Right on the grounds that this was needed to defuse the ever angrier confrontations between the two extremes; but they now found themselves in a very uncomfortable place.

This was in part owing to the fact that Pierre Laval, the current Premier, combined personal sleaziness with political dishonesty, a strong attraction to Mussolini, and a veritable passion for violent deflation, thus earning for himself a remarkable degree of unpopularity. Clearly, having Herriot and five other Radicals in the cabinet was becoming increasingly awkward; and on January 17 Léon Blum, the head of the Socialist party, analyzed the situation in a speech before the Chamber of Deputies. "It is impossible for the Radical party to face the voters both as part of the opposition and as part of the government," he said. "It is impossible to be a member of the Popular Front when one's most representative leader sits in a right-wing government."[24]

Blum was right, of course, and Herriot knew it: better to resign now than to be responsible for a debacle that the party would neither forget nor forgive. Indeed, its executive committee had just resolved that "the Premier's ideas and methods are in absolute opposition to [our] doctrine."[25]

For Herriot, it could hardly have been clearer: if he stayed in the cabinet and the Radicals did badly in the May elections, he would be held responsible. If they did well as part of the Popular Front, he would still be on the losing side; so on January 22 he resigned. Without the Radicals, the government had no majority, and so, rather than wait for a vote of no confidence, Laval promptly brought his own resignation to the President of the Republic. The question now was what sort of a government should be in office during the three-month period leading up to the legislative elections.

The answer was not easy. The new government had to have a parliamentary majority, but it could be neither too far left nor too far right. The Radicals would no longer agree to be part of a conservative government but they were clearly not ready for a prefiguration of the Popular Front. And just as important, they particularly wanted the new cabinet to do as little as possible. *L'Oeuvre,* a Radical-inspired newspaper, made that very clear: "The need is less for governing than for merely 'holding on' until the elections and the convening of the next Chamber," it announced on January 21,[26] adding the next day: "At this point in the life of the legislature, no one has any illusions left: the time of rousing enthusiasms is past, and we need only wait for [the results of the elections]."[27] Upon which the Radicals elected Daladier to the party presidency.

If the Radicals thus committed themselves, at least for the moment, to the union of the Left, it was not just because they hoped to do well in the elections. The Right, never friendly, had been attacking the Radicals steadfastly for the last two years in the hopes of gaining a majority of its own. The party really had very little to lose: as long as it was being denounced, it might as well benefit from an alliance with the Socialists and Communists. What the Right failed to realize, however, was that the violence it increasingly displayed made a mockery of its claim that it was the party of order.

The editorials in *Le Temps* were typical. Although the paper was considered to have a semiofficial position, although it was by far the most respectable, indeed the most august, of the Paris dailies, it represented only the most narrow viewpoint, that of the ultraconservative great industrialists. No wonder: ever since 1931, it had been owned by a consortium made up of coal mine, steel mill, and insurance company owners. Thus, it was altogether in character for *Le Temps* to denounce in early January "a program that turns [the Radicals], that 'party of government,' into the auxiliary of M. Marcel Cachin's revolutionary [Communist] party. Henceforth, in order to defend the Fatherland, private property, peace at home and abroad, the Radicals will team up with the Communists whose only goal is to destroy all property through an international revolution."[28]

Given the extreme moderation of the Radicals, *Le Temps*'s thundering was little short of comical, especially since the program to which the members of the Popular Front subscribed was itself very mild; but at least the paper maintained a relatively dignified tone. The same could not be said of the proliferating extreme right-wing press. That same day, *Gringoire* blasted Blum's opposition to the Nazis in the most disgusting terms: "Because you are Marxist and circumcised, you want to do in Hitler; because you are an Anglophile and a Freemason, you want to do in Mussolini."[29] In fact, the very people who accused the Communists of being non-French were themselves the tools of Germany and Italy.

Under the circumstances, it was obviously difficult to find a majority for a new government; but it seemed clear enough that there could be none without the Radicals. Logically, therefore, Albert Lebrun, the President of the Republic, called on them to form the new cabinet. The problem was, of course, that the Radicals themselves were split between Herriot and Daladier. First, the President called on Herriot, who declined; then he asked the sixty-three-year-old Albert Sarraut, whose great strength, under the circumstances, was that he had absolutely no opinions of his own, and was identified with neither Herriot nor Daladier. There now remained, however, the need for a majority. Since the thought of a Popular Front cabinet under Albert Sarraut was ludicrous, he needed supporters on his right; and, after some difficulties, he found them.

As a result, the new government was almost evenly divided between conservatives like the new foreign minister, Pierre-Etienne Flandin, and conservative Radicals like Marcel Régnier, the finance minister; noncommitted Radicals like Sarraut himself; left-wing Radicals like Yvon Delbos, the justice minister; and the leaders of a few smaller parties. Just as important, given the state of Europe, the war ministry was given to a general as a way of not choosing among the politicians.

If nothing much happened until the elections, the Sarraut government could be expected at least to do no worse than its predecessors, and perhaps even a little better. As far as the Radicals were concerned, the main advantage of the arrangement was that it allowed them to run the interior ministry — Sarraut took it on himself. Because it controlled the *préfets*, the government's representatives throughout the country, the ministry was thought able to influence the outcome of the elections. If, however, any sort of crisis occurred, the new cabinet was a recipe for disaster. It was sharply divided between right and left; its foreign minister, himself a former Premier, was not only unlikely to defer to Sarraut, he was known to espouse Laval's ideas; and finally, General Maurin, the war minister, was an elderly and reactionary incompetent whose great merit was that he never made waves.

Even so, the new cabinet had a most difficult birth, especially because Laval hoped that, if Sarraut failed, he might be called back to power. The new Premier had chosen as his chief official assistant a young and very bright left-wing Radical, Jean Zay, who was thus well placed to watch it all happen: "[Sarraut] found himself trapped by Pierre Laval's wily maneuvering. . . . It took thirty hours' worth of tortuous negotiations to put the cabinet together. Throughout an entire night, I watched the parade . . . of those who were begged to accept a ministry and who refused, following those whom no one wanted but came to offer themselves. Finally, [the conservative] Flandin, Mandel, and Pietri found themselves sitting with [the liberal] Delbos, Frossard, Déat, and Guernut. The cabinet's first meeting was tumultuous."[30]

Under these circumstances, the new Premier's declaration to the Chamber could only be ambiguous in the extreme: any precision, and half the ministers would resign. Still, on the Left at least, the absence of Laval made all the difference. "If we have tenaciously worked to end M. Laval's government," Léon Blum editorialized in *Le Populaire*, the Socialist daily, "it is because, for the last six months, we have seen his policies as a catastrophe for France and Europe, as a danger for our democratic freedoms and for peace."[31] Blum was perfectly right. By encouraging Mussolini to invade Ethiopia, by deliberately sabotaging the sanctions against him after he had done so, Laval had seriously strengthened the dictators. His deflationary policies were ruining the country; and his tolerance of armed groups on the extreme Right, the so-called *ligues*, looked very like the first step to the kind of organized disorder that had preceded the advent of both Mussolini and Hitler.

Indeed, a shocking event soon showed just how far the power of the pro-Fascist Right had progressed. On the afternoon of February 13, Léon Blum was being driven back from the Chamber to his apartment by two friends, Jean Monnet and his wife. As the car reached the rue de l'Université, it found itself stopped by the funeral procession of Jacques Bainville, a historian and, more to the point, one of the leaders of the violently reactionary and anti-Semitic daily *L'Action française;* within minutes, Blum was dragged out of the car by armed men and would undoubtedly have been killed had he not been rescued by a group of construction workers who were luckily present. As it was, he sustained a serious head wound and a number of other injuries. Here, in Paris, was a first taste of the methods used in Germany by Hitler's pretorian guard, the S.A.

The Laval government, no doubt, would have carefully ignored the incident. The Sarraut government reacted: that very evening the *ligues* involved in the assault were declared illegal, but for many of the people who mattered in Paris, the attack against a Jew and a Socialist was altogether welcome. "I was," the Czech ambassador noted, "in the most aristocratic salon in Paris. Jules Sauerwein, the reporter at *Le Matin* [a right-wing daily] came in with the story of the attack on Blum, and the guests then interrupted him to exclaim: 'But what a shame they did not kill him! At least we'd be rid of him and then maybe we'd escape ruin and war!'"[32]

This juxtaposition of war and ruin is significant. Naturally, the rich, who paid hardly any taxes, feared and hated the Socialists, who were expected to make them pay their fair share; but there was a new twist as well: the Left, which had for decades been denounced as spineless, unpatriotic, and pacifist, was now accused of being mad for war. The startling reversal was due, of course, to altered political circumstances; the dictators were seen as the extreme Right's great hope, and any resistance to their multiplied aggressions was therefore intolerable.

The three *ligues* that had been dissolved were all connected to *L'Action française,* which, although theoretically monarchist, had long espoused principles close to that of the Nazis — except that instead of a Führer they wanted a king. It was not surprising, therefore, when on February 19 Charles Maurras, the paper's editor (and theoretician) in chief, delivered himself of the following editorial: "Our patience is at an end. Ah, no! Ah, no! These Jewish masters forget the indulgence with which they have been treated of late. Sleeping Justice shall awaken. . . . *Down with the Jews!* Those whom we make the mistake of treating as if they were our equals display a ridiculous ambition to dominate us. They shall be put in their place and it will be a pleasure to do so."[33]

To be sure, *L'Action française* printed only a hundred thousand copies and actually sold fewer than that. In comparison, the two mass-circulation dailies, *Paris-Soir* and *Le Petit Parisien,* ran at, respectively, two million and a million and a half copies, while *L'Humanité,* the Communist party newspaper, sold two hundred thousand; but *L'Action française* had an influence altogether out of keeping with its circulation, and its constant and vicious anti-Semitism did much to spread that prejudice among the Parisian population. Not least important, the paper circulated widely among the top echelons of the army and helped to create an atmosphere of defeatism. Better Hitler than Blum, people said later that spring.

Just how the army felt was no secret. People in Paris knew it and so, therefore, did the German government. Already by 1936, the Nazis had spies not just in the usual places but also in the capital's salons. Thierry de Ludre, for instance, who was descended from an old aristocratic family, was received everywhere, and he was devoted heart and soul to the Führer. He had interesting things to report. Pierre Lazareff, one of the most important newspapermen of the time, saw it all:

Shortly before [the reoccupation of the Rhineland] Thierry de Ludre, in the house of friends where I was also a guest, heard General Maurin, the war minister, answer someone who was asking: "What would we do if Hitler were to bring his troops right up to the Rhine?"

"Not much and, in fact, nothing at all, I think. I know how most of my colleagues in the cabinet feel and I don't think the country would want to make war to stop the Germans from being the masters in their own territory. And it would take a war, a real war, which we would fight alone because the British would not come in."[34]

Whether or not the French would have been willing to fight is an open question; what is certain is that the army's top officers had no intention of resisting Germany.

Given the fact that the Right was making sheep's eyes at Hitler, and that much of the Left had yet to realize that its traditional pacifism was outdated, it would have been positively craven of Hitler not to have re-militarized the Rhineland. The Communists had always been virulent an-timilitarists; and although, because of Stalin's fear of Germany, their position was just then changing, they would still have been hard put to convince their followers that a military response to anything was ever justified. As for the Socialists, they, too, were traditionally pacifists, al-though they were beginning to realize that, when it came to resisting the dictators, force might well be the only option. Just recently, Blum had strongly attacked Laval's appeasement policy and demanded that the Ital-ian aggressors be punished. The previous October he had actually written that the struggle for peace could entail "the eventual application of force,"[35] but he continued to insist that any sanctions, any resistance, could take place only within the context of the League of Nations, a no-toriously useless organization.

If neither the Right nor the Left wanted to fight, that left the Radicals, and all they cared about in early March 1936 was the forthcoming election. It was then a rule of French politics that you did not threaten a war just before the voters went to the polls: the Radicals, therefore, were willing to go a very long way to avoid trouble. Finally, the three top French military commanders were all of an age to prefer peace and quiet: Pétain was eighty, Weygand sixty-nine, and Gamelin sixty-four. Hitler, who was well informed, had every reason to think he had nothing to lose by break-ing two treaties and moving the Wehrmacht into the Rhineland.

Even so, he was reported by reliable observers as showing considerable nervousness until, late on the evening of March 7, he received the message that the French army was not moving. He knew that the troops he was sending in were neither numerous enough nor well armed enough to resist if the French decided to intervene and that, if they did so, the Wehrmacht's defeat would damage the regime gravely or end it altogether; but he had estimated the Sarraut government at its true worth: the French troops never left their barracks.

For a short while, though, it looked as if they might. On March 8, Sarraut announced on the radio: "We are not willing to leave Strasbourg under the fire of the German guns"; [36] clearly, that implied action of some sort. Whether this sentence was written by René Massigli, one of the high officials at the foreign ministry (it probably was), or by Flandin, the foreign minister, remains in dispute. What is sure is that Sarraut was not just unable to write (or have his aides write) this most important speech; far worse, he was equally unable to set the country's policy.

Just what the French reaction should be was decided in a series of meetings of the Council of Ministers, the first of which took place on the seventh. Jean Zay was there and wrote in his memoirs:

> In a Council of Ministers . . . there is no example of a determined minister not being able to get approval for the solution he defends in any question that is a part of his attributions. When, on the other hand, the minister in question offers no suggestion, there is no example of the council coming to a decision by itself.
>
> As it was, M. Flandin did not propose any course of action. To be precise, he listed all the possible decisions, from the strongest to the most theoretical, from mobilization and a movement into the Rhineland to a simple diplomatic protest. . . . In his cold and emotionless voice, he then simply concluded: "Such are the possibilities that are open to us. It is for the council to decide." [37]

Zay, who was murdered by the Vichy militia in 1944, is usually a reliable witness. Flandin, who claims in his memoirs that he favored resistance, is obviously more likely to be self-serving; but, according to Sarraut himself — as reported by Lazareff [38] — he was in fact one of the four ministers present who advocated sending the army into the Rhineland, the other three being Sarraut himself (never a man to hold strong convictions or make a forceful argument); Joseph Paul-Boncour, minister of state and France's permanent delegate to the League of Nations; and Georges Mandel, who had been Clemenceau's aide during the First World War.

Obviously Mandel, who like Zay was murdered by the Vichy militia, was right: the next three years showed it abundantly. But he was fighting not merely his colleagues in the cabinet but, perhaps more important, the war minister and the army's high command. As Flandin remembered it, at the council held on March 8, "to my utter stupefaction, the war minister explained that the only plan was to activate the safety disposition of the Maginot Line and bring two divisions from the Rhône valley to the border. And he added that, in order to march into the Rhineland, the General Staff required the call-up of all men under fifty. That request met with widespread opposition: a call-up six weeks before the elections was madness, some of my colleagues asserted."[39]

General Maurin's attitude is confirmed by Albert Sarraut. That week, in the course of a lunch at Jean Prouvost's, the owner of *Paris-Soir*, he told Pierre Lazareff: "[At the council on the eighth], I asked our war minister under what conditions he would be able to move rapidly into the Rhineland a few of the divisions that were stationed near it.

"'I have consulted General Gamelin [the head of the General Staff],' said General Maurin, 'and his opinion is clear: our military system is such that we can make no movement without a general call-up. Nothing has been prepared to allow even for a partial call-up and anyway we must expect to meet a much stronger resistance than some of the ministers seem to think. If therefore, gentlemen, you wish to oppose the Germans, this council must decree a general call-up.' Everyone was appalled."

At that point, very properly, the Premier decided to question Gamelin, who would be the commander-in-chief in time of war and was, in time of peace, the head of the French military establishment. Sarraut continues: "'I can carry out the operation quite briskly,' the General told me, 'but I will not attempt it unless you give me the means to do so, and that means a general call-up.'

"Flandin, in the meantime, who had consulted the English, reported that they were increasingly in favor of accepting the status quo. The council, by a wide majority, decided to do the same."[40] After that, there was nothing left but to carry out a sorry farce of diplomatic protest. The government appealed to the League of Nations, but Germany had long since left the organization, whose powerlessness had, in any event, been made evident throughout Mussolini's attack on Ethiopia. Some years later Paul Reynaud wrote in his memoirs: "[The government] could act or do nothing; instead it took a halfway position: it talked."[41] He was right; and Hitler's troops remained in undisturbed possession of the Rhineland.

On the Right, many arguments were, of course, marshaled in favor of doing nothing; the Germans, some said, had after all only reoccupied their own territory. The Left saw things more clearly. "Adolf Hitler's Germany has violated the treaties," *L'Oeuvre* editorialized. "France does not accept this act of violence and invites the other signatory nations to carry out together their commitments. Is it even necessary to repeat that, in taking this position, France is defending not merely its own cause, but also the interests of the other European countries?"[42]

That was not the view expounded by the far more influential *Le Temps*. After protesting the breach of the treaties, it advocated the union of all the French, a hint that it would therefore not do to vote for the Popular Front, since, to the paper, "union" was a code word for rallying around the Right. That was on March 8; by the next day, the emphasis had shifted from Germany's aggression: "The question is to know how the concerned nations can most efficaciously safeguard the peace. . . . The Council of the League of Nations must meet immediately."[43] This, as the government well knew, was the equivalent of doing nothing: a war with Hitler, who, after all, hated the Communists quite as much as *Le Temps* and understood the need for authority, was not to be contemplated. It was left to an extreme Right weekly to make the point even more clearly: "The Popular Front wants war," *Je Suis Partout* proclaimed;[44] and war, as everyone knew, was the worst of disasters. With this, the Right had found one of its more rewarding propaganda themes: the Popular Front intended to comfort its political stance by starting a conflict France did not want and was in any event incapable of winning.

That was just a beginning. Two weeks later, Pierre Gaxotte, a well-known historian who belonged to the anti-Semitic fringe, wrote in the same weekly: "The mobilization of the war lovers is continuing according to the best rules of bellicist provocations."[45] The message was clear, once and for all: nothing Hitler could do would ever justify fighting him, but just in case his readers did not quite follow him, Gaxotte spoke even more plainly in April: "The Popular Front is the party of the emigrés," he explained, "German Jews, social democrats, [antifascist] Italian exiles. . . . The Popular Front wants to wage war against Germany and Italy so as to bring back the remains of [the Communist] International in the baggage vans of the French army. . . . Mussolini is a great European."[46] Coming from the very people who throughout the twenties had bitterly attacked Briand's policy of a rapprochement with Germany, and who had then demanded on every possible occasion that the French army occupy its territory, this sudden understanding of the erstwhile enemy is not without its comic side. It made perfect sense, though: in the twenties, Germany had had a democratic government; now it was ruled by a Nazi dictator.

On the Left, the reoccupation of the Rhineland met with very little more resistance. The Socialists, faithful to their long-held principles, declared that the only action of which they could approve would have to be within the framework of the League of Nations; unilateral actions would make a mockery of collective security. The Communists, on the whole, simply avoided the issue; and the Radicals were in the embarrassing position of being a major force within the government. It was thus not surprising that on March 22 Herriot wrote: "Ours is a spirit of peace. Let the men of goodwill in Germany give us the means of bringing about, at long last, a rapprochement. . . . We, too, would like to shake hands with the Germans."[47] It all sounds wonderful, but the reader was entitled to ask who the "men of goodwill" could be: Hitler, Goering, and Goebbels?

What almost everyone refused to see, in fact, was that France's foreign policy now lay in ruins. It had depended on two essential props: the first was the organization of collective security through the League of Nations, the second its Middle European alliances. As of March 8, 1936, collective security, probably always a fiction, was clearly at an end; and with France showing it would not fight even when it was directly threatened — Strasbourg *was* exposed to the fire of the German guns — no one could believe that it would care more about Romania, Yugoslavia, or Czechoslovakia than it did about itself. And if it would not fight for the safety of those allies, then not only was Hitler free to attack them (as, of course, he eventually did) but also they could hardly be counted on to deter a German attack against France.

That left Great Britain as France's only reliable ally. It was an article of faith in France that no major war could be won without British help: the recent world conflict had proved it. Of course, the United States had also played a major role, but it had, since then, retreated into isolationism, and no one in 1936 thought there was any hope of getting it to intervene a second time. Unfortunately, at this point, Great Britain was hardly dependable, owing to a mixture of feelings and circumstances. Economically, she was still ravaged by the Depression; militarily, she was virtually disarmed; politically, the peace movement had enormous strength; and, finally, a significant section of the establishment (including the Prince of Wales, very soon to become King Edward VIII) thought well of Hitler.

Thus, when he was approached, Prime Minister Stanley Baldwin made it very plain that Britain would not support France if it chose to retaliate.

As the crisis slowly dissipated in a flurry of League of Nations inactivity — there were many meetings in many places — and the French returned to what really interested them, their amusements and the coming election, France was left alone and humiliated. Hitler knew, henceforth, that he could carry out his plans for territorial expansion without having to fear the democracies; and the stage was set for the next European war.

In many ways, the collapse of France in 1940 was prefigured by her failure to react in March 1936. More than a question of arms or numbers of troops, it was a question of national will. Had the French army marched into the Rhineland, it would unquestionably have repulsed the Germans; but the Sarraut government was too weak, too distracted, too divided; the Right was too pro-Nazi; the Left had not yet shed its illusions. Three and a half years later, France and Great Britain finally decided to make a stand, but the time lost, the opportunity wasted, were irrecoverable.

Of course, there were many reasons for this failure of will — everything from the effect of the Depression to the sometimes frantic pursuit of amusement, from the flowering of the arts to the decline of the political system. For the French, the war was lost in March 1936; it merely took them four years to realize it.

# CHAPTER
# TWO

THE CENTER OF THE
WORLD

PARIS in 1930 seemed designed to please. It retained, from its prewar days, the wide, tree-lined boulevards with their shiny, sonorous wooden paving, great restaurants, a multitude of theaters, and a tradition of enjoyment. Then, adding a modern touch, there were all the developments of the twenties: rapid, if noisy, motorcars whose frequently sounding horns added a note of excitement to the scene; nightclubs, those dark, smoky bars where you could hear jazz, dance the Charleston, and drink a variety of lethal cocktails; lavish revues in which the dancers wore feathers on their heads and little else besides; and enjoying it all a cosmopolitan crowd — artists, writers, teachers from the Midwest, millionaires, and tourists of every kind — for whom the city was a close replica of paradise.

People came for many reasons. Some looked for a garret in which to write the novel that would change the course of literature; others arrived, easel in hand, because if you were a painter, Paris was the center of the world. By the thirties, among the lastingly great artists working in Paris were two Spaniards, Picasso and Miró; a German, Max Ernst; two Russians, Chagall and Kandinsky; and many others. Then there was the steady stream of clients for the dress designers; Paris was, as ever, the one place where fashion was made. Finally, there were all the visitors who were there just because the city was beautiful, its cafés were cheap, and pleasure was everywhere.

All this needed to be chronicled. For one smart American magazine which was *not* written for the old lady in Dubuque, it stood to reason that a bimonthly Paris letter was a necessity of life. *The New Yorker's* readers, clearly, needed to know what was being read, seen, worn, done in Paris; and so it was that, year in year out, a young journalist set herself to tell her fellow Americans just what it was that, indeed, made Paris such a center of civilization.

Janet Flanner was bright, assertive, opinionated. A small woman with a leonine head, a great beak of a nose, and an imperious voice, she had come to Paris in part because it was just the sort of place she found liveliest and most interesting. No one, in fact, could have been better suited to the job: this reporter who had a passion for facts, nothing but facts, and who early on developed a terse, ironic style knew just how to convey what made the city so fascinating.

When it came to learning and understanding, she went straight to the people who could educate her. If her reports on the musical scene were so good, it was because Virgil Thomson had been her mentor; if she understood fashion, it was because Mainbocher, the great designer, had explained it to her. And yet, Flanner, whose appearance was always highly soignée, was at heart a Bohemian: she lived in hotels, spent all she earned on good meals, great wines, and flowers. As a result, artists, writers, the unconventional felt at ease with her and often helped her develop those insights for which she became famous. Finally, because Paris paid no attention to sexual conventions, she was freer to live there as she pleased, with women lovers. All through the thirties, in fact, she had a complicated arrangement in which a Paris friend, Solita Solano, a country friend, Noel Murphy, and Flanner formed a trio of which she herself was the connecting center. That, in turn, put her into closer touch with a whole group of women who played an important role in the social and artistic life of the city. From Colette, the great writer, to Elisabeth de Gramont, who had befriended Marcel Proust and had a finger in many pies; from Natalie Barney, whose salon was one of the intellectual centers of English-speaking Paris, to Nancy Cunard, who liked men and women equally and was famous for her wild life and her closeness to the avant-garde, there were many well-placed gay or bisexual women who could, and did, help her to know and understand what was happening.

When, in 1931, Flanner fell in love with Noel Murphy, it was because she was so beautiful — tall, blonde, admirably elegant — talented — she sang the works of Schuman, Schubert, Debussy, Richard Strauss — and smart. Described by a friend as "a blend of Greta Garbo and Marlene Dietrich,"[1] Noel Murphy also offered Flanner an entrée into many worlds. She was a widow; her late husband had been the brother of Gerald Murphy, who was a talented painter, the hero of Scott Fitzgerald's *Tender Is the Night,* and the most admired of the expatriates. Among her friends were people as diverse as Louis Bromfield, the then immensely acclaimed novelist, Gertrude Stein, and many other Americans — most of whom, however, now appeared much less often than in the past; with the stock-market crash and the end of easy money, much of that brilliant group found itself forced to stay at home. Gertrude Stein herself, always defiantly American, was surrounded now mostly by Europeans, and rather untalented ones at that. It was, in fact, a hint of things to come: even if Paris remained as glamorous as ever, the rest of the world was sinking into the Depression.

Each of the two women had her own life, Janet in Paris, Noel at Orgeval, outside the city; but Noel came in, and Janet went out, and both were in on the latest artistic developments. In this complex world, though, one whole side of life in Paris seemed lacking in interest: politics, the two felt, was not worth bothering about. The government, after all, had nothing to do with what made Paris great. It was there, of course, but of no great interest; its members were dull, elderly men with whom one could hardly have a lively conversation; and so Flanner ignored them. Instead, she would report about a show of the latest paintings, a concert of the newest music, or parties of extraordinary glamour given by the various members of the Tout-Paris. What Flanner failed to notice, though, was that by 1930, the Tout-Paris, that blend of the very rich and members of the old aristocracy with some artists, writers, composers, and journalists, also included politicians.

Still, Genêt's attitude — that, as noted, was her pen name in *The New Yorker* — was widely shared by her compatriots. It was due in part to the general aversion to politics among the several smart sets in the United States, in part to the fact that the political and economic world in France seemed so stable, so successful that it was not worthy of attention. To these people, at first even the 1929 stock-market crash seemed like a minor accident; very few of them understood that it was the beginning of a whole new era. Certainly the French, about whom Flanner was writing, felt thoroughly insulated from such American vagaries. As late as 1933, Charles Rist, a leading (if singularly obtuse) financial expert, claimed that "France is on an isolated rock assaulted by the waves, but the other countries are floating islands. In a storm, a rock, even if it is isolated, is preferable to a floating island."[2]

For all the Americans in Paris, in fact, and for the rest of the world, it was altogether clear, on January 1, 1930, just who had won the greatest war in history. France, alone of all the Continental powers, had imposed her will on the defeated nations led by Germany and Austria. Italy, though it had fought on the right side, could hardly be taken seriously. The United States, whose help had been so essential, had turned its back on the rest of the world. Great Britain, admittedly the other European winner, had never recovered her prewar prosperity or her share of the world markets. That left just one country.

Not only had France triumphed, it was now richer and busier than ever before. Unquestionably the preponderant nation in Europe, it enjoyed the benefits of an industrial boom and a sound currency. The franc was firmly based on gold, and the reserves of bullion and currency were far in excess of requirements. The budget, which ran to 64 billion francs, was bringing in a 5-billion-franc surplus.

As a result, a little gloating was clearly in order. In its January 1 editorial, *Le Temps,* the paper which came closest to expressing the views of the government, was able to note with satisfaction: "These efforts [to overcome the ravages of the war] have been particularly successful in our country and a comparison of our situation with that of certain of our allies (not to mention the vanquished powers) is much to our advantage," and it went on to praise "the Premier [André Tardieu, who is] young, energetic, full of ideas and vigor."[3]

That was just the sort of chauvinistic crowing which Genêt found beneath her notice. Like all well-informed people, she knew that the Premier in question was having an affair with Mary Marquet, one of the country's leading actresses, but since that sort of gossip was still reserved for the happy few, it could not be reported in *The New Yorker*. The many events of the Paris season, on the other hand, were very much a part of what Genêt covered.

For the French themselves, the brilliance of the city's social life was a key part of the way they saw the world. France, they felt, was the dominant nation, economically, politically, culturally. It managed its affairs better. It was home to more great artists, writers, playwrights, architects. Its leading citizens dressed better, gave the most glamorous parties, and were wittier, more amusing than their counterparts anywhere else. And all these notions informed Genêt's columns: to read *The New Yorker* was to have a very clear notion of where the center of the world actually was.

It was typical of this mood that the two great art shows of the winter and spring were the retrospectives of Pissarro in February and of Delacroix in June. The latter was a vast exhibition that included more than two hundred of the artist's major canvases, a number of which were on loan from American museums. Both shows were huge hits; both were greeted with ecstatic sighs by the critics. That in his own lifetime Pissarro had been ignored or derided apparently worried no one: even if it took the French a while to catch up to their own geniuses, the fact that they were French was what mattered.

Conventional views were, in fact, still highly influential. Of course, there were art publishers like Christian Zervos (himself of Greek origin) and a few critics and poets who understood and praised the likes of Picasso, Braque, or Matisse; but it was typical of the mainstream, as revealed in the large-circulation papers and magazines, that among all Delacroix's superbly energetic oeuvre, the works praised most enthusiastically were his turgid frescoes at the Chamber of Deputies — vast, muddled compositions in which inflated figures in unpleasant colors occupy an amorphous space.

Still, reactionary views, when clearly expressed, were well understood to be unacceptable: they made you look old-fashioned and fusty, two qualities wholly inappropriate for a nation that prided itself on its modernity. Paris, after all, led the world because, in every field, it offered the latest and the best, whether in fashion or in art. That, itself, provoked much ambivalence: the small groups, social and artistic, that made Paris so brilliant had very few connections to the rest of the French. Their way of life, their tastes were, when known, often considered shocking. In a new development, the Tout-Paris shared with many as yet unknown artists the feeling that it was better than the rest of the nation, hardly a part of it at all, really. This sense of alienation, heartily reciprocated by the middle and working classes, still affected only small groups of people, but it set a tone; fragmentation, once begun, was likely to spread. Still, the very yearning for greatness that had once massed the French behind Napoleon now made them proud to be part of the nation that fascinated the rest of the world.

This was true in music as in everything else. Modern composers might have their work performed in Berlin or London; but it was the Paris concerts that mattered the most. And in Paris, the critics understood that, if the city was to retain its preeminence, they would have to listen to new music and like it. When, on December 31, 1929, the great conductor Albert Wolff led an all-Prokofiev concert at the Salle Gaveau, one of the city's major concert halls, Robert Brussel, *Le Figaro*'s music critic, gave it a favorable review, praising "an art which is as free as possible from all systems."[4]

In fact, musical life in Paris was nothing short of brilliant, and it was frequently mentioned by Genêt, who understood it to be an essential part of that civilized atmosphere she liked so much. She was encouraged in her listening, helped in her understanding, by Virgil Thomson: an often indifferent composer, but a brilliant and perceptive (if waspish) critic, Thomson was a great friend of Flanner's, and taught her to understand what she heard. Thus, while in the United States the rare concerts of contemporary music were ignored or derided, Genêt told *The New Yorker*'s readers all about what could be heard in Paris; and, indeed, it was splendid. Stravinsky, who had remained there after the Russian revolution precluded his return to Petersburg, offered the public at least one new work every year. In 1930, this was his *Capriccio*. Even in 1933, when the Depression had struck and funds were rare, he obviated the impossibility of paying for an orchestra by writing his *Duo Concertant,* a piece for piano and violin in which he himself played the piano; and it received a triumphant reception.

Stravinsky was not alone. Arthur Honegger, the forward-looking Swiss composer, was present for the premiere of his cello concerto. Heifetz and Kreisler gave concerts. And then there was that most flamboyant of maestros, the great Toscanini himself. When, in May, he conducted the New York Philharmonic, tickets were sold out as soon as they went on sale. The audience included virtually every important musician in Europe, Genêt reported in *The New Yorker,* "and every famous composer . . . who wasn't dead. And, judging by the face of Ravel while his *Boléro* was being played, one who wished he was dead. For Ravel's now famous refusal to rise and meet the storm of applause raging around his seat was not, apparently, caused by modesty but by temper and tempo. Signor Toscanini, it seems, had played his piece too fast."[5]

Culture was all very well; there were even some members of the Tout-Paris (and a very few politicians) who actually looked at art and listened to music; but everyone agreed that particularly prominent in France's contribution to civilization was its mastery of fashion. There could not be any doubt about it: when it came to the very latest look, only Paris would do; and its designs were eagerly copied the world over.

In the twenties, the great couturiers had revolutionized the way their clients, and the rest of the world, looked; for the first time ever, women wore skirts that barely reached their knees, pretended that they were flat-chested, and accommodatingly lowered their waists until they hovered somewhere near their pelvises. Just as important, they left the pampered atmosphere of the salon, ventured outdoors, and began to practice all kinds of sports.

Naturally, that required specific costumes, and the couture was ready to provide them. Chanel, after all, had started her career by designing sports clothes. Now this was a well-understood category. "Sports clothes have, these last few years, acquired a key role in modern life," one fashion commentator wrote. "But, in order to justify their existence, they must be above all practical and comfortable."[6]

It was through sportswear as well that the most spectacular designer of the thirties first made her mark. Elsa Schiaparelli, who was born and raised in Rome, was short, dark, exotic-looking. Her tense, enigmatic expression was in direct contrast to her sometimes brutal frankness, and her rather heavy features seemed calculated to keep people at a distance: she was what the French call a *jolie-laide* (attractive without being really pretty), but she could be enormously charming when she chose. Still, she had very few friends. As a young woman, she had made an unhappy marriage and, while she had lovers, she never again allowed a man to get close to her. "Men admire strong women, but they do not love them," she once said.[7] Instead, she relied on fortune tellers, astrologers, and her work: that, on every occasion, came first.

None of this would have mattered, of course, if she had not been enormously talented. She could dramatize the simplest article of clothing and proved it at the very beginning of her career when she designed something no one had ever seen before, a sweater in dark colors with white trompe-l'oeil bows at the neck and wrists. The moment Schiap (as she was called by the people who knew her well) herself appeared in one of these sweaters she launched a new fashion, and she never looked back, going from sportswear to dresses to evening gowns. By 1934, she was the most exciting, most innovative designer in Paris.

Her way of proceeding was in direct contrast to all that had come before. Chanel, who had started out in life as little better than a prosti-tute, had then raised herself to a higher level as a kept woman, and finally made her mark on fashion, just after the war, as a simplifier: clothes, at last, were to be comfortable, easy to wear. Other women designers — Jeanne Lanvin, Madeleine Vionnet — were noted for the refined elegance of the dresses they designed and for their mastery of their craft; and then, once they were successful, they went on to lead the kind of life that made them their clients' equals. Schiap, on the other hand, came from a good family, and, although penniless, had an easy entrée into Paris society — and that was a revolutionary novelty. Because she wore her own designs, and was seen everywhere, it was, in fact, through her social acceptability that she launched her career, something no couturier had done before her.

Most important of all, Schiaparelli had an innate sense of drama. This took several forms. Most immediately noticeable was her use of strong colors: red and yellow, orange and maroon, a brilliant pink — called shocking pink — that became her trademark; but she could make black and white look just as noticeable. Then there was her basic concept. Because the modern world was fast, aerodynamic, mechanical, she understood that clothes, too, must have simple lines.

In contrast to the twenties, when women's bodies were made to look androgynous, fashions now became soft, clinging, curvaceous; but Schiaparelli had her own view. Her dresses were designed to follow the shape, not of the flesh, but of the skeleton, the planes of the body as shaped by the bones. The result was a sleek, almost geometric look combined with a forceful slenderizing line, clothes of stylized simplicity. And in this new, harder era, Schiap's designs reflected reality: in 1931–32, she introduced big shoulder pads, which gave her dresses a bold, almost brash look, and she made up for this by making her evening dresses dramatic and aggressively seductive.

She was lucky as well; she began designing just as fashion was changing. After nearly a decade during which waists dropped and hemlines rose, a new trend was becoming visible. Dresses, *Le Figaro* noted in January 1930, "will be longer, but . . . the waist will be higher, for, having wandered from the hips to the knees . . . it is now settling back . . . where nature placed it. . . . Morning dresses are lengthening their skirts to mid-calf. . . . Dressier dresses venture even lower, all the way to the ankles. As for evening gowns, they are unquestionably long . . . and continued with a more or less serpentine train."[8]

This was momentous news, and just right for Schiap's talent, especially since Paris took its fashion very seriously indeed. The ladies of the Tout-Paris would have died rather than wear yesterday's look, and they were vulnerable because many of them made a habit of ridiculing their rivals;

the lack of charity in the Paris salons was notorious. Even in those less exalted circles where people actually worked for a living, it was well understood that fashion was paramount. The bourgeoisie followed it as closely as they could; this was the age of the talented seamstress who, for pennies, would copy (badly) a couturier model.

Every change was eagerly reported; every modification of the prevailing look copied. And by March 1930, just when Schiaparelli was showing her first sweaters, these momentous changes were becoming more evident: not only were skirt lengths changing, the look was now long and slim instead of short and square; and the very way women presented their faces was being transformed: fashion now called for a high forehead unencumbered by hair (no more bangs), with curls at the temples, shaven eyebrows, and a hat worn well back on the head.

This was hot news. Naturally, Schiap was part of it: a radical change needed new designers and, naturally, new accessories; so she provided an easy way for her clients to show that they were up to the very latest fashion. Among her innovations were thigh-length triple scarves, often in vibrant red, white, and blue. Attached together at the back, they could be twisted or braided all the way down the front; and when they were made of satin or crepe de chine, they were added to evening dresses.

Schiap soon offered her clients other ways of being distinctive: she designed trouser skirts for every occasion. These flowed like a skirt but offered the comfort of trousers; then, there were plain, figure-hugging sheaths in black crepe de chine whose impact was due to their "sunburn back": although in front they reached up to the neck, in the back they were cut to well below the waist. And, of course, there was the Mad Cap, a tiny knitted tubelike object with a pointed end that took whatever shape its wearer wanted and soon became Katharine Hepburn's favorite headgear. All these designs were thrilling because they were new; but, just as important, they reflected a new freedom. Trousers were obviously more convenient than skirts and allowed women to be themselves, because they followed the actual figure (instead of a designer's notion of what that figure should be) and allowed them to move more easily. Schiap's clothes, in fact, were not just chic: they were thoroughly modern.

Hats were, if anything, even more important: universally worn (except by the working class), they were at the same time highly visible and terribly risky: an extra centimeter of twisted silk could transform a creation of dazzling elegance into a fashion disaster, and in 1930 all existing hats suddenly became obsolete. By February, the ubiquitous cloche, still universally worn in October, was out.

Fashion was a constant preoccupation, but decoration was just as important. The French firmly discounted the influence of the Bauhaus, whose designs, critics pointed out disdainfully, were meant for those who could afford nothing better than industrially produced furniture. "The group directed by M. Walter Gropius," the critic Georges Rémon noted, "was born of the war and its miseries, of the blockade, of the revolution. . . . It is strictly utilitarian."[9] Instead, connoisseurs praised the designers — Ruhlman, Frank, Duffet, Dunand, and many others — who worked only for the very rich, and whose pieces were not endlessly duplicated. Parchment-covered walls, furniture of rare and precious woods inlaid with silver or mother-of-pearl, sharkskin-covered desks, and complex designs in lacquered straw were the order of the day, not cheap metal and inexpensive fabric.

As it had been for a decade, the yearly Salon of the Decorative Arts was an eagerly attended and eagerly reviewed event. In 1930, though, in spite of all the disclaimers, the influence of the Bauhaus was evident. Metal furniture, for instance, played a major role and tended to look like knockoffs from the originals by Mies van der Rohe or Gropius, but it was widely praised as being hygienic, easy to keep clean, and fashionably sleek.

Sleekness itself was essential: furniture was to look aerodynamic whenever possible, just like automobiles, which were now beginning to acquire curves. That implied no return to Art Nouveau, then the most despised of styles. New carpets, for instance, tended to have strictly geometric designs in which right angles broke into segmented circles so as to repeat, on a flat surface, the look of the newest building. And there was always that thrilling new metal, zinc, which was being eagerly promoted by a Spanish zinc-mining corporation.

*Le Figaro Illustré,* a monthly magazine less lavishly illustrated than its title might indicate, did not go so far as to print photos of the new zinc furniture, but it devoted nearly a full page of print to Michel Duffet's zinc room, with its "lady's desk in zinc, white maple, and green fabric [which had] . . . cylindrical metal surfaces that slide to show or hide the shelves, which are themselves circular and threaded on a tube (the leg of the desk) so that they can pivot according to the user's whim. . . . While we disapprove of using zinc merely as a surface, we will have nothing but praise for M. Duffet's handsome piece when the shelves are no longer just 'wood with a metal surface' . . . but sheets of metal."[10]

It was the done thing to look in at the decorative arts exhibition; and yet there was so much competition, so little time: you could not hope to be thought really chic if you were not away from Paris a good part of the year. Elisabeth de Gramont, the daughter of one duke and the (separated) wife of another, made it quite plain:

> The Paris season? But it no longer exists. . . . Snow and sun are the two great poles which, each in turn, attract their followers. . . . From the freezing peaks of the Pyrenees or the Alps to the burning beaches of the Mediterranean . . . here is the calendar for the fashionable: January and February: St. Moritz, Font-Romeu, or Super-Bagnères; March: Biarritz or Berlin; April: Rome; May and June: Paris; July, August, September: Deauville, Antibes, Venice; October: the country-side near Paris or Umbria; November and December: New York.[11]

Most of those places could be reached by taking one of the luxury trains, which were, everyone agreed, one of the achievements of the period. Individual compartments paneled in exotic woods, splendid meals in the dining cars, and flawless service: the very act of traveling was in itself highly enjoyable, especially since the only way to remain part of the fashionable world was to travel. Thoroughgoing luxury was also offered by the several shipping lines that provided service between Europe and the United States.

There were all kinds of other pleasing ways to show just how modern you were. You could, for instance, pilot your own plane; or, if that seemed a little excessive, you could own one of the new sports cars whose speed reached well over one hundred kilometers (sixty-five miles) an hour. Nor was it necessary for the driver to be a man: automobiles, it was generally agreed, had done even more to emancipate women than the Great War. In 1930 French car manufacturers were still among the world's busiest. Citroën, Renault, Panhard, Peugeot, Hotchkiss, and many others competed eagerly. They never failed to point out that their new, more comfortable, and safer (all-metal) models were particularly suited to women drivers.

Women agreed; and because Paris was the center of all elegance, it was immediately seen that automobiles must play their part. The result was a series of *concours d'élégance automobile* that took place sometimes in the Bois de Boulogne, sometimes in Deauville or Biarritz or the Riviera, and in which cars, often with custom coachwork and special upholstery, were either driven or occupied by smartly dressed ladies. They were not expected to exert themselves, though: a slow drive past the judges, an effective pose struck upon entering or leaving the car, were considered to be quite sufficient. In 1930, for instance, the fashion was for the glamorous lady driver to carry a full line of enameled accessories — purse, cigarette case, lighter, and so on. And when the comtesse Bernard de Ganay won the Women's Paris–Cannes race driving Renault's top of the line, a Reinastella, the fact was promptly reported.

It was no wonder that Mme de Ganay, one of the most fashionable women in Paris, drove a Reinastella. Just as, earlier, a shiny carriage pulled by a handsome pair had been an essential appurtenance of the good life, so now was a smart auto. That was practically traditional; but there were other objects that were newer in character. Cigarette cases were among them — as a cigarette ad pointed out, smoking was actually *good* for your throat — and so, naturally, were cocktail shakers. As for the cocktails themselves, they were served often and were highly popular just as long as they had an American name; Prohibition notwithstanding, it was well understood that when it came to devising new and improbable mélanges, the Americans were unrivaled. And so you could order a Three Mile Limit (one teaspoon grenadine, a dash of lemon juice, two-thirds brandy, one-third Bacardi rum), a Reverend Booth (half brandy, half Scotch, a dash of Grand Marnier) or a Reverend Barcklay (dash of Angostura bitters, two dashes of curaçao, one-third rye, one-third kümmel, one-third rum). Just how you felt after drinking these extraordinary mixtures is mercifully unrecorded.

This brilliant, often frivolous surface, which attracted Genêt and many others besides, concealed real if hidden problems. France seemed solid, prosperous, vital. In fact, much of that prosperity was as shallow as it was fragile. Even the animated, crowded life of Paris was misleading: France was not only significantly less populated than before 1914, its birthrate was also abysmally low because, to a far greater extent than any of the other contenders in the World War, it had failed to recover from the cataclysm. In the course of that most bloody of human conflicts, the country had had 1,390,000 men killed outright while another 740,000 were wounded so seriously that they remained permanently disabled. This, proportionate to the overall population, was twice as many casualties as for Great Britain, a third more than for Germany, and over sixty times more than for the United States. Given France's population of 40 million, it meant an overall loss of 5 percent, concentrated in the men of the generation then in its twenties and thirties.

The financial blow was, in its own way, quite as devastating. France lost half its merchant marine, over 800,000 buildings, some 40,000 miles of roads, and thousands of bridges. The war, in a country whose 1913 budget was 5 billion gold francs, cost 143 billion just in budgeted outlays, while the reconstruction of the devastated areas — the war was, after all, fought on French soil from start to finish — required 134 billion in rehabilitation. Set against this vast total of 277 billion gold francs were the reparations paid by Germany under the financial clauses of the Treaty of Versailles. By 1931, when they were suspended, France had received a mere 5 billion.

Part of the postwar prosperity had been due to the urgently needed rebuilding of the devastated areas, part also to the worldwide economic boom of the twenties; but, in fact, France was a little like a patient who is just getting over a very serious case of pneumonia: it tended to be feverish but not energetic. As a result, the French, almost unanimously, were pacifists: war was too dreadful ever to be faced again. This, in an unsettled world, entailed some fairly spectacular mental contortions.

France's foreign policy relied on the League of Nations, where, supposedly, all future conflicts would be resolved by arbitration, the solution then being enforced by the combined might of all the members. In the twenties, this had made some sense in spite of the absence of the United States; but it was a policy that depended on a general willingness to abide by the League's decisions. The moment a major power decided to strike out on its own, the League became powerless, a fact so obvious that it was generally ignored.

It had, however, occurred to a series of French governments; so they evolved a complementary policy that brought together the so-called Little Entente. This was composed of Czechoslovakia and Yugoslavia, with Poland as a more unofficial ally. Thus, if ever it came to war again, these countries, replacing the lost Russian ally, would provide an essential second front against Germany.

That, of course, implied that the countries in question would be willing to fight, and that their armies would be powerful enough to represent a real threat. Czechoslovakia, whose modern industrial base gave it a good deal of weight, came close to being a major contender, but Poland and Yugoslavia were lightweights. Worse, the alliance supposed that France would be ready, in case of need, to take the offensive. If it did not, then its allies would be defeated one by one; but the military strategy implemented since the middle twenties by a succession of French governments was purely defensive. It consisted of building a fortified bulwark, the Maginot Line, so strong that the Germans would never be able to break through it. Here, too, there was a dubious assumption at work: the Maginot Line stopped where the border with Belgium began, because

Belgium was France's ally. As a result, if the Germans marched through that unfortunate country as they had done in 1914, the Maginot Line would prove totally useless.

That the famously logical French should have failed to realize this says something about their terror of war and their refusal to face the most unpalatable of facts: Germany was not only far more advanced industrially, its population was half again that of France. Then, in 1930, the American credits that had underpinned Germany's prosperity were withheld. The result was a series of spectacular bank failures and a rapid rise in unemployment. That, in turn, led to political turmoil as successive chancellors tried and failed to find a way out of the Depression. One of the most ominous consequences of this new economic distress was the strong resurgence of the ultranationalist Right, which stretched from conservative monarchists to Hitler's National Socialists. These groups claimed that Germany had not really lost the war, but had been stabbed in the back by the government, which sued for peace. As for the Depression, they said, it flowed directly from the Treaty of Versailles and the reparation payments it imposed on Germany. Just as important, they laid claim to the areas lost to Poland. Here, clearly, was a new war in the making, and once it became a question of resisting German aggression, there was a substantial chance that the flaws in France's foreign and military policies would become evident to all.

From extreme right to extreme left, though, the politicians, and with them most of the French, refused to acknowledge this; for the moment, all was going well, and even if the future held disaster in store nobody wanted to think about it. This gave all the gaiety, all the brilliance of Paris a hectic, after-me-the-deluge undertone. It also served as a stimulant: great civilizations are never more dazzling than when they know they are doomed, and there was a possibility that this might apply to France. So another kind of alienation occurred: just as the artists and the Tout-Paris thought themselves different in kind from the rest of the people, so the French cut themselves off from their future. At the same time, of course, modernity was more highly prized than ever, but this did not imply a contradiction. Modernity was what was happening *now*. The future, no one knew quite how, would have to take care of itself.

In the meantime, the golden, glittering people at the top enjoyed themselves in a variety of spectacular ways. Their privileges, which included paying very little tax, were in no danger; their (unearned) income was growing larger every year. As a result, social life was more brilliant than ever. All that was needed, in fact, were new ideas for new parties, and very few people were better at providing them than a resident American.

Elsa Maxwell should have been everything that was not chic: she was fat, ugly, and poor, and she spoke French with the most appalling accent. She was a snob, too, who worked hard to reach the very top level of society; but with all that, she had an exuberance, a *joie de vivre,* that made her quite unique. She also knew how to give just the kinds of parties her friends most enjoyed and how to get someone other than herself to pay for them.

Even in a city famous for the variety and inventiveness of its festivities, Elsa Maxwell stood out. In July 1930, for instance, there was her famous Come As You Are party. The guests were told that they would be picked up by a bus at some time during the afternoon or early evening, and that when they heard its horn tooting they were to come exactly as they were. Needless to say, a great deal of planning went into the costumes in which the guests were "surprised." "The marquis de Polignac," Elsa Maxwell remembered with satisfaction,

> was attired in full evening dress save for one conspicuous omission. He wasn't wearing his trousers. Daisy Fellowes was carrying her lace pant-ies in her hand. A half dozen women . . . came in slips that were defi-nitely not shadow-proof. Bébé Bérard [a painter and highly successful set designer] wore a dressing gown, had a telephone attached to his ear, and had white make-up on his face to simulate shaving-cream. Several men who rated honor above vanity came in hair nets.
>
> I made two mistakes in my otherwise careful planning. I installed a bar in each bus and I neglected to account for Paris' monumental traffic jams. The buses began to pick people up at seven o'clock in the evening but it was nine o'clock before they arrived at Meraud Guevara's apart-ment in Montparnasse which I had borrowed for the occasion. By that time everyone was flying so high that there were drastic changes in some of the costumes. Countess Gabriela Robilant . . . lost her skirt during maneuvers. . . . Gabriela was unconcerned but Countess Elisa-beth de Breteuil . . . was outraged. "I refuse to be seen . . . with anyone in that scandalous condition," she said indignantly.
>
> "To the Bastille!" Gabriela cried, yanking off Elisabeth's skirt.[12]

And there were still other, perhaps even inspired, states of undress: one guest, for instance, came with makeup on just half her face.

The Come As You Are party was perhaps rowdier than most; but there was, at any event, no lack of competition. The ever-energetic Miss Maxwell herself gave another of the season's most amusing parties, this time at the house of the Honorable Mrs. Reginald Fellowes. It was entirely appropriate: Daisy Fellowes was the famously elegant daughter of a French nobleman, the duc Decazes, and an heiress to the Singer sewing machine fortune. Separated from the Honorable Reginald Fellowes, she lived in a splendid eighteenth-century town house on the Rue de Lille with a large, enclosed courtyard in front and a larger garden at the back. Because she was very rich, very well born, and very eager for amusement, she had become one of the leaders of Paris society, at one moment having her country house redone in the most modern style possible, and at another giving wild parties. It made perfect sense, therefore, for her to ask Elsa Maxwell to plan this particular evening.

This time, everyone was asked to come as somebody else who had to be a well-known figure; so Elsa herself came as Briand, the French foreign minister, while Daisy Fellowes was a hatcheck girl. Jean-Michel Frank, the immensely fashionable decorator, came as Marie-Laure de Noailles, a well-known hostess whose husband belonged to an august aristocratic family but helped to finance the avant-garde. This daring substitution was made more pointed by the fact that Frank and Mme de Noailles each had a large hooked nose. Many young men were costumed by Chanel and pretended they were one of the reigning beauties, the most successful being, according to the general consensus, Stanislas de La Rochefoucauld as Mme Marthe Letellier.

And the parties went on as if nothing else mattered, as if only pleasure counted, as if, indeed, it was best to have fun while you could. That same year, at the White Ball, given by the Pecci-Blunts (she was the niece of Pope Leo XIII), you could wear anything you liked provided it included something white, so Jean Cocteau and Bébé Bérard appeared wearing white plaster masks and wigs. The country ball given by the comte Caen d'Anvers took place at Champs, an exquisite house just outside Paris built and decorated for Mme de Pompadour. The several Rothschilds — the Barons Eugène, Maurice, Robert, and Henri — each gave their own dance, which, Genêt noted, "might have led to the season's being called Rothschild Week had not Catholic Paris more ironically referred to it as *La Semaine sainte* [Holy Week]."[13]

Some gatherings were a little more specialized. One party, given by the duchesse de Clermont-Tonnerre (who signed herself Elisabeth de Gramont, her maiden name) might, by those with sharp eyes, have been defined as a party by women for women: the hostess and the chief guests — Dolly Wilde (Oscar Wilde's niece), Natalie Barney, the princesse Violette Murat, and Genêt herself — having a marked preference for their own sex.

Precious metals played a major role as well. In the early summer, there was the Silver Ball given by the couturier Jean Patou. He roofed his garden over, covered the walls and ceiling with silver foil, wrapped the trees, branches and all, in silver paper, and hung huge silver cages from them in which stuffed parrots, each as large as a child, had been placed. That, everyone agreed, was pretty dazzling, but it was left to a foreigner to go Patou one better.

Elsie De Wolfe, who had recently become Lady Mendl, was an American and the most successful decorator of her generation. Although she had nearly reached her seventies, her unlined face and slim elegance gave no hint of age, and for many years already she had been a famously lavish hostess; so it was no wonder, perhaps, that she decided to give a Gold Ball at the Villa Trianon, her Versailles house. On that night she covered the walls in gold cloth and the tables in gold lamé. Gold and silver Christmas ornaments were used as centerpieces, and there were gold menus and gold ribbons around the napkins, while gold-colored champagne was served throughout the evening.[14]

This prodigious debauch of precious metals was naturally reserved for the Tout-Paris, but almost everyone looked eagerly for amusement, if only because it made it easier to pretend that the great Depression, which was causing untold suffering all through the world, would never reach France. And if there were no grand parties for the common people, Paris offered other pleasures. Of these, the newest, the most spectacular, were the talking movies. In 1930, *The Jazz Singer,* the first American talking (and especially singing) motion picture, was shown in Paris and nothing was ever the same. The public flocked in and demanded talkies of its own, while the intellectuals bemoaned the vulgarization of the medium. Mime, they said, was art: once the movies had sound, they would become mere commercial ventures — a point of view that signally failed to convince the vast majority of moviegoers. Still, when that genius of the silent films, Charlie Chaplin, came to Paris in March 1931, he was greeted with an explosion of love and admiration.

That, for Genêt, was worth noticing; it was part of what made Paris civilized, this willingness to take in the best from everywhere. Other, highly popular events she simply ignored. Although she owned a Citroën roadster, cars simply did not interest her; but the Parisians, always eager to see the newest, always anxious to lead the way, flocked to the yearly

Automobile Show. There, just as in the couture houses, the fashion was changing: the boxy look was being banished from dresses and autos alike. Instead, the new cars developed curves (again, like the dresses), took on a thoroughly modern, aerodynamic look, and emphasized that novelty, comfort. "The all-steel Citroën bodies are the prototype of the modern car, with abundant room for two on the rear banquette in the C-4F, and for three in the C-6F. Great efforts have been made to improve look and quality: . . . deeper and better profiled cushions, new door hinges, a new, much easier way to raise the windows, leak-proof floors, all designed to give the users the maximum amount of comfort," *L'Illustration* reported happily.[15]

Cars had long stopped being a rarity; but planes still seemed highly exotic — half thrilling and half terrifying. Still, if you were really modern (and willing to take a few risks), there was a truly revolutionary way to reach the new world. In May 1930 a French mail seaplane had crossed the South Atlantic: from Paris to Rio by way of Africa took just three days, and passenger versions were even then being fitted out. There was already a regular air service between Paris and London or Berlin; and if you did not mind patronizing the former enemy, you could always take that greatest of all dirigibles, the Graf Zeppelin, which, as a publicity device, had flown over Paris in late April. For the first time, at the yearly Air Show, the warplanes were in a minority; the largest passenger model was German, the Dornier Do-S, and it could carry up to twenty-five passengers. There was a problem, though. "Planes," a reporter noted, "are too expensive for the service they give. They are inconvenient, uncomfortable, noisy. Worse, they are frightening because they are not *safe*,"[16] and he went on to explain what the problem was: so long as planes depended on speed to provide lift, they would be inherently dangerous.

Planes, whatever their defects, were unquestionably modern. The French government, whatever its qualities, was not. Composed mostly of men whose careers had started well before the war, it looked back to that happier and simpler era. It was no wonder, therefore, that politics seemed boring, a leftover from a long-dead era that interested only a tiny milieu. Still, that was counteracted by the age-old French passion for discussing the latest developments and by the fact that some, at least, of the political leaders were part of the Tout-Paris. A few of these men, distributed equally from right to left, frequented a variety of fashionable salons. Others had such close ties to literature and the intellectuals that, almost in spite of themselves, they became a part of that glittering upper crust.

Paradoxically, the most authentically Parisian figure was Léon Blum, the head of the Socialist party, in part because he had so many friends among people who thought (as opposed to those who gave parties), in part because he had begun his career as a theater reviewer; and nothing was more glamorous than the theater.

None of this prevented constant attacks on the man the conservatives were determined on presenting as a bloodthirsty revolutionary. That Léon Blum seemed specifically designed to allay every possible fear hardly deterred the Right or its newspapers. Because there was, in effect, no law against slander, the press could print deliberate lies and fabrications with absolute impunity; and it never hesitated to do so. To give only a minor example of this, Blum was invariably accused of being immensely rich. He owned vast estates (it was never said exactly where), chunks of Paris real estate (it was never said exactly which), and an immensely valuable collection of eighteenth-century silver (which no one had ever seen). All three "revelations" were pure fabrications: Léon Blum lived on the income he earned as director of *Le Populaire,* the daily paper put out by the Socialists, and his accusers knew it.

None of this bothered the Right: a steady campaign of lies, its leaders felt, would prove effective through sheer repetition — a technique the Nazis were already using in Germany to great effect. Indeed, it seemed as if the more unlikely the lie, the more successful it became.

Although Léon Blum was unquestionably a Socialist who believed in the eventual advent of a society ruled by the workers, he was also deeply respectful of the laws and the constitution; in that sense, there was nothing revolutionary about him or his party. And while the Socialists until 1920 had been at the extreme left of the political spectrum, they were now pushed toward the center by the Communists.

Blum himself was one of the most civilized people alive. The son of a prosperous ribbon manufacturer, he was born in Paris in 1872 — not in Poland or Russia or Bulgaria as the right-wing press affirmed at various times. After a brilliant academic career, he had become a member of the Conseil d'Etat, the court of last appeal in cases where the French sued their own government; eventually, he left it to earn a living as a theater critic and an author. This tall, distinguished-looking man with a long intelligent face, drooping mustache, and slender white hands was nothing if not refined. His courtesy was legendary; he was scrupulously honest; but for all that, he was an accomplished debater in the Chamber of Deputies, the lower and more powerful house of the French Parliament to which he had belonged since 1919. This last quality, along with the clarity of his thinking, had helped bring him to the head of his party, a fact that, in itself, seemed somewhat improbable: why should Blum, that well-known aesthete, that man of sensibility and culture, want to lead the Socialists?

Blum himself answered that question in 1919. "We feel," he wrote, "that our happiness is not independent from that of the rest of humanity, just as our work will be useless without theirs, and that their suffering and their misery are ours, that every injustice from which they suffer wounds us as well."[17] France between the wars was the most socially backward of all the major European countries. The workers could expect no protection from the state; many industries remained ununionized; working hours were long, ten or more a day, six days a week, fifty-two weeks a year. Wages were low, working conditions dreadful. Most resented of all, perhaps, was the fact that many bosses still behaved as if they were feudal lords, and their workers contemptible slaves. Thus, when he wrote about human suffering, Blum knew just where to find it; but, while other theater critics seemed able to ignore the problem, for Blum it was intolerable, and when it came to bettering the life of the working class, one party, and one alone offered solutions. In 1906, therefore, Blum became a Socialist.

It was a startling step, but he really had no choice: the main reforming party, the *parti Radical et Radical-Socialiste,* in spite of its name was neither radical nor Socialist. It stood for the separation of church and state, the depoliticization of the army, and mild political progress, all of which had just been achieved; but it firmly refused to address social problems. Still, that a man whose family belonged to the middle class and whose education raised him still higher should have joined the Socialists meant that the Right attacked him as a traitor to his class, a denunciation with which, in the United States, Franklin D. Roosevelt would become thoroughly familiar.

Blum was also vulnerable in another, more painful way: he was a (nonpracticing) Jew, and ever since the Dreyfus affair right-wing opinions and anti-Semitism had gone together. The rise of the Nazis across the Rhine only reinforced this; and so Blum was quite often attacked simply for being Jewish, that is to say a born traitor. Jews, the Right kept repeating, were an unpatriotic group who either ruled the world through their hold on the great financial institutions or wished to spread communism and universal revolution out of hatred for better-rooted elites. That the two accusations were incompatible — bankers did not do very well in the Soviet Union — bothered not a single anti-Semite. Only *Le Temps,* the most august of the French newspapers, refrained from indulgence in this disgusting prejudice. Its founder, Adrien Hébrard, had been Jewish; its co-editor as of 1931, Emile Mireaux, was Jewish. Clearly, this was one reactionary cause it could hardly support.

Blum was extraordinarily intelligent; even his worse enemies were prepared to admit it; but he was also a good deal more than that. Pierre-Olivier Lapie, who knew him well, has left a vivid portrait of the Socialist leader:

> His method consisted of an analysis so subtle as to be almost casuistry, finely drawn but realistic. After having used the scalpel, he would proceed to an ingenious reclassification. From the political situation thus examined, he would distinguish the separate elements, one by one, would separate them, would compare them, taking care not to confuse them, hold them as if suspended in air before reuniting them or, on the contrary, opposing them to one another. All that was then organized in a logical progression toward one or several hypotheses, between which he made a motivated choice; then, he would act, seeing to it that the solution thus thoroughly matured was adopted. The conclusion he reached in this way corresponded to a deeply felt conviction. . . . At the same time, the clarity of his mind illuminated the most complex problems. . . .
>
> That deep thought, that exact logic, these implacable deductions might have made him cold, might have frozen his listeners and turned them against him. But . . . the strength of his ability to convince surrounded them, penetrated them in strange and mysterious ways. . . .
>
> As he spoke, he seemed to open himself to us, to tear himself up to reveal the depths of his reasoning; a kind of intimacy was created. . . . This moving sincerity reached the least sophisticated groups.[18]

Nor was any of this a facade: Blum, complexity and all, was just what he seemed. In private life, he was adored by his family and loved by his many friends. In politics, he earned the respect and often the affection of many of his opponents. As for his charm, it was famous — in part, no doubt, because he was genuinely interested in others, knew how to listen and empathize. Even a conservative, unemotional diplomat like François Coulondre, the French ambassador to Germany in the early thirties, who should have looked at Blum with a highly cynical eye, felt that extraordinary warmth. "Blum," he wrote, "is a charmer. His gestures, his glances, his voice envelop you, cajole you, bewitch you; you have barely come into his presence but he bends toward you, takes you by the arm, caresses you with his eyes and, more than anything, he captivates you little by little through the fluid phrases that penetrate you like a subtle perfume."[19]

None of this prevented Blum from being a highly skillful politician, however — a fact with which the Radicals, his natural allies, were all too familiar. While Blum would never support a cause he did not believe in, he was capable of just the kind of maneuvering its objects found infuriating. It was Blum, for instance, who invented the key (and diabolical) notion of "support without participation." That involved supporting Radical governments without actually entering the cabinet. Because no Socialist was himself a minister, the party owed no loyalty to the cabinet; it was free to support those policies it liked, and oppose those it disliked. The rub, as felt by successive premiers, was that when the Socialists opposed a policy, they also tended to bring down the cabinet: their Deputies, added to those of the Right, would make a majority of the Chamber, thus in turn reducing the government to a minority and causing it to fall. Of course, that made the government's life much more difficult and, on occasion, much shorter, and was much resented by the Radicals.

Although this position was extremely annoying to those who suffered from it, it remained legitimate politics and served to advance the Socialist agenda. Less easily defensible was Blum's decision to indulge his followers, even if it resulted in absurdities. Ever since the turn of the century, for instance, the Socialists, being pacifists, had ritually refused to vote the military budget. The party did not really intend to shut down the French military establishment, and its vote was just a symptom of its refusal to face reality; but, fearful of driving his followers into the arms of the Communists, Blum ritually put forth an amendment, ritually defeated, to cut off the defense credits. This posture made no sense, as Blum himself eventually realized; but it contributed to the widespread feeling that everything was modern in France except politics.

For all that, Blum had a great quality; unlike most of his fellow politicians, he refused to cut himself off from ordinary people. Throughout the late twenties, the trend had been toward an ever wider gulf between rulers and ruled. There were elections every four years, of course, but the multiplicity of parties was such as to confuse the voter and ensure that the ultimate result — the coming to power of a new government — had relatively little to do with the way the people had voted.

What the several parties advocated or promised at election time was generally unconnected to what they actually proceeded to do: partly, of course, because they felt no compunction about going back on their word, but mostly because no single party could ever hope to govern alone. France was a parliamentary democracy, and the government therefore stayed in office only so long as it had a majority in both the Chamber of Deputies and the Senate. Unfortunately, the majority in question could be achieved only by a coalition of several of the dozen or so parties among which the voters divided their favor. The result, of course, was that no single party was ever accountable for what a coalition government would do. After all, without a series of compromises, France would sink into anarchy.

The possibilities this opened for unscrupulous politicians were immense. It was often better, for instance, when faced with an unpalatable decision deliberately to provoke the fall of one's government, only to come back to power, either immediately or a few months later, with new partners and a new policy; it was always possible to blame someone else at election time. Then, many premiers, who had very little incentive to govern effectively, were well aware that their future depended on the management of the Deputies. The composition of the government almost invariably reflected this: every Deputy wanted to be a minister; the trick was to satisfy the ones likely to have sufficient support either to protect or to end the fledgling administration. And, of course, if a government fell, it meant that nonministers now had their chance.

That was bad enough. Worse, because the several parties usually advocated sharply different policies, the government often had a choice between doing nothing — thus avoiding hostile votes — or watching itself disintegrate as part of its majority deserted it on a specific question. This last danger was heightened by Blum's "support without participation." Then, as a further refinement, he invented the "support with eclipses": the Socialists would support the government on certain issues and oppose it on others.

All this required close knowledge of the way the Chamber functioned and calculations that were not infrequently far too abstruse for the voters. The result was not just that governments fell more often, but that, most of the time, the ordinary people were unable to understand what the Premier was doing or why he had fallen. The consequence was a widespread feeling that the government had become alienated from the mass of the French, and that while the politicians played their complex and selfish games the average citizen was left to suffer.

The cabinet in 1930 was composed of men of the Right; and while it kept up a barrage of attacks against the Radicals and the Socialists, it displayed the same contempt for the electorate and suffered from the same sudden eclipses that had characterized Radical-led governments. Even André Tardieu, the Premier whom *Le Temps* had praised as "young and energetic," was really neither. At fifty-four, he already had had a long and well-filled career, beginning as the writer of *Le Temps*'s own foreign policy bulletins before the war.

In many ways, however, Tardieu seemed exceptional. Tall, elegant, and disdainful, his large nose topped by equally large round glasses, he was thoroughly convinced of his superiority over practically everyone else. Any early doubt he might have had (although, in truth, none was ever visible) had been dispelled by a series of brilliant successes, starting before the war, when he wrote the daily foreign affairs column in *Le Temps*. It was then that Kidderlen-Wächter, the German under secretary of state for foreign affairs, had commented: "There are six great powers in Europe, and then there is a seventh, and that is M. André Tardieu."[20]

When, on November 2, 1929, he became Premier, he expected to remain long in office. Part of his power over his fellow politicians came from his own self-confidence, and from the generally accepted notion that he was somehow different. This was a feeling fully shared by Gaston Doumergue, the President of the Republic, who never quite knew whether he admired or disliked this peculiar man: for one thing, he went so *fast*. "He walks very quickly, with great assurance," Doumergue's chief assistant remembered. "He looks at you straight in the eye, but with a mocking air. His glasses are screwed on to his nose, his hair is black, his eyes full of laughter; his stomach protrudes a little. He reminds one of a tight spring that is about to let go. He speaks well. And then he has a peremptory way of dealing with problems, using just a few very precise words, often ironical, almost concise."[21]

As it was, Tardieu was the bright hope of the French moderate Right: alone in a group of fusty, used-up politicians, he seemed to represent the new postwar world. Instead of evading, he confronted; instead of shoring up the old, decaying structures, he trumpeted his new solutions and then insisted on their speedy implementation. The only problem was that these solutions tended to be inadequate, and at best temporary; faced with opposition, no one was quicker to change his mind than the new Premier.

That was, in part, because he often chose the appearance of power over its reality. He used few words because older politicians were long-winded; he liked to give orders because it seemed to fit the spirit of the times. Compromise was old-fashioned, iron efficiency part of the new age; and that included more than a little admiration for Mussolini, a man who had known how to seize power, all the power.

Unfortunately for Tardieu, France was not Italy, and his strutting did not make him more popular. He also quickly began losing credibility: for a strongman to be voted out of office after just three months, as happened in February 1930, was not without its comic aspect. Still, after a brief interval — the next government lasted four days — he returned to power, only to fall again in December: this kind of in-and-out hesitation waltz hardly looked serious.

The next government, led by Pierre Laval, actually stayed in office for a full year, and Tardieu was part of it. That year was just long enough for the Right to demonstrate, not just that it could not cope with the Depression, but also that its deflationary policies aggravated people's sufferings. Once again, politics seemed far removed from the feelings and desires of the electorate. It was actually a case of double alienation: the government despised the French who balked at making the kinds of sacrifices a deflationary policy required; and the French felt they were ruled by men who cared very little for them.

Things were not much better on the other side of the political spectrum. The Radicals were a tired party who had not had a fresh idea in a quarter of a century. They were still strong because they represented certain entrenched interests that brought two key groups together: civil servants and small farmers. The first of these was far more important than it might seem: because the French state monopolized all the functions that in the United States are divided among federal, state, and municipal governments, there were some two million low and middle-grade civil servants who ranged from teachers and streetcar drivers to employees in the central administration. The farmers were a major group as well. In 1930, France was still the least industrialized of any major power; its farm sector was extensive, and large holdings very rare; and so there was a plethora of small farmers, many of whom faithfully voted for the Radicals.

The party, in turn, knew just how to please them: it was firmly anticlerical; it defended the economic interests of both groups and remained, in the process, a fervent champion of private ownership; and while resisting most changes, it gave its voters the delicious feeling of being (relatively) bold and daring. Thus, for instance, the party's annual congresses could be counted on to advocate striking reforms, while its Deputies, and especially its Senators, equally reliably refused to vote for them in the Parliament.

For almost ten years the Radicals had been led by Edouard Herriot. Like so many early Radicals, he had made his way up in the world (his mother was a cleaning woman) by industry and the sort of intelligence highly prized by the men who designed school and university exams. It was as a professor that he had first entered politics. In many ways, Herriot was the embodiment of his party; a typical middle-class Frenchman, with his small mustache and large paunch, Herriot was immediately recognizable, especially since he invariably smoked a small pipe. He was famous for his violent but short rages; but he was also an adept at compromise: having vented his temper, he knew how to reach a reasonable agreement. Everything about him, in fact, seemed typical of the French middle class: his passion for good food, the rather sloppy way he dressed, all appealed to his constituency. And although when making a speech he was notably eloquent — his most famous remark, during the 1925 currency crisis, was, "We do not quarrel by the bedside of our ailing mother" — it is a kind of eloquence that today seems both meaningless and turgid.

Herriot owed his popularity, in fact, to qualities that were absolutely useless to him as a statesman. He took pride in his gastronomical knowledge and was a famous connoisseur of food and wine with a vast repertory of appropriate anecdotes. He could analyze a sauce and appraise a chef: the size of his waist was the proof of his vast experience. He was also familiar with the better brothels in Lyon, whose mayor he was, and in Paris, and was famously, if uselessly, erudite. As everyone knew, he was the author of a biography of Mme Récamier, the early nineteenth-century hostess who remained a virgin for most of her life, a piquant contrast with the professionals Herriot so enjoyed. And while certainly the visual arts meant nothing to him, Herriot kept up with the cultural life of the capital.

That was all very well; but when it came to economics, his ignorance was prodigious, and it was with a blend of bafflement and disgust that he turned to matters like the state of the currency or the drop in industrial production. Given the deteriorating state of the French economy, this was a serious lack.

Luckily for the Radicals, however, none of that mattered in 1931. As the defeated party in 1928, they could blame the Right for the slowing down of France's economy; and since it is easier to win elections with vague promises than with well worked out policies, they represented a major threat to the Tardieu-Laval coalition. As a result, the Right mounted a violent anti-Radical campaign, but, as time passed, and the 1932 elections came closer, it became clear that it was not succeeding. Moreover, the evolution of the economy obviously favored the Radicals. That was in good part because virtually no one in France understood what was happening. By May 1932 (the election took place in two rounds, on the first and the eighth), the worldwide Depression had begun affecting the country. Economic activity was slowing; industrial production, from an index figure of 100 in 1929, was down to 96, not a huge change, but one that indicated a worrisome trend, especially if it was taken in conjunction with events in the rest of the world.

Unfortunately, no one understood what was really happening. The politicians, from extreme right to extreme left, were equally ill informed. The finance minister in Tardieu's first government, for instance, was Adolphe Chéron, a supposedly wily Norman. "The cartoonists," journalist Louise Weiss noted, "never bothered to draw his face: a rounded line showing an enormously fat stomach protruding through a door was enough to identify him."[22] No one, certainly, could have been more old-fashioned than Chéron, either in his personal habits — he still wore a little beard when all young men were clean-shaven — or in his politics. He ran the nation's finances rather as if they had been a housewife's budget; all he knew was that taxes brought in such and such an amount, and that the outlays must be kept in balance. There his understanding stopped. Productivity, the rate of interest, the effect of government policy on the economy, the importance of the rate of industrial output, all that was foreign to him; and his budgets showed it clearly. As for his successors in the second Tardieu cabinet, and in the Laval governments, they were no more enlightened.

There was something new, though: in a country where leaders made speeches but parties campaigned, Tardieu and his friends emphasized the Premier's personality and achievements in a way not completely unlike that of the dictators. Walls throughout the country were plastered with posters showing a large photo of Tardieu, complete with cigarette holder, and a line in bold type, *Tardieu a dit* (Tardieu says), followed by one of his statements. Because, normally, the several right-wing parties campaigned each on its own, this not unnaturally reminded many people of the way the Fascists and the Nazis worshiped their leaders and it upset more voters than it convinced. It also reunited the Radicals and convinced them that at the next election they had better conclude an agreement with the party they had been so steadfastly avoiding, the Socialists.

In any event, the electoral system made alliances an absolute necessity, consisting, as it did, of a double hurdle. In the first round, any candidate who received more than 50 percent of the vote outright (a rare event) was elected; in the second round, a plurality was sufficient to win. Given the number of major parties, the way to win was for two or more of them to form an alliance ensuring that they would back the best placed candidate in the second round: if, for instance, the Radical had received 25 percent of the vote and the Socialist 20, and if the Socialist threw his support to the Radical, while the right-wing candidates failed to reach an alliance of their own (as had been the case in 1924, but not in 1928), then the 45 percent joint vote would be enough to put the Radical over the top.

This sort of alliance could be based on any or all of three formulas: the first a purely electoral agreement; the second an at least partial agreement on platform and principles; the third an agreement on the policy of the future government. In 1924 the second formula prevailed, and the *cartel des gauches* won the elections; in 1928 agreement of any kind proved impossible, and, under the patronage of Poincaré, the Right obtained a majority. Now the conservatives hoped that Tardieu would prove a new Poincaré, able to keep dissensions alive on the Left while uniting his own backers.

This strategy was based on red-baiting, with the role of the ogre reserved for the Socialists, and most especially for Léon Blum; and it turned out to be a mistake. Neither Blum nor the Socialists were really frightening. The Radicals, who had begun to promise better times, were eagerly heard. Still, Blum mistrusted Herriot only marginally less than Herriot mistrusted Blum. The result was a series of maneuvers in which the Radical leaders and their Socialist counterparts kept making statements in which they said the opposite of what they really meant, a spectacle the connoisseurs found highly entertaining.

All through the early thirties, therefore, the French found themselves watching two opposite pairs: on the Left, Blum and Herriot were engaging in a highly complex hesitation waltz, while on the Right Tardieu and Laval gave the always entertaining spectacle of bitter rivals who pretend they are friends. In 1931 it still made for good theater. By the spring of 1932, with the economy visibly slowing, nothing was quite as amusing as it had once been.

None of that was of any interest to those who led the fashionable world. Elsa Maxwell went on planning parties, Schiaparelli designed ever more spectacular dresses, and Genêt, in her Paris letters, concentrated firmly on social and artistic events. French governments, she felt, did not have to be taken seriously; politics was a joke, so much so that when she reported the French reaction to Roosevelt's victory in November 1932, she explained that the public had been rooting for Roosevelt — TR or FDR, she added, they did not much care which.

In this case, however, the ordinary voters proved more perceptive than the elites. They had the uneasy feeling that a major catastrophe was looming, and, except in Paris, they took the elections very seriously. What they worried about, as the Tout-Paris went on dancing, was whether they might soon be unemployed; and, for them, the election was the key to a better future.

# THREE

# A CHANGING WORLD

PARIS in 1932 did not pay much attention to the elections. Of course, there were meetings at which the politicians made speeches. The press went on at great length about the merits or shortcomings of the various parties, and *Le Temps,* ever solemn, ever reactionary, announced in lugubrious tones that France was teetering on the edge of revolution, but it convinced no one. That was, in part, because the economic slowdown was less visible in the capital, in part because the city's animation served to conceal the changes taking place. More than the rest of the country, the Parisians still refused to admit that anything had gone seriously wrong. As for the Tout-Paris, it found the subject rather a bore: parties went on as ever, the races at Auteuil were run according to schedule, and the greatest musical organizer in the city went on giving concerts at which all the listeners were her guests.

There was a good reason for that. The organizer in question, far from making money, spent it on a lavish scale and could easily afford to do so: Winnaretta Singer, who had married Prince

Edmond de Polignac, was an heiress to the sewing machine fortune and a cousin of Daisy Fellowes.

She was also a most unorthodox figure. Immensely rich, the daughter of American parents, she had been raised in France by her mother and a stepfather, who in due course raped her. Then she had been married off to the prince de Scey-Montbéliard, to whom she took an instant loathing. The Vatican, conveniently, was kind to the rich; an annulment was easily procured, and Winnaretta then found, in the person of the sixty-year-old Edmond de Polignac, the perfect husband.

It was a role that required a good deal of tact. Not only was the new princesse passionately interested in music, she was also very fond of her own sex. It was understood, therefore, that she and her husband were to be nothing more than friends, while her romances involved her with women ranging from Violet Trefusis, Vita Sackville-West's great love, to a Russian refugee; and since the only limits to her love life were those she set herself, she often found herself in the midst of dramatic scenes when her current passion proved less than faithful. This was a problem the prince was well able to understand: like his wife, he preferred his own sex.

As it was, the Polignacs were no ordinary couple. He was the great-grandson of Marie Antoinette's closest friend and the grandson of the prime minister who was directly responsible for the Revolution of 1830, and was connected to most of the great families in France. That all appeared most appropriate: he lived, essentially, in another century. Elegant, easily wearied, he was given to wandering through his wife's musicales, remarking, in a quite audible voice: "I really don't like other people."[1] He did, however, like music — he was even a bit of a composer — a taste he shared with his wife.

As for the princesse, she was an ardent music lover who gave dazzling concerts in the house she had built especially and in which José-María Sert, an immensely fashionable and equally untalented painter, had frescoed the music room. It was Mme de Polignac's great merit that her patronage went not just to famous virtuosi, but to the very best contemporary composers.

At times, she supported Erik Satie, financially and morally, almost single-handedly. She gave commissions to practically every important composer of her time, including Stravinsky; and she was advised throughout by that great lady of French music, Nadia Boulanger. All through the twenties and thirties, therefore, being invited to one of the princesse's concerts was an eagerly sought boon. Because they were private, Genêt almost never mentioned them in her Paris letters, but she was there, and they were very much a part of her musical education.

The princesse had not always been so august. At the turn of the century, young women carefully avoided her, but within a few years the support of the vast and socially powerful Polignac and Decazes families had given her an unassailable position. Tall, austere, and with the distant manners of the shy, Aunt Winnie, as her many relatives called her, had an impressive presence. It wasn't just her looks — Cocteau irreverently called her Mother Dante — she could also, on occasion, speak up sharply. When, for instance, a society woman, alluding to her lack of aristocratic birth, told her: "Well, after all, your name is worth nothing," Mme de Polignac promptly replied: "It's worth something at the bottom of a check."[2]

There was something very grand about the princesse Edmond's salon, even if the most modern music was to be heard there. The atmosphere was quite different at another great musical house. For the comte de Beaumont, out-and-out chic counted for a great deal. Mme de Polignac always invited the same music lovers and members of society to her musicales; Etienne de Beaumont, who once said that parties were given to annoy those who are not invited, saw to it that his invitations went out at the last possible moment, thus causing the greatest possible anguish to those who were not quite sure they were on his list. As it was, the Beaumonts had given some of the twenties' most successful balls, and there was a frivolous note at their gatherings that could not be found at the Polignacs. Etienne de Beaumont, very tall, very thin, very mannered, was the master of ceremonies and could count on the unquestioning cooperation of his wife, the ugly but majestic Edith. Like Edmond de Polignac, Beaumont preferred his own sex and was, on occasion, given to excess; it was long remembered that he had appeared at one of his own balls dressed as Cupid in a pink leotard, and that he had pranced around pretending to fling arrows at his guests. But he also had a sharp and accurate sense of what was new and good in painting, sculpture, and music. He owned, among other things, Picasso's stage curtain for Satie's *Mercure;* it was he who organized and financed the *Soirées de Paris,* a series of evenings that took place in a Paris theater and offered sometimes the best new music, sometimes the Ballets Russes de Monte-Carlo, the company that continued Diaghilev's tradition and eventually hired the young Georges Balanchine, sometimes daring new plays like Jean Cocteau's "adaptation" of *Romeo and Juliet.*

Among the politicians who, unlike the Tout-Paris, were paying a great deal of attention to the elections, all this appeared utterly devoid of interest. Even Léon Blum, that faithful theatergoer, cared more about literature than about the musical avant-garde; but it was part of the glitter of Paris that so much was happening at the same time, and that very different people doing very different things could be convinced that the circles they belonged to were the ones that really mattered.

When in April 1932 the campaign for the elections began in earnest, Parisians listened with half an ear to the usual mix of inflated promises and outright distortions. That the elections would make a difference seemed certain: French prosperity, once so brilliant, was looking rather tarnished, even in Paris. Clearly, a change was necessary, but that France might be on its way to a catastrophe occurred to virtually no one. The elections, as a result, sometimes seemed like another form of entertainment, a public theater in which speeches were made, villains denounced, and the suspense maintained until the very end.

It was, however, a theater for men only. Women did not have the vote nor could they be elected to either Chamber or Senate, and change was not in view. That, however, is not to say that women were completely excluded from the political process; they could influence their sons, husbands, or lovers, and they frequently did. Still, it was the men who mattered and they found that the world had become an uncertain place. The slowdown of the economy threatened the middle and working classes, while across the Rhine the full-fledged Depression, complete with bank failures and millions of unemployed, was anything but reassuring.

There was no reason to despair, though. While the conservative alliance led by Tardieu, Laval, and Flandin had obviously failed to cope with the economic slowdown, the Radicals and the Socialists seemed to offer just the right dose of reform. Naturally the two parties, in an attempt to garner more votes, never let potential supporters forget that they disagreed on a wide range of topics, but they also stood for certain common goals: helping the unemployed, giving tax relief to the lower middle classes, and ensuring the maintenance of peace as implemented by the League of Nations — all notions that had a strong appeal for a majority of the French.

On the opposite side of the political spectrum, the two major right-wing parties, the Union républicaine démocratique and the Alliance démocratique, defended their current policy of increasing taxation to relieve the deficit, ignoring the unemployed (who were just lazy) and distrusting all foreigners. And, of course, the Right kept predicting that if the Radicals and the Socialists, with their allies, took over the government, they would, in no time at all, make France a Soviet republic.

As it turned out, no one actually believed this astonishingly silly prediction: the time for a red scare had not come. And furthermore it was the Right's bad luck that its leaders (together with its policies) seemed far less appealing than their opposites on the Left. Tardieu, in spite of all his efforts, struck people as dangerously authoritarian; Laval was (except in his own district) widely distrusted, perhaps because he looked as dishonest as he actually was; and the third of the Right's leaders, Pierre-Etienne Flandin, suffered from an almost total lack of charisma. Tall, thin, reserved, he reminded many observers of an Englishman — never a popular thing to be in France. Worse, his passion for modernity, which took the form of a reliance on new technologies and the latest machines, struck his listeners as abstract, cold, and inhuman: men really had no place in his schemes. Finally, although he was given to trenchant affirmations and emphatic declarations of principle, he had been known to give up his opinions under pressure, and so he hardly inspired trust.

The Left, in the person of its leaders, had much more to offer. Both Herriot and Blum were well-known and widely popular figures, perhaps in part because they were seen as more than just politicians. There always seems to be something reassuring about men who could have a career outside politics if they chose, because they are thought to be motivated by patriotism as opposed to greed. Then, too, because they have a broader outlook, a more extended frame of reference, they are seen as bringing both common sense and a knowledge of the world to the narrow arena of pure politics; and finally, to a surprising degree, the French electorate, itself not noticeably cultivated, felt both respect and liking for intellectuals in politics. In that respect, Blum and Herriot, in their different ways, stood well above most of their colleagues. And although they disagreed on many issues, both were seen as firm supporters of democratic values, men for whom principle mattered.

Because the papers did not print much about political men's private lives (except, of course, when they decided to libel them), people who did not attend first nights at the theater were unaware that Blum was just as likely to be there as if he had still been a critic: here, in fact, was a place where two quite separate layers of Parisian life intersected. Blum's interest was in the theater itself; other politicians were more interested in actresses. Tardieu had a long affair with the glamorous Mary Marquet, the dour Georges Mandel's mistress was the buxom Beatrix Bretty. For everyone, though, the theater was still the last word in glamour. One actress, Cécile Sorel, was as famous as Madonna is today largely because she was good at playing the ingenues in Molière's plays; others were revered for their beauty or their elegance. All mattered.

First nights were still great Parisian events: they were one of the few places where a really broad cross-section of the Tout-Paris, from aristocrats to ministers, from painters to star reporters, could be seen together. Indeed, many people measured their degree of social success by the number of invitations to first nights they received. Some were more official than others: at the state-owned theaters, the Comédie-Française and the Opéra, the President of the Republic and the Premier were likely to attend. At the small, avant-garde houses, the audience would run the gamut from people like the Beaumonts and the Noailles to new authors and even painters; and then there was the *théâtre de boulevard,* performing plays written specifically to please the general public that if successful made their authors a great deal of money.

The theater was also about fashion. The greatest couturiers designed costumes, and people came almost as much to see what Schiaparelli or Chanel had done as for the play itself. They went to the theater because it was still, even after the advent of the talkies, the best known, the most familiar sort of entertainment. They went to see the stars they read about every day; they went to be amused by authors just clever enough to surprise the audience a little, and just practical enough not to surprise it too much. Some plays had thinly disguised characters, often a well-known politician, which gave the viewers the delicious feeling that they were in on a tasty secret. Others were simply standard bedroom farces in which the number of doors and closets mattered more than the motivations of the characters. And then, on occasion, there was a play of real merit from the likes of Giraudoux, Cocteau, or even Gide. Many of these are still frequently performed.

For Schiaparelli, the theater was such an important moment of social life that she had invented a new type of dress specifically to be worn on first nights; and she herself was to be seen there because it was the right place in which to be seen. Genêt also came because to her it was an essential part of that civilized atmosphere she found so entrancing. Politicians like Camille Chautemps, one of the Radical leaders, were there because it was the done thing. For all of them, the theater was the easiest way of keeping up with one of the traditions that had made Paris such a vital center.

Important new plays came in all shapes. When Jules Romains wrote his *Donogoo,* he meant to entertain with a biting satire while criticizing, in the least pedantic way imaginable, capitalism and the way it worked. On the whole, he succeeded: *Donogoo* is a funny play. It begins where an earlier Romains work ended: we are reminded that M. Le Trouhadec, a well-known geographer, has invented the city of Donogoo-Tonka in order to steal a march on his colleagues; but now he is a candidate to the Academy and something must be done to prevent exposure of his fraud. In a country where academies were still revered, it was a promising beginning.

That is where an adventurer named Lamendin comes in. When M. Le Trouhadec begs him for help, he quickly realizes that there is an obvious solution: by actually building the imaginary city, he will at the same time save M. Le Trouhadec and make his own fortune. Still, going off to the jungle and founding a city there takes money, so he floats the shares of a new corporation, something many real adventurers had done in the days of the stock-market boom, and sets off with a group of desperadoes, supposedly to find Donogoo, in fact to create it. When, in due course, the city comes into being, Lamendin promptly installs himself as its dictator and proceeds to remodel the way life is lived. He forbids all marriages, for instance, because wedded bliss is just a code word for domestic scenes and wholesale lying by both husband and wife.

*Donogoo* is no masterpiece, but its social criticism is biting and surprisingly timeless. Watered stock, that favorite twenties device, was just an early incarnation of the more recent junk bond. Academic pomposity and dishonesty still make headlines; and, as a result, the play is still constantly revived. As for the unkind things it has to say about marriage, they, too, have the ring of truth. Add to that the sharpest of dialogues, and it is easy to see why *Donogoo* was such a success. People went to laugh and, while they were at it, they gave some thought to the defects of their society.

Jules Romains, for all his funny lines, raised some important issues, and so did that most successful, most intelligent, and most suave of authors, Jean Giraudoux, in his *Judith*. A former diplomat, Giraudoux embodied a key aspect of postwar France: understated, cynical, and slightly weary, he despised bellicose patriots and the politicians whose lies were likely to bring about another catastrophe. He stood for reconciliation with (pre-Hitler) Germany, not so much at the state level, but as the result of the common feelings shared by those who had survived the great massacre. He could be sharply funny: his satire of Raymond Poincaré (under the name of "Rebendart") in *Bella,* a novel he published in the mid-twenties, stung; but he also had a streak of often melancholy poetry and looked out at a world that, having gone mad in 1914, had never really recovered.

Giraudoux was immensely popular, but *Judith* received a decidedly mixed reception. Written in a style that was so pure it seemed deceptively commonplace, his new play took up a biblical theme: surely nothing could have been more respectable. Only, by the time Giraudoux was done, the Bible looked less like a sacred book than like the kind of propaganda that blossomed during the war. The original story is simple enough: Judith, a pious but very beautiful widow, sets out to save her people who are about to be slaughtered by Holofernes, an enemy general; so she makes her way into his tent, gets him drunk, pretends to be seduced (while still, the story insists, remaining chaste), and, just as she is about to lose her virtue, she cuts off Holofernes' head with his own sword.

This, therefore, is a story about purity and heroism (Judith's) as well as about domineering braggadocio (Holofernes'): there is nothing pleasant about it but it has a stark grandeur. Giraudoux's *Judith,* as the Parisian audiences discovered, was much more modern. The epic became a story of ambition and unsatisfied love; the heroine, no longer a sainted widow, was startlingly like some of the ladies who gathered the Tout-Paris in their salons.

Rich, greedy, almost unconsciously a hypocrite, at the same time clear-eyed and passionate, this Judith becomes someone much too complex to be a standard heroine. Worse still, she kills Holofernes not to save her people, but because he scorns her love; and she is then imprisoned in the temple so that its priests can go about creating the myth that has endured to this day.

There is nothing admirable about Judith, save perhaps her determination to get what she wants; there is nothing holy about the priests who create a dangerous and deceptive myth — the kind of myth with which Giraudoux's audiences were so familiar. From "the war to end all wars" to "the stab in the back which cost Germany the war," and on to the new and particularly sickening racial theories being propagated by the Nazis across the Rhine, the postwar public had heard a great deal of this kind of phony heroism, and had no trouble recognizing it in *Judith.*

That made many people uncomfortable, as did the fact that the original story had been turned upside down; but one of the most influential critics in Paris, Maurice Martin du Gard, himself a man of conservative views, saw the play for what it is: a masterpiece. "Never has Giraudoux shown on the stage with such prodigality the spiritual wealth that makes him a moralist without peer," he wrote, going on to praise "the lively style of the text, which immediately becomes a classic, that perfect and musical language . . . that symphony where all the themes come together."[3]

*Judith* raised too many difficult questions for much of the public, and its theme was too austere. It seemed, in a way, made for the reviewers (and posterity), but there were simpler subjects that had a broader appeal. Explaining that money is evil and corrupts those it touches is an ever-popular theme, especially when the economy is in bad shape: whereas, obviously, people would rather have money, they feel better about not having enough of it if the rich can be seen as contemptible. The success of a play by Drieu La Rochelle, *L'Eau fraîche* (Fresh Water), was due entirely to this simplistic motif.

Drieu himself was a successful and ambitious young novelist who shared Giraudoux's cynicism, but he parted company with Giraudoux in one crucial way: like so many self-defined revolutionaries during the Depression, he attributed all the ills of this world to international finance (and, thus, to the Jews who were supposed to control it). He detested communism; unfortunately, he found the solution first in fascism and then in Hitler.

That was not fully apparent when *L'Eau fraîche* became a hit, but its denunciation of the rich temptress is typical of what soon followed. The play is the contorted story of a scientist corrupted by his mistress's wealth and offers some witticisms and a number of cynical (if easy) quips about the power of money. Under its modern veneer, in fact, it followed a tired and oft-repeated formula, but the style was brilliant enough to catch the audiences, and the denunciation of a certain kind of capitalist made it seem right up to date.

The two plays, each in its own way, seemed fashionably modern, *Judith* because it exploded a convenient myth, *L'Eau fraîche* because its apparent theme was the corrupting power of wealth; and so did the most successful musical comedy in Paris. The book, it is true, had been written before the war by Pierre Louÿs, but it had been thoroughly jazzed up, and the music was by a popular contemporary composer, the Swiss Arthur Honegger. The story of *Les Aventures du Roi Pausole* is simple enough: in King Pausole's realm, pleasure is the norm; no bothersome morality, no retrograde laws, are allowed to impede it. Only one thing is forbidden: passion, that curse invented by the gods to punish mankind.

Elegantly erotic, constantly amusing, daring but never shocking, *Pausole* was a huge hit. It also seemed to fit perfectly into the modern outlook: nothing was more thoroughly despised than Victorian morality (even if it went on being practiced by most of the French). In its cheerful amorality, in its firm refusal to believe in anything but pleasure, the realm of King Pausole seemed like the positive of which *Judith* was the negative.

Musical comedies were all very well, but it was another, not unrelated form of entertainment that really brought in the crowds: *le music-hall* was the French equivalent of vaudeville and offered the kind of shows that made Paris famous among the less intellectual part of the public. Even better, because most of the show was nonverbal, foreigners could enjoy themselves as they could not at the theater, and they attended in droves. Genêt herself, in a slightly superior way, was fond of it all: she knew it was not to be taken seriously, but that the right sort of slightly disdainful approval was just the attitude with which her Paris friends agreed. And since her readers, when they reached Paris, made a beeline for places like the Casino de Paris or the slightly more earthy Folies-Bergère, she covered their shows at length.

At any one of the half-dozen theaters that competed eagerly to offer these appealing spectacles, the public could see a cheerful mix of acrobats, animal acts, famous singers, and nearly nude dancers, usually crowned with ostrich plumes. There was music, there were jokes, the sets were spectacular, and the costumes, though usually skimpy, were glittering. All this was a postwar invention: there had been music-hall spectacles before, but they were neither as varied nor as undressed, and so these struck the spectators as a thoroughly modern form of entertainment — not unlike Ziegfeld's revues in New York.

What really brought people in, besides the "girls" and the animal acts, was the headliner. That was invariably a singer, rarely a man, most often a woman whose voice was the least of her assets: personality and the ability to create a mood were what really counted. The star did not have to be young or beautiful. Like the immensely famous Fréhel, she could be middle-aged, drugged, and ravaged looking; but none of that mattered when, dressed simply in black, she stood alone on the stage and opened her heart to her listeners. As Edith Piaf was to do later, Fréhel sang about bad luck, about the tough life of whores and waitresses, about love doomed from the beginning, all in a hoarse voice resonant with sincerity and a kind of desperate strength. Hers was a world of unheated rooms high up under the roof, of forbidden relationships, of lost soldiers and cheap brothels, and the public loved it.

Fréhel, however ravaged, was in her early forties; but when it came to sheer, massive stardom, she could not compete with a performer who had been on the stage since 1897 and famous since 1911: Mistinguett. Just what it was that made *la Mis,* as she was called, so hugely famous was hard to say. She was not beautiful; she was neither a really good singer nor a really good dancer; her voice was frankly awful; her material entirely predictable — but with all that she had magic.

Perhaps it was in part her directness, her utter lack of pretense or pretension: she was what she was, a girl from the lower classes who had made good but kept her accent and enjoyed her stardom. She was funny, she was sexy and had famously beautiful legs — at one point they were insured by Lloyd's for a million pounds. Even her face, with the wide mouth and the tilted nose, had something appealing about it that corresponded to her unique blend of the common and the classy. Just before the war, Mistinguett had discovered Maurice Chevalier, whom she made her partner on the stage and in bed. In the twenties, she had invented a new sort of performance. Topped with a pyramid of feathers, wearing a skirt slit to her hips but continued in back by an endless train, followed by a corps of dancers in glittering costumes, she would appear at the top of a vast staircase and sing as she slowly came down: the mix of splendor and parody seemed uniquely suited to her. Even better, she never hesitated to make fun of herself: one of her great hits of the thirties was a song in which she proclaimed, in her gravelly voice: "They say that I like aigrettes, plumes, and costumes / It's true! / They say that my voice goes off the rails when I sing my ditties, that my nose curls up / It's true! / They say that I have big teeth, that I can only sing three notes / It's true! / They say that I show off my gams / But I wouldn't be Mistinguett if I wasn't that way! / They say that, when I go shopping, I don't pay for what I buy . . . but if they made me finance minister / France wouldn't be so broke!"

No one could have been more French, more Parisian, than *la Mis,* and that, in part, was why the public loved her; but there was another performer it loved just as much because she embodied the wild and sensual appeal of a newer world. Josephine Baker had come to Paris in 1925, and the moment she set foot on the stage of the Théâtre des Champs-Elysées, wearing only a bunch of bananas, she became the toast of the town. Thin but very shapely, incredibly lithe, her skin a voluptuous shade of café au lait, she was sex appeal incarnate — and funny as well. Whenever she turned her knees inward and crossed her eyes, the entire audience shrieked with laughter. She was naive and erotic at the same time; she moved fast, furiously, and provocatively, parodying herself as she went. And having made a huge and instant hit, she remained popular year after year.

It was only in the season of 1930–31, though, that Baker and Mistinguett started a feud which provided the two stars with that essential publicity adjunct, a favorite enemy. Until then, *la Mis* had reigned unchallenged at that grandest of music halls, the Casino de Paris: now, for an entire, wildly successful year, Josephine was the star of the show. Even without that, she would hardly have passed unnoticed: she had just acquired a leopard whom she dressed up with a diamond collar and took everywhere with her. The sight of the star and the animal walking down the street to general applause was by no means rare.

Still, not even a big cat and a well-publicized feud would have been enough to keep Josephine at the pinnacle; but then it turned out that, along with her sexy figure and sexier dance style, she also had a warm, melodious, and altogether entrancing voice. Even better, the songs she sang at the Casino de Paris were instant hits. There was, for instance, *"La Petite Tonkinoise,"* the story of a girl from Tonkin and Annam (then part of French Indochina) who was the mistress of a French colonist:

*"C'est moi qui suis sa petite / Son Annana, son Annana, son Annamite / Je suis vive, je suis charmante / Comme un petit oiseau qui chante. / Il m'appelle sa petite bourgeoise / Sa Tonkiki, sa Tonkiki, sa Tonkinoise / D'autres lui font les beaux yeux / Mais c'est moi qui l'aime le mieux."*[4] (I am his own little / His Annana, Annana, Annamite / I am as lively, as charming / as a little bird that sings. / He calls me his little wife / His Tonkiki, his Tonkiki, his Tonkinese / Others may ogle him seductively / But I love him the best of all.) For all its now shocking air of colonial domination — the little Indochinese's principal merit was that, of all the French colonist's mistresses, she loved him the best — the song is catchy and funny, and Josephine's blend of naïveté and sophistication made her performance completely enchanting.

*"La Petit Tonkinoise"* was already twenty-five years old although it had never been a hit before, but it was a new song by the same lyricist-composer, Vincent Scotto, that took Paris by storm and remained Baker's signature tune. In *"J'ai Deux Amours,"* it was the star herself who seemed to be speaking directly and in the way most pleasing to her public: *"J'ai deux amours,"* she crooned, *"Mon pays et Paris / Par eux toujours / Mon coeur est ravi."*[5] (I have two loves / My country and Paris. / By them always / My heart is enchanted.) From then on, every time she left the city

and every time she returned, every time she was interviewed, every time she appeared on the stage or was heard on the radio, invariably Baker sang those appealing words set to a lilting tune.

That she should do so showed she had changed: she was no longer the wild creature who had appeared in Paris fresh from the jungles of Harlem and Broadway, and some of her fans regretted it. After praising the Casino de Paris show, Genêt went on to say:

> It is . . . as full of staircases as a Freudian dream, has . . . acres of fine costumes, the four best cancan dancers in captivity, a thriller in which Miss Baker is rescued from a typhoon by a gorilla. . . . The show even contains long glimpses of the beautiful Baker . . . [who] has, alas, almost become a little lady. Her caramel-colored body, which overnight became a legend in Europe, is still magnificent, but it has become thinned, trained, almost civilized. Her voice, especially in the vo-deo-do's, is still a magic flute that hasn't yet heard Mozart — though even that, one fears, will come in time. . . . On that lovely animal visage lies now a sad look, not of captivity but of dawning intelligence.[6]

Genêt need not have worried: greater sophistication did not spoil Josephine Baker.

In its more frenzied aspects, especially the nightclubs and the dance halls, all this night life belonged to a world in which no respectable politician could be seen. Paris, as its citizens knew, had many strata, but it was unified by a common interest in the leading politicians. It wasn't just that the survival or fall of the government had become an eagerly followed spectator sport: men like Tardieu, Herriot, or Blum were as well known, as avidly watched, as today's pop stars, and that was quite a change. In the twenties, the leading statesmen were guests in some of the great houses of Paris; in the thirties they were eagerly sought by all the hostesses, eagerly watched everywhere. For the first time, political success brought with it a dazzling social life.

The very fact that the two most famous leaders of the Left were on politically delicate terms was thus as much an object of comment as Mistinguett's latest crack. Luckily for the amusement of the public, Herriot, who liked to appear as an easygoing bon vivant, was a man who was also quick to feel he had been insulted. And when it came to attacks on his political position, he never hesitated to fight back. Unlike Blum, for whom ideas tended to come first, Herriot concentrated on personalities, his own first and foremost; and the fact that the Socialists in Lyon, a notoriously independent bunch, had tried to replace him as mayor did nothing to endear the rest of that party to him. Under those circumstances, his friendship for Blum, always an on-and-off business, faded rapidly.

Still, the two leaders, men whose differences were far greater than their similarities, were bound together, whether they liked it or not. The elections were coming up, and this time the Left could win — provided the Socialists and the Radicals came to an agreement.

Luckily, they shared certain positions. Both were in favor of peace, disarmament, and the League of Nations; both favored allowing labor unions to develop; both felt that the current tax system unfairly penalized the poor and the lower middle class. Just as important, Blum was as forgiving as he was tolerant. Inflexible on matters of basic principle, he was always willing to forget a fight or an insult, especially when the interests of the party, and therefore of the working class, were at stake. Because of that, he was the perfect partner for the touchy and self-involved Herriot: not only was Blum a great negotiator, he was also legendary for his tact.

Naturally, just as the Left could see its opportunity, the Right was aware of the possible danger. Pierre Laval, the current Premier, was a man whose ambition was happily untrammeled by principle or conviction. Born in the Auvergne of lower middle-class parents, he had retained the rough accent of his native province. A small, paunchy man with thick black hair and dark skin, Laval reminded many people of a Gypsy, and his personal habits did nothing to blunt the comparison. Seldom given to washing, he was also a heavy smoker, with a cigarette permanently stuck at the corner of his mouth and yellowed teeth and fingers. As for his clothes, they looked as if he had slept in them, and he made himself visible by always wearing a white tie, no matter what the time or circumstances.

Laval had entered politics before 1914 as a Socialist and, indeed, was a pacifist during the war, neatly evading military service by claiming a largely trumped-up disability. He had then drifted to the Right, partly because there was less competition, the conservatives having generally more money than brains, partly because he was anxious to make a fortune, and it is easier to make business connections if you are not a Socialist. Unlike Tardieu, who actually had ideas, Laval was interested solely in his personal position, and his great talent was for seducing just enough Deputies to ensure his rise. It was, in fact, a standard comment on his utter lack of principle or honor that people never tired of pointing out that Laval, spelled backward, is still Laval.

In mid-February 1932, however, one of the Premier's maneuvers went seriously wrong. It had occurred to him that the way to win the coming election was to change the voting law so as to favor the Right. This would have made perfect sense except for one awkward fact: the Radicals had a majority in the Senate.

As it was, because so many Radical Senators held reactionary views, Laval considered them his allies — and so they usually were; but when it came to the possibility that their party might be wiped out, they bestirred themselves. The new electoral law, which had passed the Chamber, was defeated in the Senate, and the government automatically fell.

Clearly, some other stratagem was needed. This is where Tardieu came in; for just as Blum and Herriot found themselves forced into an alliance, so Laval (who became a minister in the new cabinet) and Tardieu (who had been a minister in the old) were forced to work together if the Right was to have any chance of winning. Of course, Laval thought that Tardieu was stiff-necked, impractical, and difficult. As for Tardieu, that *grand bourgeois,* it is easy to guess what he thought of the corrupt parvenu with whom he was allied.

Laval could count on the absolute fidelity of the voters in his district, but he was not a popular figure. It wasn't just that he always looked as if he needed a bath (and, in fact, he did), or that when he smiled he gave the impression that the toothbrush must be an object foreign to him; his gift for intrigue, his hunger for money, and his obvious lack of principle caused him to be disliked in many quarters. At the same time, in spite of his obvious personal disadvantages, he had a good deal of charm. He knew how to talk to his fellow politicians and thoroughly understood the power of small favors. As a result, he could count on far more friends among his colleagues than the imperious Tardieu.

Because Tardieu had a (wholly undeserved) reputation for modernity and effectiveness, it was up to him to sway the voters, and one way to do that was to buy the support of as many papers as possible. That took money, of course, but then he could use the *fonds secrets*. These were the fairly ample sums traditionally put at the disposal of the Premier and of the most important ministers — the custom persists to this day — for which no accounting had to be made. In theory, the money went to pay for the sort of secret business in which all governments engage, anything from hiring foreign agents to bribing diplomats or civil servants abroad. In fact, under Laval, Tardieu, and a number of their successors, the money was largely used to improve the cabinet's prospects. Secret subventions to certain papers and certain journalists had long been a tradition; now they took on a whole new dimension, so that a "spontaneous" press campaign appeared to back Tardieu's quest for greater power.

This was possible because the French press was the shame of an otherwise civilized nation. This was true even of that most august of papers, *Le Temps*. An austere daily, all print and no photos, *Le Temps* was for many years very close to being an official paper. Although nominally independent, its owners — a consortium of industrialists and insurance tycoons — saw to it that its editorials followed the government's position, so long, naturally, as the government belonged on the Right. Thus, in 1932, it could be relied on to support Tardieu and Laval.

Even worse, France did not have a single periodical willing to print the news without slanting it. Because papers and magazines are expensive to run and seldom profitable, most of the French press reflected the views of those who could afford to support it, that is, the Right and extreme Right. Papers like *L'Action française,* which was nominally royalist but in fact ultranationalist and reactionary, and *Candide,* which expressed virtually the same opinions, attacked the parliamentary regime ceaselessly, as did magazines like *Gringoire* and, after 1933, *Je Suis Partout;* and because both of the latter also included high-quality travel and culture pages, their political message reached people who would never have read *L'Action française.*

The five main "general information" (that is, supposedly impartial) papers, *Le Petit Parisien, Le Matin, Le Journal, Le Petit Journal,* and the violently rightist *L'Echo de Paris,* which were all, in fact, very conservative, distorted the news shamelessly. Further, with the exception of *L'Action française,* these publications, together with a host of lesser papers, were usually willing to praise the (right-wing) government (as opposed to the parliamentary regime), provided they were paid to do so.

The Left, in all this, did not fare well. There were several small Radical-sponsored periodicals, but the only one of any importance was *L'Oeuvre,* which was, in fact, as close as France came to having a decent paper. Then the Socialists had their own daily, *Le Populaire,* the editorials of which were most often written by Léon Blum; and the Communists published two papers, *L'Humanité,* which came out in the morning and had a small readership, and the much more successful evening paper, *Ce Soir.* Of these, only *L'Oeuvre* had a significant circulation; the others appealed mostly to the party stalwarts, although Blum's editorials were widely read in political circles because they indicated what the position of the Socialist Deputies was likely to be.

While it was a well-established tradition that governments spent part of their *fonds secrets* on the press, the practice assumed a new amplitude under Tardieu, and he then went a step further: he used some of the money to finance the *ligues*. These groups of young men, often armed, furthered their cause by provoking and exploiting street disorders; they invariably belonged to the extreme Right. In 1930 the numbers involved were still very small, but they grew rapidly when Tardieu began secretly financing some of these organizations, and it was noticed that on his political excursions he was often surrounded by a group of toughs.

As it was, the Tardieu government took office in February 1932 with the clear intent of winning the elections three months later, but because it was nothing more than the previous cabinet, reshuffled, it followed the same ever more unpopular policies. By 1932, the worldwide Depression had finally reached France. Markets were vanishing at home and abroad; unemployment was spreading; and, inevitably, the tax yield began to shrink rapidly.

Unfortunately, no one in Paris understood what was happening. Economics was simply not a French science. It is symptomatic that Keynes was not translated into French until 1947; in the thirties, his name, though famous in the Anglo-Saxon world, was quite unknown in France. For the bankers, high officials, and academics who claimed they understood the subject, the economy as such was not even a concern: all they thought about was monetary inflation, the value of the currency on the exchange markets, and the state of the budget.

The government's response to the slowdown was, therefore, twofold. On the one hand, Tardieu, who was minister of agriculture (in the Laval cabinet) throughout 1931, tried to protect the farmers by putting a floor under the prices of certain commodities, a traditional remedy that had already been used in the 1880s, while Laval and Pierre-Etienne Flandin, his finance minister, tried to reduce the deficit by cutting expenditures, thus remaining faithful to the most rigid economic orthodoxy.

That might have worked in a booming economy, but it had disastrous effects in a downturn. As the state spent less, and took more from the producers, unemployment increased rapidly, and that in turn reduced the tax yield, which, of course, deepened the deficit. There was also a concurrent difficulty: it was extremely difficult to cut the budget. Out of a total of 50.1 billion francs, the military and the service of the debt together absorbed 32.6 billion, leaving only 17.5 billion to cover all other expenditures, and much of the latter was structurally rigid: civil service salaries (which included those of the teachers in the state-owned schools and universities) were obviously hard to squeeze.

Of course, civil servants can be fired; more difficult, perhaps, their salaries can be cut. Without going quite so far, Laval and Flandin, and then, after February 1932, Tardieu and Flandin (who remained finance minister), cut where they could but still, greatly to their surprise, they ended with a 5-billion-franc deficit. It seemed, in fact, that there was a correlation: every time the budget was cut, the tax yield, reflecting the decline of the economy, shrank proportionately, thus increasing the deficit all over again.

Tardieu and Laval were not stupid men; they simply had no notion of economics. For them, life was simple: if the budget developed a deficit, then you cut expenditures and raised taxes. The fact that the budget reflected the state of the economy, however, utterly escaped them; nor did they realize that a depressed economy needs to be reflated.

Thus, to their uncomprehending surprise, the budget of 1932 showed a growing imbalance. Like so many other politicians, however, they reacted to this unpleasant bit of reality by refusing to see its causes. They and their friends on the Right simply assumed that expenditures should be cut even more drastically, while the Radicals and the Socialists, who were happily free of office, united in denouncing the suffering of a significant part of the electorate. The stability of the franc comes first, the Right replied, cheerfully blind to the fact that, with the economy in shambles, the franc was unlikely to do well. People come first, the Left insisted. It could not have been more convenient: here was a major issue on which the Socialists and the Radicals agreed.

When, three weeks before the elections, the campaign opened, it was beginning to be clear that the Right was in trouble: the farmers, whose income was shrinking, the civil servants, threatened with salary cuts, all were ready to vote for the Radicals; the workers and some of the lower-grade civil servants, who were exploited by disdainful superiors, naturally supported the Socialists. And while the two parties could neither agree on a program nor even conclude a proper agreement, they knew just what to do. For the second round, they decided that whichever of their candidates had the advantage would receive the endorsement of the also-ran: it was a formula that was likely to be highly effective.

Tardieu naturally knew that he was in trouble. Even if the Right united as the Left was doing it was likely to lose; but, in fact, it was not about to unite. Even worse, from its point of view, there was now a new Right, influenced by Mussolini and to a growing degree by Hitler while still preserving some peculiarly French notions.

Tardieu and his friends were firm believers in the Republic and in parliamentary democracy as currently practiced; the more extreme Right, on the other hand, denounced democracy and all its works. Only a dictator, it said, could solve France's current problems and properly repress corrupting elements such as the Communists, the foreign immigrants, and the Jews.

*L'Action française,* the daily paper that most violently attacked the current regime, was itself an odd phenomenon. Born of the Dreyfus affair and still convinced that Dreyfus had been guilty, it stood for what it called "integral nationalism," a key element of which was the most rabid anti-Semitism. Indeed, Dreyfus was held to be guilty *because* he was Jewish, all Jews being, by definition, traitors and anti-French.

Charles Maurras, the founder-director of the paper and the political movement it had spawned, was a mediocre (but vastly overrated) novelist whose key notion was, essentially, that France had been great only under the monarchy; that all democracies were weak and corrupt; that the country could be properly run only by an autocrat; and that the man in question should be the pretender to the throne, the duc de Guise (the great-grandson of the last French king), whose only interest, as hereditary monarch, would be the good of the country.

The absurdity of this position hardly needs pointing out, and it was exacerbated by the fact that the duc de Guise was a thoroughly untalented mediocrity. In fact, many of those who read *L'Action française* — and it sold over a hundred thousand copies daily — were not so much monarchists as anti-Republicans; but, astoundingly, the paper and its views had a very real influence and contributed to the radicalization of the extreme Right.

Its chief characteristic, aside from the grotesqueness of its views, was the violence with which they were expressed. Almost every day, front-page editorials called for the murder of those the paper disliked; and Maurras never scrupled to invent when the facts failed to cooperate. As for Léon Daudet, his codirector, he was the son of the great novelist Alphonse Daudet, and had inherited from his father a knack for words. This talent was used solely and abundantly for invective. When seen together, the shriveled Maurras and the portly, red-faced Daudet looked distinctly comic; when read together, they were capable of producing not a little havoc.

This odd couple made its job easier by ignoring any inconvenient fact and disregarding contradictions in its own arguments. Maurras and Daudet criticized democracy for pandering to the worst elements in the electorate, for instance, while simultaneously affirming that the government could manipulate the voters as it chose. "The next elections," *L'Action française* cheerfully announced in January 1932, "will be whatever the government wants them to be."[7] This was coupled with ever-repeated predictions of the catastrophes to come. "The truth is simple," Daudet explained; "the Germans are waiting for the result of the elections to start the war. If there is a clearly . . . left-wing majority . . . , they will make the same mistake as in August 1914 [i.e., attack France]."[8] Obviously, Daudet was proved wrong, but the fact that his predictions never came true bothered none of his readers; and his influence was greatly enlarged by the creation of the active *Ligue d'Action française,* a group of well-armed young men, most numerous in Paris, who were frequently able to cause grave street disturbances.

It was under these circumstances that the campaign began. Tardieu, knowing he was unlikely to do well, resorted to a thoroughly shopworn trick: in a widely publicized speech, he announced that the Radicals and he were, after all, in agreement on the issues that really mattered; that, on the other hand, the Socialists were the real danger; and that, therefore, the Radicals should ally themselves with the Right and fight the wicked Reds.

"The Socialists, there is the enemy," the ever-partial *Le Temps* announced.[9] That view was defended by the most reactionary among the Radical leaders. Joseph Caillaux, who had been a reforming Premier in 1911, was now far more conservative than Tardieu, while still remaining in his original party. It was typical of his shade of opinion that, in a speech he made in Nantes, he should have announced that unemployment compensation was simply, "whatever people might say, a way to reward laziness"[10] — quite a statement to make at a time when the Depression was beginning to cause massive layoffs.

Naturally, the rest of the right-wing press also took up the offensive — with one exception: eccentric as usual, *L'Action française* chose the moment to publish a hymn to fascism. Daudet, having just spent ten days in Italy, returned bursting with enthusiasm. "After ten years of existence," he wrote, "fascism is now well installed and free of severity or administrative annoyances. . . . I saw a great people, pleased and even proud of its fate . . . and that nation is surely the one . . . which brings to its civic acts the coolest and most objective judgment."[11] "Coolest and most objective judgment," when applied to Mussolini and Fascist Italy, is out-and-out funny.

In the real world, the election soon came down to a duel between Tardieu and Herriot. Having tried and failed to entice the Radicals, Tardieu presented himself as the only true patriot capable of leading France. Together with this, there were standard attacks against the Radicals. One poster, for instance, showed Blum and Herriot cutting the franc in two, while, on another, the equally hapless coin was seen drowning under the weight of a Radical-Socialist alliance. The point, of course, was to suggest that, if the Left won, the postwar inflation, which most of the French remembered with horror, would be reawakened.

In his answers, Herriot, eloquent as always, denounced the misleading flash and folly of his opponent and defended the Radical platform. There was to be an "ordered economy" to offset the effects of the Depression, but the budget would be balanced, a program not unlike the one Franklin D. Roosevelt advocated during his own campaign that fall. Defense was to be reinforced, but at the same time, the emphasis on peace and the League of Nations was to be continued, thus making peace and security go hand in hand.

Nothing could have been more reassuring: there was a little touch of the new (the "ordered economy") combined with the pleasingly familiar (a balanced budget) while in foreign policy Herriot offered peace *and* strength. Of course, he never explained exactly how this admirable goal was to be achieved, and for a very good reason: his economic policy, inasmuch as it actually existed, was virtually identical with Tardieu's. Still, Herriot at least seemed more human than Tardieu, and he held out a hope for change. As for Léon Blum, he campaigned on the usual Socialist themes — disarmament, social justice — and he was heard, as usual, by much of the working class. More important, however, than all the speeches and all the promises was a stark and dreadful fact: more than a quarter of a million workers had already been laid off; the economy was visibly slowing down; and the government in power was held responsible for much of this.

When, on May 1, the votes of the first round were cast, it became clear that there had been a small but definite slide to the Left: out of an electorate of just under 10 million the Radicals and the Socialists had gained some 200,000 votes; but, even more important for the future, the Radicals, with 15.88 percent of the votes (compared with 14.52 percent in 1928), found themselves, for the first time ever, trailing the Socialists, who rose to 16.99 percent. In spite of this unpleasant shock, the Radicals followed through on their previous decision: they would observe "republican discipline" for the second round. This, in fact, was to their advantage as the Radical candidates in first place were more numerous than the similarly placed Socialists; and the Socialists collaborated because they knew that their failure to do so would produce another right-wing Chamber.

On May 8, the final results confirmed the defeat of the Right. Overall, the Left had gained 78 seats, and it led the Right by over a million votes, 4,895,023 to 3,880,717. As a result of the withdrawal of the Socialist candidates who had placed second in the first round, the Radicals gained 48 seats for a total of 157, thus becoming, by a wide margin, the largest party in the new legislature. The Socialists progressed to 129 (from 112); and the third component of the new majority, the moderately leftist Républicains socialistes, with 37 seats, posted a gain of five, while on the far Left, the Communists, who went from 10 to 12 seats, actually had 300,000 votes fewer than they had in 1928; and a new Trotskyite party managed to get six of its men elected.

On the Right, the several parties lost a corresponding number of seats, with, however, one exception: the Union républicaine démocratique, Tardieu's own party, clearly benefited from his campaign and went from 83 to 98 seats. As it was, however, the parties of the non-Communist Left, Socialists, Radicals, and Républicains socialistes, with their minor allies, held 334 seats, while the former majority was down to 259. On the face of it, therefore, it should have been easy for the Radicals to remain in power throughout the legislature; but, in fact, the Républicains socialistes, whose name was wholly misleading, were terrified of change, and not unlikely to defect on any number of possible occasions. And, of course, there was always the Senate, where many of the Radical members held highly conservative views.

None of this was immediately apparent to the voters, though; as far as they could see, the former right-wing majority had been replaced by the Radical-Socialist alliance. Reforms were expected, economic improvement eagerly awaited. The people could apparently make a difference after all; the sense of alienation, which had grown so strong, gave way to a brand-new hope. The haughty leaders of the Right were out; men who understood how and why the unemployed and underemployed suffered, had replaced them. Democracy had proved itself once more.

Of course, the politicians knew better. The Socialists were afraid of being compromised by the Radicals; the Radicals dreaded the reforms the Socialists were sure to demand; and, to make it all more interesting (for the professionals, at least), the Radicals themselves were deeply divided. This was nothing new. It had long been a party tradition to split on issues, so that, in the past, Radical-led governments had frequently been brought down by the Radicals themselves; but this phenomenon, which had once seemed perfectly acceptable and even, on occasion, entertaining, was likely to prove highly unpopular in the midst of the Depression.

The battle among the Radicals began promptly. It was understood that Herriot, the party's president, would become Premier. During his previous (and disastrous) tenure of that office, however, he had presided over the collapse of the franc and was now thoroughly convinced that the only way to remain in power was to practice the most rigid financial orthodoxy while constantly appeasing the major banks and great industrialists. That, of course, meant pursuing the deflationary course set by Laval and Tardieu, something that was anathema to about half the Radical Deputies.

At the same time, Herriot had a younger and rabidly ambitious rival within the party: Edouard Daladier, once his protégé, and now eager to succeed him as leader. Daladier, who was twelve years younger than Herriot, was just as adept as his former protector at the kind of scheming for which the Radicals were famous; but since Herriot was known for his conservative views, Daladier positioned himself on the left of the party. Then, too, Daladier made it his business to seem frank, open, almost clumsy in his honesty in contrast to Herriot's well-known talent for equivocation. Even his nickname, "the Bull from the Vaucluse," depicted him as a force of nature. No impression could have been more misleading, though. Daladier, who was almost pathologically indecisive, had a genius for intrigue and stopped hesitating only when it was a question of plotting against a rival. In 1932 his one obvious rival was Herriot, whose position Daladier coveted: everything was in place for the beginning of what their contemporaries called "the war of the two Edouards."

Herriot could thus expect two oppositions within his own party, the first based on principle, the second on Daladier's ambition, a situation that may have remained obscure to the electorate but was well known to the Paris salons. Here, indeed, was a mini-war everyone could enjoy; and it was at this point that politics became a standard subject of conversation and politicians an ever more noticeable element of the Tout-Paris. Where once the affairs of one's friends had been a major topic, now the hostesses produced politicians able to convey the very latest gossip — what Daladier had said about his admiration of Blum (that was sure to annoy Herriot) or the dig about insufficient patriotism made by Herriot, which was clearly directed at Daladier.

Just to make the situation more complex still, a major event had taken place between the two rounds of the election. On May 6, as he was inaugurating an exhibition of books by war-veteran writers, President Paul Doumer was assassinated by Pavel Gorguloff, a Russian refugee. Gorguloff was insane; there was no deep-laid plot, he had no accomplices, and Doumer was hardly a major political player; still, a new President of the Republic had to be chosen.

Because the new Chamber of Deputies was not, by law, to meet until June, it was the lame-duck, conservative Chamber that, together with the Senate, elected the new President. Naturally, it chose one of its own, the current president of the Senate, Albert Lebrun, a man distinguished chiefly by his complete absence of personality.

Lebrun, who had become president of the Senate because he could be counted on to offend no one, was a small, mousy-looking man whose large brown eyes looked at the world with a permanent expression of terrified surprise. A former engineer, he displayed none of the efficiency often found in that profession and seemed singularly lacking in both poise and resiliance; but his very lack of personality concealed the fact that he tenaciously held highly reactionary views.

Even worse, Lebrun lived in a world he found utterly incomprehensible: like so many others, he had never adapted to the changes wrought by the war. As a result, he was constantly startled, constantly appalled, constantly terrified. All in all, it would have been hard to pick a more inadequate figure even for this relatively unimportant position.

One of the ministers who had many occasions to watch him preside over the Council of Ministers described him thus: "President Albert Lebrun only offered opinions on foreign policy, a topic he followed attentively and with great emotion. When the news was bad, he would raise his arms to heaven and then drop his head into his hands. He showed with candor that he was frequently startled." [12]

Thus, as the new Chamber met in June 1932, the future of France was in the hands of one man, Lebrun, who understood nothing, and of another, Herriot, who understood that he understood nothing, at least in economics, but was determined to govern France anyway. That, combined with the state of the economy, did not bode well for the future.

For the moment, however, the Tout-Paris remained both unconcerned and unbowed. It was, from its point of view, deplorable that the Right had lost the elections, but then again, neither Herriot nor the Radicals were really alarming. It was very much more annoying that dividends and the income from country estates was shrinking — but then, prices were going down and it was still entirely possible to live very lavishly.

There could have been no better proof of this than the ball given by the baron Nicky de Gunzbourg in June. His house near the Bois de Boulogne "was transformed into a glorified farmhouse by . . . Christian [Bébé] Bérard, who painted a fantastic farmyard on wood frames and covered the entire house with blue satin. Cole Porter had composed a special score for the orchestra and Lauritz Melchior and Frieda Leider sang the love duet from *Tristan and Isolde*. [The ballet dancer] Serge Lifar made a grand entrance on a white horse, his body painted entirely in gold," Elsa Maxwell remembered, adding, with quite stupefying insensitivity: "There would be far less unrest abroad in the world if all farmers were as gay as our four hundred 'peasants.' The Cole Porters arrived in a Sicilian donkey cart loaded with orchids and gardenias. Daisy Fellowes came as Circe with the Baroness Lillian LoMonoco as her bewitched swine."[13] Indeed, it was understood that the guests were to arrive only on foot, in a cart, or even on a bicycle, and, in the front courtyard, papier-mâché lifesize farm animals were carefully arranged to give the impression of a real farm.

Farms were just unusual enough to provide a good theme for a ball. The ocean was even better. At Etienne de Beaumont's one night, the reception rooms were transformed by huge aquariums filled with goldfish and undulating jellyfish. "The comtesses d'Andlau, de Mortemart, and de Caumont appeared, imprisoned in a net," one of the guests reported; "the princesse Robert de Broglie was dressed as a coral reef and Lady Abdy was the fog. As for Princess Nicolas of Greece, she justified her inky gown by announcing that she was the Black Sea!"[14]

All this frenzied frivolity struck no one as odd; but then, the guests were quite clear about the purpose of life, which was to find amusement in the most glamorous surroundings possible, and when it came to providing glamour, Lady Mendl, herself one of the guests at the Gunzbourg ball, was unsurpassed, even if the sumptuous look she favored was a little old-fashioned. In one respect, though, she was thoroughly modern: the most remarkable room in her new apartment on the avenue d'Iéna was the bathroom, and the Tout-Paris came to gape.

What Lady Mendl had created, in a country where bathrooms were few, and often spartan, was a wholly new kind of setting, where utilitarian objects like a bathtub took their place in what was also part drawing room and study.

In that famous room, the mirrored frieze below the ceiling was etched in black with mermaids, dolphins, tropical islands, and palm trees, while, lower down, other friezes were engraved in a pattern of ocean waves. Naturally, the fireplace mantel was also mirrored, and so was the cocktail table, set on a mirrored globe adorned with the signs of the zodiac; and near that was a long couch covered in zebra skin. For contrast, there was a white velvet carpet near the bathtub — it was, after all, a bathroom — which was surrounded by mirrored columns, sheltered by metallic silver curtains, and lit by a lamp made of oyster shells and mother-of-pearl.

After all that, it was no wonder that Lady Mendl often chose to receive her guests in the bathroom; but it was not for lack of space. There was also a salon where the parquet floor came halfway up the walls to meet antique wooden wall paneling, on which were hung a number of eighteenth-century drawings that included an Hubert Robert, a Gainsborough portrait, and a Fragonard landscape, while the chairs, covered in sixteenth-century blue velvet, were signed Cressent, one of the greatest of the French rococo cabinetmakers.

The dining room was just as grand. The view was ugly, so a trompe-l'oeil scene of a garden covered the windows. There were, on the table and sideboard, rock crystal obelisks, a coral and ivory pagoda almost three feet high, and a sixteenth-century Nuremberg unicorn of silver coated with gold; but all this paled in comparison with the table centerpiece: a coach and its horses, made in 1760 of solid gold, with diamond studs on wheels and harnesses and a tiny clock; and there was even a mechanism that set the horses galloping. As for the flowers, that indispensable adjunct to an elegant decor, they were simply, and in great profusion, white orchids.[15]

It was, perhaps, just as well that the dining room gave the eyes so much pleasure. Lady Mendl was famous for the sparseness of her dinners and the lack of quality of her food. Still, the conversation provided another distraction; there was nothing kindly about the former Elsie De Wolfe, and the most acid gossip was usually the order of the day.

There was something slightly passé about Lady Mendl's luxury, though. Schiaparelli, whose dresses she wore, knew better. When it came to decorating her apartment on the Boulevard Saint-Germain, Schiap called in that supremely fashionable decorator, that apostle of the elegantly empty room, Jean-Michel Frank; and the results were appropriately striking.

First, Frank stripped the apartment bare, leaving only the arched bookcases, and he painted the now smooth walls a pure white. Then, in the living room, he hung curtains of black, shiny rubber; there was an enormous orange leather couch, two armchairs covered in emerald-green rubber, and, as a contrast, other chairs upholstered in bright yellow chintz. The bedroom was scarcely less austere; while the walls were covered with blistered lavender fabric, there was a footstool made of the hipbones of a horse and bronze Diego Giacometti lamps. It was in the dining room, however, that Frank outdid himself. There, instead of one large table, he installed small, black, glass-covered tables just large enough for four; the sofas were chartreuse, the plates were black porcelain, the silver Swedish, modern and geometric. All in all, it may perhaps have seemed less than cheerful. Chanel, who was a guest at the first dinner party Schiap gave in her new apartment, remarked acidly that she shuddered as if she had been passing a cemetery, to which the hostess, on being informed of this, answered: "Chanel, that dreary little bourgeoise . . . specializes in cemeteries,"[16] thus neatly putting down her rival's dresses.

Still, Schiap knew that modernity was a key part of her own image and never forgot that her guests were also her clients. Chanel merely gave herself the look of success in her apartment; Schiap made sure that hers reminded everyone of her designs. It was also the perfect background for them: all that black and white was the ideal setting for costumes like the one worn one night by the hostess herself: a shocking pink, very fluid, long skirt with a train, and a big-shouldered wine-colored velvet jacket with grape motifs embroidered in red, yellow, green, and gold, and bunches of grapes in red and orange colored glass.

Schiap had chosen Jean-Michel Frank as her decorator because, when it came to sheer, overpowering chic, he was unbeatable. A strange, sprite-like man with a big nose and a worried expression, Frank simply reinvented what an interior was supposed to be: not lush and full of silk, velvet, and deep carpets, which was what Lady Mendl preferred, but stark and yet utterly luxurious.

"For our friend," Jean Cocteau remembered, "luxury was simplicity. It was simplicity that defined the lines and materials of his luxury. He liked the invisible quality of true elegance. . . . Leather, straw, parchment, marble, rare woods, bronze, copper, or the unreal plaster obeyed the orders of this lyrical geometrician. Here, there was nothing frivolous."[17]

The emptier, Frank said firmly, the better: his clients just had to send many of the family antiques off to the warehouse. Colors, too, were kept firmly in check: his palette often extended no further than white, ivory, beige, and brown; the touches of brilliant color in Schiaparelli's apartment were a concession to the designer's taste. But then, as compensation, all the materials used were utterly luxurious: the walls were covered with parchment, or natural-colored leather hand-sewn into place, or panels of rare and precious woods, sometimes even with marquetries of woven and varnished straw that looked a little like part of a Cubist painting. The straw, in particular, was immensely popular among those who could afford it; the delicious paradox was that this cheapest, most perishable of materials became, after it had been transformed, enormously expensive. And within these empty rooms, the few pieces of furniture were covered with the rarest, choicest materials: ivory, often, or sharkskin, or the very highest grade of leather whose luxury nicely balanced the very simple lines on which Frank insisted.

It was the right look for a society that took pride in its modernity. Speed was the catchword; Jean-Michel Frank's luxuriously simple apartments had something in common with the new cars, aerodynamically designed and more powerful than ever before. It was a new world in which slow conversation and leisurely drives seemed hopelessly passé. "Speed," the writer Philippe Soupault noted, "helps us to clear out the fog and dissipate legends. Speed makes us see clearly. . . . It resembles music because it activates our thinking, demands our attention, helps us to know and conceive." [18]

How, in fact, could you want anything but a simple interior when even cars seemed a little slow? It was clear enough. "Soon leaving the road, everyone will have his plane traveling across the sky," a journalist predicted. [19] For all that, some parts of life remained comfortably unchanged: eating was one. The French (or rather, the French upper class) might like to go fast, but it also insisted on superb meals.

Those same people who paid such close attention to the decor in which they lived thus naturally gave deep and prolonged thought to the arrangement of their dinner tables. All was possible. Cécile Sorel, a hugely famous actress who had become a countess by marriage, had a marble-topped dinner table on which fruit, sometimes arranged in great silver bowls, sometimes set directly on the table, took the place of flowers. Flowers, in fact, were almost too normal as a centerpiece: the marquise de Jaucourt used Meissen porcelain instead and Mme de Beistegui her museum-quality antique silver, while Chanel, at the center of the three tables for six where she seated her guests, put antique crystal candelabra and silver-gilt plates full of salted almonds — all very different from Schiaparelli's almost unrelieved black.

Of course, there were less daring hostesses: the comtesse Henri de Mun, who was famous for the excellence of her dinners, covered the center of her table with flowers whose colors harmonized with those of the place mats, which were changed with every course, while at the house of the princesse Lucien Murat, the flowers took second place to the porcelain and linen in tints of lapis, turquoise, or gold.[20]

All these ladies lived in a world that, although it was more open than before the war, had, until very recently, remained closed to most intellectuals and most politicians. Léon Blum, who circulated a good deal, avoided society as such; Herriot's deliberately lower-class manners were not such as to make him welcome; but Daladier, his great rival in the Radical party, was making his way into the Tout-Paris, and so were many others.

For them, and for many of the French, just what was going to happen as a result of the elections mattered a good deal more than the latest decor or the most amusing party. Everybody knew that President Lebrun would call on Herriot to head the new government, none better than Herriot himself. That, however, was just a beginning. Herriot was too familiar with the vagaries of the system to think that his government would last as long as the legislature, but, whether at the head of the cabinet or not, he was determined to be the main power in France.

As he waited for the new Chamber to hold its inaugural session, Herriot found himself faced with two urgent problems, one familiar, the other new. The first of these was that he would have to rely on the Socialists for a majority, the second that the country was slipping into a deepening depression. Firmly ignoring reality, he concentrated instead on what he knew best, that ritual hesitation waltz in which he and Blum withdrew when the other advanced and vice versa.

At first glance, the situation seemed simple enough: by concluding a firm alliance with the Socialists, Herriot would ensure the survival of his government. That, however, would have meant asking them to join the cabinet and Herriot was resolved to keep them out, partly because he had no intention of favoring reform, partly because Daladier, who had called for an alliance with the Socialists, would have been vindicated, and Herriot was not about to help his chief rival.

Here was just the kind of politics Herriot enjoyed: it called for fast footwork, dishonesty with a candid face, and the planting of knives in a variety of defenseless backs. The trick being to keep the Socialists out of the government but in the parliamentary majority, the premier-to-be set about pretending that while he was prepared to welcome a Socialist group into the cabinet, it was precisely those same Socialists who refused to join it. Since, until then, the Socialists had claimed that joining a bourgeois cabinet would be a betrayal of their principles, Herriot's pretense seemed safe enough.

Never a man to admit that he had been less than selfless and statesman-like, the Radical leader kept up the charade in his memoirs. "I thought," he wrote, "that my duty was to accept, in the future government, the collaboration of the Socialists, but without any preconditions on their part."[21] The key word here is "preconditions": if, that is, the Socialists were willing to abandon everything they stood for, they could join the government; but if they were to insist on certain specific principles or measures, then they were not wanted. Knowing the Socialists as he did, Herriot could not have had any doubt as to their answer.

As expected, in fact, the Socialists were not at all eager to enter the government. The old shibboleths about class conflict and the sin involved in being part of a bourgeois cabinet were alive and well; on the other hand, it was clear that if they did agree to share power, the Socialists might be able to carry out some of the reforms they had just been advocating in the campaign. The trick was to make participation impossible while appearing to yearn for it. The stage thus being set, the two partners were ready for the comedy to begin.

Blum himself was a thoroughly honest man, but he was deeply convinced that it was essential to ensure the survival of his party as the best hope of the working class. Participation, he feared, would split it; so, bowing to a higher necessity, he proceeded to join the game: to Herriot's delight, he set about making such conditions as the Premier-designate was bound to reject; and both parties kept absolutely straight faces.

A lot of pretense was still necessary, though: it would never do if the voters realized they had wasted their time when they supported the Left in the second round of the elections. On May 30 and 31, therefore, the Socialists set out a minimum program: if the Radicals agreed to implement it, the Socialists would join the government. The hitch was that the program in question was unacceptable to the Radicals and everyone knew it.

This suited both Blum and Herriot perfectly while keeping up the charade that the two parties really wanted to join forces in the new government. Herriot promptly let it be known that if the two parties were in basic agreement, there was no need for these formal preconditions; but that he could not agree to many of the elements of the Socialist program.

After that, the road was clear, and the Socialists decided to support, but not enter, a Radical government.

On June 3, Herriot thus came into office. His cabinet showed clearly just how conservative he really was, and how devoid of new ideas: the two key ministries, finance and budget, went to Germain-Martin, who had been minister of the budget in a Tardieu government (March–December 1930), and to Maurice Palmade, who was known to hold rigidly conservative views. It could not have been clearer: the Premier of the newly victorious Left was about to continue the reactionary and ineffective financial policies of his conservative predecessor.

There was a complication, though. Herriot was dependent on a Radical-Socialist majority, which might conceivably be unhappy if it saw him continuing Tardieu's policies, and the Socialists were almost bound, eventually, to vote against him. Still, if the Premier pursued a conservative policy, then he might garner enough votes on his right to offset defections on his left. It was as neat a denial of the voters' will as can be imagined; but, nothing loath, Herriot went right ahead. From his point of view, there was yet another advantage to this shift of the majority: by looking to the Right, he was also protecting himself from Daladier. Given that, and his own conservative views, the new arrangement was a positive blessing.

Now it was only a question of pretending that these maneuvers, and the continuity in financial policy, were for the good of the country. "At the [first] Council of Ministers," Herriot wrote, "Germain-Martin told us that the Treasury's balance was down to 56 million. He explained the serious measures that must be taken to improve our financial situation."[22] Naturally, the conservative (and incompetent) finance minister proposed conservative measures; the fact that they had already been seen not to work did not stop him for a second. Nor did he worry about the sufferings of the unemployed. Fiscal orthodoxy came first.

All these games, satisfying though they were for the politicians, were an outright denial of the election results. For a while, during the campaign, the people had felt less alienated from the politicians; they had been encouraged to hope. Now all this was forgotten. By opting for business as usual in the midst of the Depression, Herriot was betraying a trust. By playing the kind of politics with which he was most familiar, he ensured not only the failure of his policies, but the deepening of the chasm between the governing and the governed.

It thus seemed particularly appropriate when, in October, an explosive first novel was published, *Voyage au bout de la nuit* (Trip to the End of Night). The author, Louis-Ferdinand Céline, was a thirty-eight-year-old physician who had been badly wounded in the shoulder and arm during the great battles of September 1918, and who had never recovered the full use of the limb. Upon being invalided out of the army, he had practiced medicine in the French African colonies and in the United States, most notably in Detroit, where he had studied labor injuries at the Ford factories. There was much misery, much exploitation, to be seen in both these places; and when he returned to France and started his own practice, it was in a working-class suburb of Paris where life was no pleasanter.

His most immediate reaction to what he had seen and experienced was one of mingled pity and disgust — pity for the mass of humanity condemned to live in appalling conditions, disgust for the governments and the businesses that so cheerfully organized these varied hells. And with the disgust came a searing anger.

All these feelings were expressed in *Voyage au bout de la nuit,* and they took the form of a series of graphic descriptions of life in the army, in Africa, in France among the sort of lost people who, until then, had been considered beneath interest: blacks, workers, drifters, the elderly poor. Even more striking, the book was written in a new and shocking style, half slang, half elision in which whole sentences are often replaced by fragments connected by three dots, so that the very page seems breathless with pain and fury.*

It was clear from the moment *Voyage* was published that it was a work of genius; it was equally plain that the author was horrified and disgusted by the world he saw; that, for him, not just the governments, but civilization itself had failed; and the chief note, after anger, is utter hopelessness. It is strongly expressed just before the end of the book:

> Over there, far away, there was the sea. But I had nothing more to imagine about it right now. I tried hard to lose myself so that I wouldn't find myself in front of my life, but I saw it everywhere. I came back to myself. My carryings-on were well over. Let others do it! . . . The world had closed up! . . . At the end, that's where we got to! . . . Like at a party! . . . Being hurt, that's not all, you'd need to start the same tune over, to go and get more pain! . . . But that's for someone else! [. . .] Anyway, to bear more, I wasn't ready for that either![23]

*Celine's use of the dots is followed in the quotations from his writings. Cuts are indicated by [. . .].

The keynotes here are despair and alienation. Until then, these two emotions had been reserved for a small minority of the French; but, just as Céline's book was coming out, it began to look as if they might, in fact, dominate the decade. Suddenly, incomprehensibly, the world had changed; that fine self-assurance with which France had begun the decade was gone. In May, hope had seemed as green as the spring. In October, although Paris was enjoying one of those golden autumn moments when the sky is pale blue, the air cool, and the leaves of the plane trees flutter down gently, it was already becoming clear that, bad as thing were, worse was still to come: not just winter, but economic disaster.

# FOUR

# THE DANCE OF THE MINISTRIES

THE WORLD, by the end of 1932, was beginning to look distinctly unappealing. In New York, the lines of the unemployed were everywhere; London was not much better; Germany, ravaged by bank failures, was undergoing convulsions of its own; but, as Genêt testified twice a month, Paris remained as lively as ever. Even if the Depression was finally catching up with the French, it was hardly visible in the capital. Indeed, it seemed as if the Parisians had decided, once and for all, that clinging to old customs would prevent change. Modernity was still chic — for that matter, chic was still chic, when, elsewhere, a new, more proletarian aesthetic was beginning to take over. Even in the political world, the game went on as before: intrigues multiplied and governments fell as if all were still well. After all, the cafés were still cheap, and still full of people sipping and looking; the bars served their usual lethal mixtures; the theaters offered new plays; and, as if to show that frivolity was alive and well, there was the latest craze: you could hardly walk down a boulevard without seeing dozens of yo-yos, maneuvered by adults and children alike. In fact, Genêt told her readers, they had become an epidemic. She went on:

> The papers print editorials about [the yo-yo], praying for its finish and discovering its beginning. Now bearded gentlemen waggle yo-yos over the back platform of tramcars; café terraces are plagued by yo-yo merchants; the gourmet's Club des Cent played yo-yo over their partridge at their first game dinner; the young Sultan of Morocco, on his recent visit, flaunted one at the feet of the President of the Republic during their official introduction; and Cartier sells yo-yos in gold (280 francs) large enough to be practicable but small enough to wear as a bracelet bangle after the craze dies down.[1]

Everyone could afford a yo-yo, provided it was not made by Cartier; only the privileged few could order their clothes from Schiaparelli; but she, too, helped to sustain the note of determined frivolity that seemed so much a part of the times. Suddenly her clients, led by Lady Diana Cooper, appeared in evening pajamas: it was the latest rage, a note of chic informality that was, apparently, irresistible. And then there was the dress Schiap designed for Marlene Dietrich: it had tall black rooster feathers shooting up from the shoulder straps. Indeed, even if rents and dividends were no longer quite what they had been before, the Tout-Paris still carried on its glamorous life.

Fashionable dresses were expensive, of course, especially since they could be worn only for the current season. It was a matter of line, length, décolletage, and most important, color. In the winter of 1932–33, for instance, perhaps because fashion had changed so dramatically in the past two years, restraint was the order of the day. "The alliance of white and black is indicated for this period of settling down. . . . A mere touch of color will prevent this from having a semi-mourning look,"[2] a magazine noted. Clearly the writer had been looking at Schiap's collection; at Marcel Rochas, the preferred combination was blue and white. And while in the winter of 1932 low-cut dresses were still acceptable, by 1933 only a high front and a very low back would do.

More than ever, the great couturiers understood that their prosperity depended on their social presence. Even if everyone was pretending that all was well, there were far fewer clients buying couture dresses. Most of the Americans were gone, and so were most of the British, the Austrians, the Germans; even the French were not as numerous as they had once been, so the edge given by social success was particularly important. Schiap herself hired beautiful, well-connected young women to wear her dresses at fashionable events: the princesse Thérèse de Caraman-Chimay, the princesse Cora Caetani, the princesse Paulette Poniatowska, made sure everyone realized where true chic came from, while a beautiful young American, Bettina Jones, looked after her compatriots. Other designers gave parties that made a huge splash. Jean Patou, for instance, at his geometric ball had cards of different colors and different shapes distributed to the guests; the first couples who discovered they had identical cards received prizes. As for Chanel, always loath to give up the lead, she simply invited the Tout-Paris to a great ball at the Hôtel des Bains in Venice.

Indeed, as unemployment grew and the international situation became more worrying — Hitler had become Chancellor of Germany in January 1933 — Paris society seemed more determined than ever to show how splendid it could be. The extravagance, the frivolity, the determined continuation of the life-style of the twenties, seemed to offer Paris society a sort of magic protection against the onslaught of the Depression. If everyone gave enough parties, danced as late as possible as often as possible, lived as spectacularly as possible, then, somehow, everything would be all right.

Balls took place in people's houses, and so were relatively discreet; but that key feature of social life, the competitions of automobile elegance at which the most elegant woman in the most elegant auto won first prize, became ever more spectacular; and they naturally took place outdoors and in the midst of throngs of watchers.

"There was the year of the reptile skins used to upholster the interiors [of the cars] and the outside of the lady drivers," a frequent judge noted. "Another year, the fashion was for the switch which, if merely touched, would produce an already lit cigarette or a powder puff. Naturally, the dresses, the hats, the personal attraction of the competitors [all mattered] . . . as well as the presence of an impeccable chauffeur — preferably a black chauffeur. . . . Here, a blonde would wear an almond-green ensemble, there a brunette would be in a pearl-gray dress striped with silver."[3]

Even so, the huge cars with the custom bodies were becoming rarer, and most manufacturers began to produce smaller, cheaper models. Every day money was becoming scarcer, even if the working class was far more affected by the economic crisis than the bourgeoisie. Because so many members of the middle class had capital, they still drew an income from it — smaller, perhaps, but then, prices were dropping: by 1934, on a base of 100 for 1929, retail prices were down to 82. Workers who lost their jobs,

however, economics came first, and that was more than he was prepared to face.

While Herriot understood nothing about the Depression or how it should be fought, he knew all about the power of the banks. In 1925, his government had fallen because the value of the franc, relative to the pound and the dollar, kept dropping; and that, in turn, was caused by the mass of floating short-term government paper and the budget deficit, which, in a period of full employment, was a cause of inflation. At the time, Herriot had utterly failed to understand what was happening; but, after he had left office, he finally caught on to the fact that the major banks, including the Bank of France — which was privately owned but responsible for the currency and the interest rate — had been deliberately pushing the franc lower so as to bring in a more conservative government. Over the years, he did not forget that they had succeeded in pushing him out of office. Now, in order not to let that happen again, he was determined to heed the banks — hence his appointment of the ultraconservative ministers of finance and the budget.

Unfortunately for Herriot, in 1932 the great French bankers understood the economy no more than he did. Like him, they were fixated on balancing the budget, terrified of inflation, and determined to maintain the parity of the franc. Even worse, the only means they could see of achieving their goals was a dose of stiff deflation. Because they were quite as ignorant as the Premier, they were incapable of realizing that a procedure which was beneficial in an overheated economy would only worsen the current Depression, whereas deficit spending, far from being inflationary in a period of rapidly falling prices, would help create jobs and thus, in the end, help to balance the budget. Nor were they capable of learning.

The problem, though, was that a majority of the French had voted for the opposite policy, and, in consequence, many of the Radical Deputies were not prepared to accept the huge cost in human suffering that went with further deflation. Even worse, from Herriot's point of view, they held that the welfare of the people came before that of the bankers. This attitude was expressed vividly and succinctly in a letter to Herriot from Gaston Bergery, a young and brilliant Radical who was about to marry Bettina Jones, Schiaparelli's American assistant. In March 1933, after yet another cut in the salaries of civil servants, he wrote: "This is not just about a few dozen francs to be withheld every year from middle-grade state employees; it is a coherent policy, tirelessly advocated for the past few years by the reactionaries, which makes the working classes bear the brunt of a crisis for which they are not responsible after a time of prosperity from which they were excluded."[4]

All this was more than Herriot could cope with. Instead of presiding amiably over a do-nothing government, he was being forced to make decisions; instead of absorbing himself in the ever more subtle game of balancing the various components of his party against one another, he was faced with unpalatable choices. Either he could pursue the deflationary policies put in place by Tardieu, Flandin, and Laval — but then the Socialists and many Radicals would vote him out of office and resent him for a long time afterward; or he could forget about the deficit and try to reflate — but then the banks would see to it that the cabinet fell. It was an impossible position.

It took Herriot just six months to realize this; and having done so, he resorted to an old trick. It had long been understood that if you felt your government was about to fall, it was best to provoke a no-confidence vote on a side issue, thus preparing the way for an early return to power since no major policy had been involved; and this is just what Herriot proceeded to do. As luck would have it, he had the perfect excuse.

Because the German economy had collapsed, an international conference had suspended the payment of reparations to France and Great Britain; at the same time, President Hoover and the U.S. Congress took the view that this should have no effect on interallied war debts because the latter had been contracted voluntarily. Thus, the yearly repayments that France and Great Britain made to the United States were expected to continue whether or not they were themselves receiving reparation payments from Germany. One such installment was due in December 1932. The question was now whether France should pay "for the uniforms in which her sons had died," as the press usually put it. Given the economic situation, and the suspension of Germany's payments, the answer was clear: the Chamber would vote for default.

Here was Herriot's ideal pretext: by insisting that France must honor her word no matter what, he would look statesmanlike, gain friends abroad, and fall on a minor matter, not on the failure of his economic and financial policies. There was thus every prospect that, after a short interim cabinet, he, Herriot, would regain the premiership. It was a typical Radical maneuver, subtle, effective, and wholly unrelated to the needs or demands of the country.

So it was that, as planned, the Chamber, in spite of an eloquent but empty speech by Herriot, refused to vote the credits necessary for the loan payment. On December 14, 1932, the cabinet fell. After that came a series of revolving-door cabinets. One Radical succeeded the next, not a single problem was solved, and, watching this cynical game, the country grew angrier week by week.

First, there was Joseph Paul-Boncour, who was the perfect temporary Premier. He looked well, and was instantly recognizable by his great shock of white hair crowning a young face. He also did nothing: after all, his government lasted a bare forty days, thanks to the incredibly fat and even more stupid Chéron, who had been Tardieu's finance minister and now held the same office under Paul-Boncour. On January 28, 1933, in the course of a debate, Chéron told the Deputies: "The current situation is, by and large, not the result of the Depression, but that of our own mistakes,"[5] upon which he asked for a stiff dose of deflation. That was more than the Chamber was willing to take: in the vote that followed, a majority voted against the cabinet.

Now, to Herriot's indescribable fury, President Lebrun called on Daladier to form the next government. Small but square-shouldered, with dark hair, a Roman nose, and an intense expression, Edouard Daladier, Herriot's chief rival within the Radical party, gave an impression of fierce energy barely controlled. He liked to mention his principles, his unbreakable principles, and was generally thought to be strong where Herriot was subtle. With Daladier as the new Premier, clearly, something would be done. Soon, however, those who knew him well began to whisper that there had been a mistake: Daladier was even more indecisive than Herriot. Even Paul-Boncour, a man not easily given to criticism, noticed it: "M. Daladier, in spite of his appearance of sometimes rather brutal firmness, was highly sensitive to the campaigns in [the Chamber's] lobbies and to all kinds of rumors. He was sometimes hesitant in carrying out his decisions."[6]

Even worse, he had trouble making those decisions in the first place, in part because, aware as he was of his own incompetence, he was easily cowed. "Edouard Daladier," Blum wrote, "was assailed the whole day long [on which he was putting his cabinet together] by the emissaries of the banks. By six that evening, he was terrified, crushed by the need, which he could no longer face, of resisting the power of the financial institutions . . . and in order to justify himself, he claimed that only the banks could absorb the bonds needed to meet the deficit."[7]

Naturally, therefore, deflation remained the order of the day. Daladier chose a fellow Radical as his finance minister, the sharp, ambitious, and unscrupulous Georges Bonnet, whose main complaint was that the previous cabinets had not deflated *enough*. Indeed, Bonnet was typical of the party's right wing: on most subjects, his views were quite as conservative as Tardieu's or Flandin's.

He made this very plain at the Radical convention that fall. "It is obvious," he said, "that we cannot ask that sacrifices be borne only by government employees. They must be more widely spread. . . . It is a colossal error to believe that, tomorrow, after we have made whatever reductions [in civil service salaries] will be necessary, the shopkeepers, the industrialists, and the farmers will be entitled to sell their production at the same price as before. Our policy of budgetary deflation must, if it is to succeed, go together with price deflation."[8] The only problem with this logic was that the policy it inspired served considerably to worsen the Depression.

In fact, prices were already much lower than in 1929. The index of wholesale prices, from a basis of 100 in 1900, had reached 129 in 1929–30. By 1933, it was down to 81, a drop of nearly 40 percent. While this helped all those who lived on fixed incomes, it spelled disaster for commercial, agricultural, and industrial producers. And Bonnet now wanted more, much more, of the same. The tax yield had shrunk from 53 billion francs in 1929 to just under 43.5 billion in 1933, and so he was determined to cut outlays brutally.

In his own domain, defense, Daladier proved to be equally incompetent. Pertinax, one of the foremost journalists of his time, soon discovered this. "I went to chat with [Daladier] from time to time when he was Premier for the first time," he wrote, "and I was shocked by the lack of intelligence and the limited character of his remarks. I can still hear him, as war minister, saying that it was an indisputable truth that the last word of the art of war was to build entrenchments and hold them solidly. All the rest [he would say] . . . is just words."[9] Sadly, the idiocy of this remark showed a certain capacity to learn: it reflected the doctrine held by what may well have been the most incompetent General Staff in French history.

As it was, incompetence notwithstanding, the Daladier government set a record for the legislature: it actually lasted nine months, thanks to the Premier's ability to do everything and its opposite. Then, with Herriot plotting in the background, the government was defeated on October 24 by 329 to 241 votes.

Obviously, it was time for the delighted Herriot to return to power as a cover for a major shift to the right: "This is your triumph," President Lebrun told him.[10] Unfortunately, however, the potential Premier was gravely ill, and although expected to recover, as eventually he did, he was clearly in no position to lead a government. Since it was just a question of waiting for a few weeks, another temporary cabinet was needed. There was no hesitating: when a perfect nonentity was wanted, the cry went up for Albert Sarraut — as it was to do again in 1936.

Of course, Albert Sarraut was wholly unfitted to be Premier, a distinct advantage under the circumstances, since it was understood that he was only a stopgap, merely filling in until Herriot could take over. All the key ministers from the previous government remained in place. They were Radicals, after all, and just because the governments kept falling was no reason for them to lose office. Thus the personnel of these tumbling cabinets remained remarkably stable, a fact the public noticed and resented.

Perhaps this time the maneuver was a little too cynical. The Sarraut government, which took office on October 26, was gone on November 23.

At this point, the government-forming process had begun to look like a farce, an impression not corrected by President Lebrun's next choice. Camille Chautemps held the distinction of having, a little more than three years earlier, been Premier for four days, an unquestioned record of its kind. Lebrun, in fact, was merely following Herriot's advice. Although he was now convalescing, the president of the Radical party was not yet well enough to take on the premiership, so another substitute was needed. For that, Chautemps was the perfect choice.

A tall, willowy, elegant man with a small clipped mustache and a perpetual smile, Chautemps was the professional politician par excellence. Always eager to please, always fearful of offending, he was a born compromiser, an aptitude that had served him well within the Radical party. He had been minister of the interior in the four previous governments, and kept the office now. Because it controlled the police, the actual administration of France, and the electoral machinery, this was a key position, and one in which Chautemps could do much that required subtlety and a light hand. He was also a man who understood just how far the perks of power might be made to stretch: you could, at the very least, feather your nest and protect your friends while taking care never blatantly to break the law.

As Herriot's close and faithful follower, Chautemps had done well within the party; to the rest of the French, however, he was a little too much the archetypal Radical. "At the Opéra Comique, yesterday, Camille Chautemps, the Premier, sat in a box next to mine," Pierre Lazareff, a highly successful journalist, noted. "I spoke to him. He is a clever, too clever Radical. He makes appealing phrases, splits hairs, never answers any question precisely. Since he could not quite remember who I am, or what my political positions are, he came up with this: 'In brief, I think that all will come out right thanks to honest and energetic Frenchmen like yourself. By the way, forgive me, I see so many people, how do you spell your name, my dear friend?'"[11]

Of course, everyone who mattered understood that Chautemps would soon give way to Herriot. Once again, this was to be a transitory cabinet in which the key ministers remained in place when the Premier changed. At the best of times, this would hardly have been an efficient way to govern; with the economy collapsing and Hitler ranting across the Rhine, it was altogether disastrous. For all the speeches in which they claimed to put the welfare of France first, in fact, the politicians were behaving, in their own domain, just like society: perhaps if they did just what they had done before, only more so, the problems would go away. So instead of giving balls, they plotted the replacement of the Premier, a game more than a little reminiscent of those popular yo-yos. And throughout it all, the voters grew progressively more alienated from the politicians whose preoccupations, it seemed evident, were wholly self-centered.

These constant changes, and the intrigues that went with them, made for the most entrancing gossip, however. With perhaps the single exception of Léon Blum, French politicians seemed unable to keep a secret. Some of this chatter was due to a desire to look important; more often, it was part of various complicated strategies aimed at discrediting rivals. In every case, it furthered the sense that France was split between two radically different populations: that of the privileged, who had access to the latest news, and the rest.

By 1933 there was a new development. With the exception of Léon Blum and his friends, most major politicians were welcome in those exclusive circles which, only ten years earlier, would have cut them dead. Indeed, for the first time, people of widely divergent opinions came together, united by the feeling that they belonged to a superior order. Journalists like Pierre Lazareff, who was editor in chief of *Paris-Soir*, the paper with the largest circulation in France, or the political columnist Geneviève Tabouis, whose specialty was access to the deepest of secrets; leading politicians like Daladier, Laval, Paul Reynaud, the most intelligent among the Conservatives; artists, usually of the third rank; intellectuals like Paul Morand, Paul Claudel, François Mauriac; the very rich, men like the textile magnate Jean Prouvost, who was also the owner of *Paris-Soir*, the steel-making Wendel family, and, of course, the Rothschilds; bearers of the great names of the French aristocracy — all came together to form a magic circle where the latest gossip was avidly traded and the rise and fall of governments was discussed very much as if it had been a sporting event.

No salon could be really successful without the right mix of luxury, the newest information, and a few famous men. Discretion was unknown: ministers coming straight from the council would reveal what had been discussed. Frequently, the Premier himself would talk about French policies with an openness that struck the occasional foreign observer as nearly treasonable. Of course, the fall of the government was a standard topic of conversation, with people betting about the date and occasion on which it would happen; and the men who made these bets were those very ministers who were supposed to be governing the country.

The result was, on occasion, some very strange juxtapositions. The duchesse d'Harcourt, for instance, belonged to one of the most ancient ducal families and resided, when in the country, at her eponymous Normandy castle. She was also an eager huntress; and having attended the Hunting Congress held in and outside Berlin under Goering's patronage, she became, along with her husband, violently pro-Nazi. Indeed, the duke was soon one of the leading lights of the Comité France-Allemagne, a Nazi organization run by Otto Abetz. Ostensibly, the Comité simply encouraged the development of friendly relations between the two nations; in fact, its task was to convert the greatest possible number of influential people to the Nazi ideal so as to weaken France. As it was, the Harcourts were easily taken in: as far as they were concerned, hunting was about all that mattered. Others who were both brighter and better informed than the ducal couple knew better than to join the Comité France-Allemagne; but that did not mean they despised Hitler. François de Wendel, a great industrialist, the head of his family, a multimillionaire, a co-owner of the ever-influential *Le Temps,* and a Senator, watched Hitler's proceedings with approval. Late in 1933, he told Jules Jeanneney, the president of the Senate, that the Führer's success was "the proof . . . that the masses can yield today, just as they did in the past, to a firm will. . . . This proves that Maurras is right, except for the return of the monarchy," and he went on to praise Mussolini as "the most important person in Europe." [12]

Of course, not all society women were as gullible as the duchesse d'Harcourt. Some eventually closed their doors to avowed pro-Nazi guests; but for most, life went on as usual, and the trick was to gather as

many important or well-born people as possible. By 1934, there were a
few specifically political salons, two of which were headed by ladies who
had decided that, in order to catch a politician, all means were legitimate.

The comtesse Hélène de Portes had, as a young woman, married into
an aristocratic family by virtue of having a huge dowry — her father was
a plebeian but colossally rich contractor. Soon, however, she realized that
in Paris a minor title was not enough to carry her into the very first circle
of society; so she considered carefully, and decided that what she needed
to establish herself as one of the great Paris hostesses was the support of
one of the country's leading politicians. She was young, she was beautiful (if singularly bad-tempered), she was ambitious: all, therefore was
possible.

The political leader she decided to conquer was Paul Reynaud. This
tiny little man who stood so straight he appeared almost medium-sized
was modernity incarnate. He practiced a variety of sports; he spoke English fluently; alone among the French political leaders, he knew enough
economics to see where further deflation was likely to lead; and he was
intensely ambitious. Starting as a brilliant young lawyer, he had married
the daughter of one of the great men at the Paris bar, and proceeded to
be endlessly unfaithful to her. Naturally, he had gone into politics, quickly
becoming finance minister under Tardieu. No one doubted he would, one
day soon, become Premier: he was already among the group of four or
five men who led the conservatives in the Chamber.

Mme de Portes set to seducing Reynaud; Reynaud was delighted to
be seduced. Not only was his new mistress pretty and rich, having a salon
at his devotion was a major help to his political career. Deputies could be
wooed, journalists flattered, propaganda made. Anyone who went to one
of Mme de Portes's dinners was likely to come away with the feeling that
Reynaud alone would save France; and Mme de Portes not only glowed
in Reynaud's refracted light, she confidently expected to rule the country
when her lover became Premier. With all his many qualities, Reynaud was
easily influenced by a determined woman, a fact his mistress never forgot.

Life, in fact, would have been a bed of roses for Mme de Portes had it
not been for a most annoying rival. The marquise Jeanne de Crussol was
not unlike Mme de Portes. She, too, came from a plebeian family. Her
father owned fleets of sardine fishing boats; she, too, had used a vast
dowry to snatch an aristocratic husband (thus giving rise to a punning
description: she was, people whispered, "*la sardine qui s'était Crussol* [*cru
sole*]," the sardine who took herself for a sole / a Crussol). What annoyed
Mme de Portes was that the marquis de Crussol, who was a relative of

the duc d'Uzès, came from a much grander family than the comte de Portes; but even that was not as bad as Mme de Crussol's successful appropriation of Edouard Daladier.

Like Mme de Portes, Mme de Crussol understood that the easiest way to catch a really important politician for her salon was to become his mistress; so she looked around and settled on Daladier. It was an inspired choice. The son of a baker, Daladier was ambition incarnate, both socially and politically; but he hid this often unappealing characteristic under a look of apparent simplicity. For him, of course, Mme de Crussol represented the ne plus ultra of Paris society. Still, he did not want to be known as a social climber, always an unfortunate thing for a left-wing politician to be. Because Mme de Crussol was known to be his mistress, however, his constant presence in her salon made him look like a successful ladies' man instead of a snob.

Naturally, Mme de Crussol worked hard on behalf of her lover: her salon was used relentlessly to push his prospects; and there she scored a significant triumph over Mme de Portes. While Reynaud was out of office from 1932 to 1938, Daladier, during that period, was frequently a minister and even, on (brief) occasion, the Premier, thus giving his mistress's salon a marked advantage. Naturally, it was Mme de Portes's great object to plot Daladier out of office, and Reynaud into it. Nothing could have been more coldly ferocious than the rivalry of the two hostesses; and since Daladier was just as easily influenced as Reynaud, the two men were, under a pleasant exterior, deadly enemies, a fact that within the next five years significantly contributed to the collapse of France.

There were other successful salons, of course, chief among them that of the comtesse de Montgomery. The heiress to a liquor fortune, Minou de Montgomery was not just rich, she was beautiful as well. Her ash-blonde hair, piercing blue-green eyes, and dazzling complexion were much noticed, and the highly fashionable clothes she wore added to her glamour. "She gave artfully planned parties in a stunning decor — there were white walls and curtains, very low purple couches, wide screens of Chinese lacquer, black and gold bronze Venetian pages, all in vast rooms perfumed by huge bouquets of white flowers and lit by multicolored candles," one of her guests noted.

Several ambassadors . . . were Minou's most faithful guests, together with French politicians like Georges Bonnet [and Paul Reynaud], French and foreign press magnates like Jean Prouvost [of *Paris-Soir*], Pierre Guimier [of *Le Journal*] and Lord Camrose [of the London

*Daily Telegraph*], famous dress designers like Chanel and Schiaparelli, society people like the duc and duchesse d'Ayen, the Hon. Mrs. Fellowes, Lady Mendl, bankers, great industrialists, etc. Minou was the authoritarian editor in chief of *Marie Claire,* the most popular of the women's magazines. . . . Unknown by the general public, she was still rightly considered as one of the most important powers in the world of politics.

That same Tout-Paris one met at Minou's could also be seen in the sumptuously decorated . . . private house of the comtesse Marthe de Fels, who was married to the young and immensely wealthy Deputy André de Fels. A tall, shapely, and cordial woman, she was unrivaled when it came to planning subtle maneuvers and moving her men on the political and diplomatic chessboard. The star of her salon was Alexis Léger, the general secretary of the foreign ministry [its highly powerful top civil servant], whom one liked to hear explaining his views on foreign policy with great charm and a wealth of poetic images [Léger, under the pen name St. John Perse, was a considerable poet who eventually won the Nobel Prize for literature]. One had dinner at Marthe de Fels's, one had lunch at Minou's, one had supper in the underground hall, paved with white marble, of the highly modern apartment of the beautiful Florence Jay Gould, who had married an American. The next day, one might meet at a ball in the gardens of the Versailles villa that belonged to Lady Mendl, that obstinately juvenile octogenarian [*sic*], who was also a highly successful decorator and whose husband was a British diplomat. . . . Otto Abetz soon made his way into these circles, where he could further the Führer's propaganda, but also . . . overhear many a state secret: the politicians, in order to dazzle a pretty aristocrat . . . often gave exact accounts of government deliberations.[13]

The very unreality of so much of any government's activity, the feeling that it was all a game to be enjoyed by those in the know, all that contributed to the ministers' indiscretions. It was also a reflection of the deliberate blindness to the real world that pervaded the top echelons of Paris society.

Politics was not the only topic in these salons, although it kept gaining in importance with every year that passed. There was gossip of all kinds — who slept with whom, who had just been unfaithful, who had embarked on a new liaison — stories about theater and movie stars, even an occasional conversation about the latest play. It was the done thing, after all, to go to the opening nights of new plays. Not to be seen there was as shameful for men like Reynaud and Bonnet as it was for people like the duc and duchesse d'Ayen. And even when the play in question was rather too difficult for most of the Tout-Paris, it was discussed (briefly) with an appearance of interest and an illusion of information. That was the case for André Gide's *Oedipe*. An austere work centered around the dialogue between Oedipus and Tiresias, the priest, it argues that no matter how harsh our fate, we may still save ourselves without the help of any established religion. Tiresias believes, and insists, that we cannot alone and without the Church find salvation; Oedipus, refusing to kneel in front of men who claim that they represent the divinity, confesses his fault — marrying his mother — in public and relies on this soul-cleansing action, as well as on Antigone's purity, to reach beyond his doom. Through the expression of its belief in the independence of mankind and its refusal to give in to the fears invoked by the priests of every religion, *Oedipe* was, in fact, a major political statement. In Italy and Germany, the people already had abdicated in favor of lay equivalents of Tiresias: the dictators were the all-powerful interpreters of their own brand of divinity. In France itself the growing wave of antiparliamentarism sometimes took the form of a wish for a strongman. In all the beauty of its spare and musical language, *Oedipe* was a cry for democracy and freedom of thought.

This obviously was not an easy theme; nor does the play, in its simple grandeur, make for an "amusing" evening; but anything that came from Gide's pen was received with respect and attention. Indeed, the novelist had come to be something like the literary conscience of France: what he liked was read, what he talked about was interesting. The publication of segments of his diary was eagerly awaited. Oddly enough, however, this puritan whose style was marked by the most sophisticated simplicity, this eagerly sought writer who firmly refused to become part of the Tout-Paris, was also a hedonist and a man of courage, the first homosexual in French literature to publish a book that was also a hymn to his kind of love. And while, except for *Oedipe* and his diary, he published little in the early thirties, he remained the genius by whom all others were judged.

*Oedipe* was briefly a subject of conversation for those who were the guests of Minou de Montgomery or Hélène de Portes. They knew they were supposed to be interested in Gide's work because they liked to think of themselves as cultivated; but nightclubs were of far more immediate interest to them. Although Le Boeuf sur le Toit, that most fashionable of the twenties' clubs, still existed, it was no longer the place to go. Now there was a whole new generation of clubs each of which for a short time was what the French called *un must.*

Much the most famous of the nightclub singers, Lucienne Boyer soon reached national celebrity. Always dressed in a tight black velvet dress, she was a modern beauty whose huge eyes and generous mouth went with a tough, sensual manner. She sang, in a husky mezzo voice and with a blend of modesty and sensuality, love songs that relied on suggestion rather than frank eroticism, and always seemed addressed to just one listener. Her career started with a huge hit, "*Parlez-moi d'amour*" (Talk to me of love, tell me tender things . . .), but most of her songs were about women who were about to be left or who had just been left by a lover; and for all her success she performed mostly in small clubs of which she was at least part owner — Les Borgia, Chez les Clochards, Chez Lucienne, Chez Elle. Her New Year's Eves were famous; and at her successive clubs, all through the year (except, of course, during the summer, when no one who mattered was in Paris), she drew in all that was fashionable in the city. It bothered no one that the decor often seemed like an insult to the poor (Chez les Clochards was decorated with pictures of the shacks of the homeless on the river's quays); in fact, it only added extra piquancy to the singer's sad ditties.

There were all kinds of nightclubs. Some were large, exotic, and cheap, like the Boule Blanche in Montparnasse, where West Indian blacks put on dance shows and white Parisians could give themselves a frisson by twirling about with someone of another color. Others, like the Marine, offered three-piano jazz and though inexpensive attracted the Tout-Paris. Some insisted on poverty made exotic and palatable: at the Place du Tertre there was a faithful reconstitution of the Montmartre square, with awnings, trees, and a trompe-l'oeil sky. The waiters, instead of being all in black, wore corduroy trousers — a fabric normally seen only on working-class men — and the orchestra was suited up in apache costumes. There was no danger, however; the so-called apaches, once in fact a group of petty criminals, were now nothing more than a convenient fiction, so the rich could feel brave in perfect safety. The situation in the real world was the exact opposite: there, problems and outright perils multiplied, so it was particularly relaxing to appear to be taking a risk.

All these places were French; but, thanks to Prohibition, it was well understood that there was no rivaling New York when it came to the really hot night spots; and when an American opened her own place, Paris went mad.

"Times being hard, those who failed to squeeze in at Bricktop's opening of her new Rue Pigalle *boîte* crammed the staircase, filled the lower foyer and overflowed as a mob of top hats and ermine into the street," Genêt reported.

> Chairs had to be borrowed from neighboring bistros to seat a chic international crush that included the Princesse de Faucigny-Lucinge, the Duchesse d'Ayen, the Comtesse de Vogüé, Elsa Maxwell and Harry Thaw. The decors, designed by Baron Hoyninguen-Huené, and executed by Neil Martin, are, for once in a nightclub, becoming to humanity — black-and-mercury glass tiles and black oilcloth, with concealed lighting in a white wall ramp which, throwing heads and shoulders into silhouette, turns even drinkers into charming decoration. Bricktop's automatically becomes not only the newest but the smartest club to see or be seen in of all Montmartre.[14]

A year later, nothing had changed, and Janet Flanner described the scene with as much enthusiasm as ever. It was part, she felt, of what gave Paris its uniquely civilized quality, along with great music, great art, and great literature. It was also one of the very last links to the golden twenties, a time when Americans had felt that Paris and Heaven were actually the same thing, and money flowed as easily as champagne.

"The nightclubs have opened again, doubtless on the theory that after midnight the wolf is so tired you don't have to keep him from the door," she informed her readers. "Bricktop is back in her top hat . . . on the Rue Pigalle. The Melody Bar, Bagdad and all the various rum-and-rebellions that mark the Martinique Montparnasse season are in full swing."[15] Indeed, the *boîtes*, as Genêt usually referred to them — the word was short for *boîtes de nuit* — were flourishing more than ever, even when they seemed too inexpensive to draw in the Tout-Paris.

> As a means, perhaps, of carrying on the old family tradition, Suzy Surcouf, supposed descendant of the popular pirate of that name, has just opened a new nightclub, La Vie Parisienne on the Rue Ste.-Anne. To her original corsair equipment, she adds the original booty of a bounding baritone voice, fine blond hair and what the artists call one of the best backs in Paris. Excellent views of it by Van Dongen, Kisling, Foujita and Laurencin, among others, serve as the club's modest decoration. Though not dressy enough to be chic, the *boîte* is oceans of fun, heavily frequented, even, by some of the right people, and above all has the sultry emotional quality of boom days, when couples were interested enough in having a good time to quarrel about it.[16]

Among those "right people," of course, was Genêt, who wrote this description. To her, nightclubs were a place where you could feel at home.

Even the nightclubs, even all the delicious gossip, failed to conceal that life was rapidly taking a turn for the worse. It wasn't just that, as Genêt noticed, the wolf was at the door, or, in fact, already in the house; events in Germany were taking a new and unpleasant turn. Most commentators assumed that Hitler would not last, that the reign of the Nazis was just a passing phase; still, a number of rather worrying events were clearly taking place on the other side of the Rhine. Suddenly there was a great influx of Jewish refugees, many of them wealthy, some of them the cream of the German musical world. Most audiences simply considered themselves lucky; but there was one ugly, and not unrepresentative, incident in which the French composer Florent Schmitt, a man of indescribable mediocrity, stood up as one of Kurt Weill's pieces was about to be played and shouted: "Long live Hitler! We don't want all those Jews over here!"

For another group of people, however, life seemed to go on as usual — except that many of them found themselves almost penniless — the artists. For some renowned painters like Picasso and Matisse the Depression did not matter so much: their work was still selling, if a little more slowly, and they had prospered long enough to have very substantial reserves. For others, though, who were neither as well known nor as well established, money was very hard to come by. Some, like Miró, went home temporarily; others, like Max Ernst, stayed on, the latter all the more eagerly since there was no room in the new Germany for avant-garde artists.

Still, no worthwhile artist paints just to earn a living. Miró, back in Barcelona, had such a small studio that he could work on no more than a single sizable canvas at a time. Ernst, in Paris, had more room but made up for it by being unable to pay the rent. In spite of all that, both went on producing work that was as new as it was beautiful.

They were encouraged to do so, in part, because of their allegiance to Surrealism. The successor of Dada, many of whose ideas it borrowed, Surrealism was invented by the poet André Breton, who ran the movement with an iron hand. Artistically, it was based on the direct expression of the unconscious and dreams; it rejected all traditions, all established formulas, all official approval. One consequence of this was a dramatic and frequently voiced rejection of French society as it stood; so the Surrealists got very close to the Communists. That made perfect sense since Stalin had yet to start on his massacres and it did look as if the Soviet Union might genuinely establish a classless society. As a result, a number of important texts were published in a magazine, *Le Surréalisme au service de la Révolution* (Surrealism at the Service of the Revolution), which was printed by the party presses. Still, there was much to differentiate Communists and Surrealists: faithful party members were expected to be obedient and conventional; Breton's followers, all of them thorough individualists, were not about to take orders. Even in their private lives, the Surrealists (except for Miró) defied conventional morality. Partners changed frequently, group sex was not unknown, marriages were few and brief.

All that suited Ernst perfectly. A rebel by nature, he thought, as John Russell has aptly noted, that the artist was a natural and permanent outcast. His own situation confirmed this. As a German who loathed the Nazis, he was, from 1933 on, a stateless person. As a husband, he had soon tired of his wife and was currently in love with another Surrealist, the beautiful Belgian poet Meret Oppenheim. As it turned out, Oppenheim proved resistant; but that was an exception: Ernst was one of the great seducers of his time. Slim, standing very straight, he seemed taller than he really was and had a tremendously imposing presence. His hair, first blond, but very soon white, was wavy, his skin very white, his nose beak-like, and his eyes a translucent and fascinating blue. That, his evident refinement, his sly sense of humor, his sharp intelligence, and his fascination with women, usually ensured his success.

There was no convention that Ernst hesitated to mock, no power block he feared to offend. An article, "Danger of Pollution," that he wrote in the summer of 1932 for *Le Surréalisme au service de la Révolution* was typical. "The confessors have done their work well," he explained. "If mankind has become more and more ugly, more and more redoubtable, it is because for centuries men have given in to the mother of all vices: the confessional. The anemic body of the Savior has thrown their digestions out of order. Their sexuality has been enfeebled by the suppression of pleasure and the duty of procreation, and their passionate impulses have been tamed by the necessity of praying to a Virgin. . . . The virtue of pride, which was once the beauty of mankind, has given way to that fount of all ugliness, Christian humility. Love, which should give meaning to life, is under supervision day and night by the clerical police. . . . Love — as Rimbaud said — must be reinvented."[17] This was an attack on the Catholic Church, of course, but it applied well enough to the Protestants; and while its rejection of Christian repression is fairly elementary, it could still, in 1932, shock a great many people.

Still, if Ernst had merely been the author of unconventional articles, he would not be remembered: it is, of course, his art that made him famous. On one level, his paintings were wholly new: dreamlike, semi-abstract landscapes, unlikely creatures, often birds, in impossible roles and shapes, highly suggestive textures produced by frottage (the rubbing of paint on canvas or paper) all contributed to the formation of a strange and haunting universe.

By 1933, that universe was clearly about to undergo a cataclysm of huge proportions: impending doom could be felt in much of Ernst's work. An immobile sun or moon, eerie lighting, and above all vegetation apparently possessed by a malevolent life hint at danger and destruction. In *La Forêt* (The Forest), for instance, the outline of a huge but transparent bird is superimposed on creeping growths while the sky holds the half-circle of the sun.

That is alarming enough; but *Europe after the Rain I,* painted a little later that year, goes a good deal further. In this large canvas, we see a smudged, altered, and generalized map of Europe, with dark, encroaching seas and arbitrary national boundaries. The surface seems eroded, torn, crushed by a vast catastrophe, as if the whole continent were seen after a rain, not of water, but of deadly fire. Here was premonition indeed: the events predicted by the painting did not take place for another seven years, but in his interpretation of unconscious dread, Ernst proved himself a far better prophet than the statesmen and the historians.

That a catastrophe loomed near was made just as tangible in another work, the first version of *La Ville entière* (The Whole City), in which we see a crumbling fortress devoured by a malevolent growth, half-vegetation, half-insect and reptilian, under an unnatural sky: civilization, life as we know it, has given way to a mindless, devouring horde of unthinkable creatures.

*La Ville entière,* like *Europe after the Rain,* is painted in somber colors — browns, grays, dark green. For all its brightness, however, the *Jardin gobe avions* (Airplane-Swallowing Garden) is no more cheerful. Here, strange geometric plateaus form the setting for frottage objects, part leaf, part feather, part scurrying insects painted in brilliant pinks, purples, greens, and whites; and the feeling we get is one of devastation and uncontrolled unconscious life. As it is, the work is threatening enough, but the title makes its meaning even clearer: planes are the obvious symbol of modern civilization, and the eerie garden has swallowed them as it will swallow us. This is yet another remarkable example of a great artist so closely in touch with the major forces of his time that he sees what others will only discover later; and yet the work is also timeless: people who saw it in the fifties could associate it with nuclear destruction; to us, it evokes irresistibly a thousand terrifying images seen on the evening news.

There were other ways as well in which Ernst made the viewer rethink his world. In a whole series of collages, he combined elements of turn-of-the-century catalogue illustration to create improbable, haunting images — a woman with the head of a bird, a man whose body is in part replaced by a washboard. Nothing here is as it seems. The most conventional images lead us into an impossible world where anything may happen at any time; "scientific" reality gives way to all the fears and symbols of the psyche. The conventional world is mocked by its own tools: here, too, we see the end of a civilization in which the artist sardonically enjoys the nightmare he pictures.

Joan Miró also used illustrated catalogues, but in a very different way. While Ernst created hallucinations, Miró reduced the tools offered by hardware manufacturers to abstract symbols organized at random on a white page; and he then went on from this to produce paintings that were more abstract than, but just as evocative as, Max Ernst's.

In one of these works, for instance, the ground is bright blue and green, and against it various forms, one of them almost recognizable as an ax, stand out in black, white, orange, and yellow. Although the threat here is not as clear as in Ernst's work, the result, in spite of the bright colors, is a sense of mystery, of disconnection. Even when we do recognize an object, it is so removed from its usual context that it offers not reassurance, but the warning that, for Miró too, nothing is what we think it should be.

That these alarming and wholly original paintings should have been the work of Miró seems almost impossible. A small, bright-eyed, meticulously neat man with old-fashioned manners, Miró, while radically rejecting conformity in his work, was otherwise entirely respectable (if poor). A model husband and father, he shared the Surrealists' cultural attitudes but not their way of living. To meet him was to wonder, for a while at least, whether you had made a mistake; surely this was a bookkeeper or a bank teller; but within a few minutes the painter's bold, unconventional intelligence became manifest.

The very technique he used showed it clearly. Until Miró, form had always been defined by color contained within a boundary; but this was a restriction that he rejected. Although he used flat surfaces of color as a means of illuminating clearly marked shapes, he would subject the forms themselves to violent changes of color: as one shape passes across another, its hue changes abruptly. Within this startling system, there are often figures that may seem abstract at first but then are seen to have familiar anatomical elements — only distorted, elongated, pulled about.

This, too, was ominous: the bodies we see are no longer those we know. They have endured immense pressures, radical transformation; they have been tortured almost beyond recognition. By 1934, this had become even more clearly manifest. Female monsters in brilliant colors people Miró's canvases, and their faces are pulled out of shape by fierce grimaces. There are openings in the bodies where we do not expect them, tiny, strange-colored eyes, streaming, simplified hair often coming from what looks like the wrong part of the figure, screaming boxlike mouths, and vast, distorted limbs, so that a foot or the splayed fingers of a hand are larger than the rest of the body; and all that in oranges, acid yellows, violent blues and blacks.

It is, in fact, the same world that is depicted in the works of Ernst and Miró. With Ernst we see blasted landscapes, with Miró monsterlike figures; but both share their premonition of a looming disaster. Of course, the two artists also shared the Surrealist fascination with the unconscious, and so they were unusually sensitive, not just to their own psychic goblins, but to Europe's slide to catastrophe. What we block out of the conscious mind, all the signs and warnings, remains in the unconscious. To most people, that becomes available through dreams: for Ernst and Miró, it was manifest on canvas after canvas. Here, in fact, was a new and disturbing aspect of modernity. The designers of the Bauhaus had thought that a new world could be a better, more rational place. The people who bought fast cars and took airplane rides saw the new as thrillingly fast. Now, two great artists depicted the place where that speed was leading, and it was anything but reassuring.

One artist, insulated to a large degree by the magnitude of his genius, continued unchanged, at least for a while longer. For Picasso, his own life was what mattered. When he was happy, which is to say in love, then his work was all tenderness; when he was unhappy, horror filled the canvas. Never a Surrealist himself, he was perhaps not as closely connected to the unconscious, and he generally cared very little for the world outside: not until *Guernica,* in 1937, did he suddenly notice that all was not well.

In 1931, however, all was proceeding nicely. He had found and bought a small château at Boisgeloup, in Normandy, the first of the old houses in which he was to live henceforth. With the exception of a handsome

Gothic chapel, Boisgeloup was a classical seventeenth-century castle. There was a great courtyard framed on each side by a long row of stables and coach houses, which the artist promptly converted into studios. The immediate result was a vast new creative leap. A press for etchings was set up so that Picasso could work on engravings whenever he felt like it. There was room for sculpting as well, and it was then that Picasso started using found objects that he transformed into his own creatures. Part of a rake would become a figure's hair, for instance, while roots, branches, an old glove, or a child's broken toy would either be used as abstract elements or combined to form part of a figure.

By the time the artist's retrospective opened at the Galerie Georges Petit, it was clear that something else had happened as well: there on the walls was a series of highly sensuous female nudes. There were sleeping figures with arms folded around their heads; but sometimes the sitter was awake and looking out at the viewer from the cocoon of a series of curves in which forehead and nose were united to a pair of sensuous lips. It needed no great acuity to see that Picasso had, yet again, fallen in love.

The lady, this time, was Marie-Thérèse Walter. Young, blonde, voluptuous, with Nordic good looks, Marie-Thérèse was also everything Olga, Picasso's wife, was not. Olga wanted her husband to live and dress like a *mondain,* a society man. Attendance at the balls given by the comte de Beaumont and the vicomte de Noailles were the order of the day; life was to be lush and conventional. Unfortunately for Olga, though, Picasso was a Bohemian through and through. Nothing interested him less than a well-cut suit, nothing bored him more than a grand party, especially when he wanted to be in his studio; and so the marriage deteriorated very rapidly. Marie-Thérèse, on the other hand, was robustly coarse and unconventional, unquestionably sensual, and at the same time capricious (like Picasso himself) and unpredictable. Because of that, there was something a little mysterious about her, and that was yet another attraction.

That she was the right woman for Picasso came through clearly in the exhibition. She could be seen looking at her duplicate curves in a mirror against a mosaiclike background of brilliant colors; she reclined nude on a couch, the rounded outline of her body flowing from hip to breast to arm to head. Never before had Picasso's work been so unabashedly sensual, never before had he painted so inviting, so peaceful a universe.

Even so, another element was creeping into the oeuvre. "When you work, you don't know what is going to come out of it. It is not indecision. The fact is it changes while you are at work," Picasso told his friend Roland Penrose.[18] That, of course, is bound to happen to any non-academic artist. Like the Surrealists, Picasso let his unconscious come through, only in a more controlled way; and one aspect of his work in 1933 showed it clearly: the prints in which minotaurs are the main themes.

Like the good Spaniard he was, Picasso had always been interested in bullfights, but they had not, for a very long time, been among his images. Now they reappear, thoroughly transformed in a series of engravings whose almost classical purity of line makes their content more shocking. The Minotaur, a man with the head of a bull, was a mythical Greek monster who had to be fed live virgins at regular intervals. There is something left of the ogre in Picasso's Minotaur, but it is an almost civilized, almost human ogre: we see him playing, making love to a woman — or raping her — fighting, dying in the arena as a row of pitiless faces watches. Here is a dark instinct, an uncontrolled passion made visible; but while we should yearn for the Minotaur to be controlled and defeated, his own awareness of himself makes us sympathize with him, and so does his unbounded vital energy. In many ways, the Minotaur is the symbol of a wild and exuberant freedom, and without him the world is not just duller, but also dangerously regimented. That, of course, can be taken as a comment on the standardization of the modern world; but, more pointedly, it could also be seen as referring to the crushing sameness imposed by the dictators on those they ruled.

Although Picasso was hugely famous, Genêt paid very little attention to him. Indeed, she frequently equated him, in terms of column space at least, to such third-rate painters as Foujita and Kisling. That was in part because she lacked the sort of mentor she needed: there was no Virgil Thomson to teach her about the visual arts, and so she never quite understood the difference between a great artist and one that was merely fashionable. Still, she dutifully reported Picasso's exhibitions; not only were they Parisian events, they enhanced two of the aspects of the city she most cared about: civilization and modernity. Here, too, Paris was leading the world — and that was worth noting.

That the behavior of the Tout-Paris might have very little to do with how ordinary people felt, however, was not something that often occurred to her; and so, when, in February 1934, the city exploded, she was both surprised and rather shocked. Even the cause of the explosion, the most sensational scandal in half a century, struck her as just another instance of government corruption, but this, after all, was not, she felt, anything that really mattered. She was wrong, though. Paris society and the top politicians had tried hard, for nearly two years, to ignore the real world. With the riots, that world reasserted itself, and it was suddenly seen to be far more dangerous and unpleasant than anyone had thought. For the French, the Stavisky affair, which provoked the upheaval, was a watershed just as the Dreyfus affair had been in its time. Having exploded violently, it changed France forever.

# CHAPTER
# FIVE

# MURDER AND MYSTERY

PARIS until 1934 had seemed isolated from the rest of the country. It was, unlike the provincial cities, the center of all cultural and artistic life, and that in itself made it different. More important, though, its most visible citizens were people who refused to admit that anything had changed, and whose social and political life continued unaltered. On February 6, however, the Parisians themselves made it very clear that they, too, had had enough.

"By dinner time," Genêt wrote on the tenth, "the Place de la Concorde was a lurid lithograph of burning bus barricades, hamstrung horses and men and women stoning [and] shouting. . . . Both the populace and the troops showed a dreadful courage. . . . It is not unlikely that the Third Republic *will* fall."[1] For a few hours, in fact, it looked as if it might — and all because of Alexandre Stavisky, a second-rate crook who had died a month earlier.

The man had, furthermore, been a considerate crook: unlike so many of his colleagues who defrauded the public, Alexandre Stavisky had victimized banks and insurance companies — businesses not usually popular with those who are not their shareholders. There was, in fact, something positively appealing about him. With the money he stole, he and his beautiful wife, Arlette, lived a glamorous life in Paris, complete with limousines, furs, jewels, and dazzling parties. Of course, the funds he was spending were not his own, but it was a kind of Robin Hood act, taking from the rich to live like them.

Stavisky himself had the kind of charm it takes to be an effective confidence trickster. Joseph Kessel, a tough reporter and adventure writer, found him altogether appealing. "He seemed pleasant to me, with a lively, well-informed mind, and the possessor of experiences both brutal and subtle," Kessel noted in March 1934. "Flexible and supple, dressed in the smoothest of suits, he moved easily, like a young man. . . . His smooth complexion showed he took good care of himself. He liked to show off his straight, sharp, even, dazzling teeth by smiling with his thin lips. Below the well-shaped, but slightly inclined forehead, shone black, silky eyes . . . but the top half of his face, which was energetic, firm, almost beautiful, was given the lie by the bottom half, by the softness of the chin, by the movements of the mouth, which was weak and cunning when it was not set into the smile that Alexandre used so often."[2]

It was no mean achievement for Stavisky to have become friends with someone like Kessel; but then, he was a highly skilled con man. The son of a Russian dentist who had emigrated to France and settled in Paris in 1890, young Alexandre, at an early age, showed both a taste for money and a tendency to take it even when it belonged to someone else. By the time he was twenty-three, in 1909, he had already defrauded the investors in a little theater, engaged in various other shady operations, and shown a remarkable talent for having his trials postponed. Still, by 1914, he was beginning to run out of luck and so the war came as a splendid opportunity. The twenty-eight-year-old Stavisky promptly volunteered, thus neatly removing himself from the reach of the civil courts. By January 1915 he had been wounded and returned to civilian life; but that was also when he discovered a new, even easier way to take other people's money. He became the lover of an aging but wealthy singer, and for the next eleven years he lived off a series of easily bilked women, with occasional excursions into the drug trade and the setting up of phony corporations, one of which, the Cinema Trust, fooled a few investors.

It was thus not until 1926 that Stavisky discovered that it was easiest, after all, to get the money where it was to be found in the largest amounts: the stocks and bonds of corporations, which could be either forged or stolen. His first attempt worked out splendidly. By the time he was caught, he had hired some of the best and most politically connected lawyers in Paris and had fallen in love with one of Chanel's models, the beautiful Arlette Simon. And then, most inconveniently, he was arrested on July 22, 1926.

At least Arlette remained free. She was, in fact, innocent; but it no doubt helped that her lawyer, hired by Stavisky, was none other than Joseph Paul-Boncour, the future Premier. Stavisky himself did not have such an easy time of it. Now that he was safely in jail, the various indictments going back to 1909 began to catch up with him; by December 1927, a year and a half later, he was still awaiting a cascade of trials. That did not stop him from bribing a corrupt police detective to steal as many of the incriminating documents as possible. It was a smart move: the baffled prosecutors were forced to postpone his trial; then, on December 28, he was released for medical reasons. Clearly, (bought) influence had been brought to play.

No sooner was he released than he married Arlette, who, in due course, bore him two children; and, as an elementary precaution, he changed his name to Serge Alexandre. Having done so, he entered a new business. In no time a string of jewelry stores, the Etablissements Alex, was ready to buy stolen gems, which were then hocked at the municipal pawnshop in Orléans. The problem was, however, that not enough jewel thieves offered their provender to the Etablissements Alex; and so, instead of bringing real, but stolen, goods to the pawnshop, Serge Alexandre, having bribed the local officials, started pawning fake stones. By 1929, that institution, which was owned by the city, had given Alexandre 30 million francs (20 million 1993 dollars) in supposedly secured loans.

Obviously, there was no reason to stop: in June 1929, Stavisky brought in 10 million francs' worth of false emeralds. And then bad luck struck. Because the pawnshop had made so many loans in a very short time, it was audited by outside experts sent in by the state: obviously, they would notice that much of the pledged jewelry was fake. In order to withdraw it, 17 million francs were needed: Stavisky raised the money by selling forged notes. Even so, one of the employees talked. Yet another indictment was on the way.

By then, however, it hardly seemed to matter. A mysterious force had apparently suspended the normal course of justice — so much so that in 1931 a magistrate was appointed to find out why Stavisky was still at large; but the report he produced, recommending an immediate arrest, proved to be as void of effect as the earlier indictment. As for the trial begun in 1926, it had been suspended and was postponed no less than nineteen times. Even today, it is not altogether clear just who was bribed, and through whom Stavisky did the bribing, though the probabilities point to Camille Chautemps's family, particularly his brother-in-law, and perhaps even some sections of his entourage. What is certain, however, is that highly placed (and corrupt) officials saw to it that Stavisky remained safe.

Sure that he was invulnerable, Stavisky now reached for even larger amounts of money. Within weeks of the Orléans debacle, he was setting up a whole network of dummy corporations that promptly floated valueless bonds. That the bonds found a ready market among banks and insurance companies may seem astonishing: in spite of many instances to the contrary, these institutions are, after all, supposed to have a certain financial expertise. In this case, they were reassured because the board of directors of the main holding company was so eminently respectable: it included a former prefect of police, a close friend of then Premier Pierre Laval, a retired high-level civil servant, a general of reactionary views (that somehow made him seem even more reassuring), and a former ambassador.

Even better, this board reassured the attorney general's office: clearly a man surrounded by such massive respectability could not be a crook. Once again, the Stavisky indictments were tactfully forgotten.

There seemed to be no reason why this could not go on forever: as Stavisky stole money, so he spent it. By 1933, if perhaps not quite a member of the Tout-Paris, he had nevertheless become a well-known Parisian figure. He lived in a vast suite at the Claridge, a luxurious hotel on the Champs-Elysées; he gambled, he was seen at the horse races on the right days, he gave brilliant dinners, attended by ministers, Deputies, and newspapermen, at which champagne flowed and mountains of caviar were consumed; and just as important, the beautiful Arlette, his wife, dazzled all the men. Swathed in furs or covered with jewels, she was unquestionably one of the most elegant women in Paris. Her cars were as chic as her dresses; soon she was seen at first nights and charity galas; and even if she had yet to receive an invitation from one of the great Parisian hostesses, it seemed likely that day would not be long delayed.

Indeed, Serge Alexandre was becoming a magnate of the most conventional sort. He backed a newspaper, *La Volonté,* whose readership was minute, but whose editor, Albert Dubarry, was close to several of the Radical ministers and played a significant role in the party's intrigues. He bought one of the largest theaters in Paris, L'Empire, and put on the most lavish musicals — one, *Katinka,* was Russian-inspired, another, *Deux Sous de fleurs* (Two Pennies' Worth of Flowers), imitated the shows to be seen at the Casino de Paris. Both lost vast sums, clear proof that M. Alexandre was so rich that he could afford the loss. By 1933, in fact, he had reached a new high: he owned and raced his own horses, another notoriously expensive amusement.

Nor were these spectacular activities reserved for Paris. In the summer, the Alexandres were off to the fashionable resort town of Bayonne, where the husband gambled, and lost, vast sums at the Casino while the wife was a key participant in all the *concours d'élégance*. This was easy: the couple owned two Marmonts, a Buick, and a Hispano-Suiza, a car just as grand and glamorous as a Rolls. And of course Serge and Arlette were seen in all the best restaurants and nightclubs. It was all more than enough to impress Jean Garat, the Deputy and mayor of Bayonne. He and the Alexandres soon became fast friends.

This sort of life cost a great deal of money, but the market for worthless bonds was limited; so Stavisky now decided to work a new wrinkle on an old scheme. Instead of merely pawning jewelry, he would create a pawnshop of his own that would then sell notes backed by the objects it held as collateral: this was a perfectly normal way of doing business. The borrowers who pawned their jewels would pay a higher rate of interest than the institution. The difference between the rate of interest on the notes and that paid by the borrowers was net income. The notes themselves, because they were normally absolutely secured by the objects pawned, were a favorite form of investment for insurance companies and banks.

The hitch was that pawnshops in the thirties were a municipal monopoly; so Stavisky looked around for a city without a pawnshop — it was called a *Crédit municipal* — and conveniently found it in Bayonne. As for the authorizations he needed, they would come from his friend Garat. And just in case that officeholder had any doubts, they would have been stilled by a letter warmly recommending the project written by Albert Dalimier, a fellow Radical who was then minister of commerce.

The letter in question was the proof of Dubarry's usefulness; it was the newspaperman who had convinced his good friend Dalimier to write it. Still, there were quite a few people who knew that Serge Alexandre was really Alexandre Stavisky — especially among the police — and they saw no reason why they should not say so. That, obviously, was a clear and present danger, but M. Alexandre's connections were such that the problem could be solved. Once again, the useful Dubarry was put to work. He went to see another old friend, Jean Chiappe, the prefect of police. Amazingly, in February 1933 the man who ran the Paris police agreed to see the indicted but not yet tried crook. What happened in the course of that brief meeting is far from clear; but it is certain that those police inspectors who might have felt suspicious of Serge Alexandre's new endeavors remained absolutely silent. Stavisky had now reached the pinnacle: he could go ahead and use the new *Crédit municipal* of Bayonne, an establishment guaranteed by the city itself, to pass worthless notes.

This was very convenient; but M. Alexandre now set up an even more glamorous scam, one that involved nothing less than the European Great Powers. When, in 1920, the Treaty of Trianon settled the borders of the new Hungary, a number of Hungarians whose land passed to other nations were left dispossessed, with the understanding that they would be compensated for their loss by the powers; and in earnest of this intention, they were given notes payable when the powers had set up a fund to do so. Fourteen years later, the powers had yet to pay a penny. Still, there were those notes, and M. Alexandre proceeded to buy them for peanuts.

Now he had to resell them, and, once again, his political connections proved to be extremely useful. By hinting that an agreement to set up the fund was imminent, he could resell the notes, not at par, certainly, but for vastly more than they had cost him; and that is just what he proceeded to do. This time, however, he was dealing not just with incompetent bankers but with governments. Where before he had been able to obfuscate reality sufficiently to make his valueless bonds pass for good, the French government knew very well that no Hungarian compensation fund was about to be set up. The police, following this up, decided to question M. Alexandre about the Hungarian notes and their suddenly active market. On December 22, 1933, they sent for him.

From Stavisky's point of view, nothing could have been more disastrous, especially since, in Bayonne, his scheme was also on the verge of exposure. Unfortunately for Stavisky, the accounts of all the city-owned pawnshops were periodically reviewed by the national Treasury. Already in November, an official, worried by the high volume of loans made in the past few months — they came to well over 100 million francs (a little under 70 million 1993 dollars) — had repeatedly warned Mayor Garat that something looked suspicious. Garat, however, fully trusting his friend Alexandre, simply dismissed the successive warnings.

That did nothing to reassure the Treasury; its chief official in Bayonne now proceeded on his own and on December 15 sent an examiner, unannounced, to the *Crédit municipal*. With that, the fat was in the fire. By the end of that afternoon, it was already clear that large-scale fraudulent operations had been taking place.

Even so, nothing yet seemed to involve the glittering M. Alexandre. Instead, suspicions were centered on Garat, who simply stonewalled; but then, on December 21, one of the insurance companies that had bought the worthless notes swore out a complaint, and the chief cashier of the *Crédit municipal,* one of Stavisky's men, disappeared with his mistress. Two days later, he came back, was arrested, and claimed that he had merely been obeying Garat's orders, thus shielding his real boss to the last. The next day, Stavisky was sought by the police in connection with the Hungarian notes. It was obviously a matter of days, perhaps hours, before a connection was made between the two frauds.

At that point, Stavisky broke down. In a meeting with his lawyer, Me. Guiboud-Ribaud, he literally collapsed, admitting the truth not just about the Hungarian notes, but about the Bayonne frauds as well. As usual, of course, he had chosen his lawyer carefully; aside from his legal work, Me. Guiboud-Ribaud was an aide of Georges Bonnet, the Radical finance minister. With any luck, he would have the influence, at the very least, to contain the scandal a little longer; and then, there was also Dalimier, now minister of the colonies; he was sure, Stavisky felt, to protect him.

It is not hard to see why Stavisky took all this for granted. Guiboud-Ribaud's advice to his client was not to go to the police and make a clean breast of it all; instead, he called up René Pigaglio, Stavisky's chief henchman, and told him to take his chief away to where he would not be found for a while. Of course, that required money. Stavisky did have 10 million francs' worth of jewels taken from the Bayonne pawnshop, but it was late afternoon on December 24, no jeweler who would buy without asking questions had that sort of cash on hand, and in the end Stavisky left Paris with only 50,000 francs (about 32,000 1993 dollars).

After that, what had begun very like a story by Dashiell Hammett turned into one of Agatha Christie's more convoluted mysteries. Stavisky and Pigaglio left Paris in a hurry, driving through a storm; the car broke down; leaving it behind, they continued by train, finally reaching Chamonix, a skiing village in the French Alps, where Pigaglio had a villa. No sooner did they walk in, however, than they saw that the pipes had frozen; so they rented another villa, and there Stavisky closeted himself, still believing, for a few days, that Dalimier, who was a close friend of Premier Chautemps, would protect him, or perhaps that Georges Bonnet would do so. That would have been enough; these two Radical leaders were also among the most powerful men in France; but by the beginning of January, newspaper headlines dispelled that illusion; and on the sixth, after writing Arlette, Alexandre Stavisky died.

This is when a fraud and corruption scandal turned into a murder mystery. To this day, it is impossible to be sure whether Stavisky committed suicide or whether he was killed by the police in order to avoid the kind of testimony that might have incriminated high civil servants, Deputies, and ministers.

On the side of suicide, there is the fact that Stavisky was known to dread returning to jail, and the letter to his wife, which was found in his room, said: "I consider it my duty to go . . . for you, for the children. I would be away from you and them for years, perhaps forever. It is best therefore for you to be free, for me not to be an obstacle to their education and position in life."[3]

Against suicide, many people argued that it was all too convenient; that the medical evidence was ambiguous — the bullet found in the wall must have had a trajectory that was impossible considering the body's position — and that it had probably been tampered with; and, finally, that when Stavisky wrote he must "go," he simply meant to run and hide. A well-informed satirical weekly, *Le Canard enchaîné,* put it succinctly: "Stavisky kills himself with a bullet which was shot at him at close range,"[4] its headline proclaimed.

What is at any rate certain is that Stavisky lived for some twelve hours after the shooting; that he was left in the house for two hours after being found by the police before he was transferred to the local hospital; and that death was caused by loss of blood. Obviously, even if he did actually try to commit suicide, he could have been saved; just as obviously, no one wanted him to live.

Naturally, this sordid but spectacular story made for banner headlines, and the mystery surrounding Stavisky's death added greatly to the interest of the affair; but all that was as nothing compared to the real questions: What did Chautemps, Dalimier, and their associates know about the multiple trial postponements? How long had they known it? What had they done to protect Stavisky, and how did they do it? Soon the questions were asked not just about the Premier and his minister of the colonies, but about all the leading Radicals.

Ever since June 1932, the French had watched as the Radicals wrought their own peculiar brand of political magic in which cabinets disappeared and reappeared in different forms, and they were angry, an anger further

fueled by the growing Depression. Now, every day, there were new revelations — about the full extent of Stavisky's depredations, about the nineteen postponements of his trial, about his friendship with a number of
leading politicians headed by Garat and Dalimier, all of whom were important Radicals. Even worse, it soon became evident that the man responsible for not bringing Stavisky to trial, Pressard, was Chautemps's
brother-in-law. As the head of the financial section of the Paris attorney
general's office until 1926, and then as attorney general himself after 1928,
it was up to Pressard to see that indictments resulted in a prompt
trial — instead of which there had been those nineteen postponements.
From there to implicating the Premier himself, even though he was innocent, was a very small leap. Here, neatly summed up, was everything
that seemed to be wrong with the Radicals and, indeed, with the regime.
All the alienation people had been feeling, the evident fact that the political process was controlled, not by the voters, but by those in power, had
set the stage. The Stavisky affair was now taken as the paradigm of the
decadence and the corruption of the leading politicians.

Even the usually mealymouthed *Le Temps* sounded that particular
note: "The scandal of the affair," it editorialized on January 7, "is not the
theft itself . . . but the astounding facilities given the crook, the complici-
ties he found in the most unexpected circles, and the blindness, whether
sincere or pretended, of those whose task it is to protect the public's sav-
ings";[5] two days later it went on to advise the government to resign. As
for *L'Action française,* it minced no words. On January 7, its banner headline read simply: "Down with the thieves!";[6] on the ninth, it became:
"Down with the thieves! Down with the murderers! All, tonight, before
the Chamber!"[7] — meaning that all the Parisians should be on the square
in front of the Palais-Bourbon, where the Chamber sat, in order to demonstrate against the government; and on the tenth, with its usual disregard for truth, it went one better. That day, the headline, in huge type,
read simply: "Camille Chautemps is the head of a band of thieves and
murderers!"[8] For the first time, it began to look as if the extreme Right
had found the perfect cause: all through January, the street disturbances
multiplied.

Naturally, the government tried to stem the tide. On January 7, Garat
was arrested; on the eighth Dalimier was made to resign after the explanation he tried to give the Chamber was covered by boos and hisses; but
that left Chautemps himself all the more exposed, since there was no
longer anyone he could fire. To make his position even worse, very few
people believed him to be innocent. Not only was his brother-in-law di-

rectly involved, he himself was known to have an extremely supple sense of morality. From that, it was a small step to the belief that France was run by Stavisky's accomplices. And what everyone forgot in all the brouhaha was that, in fact, no private person, no widow, no orphan, had suffered from Stavisky's depredations: the victims had all been incompetent financial institutions.

Revolutions in France have always come from the Left; but as January passed into February, it looked as if this time the Right might stage a violent takeover. All through the month, with considerable success, *L'Action française* (together with its *ligue*) saw to it that the demonstrations were virtually permanent while its editorials reached a new pitch of rage. "We await the croaking of this regime of thieves, of procurers of both sexes, of murdering policemen called Republic, or Democracy," Léon Daudet wrote in a front-page editorial on January 13,[9] and he kept up that note for the rest of the month. By the twenty-second, the paper was proclaiming: "French citizens will no longer accept this corrupt and criminal dictatorship. Tonight . . . they will go massively before the Chamber and demand the end of . . . this dishonored regime."[10]

That sort of excess was typical of *L'Action française;* usually, the rest of the press struck a very different note. Now, however, no one was willing to defend the government, and the appearance of guilt was enough to tar a man. Herriot, himself notoriously honest, feared being a target, and, although just a Deputy, promptly made public the state of his nonexistent fortune.

As for Chautemps, he was pursued by bad luck — or the habits of his party. Although he survived the demand of a commission of enquiry into the affair on January 12 — the Left united behind him — he received a new blow exactly a week later, when it became evident that his minister of justice, Eugène Raynaldy, was involved in a scam operated by a dishonest banker. On January 27, Raynaldy was forced to resign, the second minister to do so because of corruption; and it became clear that the government could no longer carry on. The Republic survived, but Chautemps, the first target of the now rabid Right, fell. And although he was obviously a victim of the affair, he owed his fate just as much to the fear that the daily street manifestations might turn into a general rising.

It was not an unmotivated fear; the situation looked very bleak indeed. Even Genêt, who usually found politics a bore and ignored them, devoted her whole Paris letter to the affair, going on to say: "Herriot's Radicals are covered with mud, with side splashes for every other party, and parliamentarianism in general; a military *coup d'état* was rumored; and there was an ugly evening of rioting in the Boulevards Saint-Germain and Raspail, in which skulls and street lights were broken, shock troops guarded the Chamber, and the Concorde bridgehead was barricaded against the mob, led by Royalist agitators, as usual."[11] Genêt's text is dated January 18; by the time it appeared in print, two weeks later, the disorders had grown in frequency and violence.

That was in part the doing of one man. Jean Chiappe, the prefect of police, was supposed to maintain order in the streets of Paris, and throughout January it could have been done without much trouble. The point was, however, that the prefect ordered his men to attack any left-wing group but to let the *ligues* and their friends carry on as they pleased. Chiappe himself was well known to hold rabidly conservative views, to have a great many close ties to the leaders of the extreme Right, and to harbor great ambitions. Here, obviously, was a situation tailor-made for him; and so the riots grew in violence.

Although the riots were not primarily responsible for the fall of the Chautemps government, they seriously complicated the task of finding a replacement: as if putting together a parliamentary majority were not hard enough, the new cabinet would also have to pacify the streets. Since most of the demonstrators belonged to the extreme Right, the Deputies on the right of the Chamber thought that President Lebrun might call on one of them; but that ever-fearful magistrate was also a firm believer in constitutional propriety. The Radicals were still the largest party in the Chamber, so, on January 29, he turned to one of their leaders. Because Daladier was well known to be personally honest, because he had no involvement with the affair, he seemed the perfect choice.

That, of course, was not how Herriot saw it. To him, Lebrun's move was an outrage, and he promptly began scheming against the new cabinet. As for Blum, his trust in Daladier was limited by the fact that the new Premier was currently trying to bring the Right into his cabinet — a maneuver that almost immediately proved both futile and self-defeating — so the Socialists refused to join the government. That left Daladier with an almost purely Radical cabinet. Still, he seemed assured of a majority: faced with an attempt at a right-wing revolution, the Left within the Chamber would obviously unite behind the new Premier. Thus, for once, the problem was not how the Deputies would vote: it was whether order could be restored in the streets outside.

Perhaps a few firm words would do it, so the Premier called in the press and announced: "It is time to end, fast, brutally if need be, . . . the errors that have troubled our country."[12] At the same time, he put pressure on Chiappe and actually got him to hold some of his friends back. The Right, however, was not to be bought off so cheaply. Its more reasonable elements wanted a conservative government; its extremists were hoping to replace the Republic by a dictatorship (just who the dictator was to be never became quite clear). Daladier's attempted pacification had failed.

Now he needed the Socialists more than ever, and they had their price: they would not vote for him unless he replaced Chiappe as prefect of police. Like the good Radical he was, Daladier promptly agreed to what seemed a standard political trade; and it was then that events spun out of control.

When Chiappe was fired, the restraints agreed to by his friends naturally came to an end; more, the Right, having found its pretext, called for relentless and violent protests. In the Paris City Council, a majority of extreme-Right members demanded an attack against the regime, while, in the Chamber itself, Tardieu and his friends launched a series of assaults on the new government.

Everything was now set for the most serious street violence Paris had seen in three-quarters of a century. On February 5, the *ligues,* several right-wing veterans' organizations, and the city councillors called for a general uprising the next day — and so did the Communists, who, as usual, were a little slow to catch on. The plan was that the rioters would gather on the Place de la Concorde. Then they would cross the bridge that led directly to the Chamber of Deputies, assault the building, and take it over. After that, the plans were vague; but the general idea was that the Radicals and the Socialists were to be beaten up, their colleagues expelled from the building, and an emergency dictatorial government was then to be set up.

Of course, Daladier knew what was being prepared, and he ordered the army to bring tanks and machine guns into Paris — none of which, in the end, were used, partly to avoid a massacre, partly because no one was quite sure whether the troops would obey orders to shoot. It was, in the end, left to the police to defend the bridge; and it did so with inadequate means. The result was that, for much of the afternoon and early evening of the sixth, it looked, time and again, as if the rioters might break through. It was not until five o'clock that the real violence started; by then, on that dank winter evening, it was already night, and the darkness only added to the confusion. The rioters were armed mostly with pieces of cast iron, paving stones, and firecrackers — the latter being used against the horses of the mounted police — but soon knives and a few handguns appeared. At six-thirty, the two dozen or so buses stuck on the Place de la Concorde were set on fire, and their lurid silhouettes did much to create the impression that the mob was out of control. Just an hour later, it looked as if that were indeed the case: the rioters had already reached the middle of the bridge, and the police, outnumbered and poorly armed, were falling back and fired their first shots. This time the mob retreated; but it returned again and again, most effectively around ten. By the time it was all over, around two-thirty in the morning, the police barriers were still in place; but 338 wounded, ninety-two of them policemen, were in the hospitals of the city, and fifteen men, one of them a policeman, had been killed. It was soon discovered that all fourteen civilians were members of the *Ligue d'Action française.*

While all this was happening outside, the events inside the Chamber were almost as dramatic. This was the date set for the debate at the close of which the Chamber would give, or refuse, its support to the new government. The day's session opened at three P.M.; by then, columns of rioters were already filling the Place de la Concorde, and the ever-hopeful Right did its best to provoke corresponding disorders within the Chamber, both by continually invoking points of order and by shouting, and even, on occasion, by assaulting some fellow Deputies. At seven, finally, the government asked the Chamber to agree that the debate must end soon, and it won by 302 to 204; but by then the sound of shooting could be heard, and it was in an atmosphere of incipient civil war that the debate continued. Much of what the Premier said was inaudible over the shouts of the Right; but finally the vote took place, giving the government a majority of 360 to 220. For the moment at least, the attempted revolution had failed: neither the cabinet nor the regime had fallen.

What the mobs could not do with their utmost effort, however, Edouard Herriot managed with the greatest of ease. He had, naturally, refused to be part of his hated rival's cabinet; as he remarked sourly: "I had no reason to be concerned with a ministry about which I had not been consulted."[13] A more generous man might have thought that saving the Republic required a temporary end to personal rivalry; but Herriot, firmly concentrating on his revenge, decided instead to oust Daladier. For so seasoned a politician, it was a simple maneuver, especially since he had an accomplice in a key position.

President Lebrun had deplored the results of the elections in 1932. A conservative himself, he yearned for the return of the Right to power, but was at the same time far too aware of his duties to shirk them. Luckily, given his narrowness of understanding, these duties were few. Aside from various ceremonial functions, all the President of the Republic had to do was chair the Council of Ministers, always remembering that it was the Premier who had the real power. The President also selected the new Premier when the current government had either fallen or imploded.

It was this power that now made him such a precious ally for Herriot. Together with Lebrun, he could pressure Daladier into resigning so as to avoid a repetition of the previous night's riot and deaths, and he happily recalled the moment in his memoirs. "In the morning, I was sent for by the President of the Republic," Herriot wrote. "'This is your triumph,' he exclaimed. . . . Having told me the number of the dead, he asked me to advise Daladier that he ought to resign. . . . In Daladier's office, . . . I was at last asked for my opinion. I told the Premier that I could not advise him to go forward with an adventure [i.e., staying in office and declaring a state of siege] that would cause blood to flow. . . . Daladier told us he would resign."[14] Herriot had indeed triumphed, and so had Lebrun. He was now free to call on an old-fashioned conservative under the guise of restoring national unity. By the end of the morning of the seventh, Gaston Doumergue, a former President of the Republic, had been appointed Premier, with Herriot and Tardieu as his ministers of state. To all intents and purposes, the result of the 1932 election had been canceled and the Right was back where it felt it belonged — in power.

That meant, of course, that the Premier was no longer a Radical; but for Herriot, the new government had several major advantages. He was a minister once again, and something of a power behind the throne; four of his friends had been given ministries as well; and Daladier was obviously out of office for the rest of the legislative term. As for the fact that democracy had just been wounded, Herriot cared not at all.

Doumergue himself was nothing if not emollient. He announced that he would see to it that all the facts in the Stavisky affair were made public; he proclaimed his intention of balancing the budget; and he declared that he would ask the Chamber and Senate to amend the constitution so as to give the executive greater power. Within days, all was back to normal — or almost: on February 12 a massive Socialist-Communist demonstration denounced what it called the "Fascist riot" of the sixth.

For the first time since the war, outside events had disturbed the activities of the Tout-Paris — it is awkward to go out to dinner in evening dress when a mob is rioting — but by February 10, that was all over. In spite of Genêt's dire predictions, in fact, normality returned with astonishing speed. Even in January, her Paris letter had quite rightly mentioned a concurrent sensation that had nothing to do with politics: the publication in French of William Faulkner's *Sanctuary*. Here, for the French readers, was a whole new and fascinating world. "Among the critics," Genêt noted, "the sound and the fury of praise have only been less loud than the confusion. No English-language work since and except James Joyce's *Ulysses* has ever caused such an uproarious volume of comment in literary France."[15]

Many of the intellectuals who realized that in Faulkner they were discovering an author of genius had other preoccupations as well: fighting fascism was one, helping to organize a common front against the Right was another. Society, on the other hand, reassured by the arrival of Doumergue, went straight back to its usual amusements. Music, as always, was important — as long as it was carefully selected and performed for the right people. This was most definitely the case of a series of chamber music events called the Sérénade concerts.

Although they were given at the Salle Gaveau, one of the city's larger halls, the concerts were ruled not by public taste or demand but by a foundation whose working committee made the actual decisions and included a number of important composers — Milhaud, Rieti, Auric, Poulenc, Sauguet, and the young but brilliant Nicolas Nabokov. They could be trusted to come up with interesting programs of new music. As for the foundation committee, it was the acme of social glamour and included not only the inevitable princesse Edmond de Polignac, but also Etienne de Beaumont, Marie-Laure de Noailles, and even Coco Chanel. It was typical of these concerts that a single program included a Sauguet piece, another by Hindemith, a Poulenc sextet, and even a Milhaud suite written for the very first electronic instrument ever devised, the Onde Martenot.

That Marie-Laure de Noailles should be part of this surprised no one. She and her husband, Charles, were not only among the most glamorous people in Paris, they were also enlightened patrons of the avant-garde. This could take minor forms — it was Jean-Michel Frank who had redone the entrance and salon of their house on the Place des Etats-Unis — but also stretched a good deal further. It was the Noailles, for instance, who financed Buñuel's first film, *L'Age d'or*.

Marie-Laure de Noailles, who played a leading role in Paris society for more than half a century, was never a beauty (by her late fifties she had begun to look strikingly like the aged Louis XIV); but she was intelligent, eager to learn, to see, to hear, and willing to spend part of a large fortune to subsidize the arts — as well as to give balls, invitations to which were eagerly sought.

She herself was a curious mix. Her grandmother Laure de Chevigné belonged to an old aristocratic family, one of whose relatives was none other than the marquis de Sade. Mme de Chevigné was not a beauty — her thin and beaky face reminded everyone of a bird, and her voice was loud and hoarse — but with all that she had a dazzling natural chic that gave her the most glamorous position among those who knew her, and then for all time, for Proust used her as one of the principal models of his duchesse de Guermantes.

With all that, the comtesse Adéhaume, as she was known, was not at all rich; so she married her daughter Marie-Thérèse to an extremely wealthy but tubercular young man, Maurice Bischoffsheim, the scion of a Jewish banking family. In due course a daughter was born to the young couple and named Marie-Laure; and then M. Bischoffsheim died. Twenty years later, in 1923, when it was time for Mme de Chevigné's cherished and immensely rich granddaughter to marry, she effortlessly rejoined the world of her maternal family by accepting the proposal made to her by the vicomte Charles de Noailles.

The Noailles themselves were very grand. There were three dukedoms in the family (Noailles, Ayen, Mouchy), and they counted several cardinals, marshals of France, and First Gentlemen of the Bedchamber among their ancestors; and at first the young Marie-Laure's social life was spent among the members of the old aristocracy to whom she was related through the Chevignés as well as the Noailles. It cannot have been very amusing, and as people soon discovered, the new vicomtesse did not like to be bored. She also had a taste for modernity. When the Noailles decided they wanted a house at Hyères, on the Riviera, they commissioned Alfred Mallet-Stevens, a modernist architect whose style was stark, geometric, and spectacularly new. Then they began seeing artists, intellectuals, composers, many of whom were part of the Surrealist movement. It was typical, for instance, that when Man Ray wanted to shoot his own film, *Les Mystères du château de De,* they offered him their house to be used as the set.

Because Marie-Laure liked music, she became one of its patrons in Paris. Although neither as knowledgeable nor as musically sensitive as the princesse Edmond de Polignac, she knew quite enough to finance performances of first-rate new work, either in concert halls or in her own ballroom. It was, however, the scandal provoked by *L'Age d'or* that defined the Noailles as daring patrons of the avant-garde. The collaborative work of Dalí (before he had sold out) and Buñuel, already a director of genius, the film was not kind to the principles held dearest by the establishment. What happened next was described by one of the spectators, prince Jean-Louis de Faucigny-Lucinge:

> The evening of the [film's] first showing, in the great ballroom of the Noailles's house, now equipped with a "talking" projector, the bomb burst forth in our poor friends' faces. As they watched bishops being thrown out of windows and Christ as the hero of *A Hundred Days in Sodom* [the marquis de Sade's book], the shocked, terrified, and revolted guests drifted out. At first, the Noailles held firm. The film was shown in public, but its triumph only worsened the scandal. Chiappe, the prefect of police, banned *L'Age d'or*. There were rumors that Charles was going to be excommunicated. Etienne de Beaumont, who had been worrying that the Noailles were . . . beginning to make him seem old-fashioned, had, it was said, charitably warned the Arch-bishop of Paris about the film. At the Jockey [the most aristocratic men's club in Paris], the duc de Mouchy had the unpleasant task of telling his brother he had better resign.[16]

Obviously, Paris society was not yet ready to abandon its reactionary ideas; since then, however, *L'Age d'or* has been universally recognized as a masterpiece. And already the Noailles had financed another important film, Jean Cocteau's *Blood of a Poet*. Full of the poetic, Surrealist images that became the trademark of Cocteau as a director, this film about the life and death of a poet — or more exactly, perhaps, his unconscious — caused no scandal. No one could be really shocked by a hand with a mouth in it, or figures rising and moving through the air.

The story is, in a sense, that of the conception of a poem, a visual equivalent of the poet's inspiration. It is, said Cocteau, "a realistic documentary of unreal happenings," and although he insisted that these dreamlike images are beyond interpretation, he himself eventually provided an explanation:

> I might tell you that the poet's solitude is so great, that he lives so intensely what he creates, that the mouth of one of his creations lives in his hands like a wound, and that he loves this mouth, that he loves himself, in short that he wakes up in the morning with this mouth beside him like someone he met by chance and brought home and tried to get rid of, and that he does rid himself of it by passing it on to a dead statue — and then this statue comes to life — and it takes revenge and involves him in ghastly adventures . . . [but] while I was working

I thought of nothing and that is why you must expose yourself to the film just as you do to Auric's noble music which accompanies it."[17]

For all its daring, *Blood of a Poet* does not innovate in the same way as *L'Age d'or*. There are no attacks on the Catholic Church in it, no scenes that imply a rejection of society as it is. It was possible, therefore, to be agreeably surprised by the many unconventional images and by the lack of a plot, while feeling that this sort of avant-garde was altogether acceptable.

That carefully managed compromise between the new and the conventional was typical of Jean Cocteau, who was himself not just a charter member of the Tout-Paris and a famous Parisian figure, but also a writer, playwright, and film director of considerable if often flawed talent. This man who loved fairy tales (and made *Beauty and the Beast* into a film full of magical images) seemed himself to have come right out of the story in which all the fairies have been invited to see the king's newborn son. One after the other, they endow the baby with a multitude of talents; but then comes the forgotten old crone whose curse cancels out the gifts of the other fairies. In Cocteau's case, the curse was an irradicable frivolity.

With that went an extraordinary talent for words. The most brilliant conversationalist of his generation, Cocteau could fascinate a roomful of the most difficult people in Paris whenever he chose — and he knew just how to use his physical appearance. Tall, very thin, with a long nose and a sharp profile, Cocteau was above all proud of his long, slender hands, and used them to great advantage when he talked. He understood art, to a degree at least: he had caught on early to the fact that Picasso was the century's greatest artist, but he also though very highly of the insipid compositions of his friend Bébé Bérard. He was a discerning music lover and a fixture at the concerts given under the auspices of the princesse Edmond de Polignac and of the Noailles. Indeed, he was a friend of Stravinsky's — or at least so he thought. He understood, before the war, that real talent was to be found only in the avant-garde, and acted in consequence. It was largely thanks to Cocteau, for instance, that *Parade,* that stunning ballet with music by Stravinsky and sets and costumes by Picasso, came into being. The trouble was that he loved society almost as much as the arts, and led a life of relentless chic; and that his own considerable talents fell short of real genius, perhaps because he lacked boldness and true originality. Naturally, he liked to shock, having understood that in our century shock is the natural effect of any important work of art — but he could not bring himself to do anything that might alienate his elegant friends. Finally, there was his talent for knowing just what was in. He took opium when it was fashionable to do so (and eventually discovered that, having started, it was not so easy to stop); he tried very hard to become close to the Surrealists (but Breton despised him) and took over a number of their ideas; but all that was always done from the outside. Cocteau could look at other people's achievements and imitate them; the imitations frequently had very considerable merit; they usually stopped short of being work of the very first rank. Thus, *Blood of a Poet* was typical. Its bold images were clearly inspired by the Surrealists and so was its exteriorization of the unconscious. It was and is a successful film; but the ideas were not really Cocteau's own.

It is often characteristic of a disturbed period that its artists reach back to the great classical stories in order to impose order on the chaos around them. Not surprisingly, the thirties were just such a time. With barbarism of the most primitive, odious, and bloodthirsty kind triumphant in much of Europe, many artists resurrected Greek and Roman forms. We see it in Picasso's Vollard suite, those engravings in which line is used (but with inimitable originality) in a way inspired by classical sculpture, in Gide's *Oedipe,* in Giraudoux's *Judith*. For Cocteau, who knew how to adapt but sometimes had trouble inventing, these kinds of borrowings were the perfect solution. In 1924 he had written the libretto for Stravinsky's cantata *Oedipus Rex;* in 1934 his play based on the same myth, *La Machine infernale,* was one of the great successes of the Paris season.

It opened on April 10, 1934, at the Comédie des Champs-Elysées, and starred the great actor Louis Jouvet, then unquestionably the best and most famous in France, the young, handsome, and talented Jean-Pierre Aumont, and Cocteau himself as the Narrator. Naturally, Genêt was there, and, as was so often the case, she understood exactly what was happening:

> It would be a relief to a lot of Parisians if Jean Cocteau never wrote another theater piece, for then they would not have to endure a fashionable *première* where they are certain they're dressed up but not sure what they are to think. Perhaps because we wore only our simple business suit we thought that *La Machine Infernale,* or Cocteau's rewrite of Sophocles's *Oedipus Rex,* added little to the rare quality of either gentleman's great reputation. The lovely lotus which is Cocteau's creation when his brain best blooms we failed to find except in the platform speech of the Sphinx, nor did we hear those hidden meanings usually so audible in his smallest phrase. In his rewrite he follows the Sopho-

clean tradition — aside from the fact that the Cocteau Sphinx doesn't ask Oedipus the riddle but tells him the answer, that Oedipus is played by an obscure motion-picture star [Aumont, who soon gained great fame] and that Jocasta is played (with magnificent vulgarity) by Marthe Régnier, ordinarily a good old comedienne. The costumes and sets by Christian Bérard were neo-classic and neo-perfection — with soldiers in polka-dotted tights, the immense tragic mythology of Greece encompassed in one beautifully broken papier-mâché Ionic column, and a sense of architectonics suited to theatre rarely seen on any Continental stage.[18]

Genêt was entirely right. What Cocteau had done was to cheapen Sophocles' tragedy by removing the poetry and bringing it down almost to the level of a situation comedy. Even the title, La Machine infernale, suggests a kind of empty portentousness: a machine infernale is a time bomb — not really what the story is about. In fact, all the poetry, all the deep meaning of the myth, have been left out of Cocteau's play. Jocasta is simply a silly royal who knows she is no longer young and has developed a taste for young men; Oedipus himself is recast as an empty-headed adventurer whose good looks seduce a bored Sphinx into telling him the answer to the famous riddle; and most of the first act is spent on the dialogue (in slang) of two soldiers who occasionally see the ghost of Jocasta's dead husband, come to warn her not to marry Oedipus.

Much of the play is spent on talking (like Genêt) about the goings-on in les boîtes, the nightclubs; the weight and inconvenience of royal costumes; and the general ordinariness of life. Gide's Oedipus is a great tragic figure, that of a man brave enough to take sole responsibility for his own fate. Cocteau's Oedipus is not unlike the handsome young men who made a good thing of their looks and were supported by richer and older lovers. That, indeed, may well be the reason the play was a success; there was something singularly comforting in being told that tragedy was no big deal, after all. By shrinking the myth to an everyday story, Cocteau was saying that, finally, nothing is so terrible. To an audience, fresh from the Sixth of February, and aware that Germany was rearming, it was reassuring to be told that daily life is all there is.

For the rest of the decade, a new Cocteau play was always a great Parisian event, even if, on occasion, it plunged to new levels of mediocrity; but it was only one of the many occasions in which Cocteau kept up his social and intellectual role. There were, for instance, the entrées he designed for the costume balls that were so much in fashion. An entrée consisted of two or more people in costume who were supposed to represent a scene germane to the theme of the evening. They would enter the ball together, sometimes even enact a little story. At the comtesse Pecci-Blunt's White Ball, for instance, Cocteau had designed an *entrée* for Marie-Laure de Noailles that represented the waking of Ariadne and in which masks of white plaster played a prominent role.

Even if he just went as himself, Cocteau never missed a really important party, though he might well have been a greater artist if he had gone to fewer balls and designed fewer *entrées;* but one minor aspect of his activities was entirely apposite and a great success: that was his collaboration with Schiaparelli. From the very beginning, the poet had been fascinated by fashion and those who created it. He was a friend, and often a protégé, of Chanel, who, on several occasions, paid for the treatments that were supposed to end his drug dependency. With Schiaparelli, however, Cocteau had a very different relationship. Not nearly as generous financially as her great rival, Schiap was also more interested in the arts and thought very highly of Cocteau's drawings. Even today, it is easy to see why. Although certainly not a draftsman of the first rank, Cocteau had a fluid, persuasive line that suggests more than it defines. His repertory was small — about three profiles, stars, suns, moons, and the odd boat or architectural detail; the origin of his style is clearly Picasso's "classical" drawings; but, in spite of all these limitations, Cocteau's drawings have a suggestive magic.

Schiap understood this and as she began to add more and more embroidered motifs to her designs, she realized that artists could make a major contribution to her dresses. Cocteau was not alone in being approached. Dali, Bérard, Vertés also worked for her, but Cocteau's designs were very much the most successful — perhaps because they retained an aura of poetry. There was, for instance, the jacket on which a woman's head in profile was embroidered: her long blonde hair swept down the sleeve in a Melisande-like effect, and made a piece of clothing into an evocative and enchanting object. The same was true of another embroidered design: two columns of gold stripes were topped by two gold profiles with red lips and blue eyes; the space enclosed by the two profiles formed an urn topped with a bouquet of three-dimensional pink silk roses. Because you could read the profiles as merely the outlines of the urn, or the urn as the void between the two profiles, because there was such a contrast between the flat embroidery and the thick satin roses, the effect here, too, was ambiguous and very appealing.

Schiaparelli herself triumphed more than ever. For her, the Sixth of

February was a temporary inconvenience. As soon as it was over, her clients flocked back, and well they might have; if any single designer gave a look to the thirties, both in Europe and in the United States, it was Schiaparelli. That was partly because her designs were so original, partly also because several of the greatest stars of the period were dressed by her. It had started with Marlene Dietrich, of course; soon Joan Crawford realized that the Schiaparelli look was just right for her kind of robust beauty; even Mae West was costumed by Schiap in one of her films.

Just as important was the designer's sense of line. The simple black wool trouser suit with a box-shaped jacket and a vividly striped or checked waistcoat or a bright plaid blouse managed to be at the same time comfortable, modern, and striking; the same was true of the much more fluid evening pajamas. But Schiap never hesitated to complicate. The Typhoon line in 1934 made its wearers look as if they were birds caught in a hurricane: there were winged berets, big shoulder wings, winged capes on day and evening coats, large pointed lapels, and featherlike embroidery; and then, six months later, the Celestial line molded the figure in soft, spiral silk folds. Every woman who could afford Schiap's prices could find the look that was right for her while being immensely fashionable; and for the millions whose dress budget was severely limited, Schiap's sharp, clean designs made for adaptations that could be found even in the cheapest of stores.

And then there was that major technological innovation, the zipper. Earlier, dresses generally came in two forms: either they had hard to close buttons or laces or they came in one piece, and then you had to pull them over your head, with often disastrous results to your coiffure. In both cases, they were inconvenient. Now, with a zipper, it was possible for a woman to dress herself, and Schiap was the very first designer to use it as a key part of her look. Like so much of her work, it was a piece of shrewd business, but it was also stylish: just because the new device was practical did not mean that Schiap would use it only when absolutely needed. Suddenly, zippers became a major decorative element: dyed in contrasting colors, adorned with baroque pearls or Indian tassels, they appeared everywhere.

Exoticism was also important. There was a whole collection with sari-like dresses made of Indian silks. There were housecoats, usually worn with evening pajamas, that were inspired by Moslem gowns and were worn with sumptuously jeweled headdresses, while others were reminiscent of the brocade robes worn by the doges of Venice. As the decade progressed, in fact, Schiap's designs became increasingly splendid: the fabrics were lusher and brighter, the embroidery richer and more complex, spreading over the bosom and the hip pockets, occasionally taking the form of a stylized bra or, as in a design by Bérard, a carefully positioned double sunburst. Of course, Schiap still made those famously simple suits for the day; but the search for the *moderne* that had characterized her early collections was clearly a thing of the past. It was as if her dresses were to be a protection against the ever more worrying present by taking their wearers and viewers to distant and sumptuous places.

Not that she was above a comment on the latest news: soon after the riot on the sixth of February, Schiap designed a hat with a policeman's visor. Most of the other hats were far less contemporary, however. There were turbans and Marco Polo hats (with a wide brim), François Villon hats (a toquelike affair similar to that worn by men in the 1480s) and Dick Whittington hats with forward-jutting brims, huntsmen's caps, modified tilted top hats, even bowlers — as well as a hangman's hood and a Mongolian tribesman's hat. And under this exotic headgear were coiffures that were quite as artificial.

Working with Antoine, the most fashionable hairdresser in Paris, Schiap designed new hairdos that were stiffened with lacquer so they looked almost like wigs. Soon, she recommended that women wear actual wigs — the ones, naturally, that she had designed. There were silver, ash-blonde, and red wigs for the evening, waterproof wigs for sport, some, black and shiny, that looked as if they were made of wrought iron, others silver-colored with curls at the temples and on top of the head. And when a few women were bold enough to ask what was wrong with their own hair, Schiap pointed out that wigs had been worn during all the great periods in history. "Can you imagine Voltaire or Catherine of Russia without a wig?" she would ask imperiously.[19]

Well might Schiaparelli advocate wearing wigs and extraordinary hats; that was just the same as her predecessor Rose Bertin had done in the 1780s. Historicity is, after all, just another way to forget about one's own times; and so, of course, is travel. In 1931 Elisabeth de Gramont could still easily list the dozen or so places where the Tout-Paris went for its holidays. Now, that had all changed, and the general idea was (if you could afford it) the further, the better.

"The fashion is no longer to spend one's holidays like everyone and with everyone," a chronicler noted. "Today, it is far more chic to do something unique. He who returns to Paris saying that he has been hunting vicuñas in Peru . . . or fishing for sturgeon in the Kuban . . . is obviously . . . fashionable. If you claim to like music, you will go to Salzburg for the Festival, swear by Bruno Walter or Clement Kraus, no longer mention the *Nozze di Figaro* but always *Figaros Hochzeit* and wear a little gray felt hat bought in Bad Ischl from the former hatmaker to the House of Austria. . . . Those who like exercise will hunt grouse in Scotland, partridges in Hungary or in Czechoslovakia, and fish for salmon in Ireland or swordfish off the Canaries."[20]

In one respect, though, modernity was chic. Those who could afford it now preferred to fly, so that in a single year Air France had what seemed the huge number of one hundred thousand passengers. It was no wonder: you could go from Paris to Stockholm in a mere six hours; the same amount of time would get you from London to Cannes, queen of the Riviera, via Paris. It wasn't just that the airline had six daily flights between Paris and London, the most heavily traveled of its routes; it flew to Berlin, Warsaw, Bucharest, Algiers, Tunis, and with refueling stops on to Saigon, Buenos Aires, and Santiago. Only the rich could hunt the vicuña; but now they could get to the Andes a lot faster.

Another innovation was holding fast as well: fitness and exercise. There was no return to the prewar buxom look for women, or the early paunch for men: it was the done thing to look (relatively) slim, young, vigorous — so much so that *Le Figaro Illustré*, in 1934, started publishing a monthly page on which specific exercises for women were described and illustrated. Still, no one expected the new slenderness to make inroads into that key French preoccupation, eating well.

Just as Schiaparelli's designs veered to the sumptuous and exotic, so interest in gastronomy was back in fashion. Even if Hitler made menacing speeches, even if, in France, the Depression deepened, those with means could still enjoy one of the great pleasures of life. And just in case you were foolish enough to think that six- to eight-course meals might cause you to gain weight, there was prompt reassurance: "We now know that it is not *gourmandise* but laziness that makes us fatter," a columnist reported. "It is all right to eat well. . . . Food is in fashion: enjoy it!"[21]

And people did. There was no nonsense about sparing the butter or replacing the cream with yogurt; in 1934, the general theme was the richer, the better. Of course, there were some recipes that were spectacular looking without being spectacularly fattening. At the marquise de Crussol's, for instance, food was almost as great an attraction as Daladier, and she (or actually, her cook) was famous for her *Jambon exotique* (exotic ham). The ham came to the dining room invisibly sliced. When it was opened it revealed a mosaic of pineapple, mandarin oranges, cherries, and prunes adorning every slice, the whole bathed in a sauce made of several exotic wines.

Other hostesses relied more firmly on traditional French recipes. There was, for instance, the *Poularde à la Valençay*. First you had to make an oval puff pastry case large enough to hold a large pullet and bake it until it was beginning to color. Then you poached the pullet in chicken stock; you sautéed minced mushrooms in butter, then added cream to make a sort of purée. Separately, you made a cream sauce to which you added raw mushrooms chopped fine enough to go through a sieve. Next, having carved the pullet and put it back together, you garnished your puff pastry case with a bed of the creamed minced mushrooms, installed the pullet on top of them, and covered it with the cream sauce. Finally the whole construction was gratinéed in a very hot oven. Add to that the fact that this masterpiece of richness and complication was only one of possibly six dishes — soup, fish, the *Poularde,* a complicated salad, foie gras, cheese, dessert — and it will be clear that dieting was not exactly the order of the day.

Eating well was so important, in fact, that even Lady Mendl realized that she had to make an effort. The dinners she gave either at Versailles or in her grand Paris apartment had long been famous for the excellence of the guests and decor and the paucity of the usually dreadful food. Now, though, she came forth with her very own American recipes for an oyster soup that served six people. It was as simple as it was rich: poach six dozen oysters in their own juice. Take six egg yolks, add milk and the oyster juice, and cook gently to make a custard. Add the shucked oysters and serve immediately.

There was a very great deal of splendid food to be had in Paris, both in private houses and in restaurants, but, because communications had become much easier, this was also the time when it became fashionable to find first-rate restaurants outside the city. Some were merely in the suburbs, like the Coq Hardi in Bougival; others were as far afield as Burgundy; and motoring to a place recommended mostly by a superb restaurant now became a recognized form of elegant self-indulgence.

Still, nothing could outshine Paris. Lunch in the country was permissible; a retreat to a country house was expected when the season was over, at the beginning of July; until then, leaving the capital meant missing out on the latest fashion, the latest gossip, and the latest spectacle.

Sports were important and fashionable; the international tennis, polo, and flying competitions were widely attended; but no season could be a real success without one good, enjoyable flop. In 1934 it was Ida Rubinstein who provided it. Twenty-three years before, Rubinstein had dazzled Paris by her combination of mystery and ambiguous sexuality, the luxury of her costumes and the eloquence of her dancing. Now she was decidedly past her prime, but, naturally, Genêt was there. "After the war," she wrote,

> Ida Rubinstein was, despite her un-French Polish accent and her un-fashionable length of leg, one of the Parisian theatre's great ornaments. Bakst, Debussy, D'Annunzio, Diaghilev all worked hard for her and must have worked hard *on* her, judging by the disappointingly different results now obtained by her when she labors alone. Still a rich woman, she has lately been accustomed to hire the Opéra for a spring gala series of ballets, talky dances and musical philosophical mimings specially written, composed, choreographed, costumed and directed for her by the best men in Europe today. Maybe men aren't men anymore, judging again by this year's result. With Stravinsky, Ibert, Honegger, Florent Schmitt, Gide and (as an exception) Elisabeth de Gramont, formerly Duchesse de Clermont-Tonerre, Paul Valéry and Ravel as word and music writers, with Fokine and Joos for choreographers, sets by Benois and stage management by the great Copeau, Mlle Rubinstein still managed to flop artistically. Apparently it would take an army to hold her up.
>
> The fashionable first-night Opéra house received her performance with mixed snickers and applause. . . . The main musical interest, naturally, centered in the Stravinsky self-conducted premiere of his *Perséphone*. Like his "Psalm" Symphony, it is noble, massive music, nearly religious and clearly not to be appreciated on its first audition. Especially with a stage cluttered with one male, one female, one children's chorus, Rubinstein miming when she wasn't reciting, the ballet prancing when she wasn't doing all three and, far to the back of the stage, a tenor on a pedestal singing about what Perséphone felt like when she was going through Hades. The tenor probably knew.[22]

A really silly performance was always amusing, but it could hardly compare to serious fun, like the first night race ever at Longchamps, which was celebrated by a very grand supper served in a vast tent and for which Daisy Fellowes suggested forcefully that light dresses and big hats were in order. On that same order of desirability were Mrs. Fellowes's own garden parties, and the immensely rich Lady Deterding's ball at the Hotel Crillon, where all the party rooms were sprayed with the hostesses's perfume, champagne flowed in unheard-of quantities, and, for the first time since the beginning of the Depression, society women wore their pearls and their diamonds.

It was wholly appropriate for Lady Deterding to have chosen the Crillon: it had just recently become more chic than the Ritz. Genêt, never one to ignore a really good bar or a really new hit, promptly described it for her readers:

> For cocktails and lunch, the Crillon bar is now crammed as the Ritz used to be, isn't anymore and will soon be again if the Crillon's food and service don't go back to the high standard which made the bar a quiet joy for selecter souls in the pre-popular period. However, the cocktails mixed by Emile . . . are still Grade A. If you're interested in vital statistics, what he makes most are Martinis; then, in a descending scale, Champagnes, Sidecars, Manhattans, White Ladies and Bronxes, ending up at the bottom with Bacardis. He also reports two apéritifs as snobbishly going up in American favor: Pernod and Americanos.[23]

All these amusements put together, though, did not catch a tenth of the amount of attention still focused on the Stavisky affair. That was in part because, in March, it turned, finally and forever, into that most fascinating of stories, a double murder mystery. On February 20, 1934, just two weeks after the riot, Albert Prince, a judge of the Assize Court, was found dead, run over by a train at La Combe aux Fées, near Dijon. He had been involved in the many postponements of Stavisky's trials, and the first assumption was that he must have been murdered so as to prevent him telling what he knew. To make it all worse, the next day Albert Sarraut, the minister of the interior, and as such the head of the national police, announced: "M. Prince has been murdered. It makes one believe that there must be a real mafia that eliminates all those who know too much."[24]

As usual, Albert Sarraut was demonstrating his incompetence; there was no sign at all of foul play, and on the face of it, Prince's death looked far more like suicide. But after the minister in charge blithely referred to it as murder, no one thought it could be anything else — especially since Prince's immediate superior was none other than Pressard, Camille Chautemps's brother-in-law, and the man ultimately responsible for not stopping the postponements. From then on, the French could feel, with good reason, that they were living inside a murder mystery.

Naturally, the death made huge headlines; and the headlines continued when it became clear that the police were incapable of finding the murderer, and not even sure that Prince had not committed suicide. Of course, the arguments raged back and forth. Pro-murder enthusiasts pointed out that the body had been tied to the track; pro-suicide believers answered that the position of the rope was consistent with Prince's having tied himself up in order to make sure he would not quail at the last moment; and so it went, with the pro-murder camp much the more numerous. Conspiracy theories have always been popular in France; and a new suicide, after Stavisky's own ambiguous end, seemed a little much to swallow.

Because no one talked about anything else, Genêt's Paris letter, which had already featured the political situation all through January and February — a most unusual step for her — now focused firmly on this latest sensation. "Politics here are apparently being run by the late Edgar Wallace [an author of murder and spy thrillers]," she wrote. "A few more horrors such as the tying of . . . Prince to a Dijon railway track and the French public won't be able to sleep at night. Stavisky's suicide — if it was — was bearable as the first installment in a serial thriller dealing with counterfeit bonds, blondes and big bugs. The subsequent chapters, with their killings on the Concorde, poison-package party politics, stranglings of justice, threats, calumnies, briberies, protected perjurers, counterplots of police against police and consistent triumph of the evildoers would long since have been tossed aside as bad fiction if it hadn't been worse fact."[25]

Genêt was obviously right. It struck everyone that the French were living out a really bad murder mystery, and that, as is traditional in the genre, the police were quite unable to provide a solution. To a generation raised on the triumphs of Sherlock Holmes, the answer was obvious: only an English detective would do; and so *Paris-Soir,* the paper with the largest circulation, started out by offering a huge reward to any amateur sleuth who solved the case and then, perhaps because Holmes was, sadly, a fictional character, it hired (after getting him a fortnight's leave) a whiz from Scotland Yard. Real life being notoriously trickier than fiction, though, the detective got nowhere; but then, anyone could have told *Paris-Soir* that Inspector Lestrade, in the Conan Doyle books, was a model of self-satisfied incompetence.

All this naturally kept the now double affair at a simmer; and as headline followed headline, the mystery remained unsolved. Beyond its immediate fascination, however, its chief effect was further to deepen the rift between the French and their leaders. That politics — and politicians — were corrupt was now taken for granted; that the deputies cared nothing about the people was, if you read most of the press, equally obvious. For a while Doumergue, the new Premier, enjoyed a solid following, in part because he was old and the French love a father figure, in part because he was so clearly innocent of any involvement in the affair. But he was virtually unique, and below the surface the rumblings of discontent got louder with every passing month.

That the police should be unable to solve the mystery was taken by most people as a proof, not just of its incompetence, but of its corruption. Under Chiappe, the Paris police, the great rival of the national police, had recruited some very odd officers. Corruption was, indeed, far from unknown; the ties to the underworld were real; and much of that came tumbling out as part of the affair.

In the end, Prince's death was never explained. Today, in looking back at the facts contained in the archives, the solution seems, if not certain, at least extremely probable. Prince did in fact bear a heavy responsibility in the postponements, not because he was protecting Stavisky, but through sheer neglect and incompetence. There was a lot going on and he had paid very little attention. Even when the case had been brought to his attention and he had, in turn, mentioned it to his immediate superior, Pressard, he had again let it drop. That, undoubtedly is what Prince discovered as he himself checked the files in an effort to supplement his memory — and he checked the files because he was now asked to account for his dereliction of duty.

For someone who had risen from a humble background, and to whom his high position within the judicial system was everything, this was a dreadful blow. Although he was innocent in one sense — he had not meant to help Stavisky — Prince was guilty of not having done his job; and that was obvious to him on February 19, the day on which, as a judge, he tried a case where a young woman had been thrown onto a train track. It seems clear enough, given all this, that Prince in fact committed suicide; but few people in 1934 believed that this was even a remote possibility.

Stavisky would have laughed, no doubt, had he known that he would shake up the Republic, cause a change of government, and become the most famous man of his time among his compatriots. He might have laughed even harder at a last, ironic touch. Later in 1934, Alexis Léger proposed Igor Stravinsky for the Legion of Honor.[26] Promptly displaying his unparalleled talent for doing the wrong thing at the wrong time for the wrong reason and in the wrong way, Albert Sarraut quashed the nomination on the grounds that Stravinsky sounded too much like Stavisky and that the public might thereby be misled. It was funny, of course: even in 1934, Stravinsky was a famous figure; but it was also sadly typical. Paris itself might continue, apparently unaffected by all the disturbances, to make cultural history. France, with its government of incompetents, was beginning to look like an innocent lost among ferocious beasts.

CHAPTER

# SIX

## THE DIVIDE DEEPENS

IN 1930, the French had looked to the future with pride and confidence. Four years later, the world outside their borders struck them, with good reason, as a savage and unfriendly place, while they found that the greatest enemy of all was right in France itself. It was not just the Depression, which starved the working class and terrified the bourgeoisie; the riots on February 6 and the consequent setting up of the Doumergue government sharply split the French between Right (the conservatives, reactionaries, and Fascists) and Left (the Communists, Socialists, anti-Fascists, and some of the Radicals). For the Right, the new cabinet was a useful first step, but they wanted to do much, much more, everything from setting up a dictatorial executive and severely curtailing civil liberties to concocting a much stronger dose of deflation. For the Left, the Sixth of February was the first step on the road to the kind of regime that ruled Germany.

Ever since the Revolution of 1789, the French had been split between those who thought it a good thing and those who yearned for something like the old order. On occasion — the

World War was such a time — the two camps had come together. Now, it seemed clear once again that the most dangerous, the most hateful, enemy was within. Bad as Hitler, Mussolini, or Stalin might be, the first priority was to beat the other side within France itself.

This, on the face of it, was hardly wise. Much of the rest of the continent was ruled by tyrants — the Soviet Union by Stalin, Poland by reactionary and anti-Semitic colonels, Germany by Hitler, Italy by Mussolini, Hungary by the ultrareactionary Admiral Horthy, the Balkan countries by a variety of homegrown dictators. In such a world, France was hardly safe. Most of the political leaders, from Tardieu to Blum, and even including the ineffable Laval, were aware of the danger; but for them also, interior politics seemed more urgent, more important, more absorbing.

It was no wonder, in a way. French politicians lived in Paris, a city that remained what it had long been, one of the most beautiful urban landscapes anywhere, ringed by a mix of slums and factories of peculiar horror. Extreme poverty, ruthless exploitation, and pollution of the most visible kind were the rule in the working-class suburbs. As for the population, it led a life without hope or relief. Workers — men, women, children over twelve — were on a ten-hours-a-day, six-days-a-week, fifty-two-weeks-a-year schedule. There were no paid holidays, no days off allowed for illness, no fringe benefits of any kind. No work meant no pay; and the pay, pitifully little to begin with, had been steadily cut since the onset of the Depression, so that it was hard for even a fully employed worker to survive. Few, however, had full employment; many jobs were part-time. Then there was the great mass of the unemployed who survived as best they could — or died: unemployment relief came to minute numbers in minute quantities, medical care was virtually nonexistent.

None of that mattered to Paris society, or, indeed, to those whose love for the city was based on its many pleasures. "While Rome is capital of Italy, Vienna capital of Austria, and Berlin capital of Hitler, Paris is still capital of Europe for a kind of obstinate civilization, cerebral style, ideology, and suave, formulated, independent, liberty-loving living," Genêt wrote in the fall of 1934.[1] She was still right, especially since a flood of immensely talented refugees from the Third Reich gave the city an even more cosmopolitan feel than usual. At the same time, all this brilliance felt increasingly fragile.

Genêt never wrote about the life of the proletariat; it would hardly have been the right fare for *The New Yorker*. A few writers took the trouble to look at, and cared enough to describe, this grim underworld, as Zola had done fifty years earlier; but they were themselves middle class, with middle-class values. From 1932 to 1936, however, a very different kind of novelist was busy writing about what it felt like to be poor in Paris, about the suffering and the hopelessness. Céline, fresh from the triumph of *Voyage au bout de la nuit,* continued his autobiographical stories. Himself the son of working-class parents, he understood poverty very well, and he wrote about it in *Mort à crédit* (Death on the Installment Plan) as no one had before. He also, while he was at it, reinvented the French language.

Although Céline was unquestionably a novelist, he belonged to that small group of writers whose subject is invariably their own life, slightly rearranged. The war and his experiences in the twenties had provided the material for *Voyage;* now he went back further in time to his childhood and adolescence, and the story is grimmer still. It begins with a death, that of the narrator's concierge; then, in a fit of fever-induced delirium, Bardamu (the same figure as in *Voyage*) relives his early years.

We read about the family shop in the Passage Choiseul, that covered street where the sun was never seen, about the long hours, the grotesquely poor food, the lack of fresh air, the constant and desperate need for tiny sums of money, the grind and hopelessness of poverty as it afflicts those who know that their position will neither change nor improve. We meet the narrator's mother, a lace repairer, who toils fourteen or fifteen hours a day on her incredibly delicate, incredibly ill-paid task, and whose rich clients forget their bills; we are told about the everlasting boiled noodles, the family staple chosen because they are odorless and thus will not contaminate the lace. We go on to the wretched school in England where the narrator is sent to learn the language, and to the rich eccentric who takes him in, gives him a job as assistant on scientific projects, but then dies, leaving him as poor as ever. From page to page, the book describes a closed and stifling world, one in which the delicateness of the bourgeoisie does not apply. Indeed, when the first edition came out in the spring of 1936, it bore a number of blanks because the printer had found the language too shocking to print.

*Mort à crédit* is a great book because Céline is a great writer, one of the best of the century; but it is also firmly anchored in a time that was just beginning to perceive that certain degrees of misery are simply not acceptable to the rest of the community. For Céline, what matters is individual suffering, of course, but even worse, the utter degradation of the individual. If the characters of the novel use obscene or scatological expressions, as they sometimes do, it is because the life they lead has stripped them of all dignity. And because Céline himself, as a physician, was thoroughly familiar with the humiliations inflicted by sickness, especially on the poor, that, too, is a vivid part of his world.

The story of the novel, in fact, is one of suffering worsened. At first the child suffers passively, almost unconsciously; as soon as he reaches his teens and begins to work, he is exploited by a ruthless employer; and, though still naive, he understands his pain. The next step is retreat into the self: at the ironically named Meanwell College, the narrator becomes obstinately silent and withdrawn; by the end of the book, he is ready to join the army because, knowing that he can expect only the worse kind of life, it offers him a shortcut to an early death.

Death, indeed, is always present, and always desirable; besides, it goes together with hatred born of extreme poverty. From the very beginning of the book, the twin themes of hatred and death are interlaced: "I could myself tell all about my hatred. I know. I will do it later if they don't return. I would rather tell stories. I will tell such stories that they will return, on purpose, to kill me, from the four corners of the Earth. Then it will be over and I will be really pleased."[2]

*Mort à crédit* is not an easy book: uncompromising in its pain and despair, unflinching in its depiction of the degradation of its characters, utterly devoid of hope, redeeming figures, or happy endings, it is also immensely powerful, a dark world that encompasses the reader — not least because of its revolutionary style. Even more entrancingly than *Voyage,* this is written in a new language, full of slang, sometimes of the author's invention. Here grammar is continually raped. Ellipses, exclamation points, fragments of sentences, all are utterly different from the stately prose used by other French authors.

At first glance, the language of *Mort* seems to be that of life itself in the underclass, among whose members pluperfects of the subjunctive or careful subordinate clauses are not readily found. In fact, just like Proust's immense, sinuous sentences, Céline's fragments are striking, imaginative, poetic, contrived with the most immense care. Never, perhaps, has the appearance of spontaneity, of a flood of consciousness, been more misleading. The very few people who were close to him knew it well.

"To see him at work was a miracle," his secretary recorded. "He was never short of inspiration. If he decided to change a word, he was never satisfied with just replacing it. He would completely rewrite the whole sentence, and sometimes all the surrounding sentences, to fit the demands of his 'rhythm.' Sometimes he counted the syllables on his fingers as if it had been a line of verse. Almost every time, these changes . . . entailed growth and enrichment. Sometimes he would go over the same passage, hours, a night, several days later. . . . What torture that need to create form and content together would entail!"[3]

The result was a style wholly unlike anyone else's, a style that violated all the rules; and that, quite as much as the content and the occasional obscene passages, was what upset the critics, and many other people besides. A great artist, Jean Dubuffet, who shared with Céline his contempt of the conventional and the orderly, understood just why. "The dogma of the beautiful style is a key piece of the defense of the bourgeoisie," he explained. "If you want to strike this punishing caste in the heart, strike its subjunctives, the ceremonies of its beautiful empty language, its aesthetic coquetry."[4]

Dubuffet is right. Even more than the content, it is the style of Céline's books that is subversive since it ignores all the amenities of middle-class decorum; and in doing so it utterly rejects the world in which unpleasant facts — and exploited people — are genteelly ignored. As for the author himself, most of those who met him found him quite as disconcerting as his books; even Robert Denoel, his publisher, thought him anything but reassuring: "He talked to me for almost two hours like a physician who has seen what life has to offer, in terms of extreme lucidity," Denoel noted. "He was coldly desperate and yet passionate, cynical but full of pity. I can still see him, nervous, agitated, a hard, penetrating look to his blue eyes, with a slightly haggard expression. . . . The notion of death, his own and that of the world, came back in his speech like a leitmotif. He described to me a humanity thirsty for catastrophes, in love with massacres. The sweat ran down his face, his eyes seemed to burn."[5] Considering the fact that this conversation took place in 1935, we can give Céline credit for sound judgment: Stalin's purges were getting under way, the Holocaust was just ahead; and even as this anything but dispassionate observer pitied the victims, he was fully aware that the killers and torturers were more numerous than is often supposed.

When Céline was asked about his political convictions, he invariably answered that he was an anarchist: the world as it was was beyond fixing, only a complete breakdown of its structures offered any hopes. Unfortunately, to the hatred for real oppressors, he soon added an even greater loathing for imaginary tyrants. When *Voyage* was published in 1932, it looked as if its author might win the Goncourt, that most illustrious of French literary prizes. In the event, he had to settle for the next most prestigious award, but one man on the jury for the Goncourt had fought hard for the book: Léon Daudet. And having done so, he became Céline's friend.

Léon Daudet was a curious blend of opposite qualities. He had a good eye for literary talent, and a quick appreciation of even so unconventional a book as Céline's; he was unquestionably bright and could be very funny; but he had also become so engulfed by his extremist political views as to lose all sense, first of proportion, then of reality, and finally of humanity. It was Daudet who called daily for the murder of Blum, Daladier, and a few others on the front page of *L'Action française,* and it was not hyperbole: he really meant it. It was Daudet who remorselessly slandered those with whom he disagreed. It was Daudet, finally, who was the most tenacious and most violent anti-Semite in France, a country where anti-Semitism was by no means rare.

In January 1934, for instance, Daudet wrote a series of articles entitled "The Jewish Problem" based on what he presented as an incontrovertible fact. "Every reasonable person must recognize that the Jewish problem belongs to what Balzac called 'the pathology of societies,'" he explained. "The Jew is a yeast thrust into the bodies of nations among whom he roams without taking root, a yeast which, under certain circumstances, becomes pathogenic."[6] That these circumstances had arisen in France was amply evident, Daudet went on; and a solution was needed. That, once the monarchy was restored, would probably mean that some Jews would be expelled from the country and others would be constrained to live in a sort of ghetto, while being forbidden to practice most professions, including, of course, politics. If France was in such a sorry state, Daudet explained, it was in large part the result of a Jewish conspiracy aimed at taking over the world (Jews being, by definition, unpatriotic and internationalist) and destroying the country.

For a man like Céline, who loathed society as it was and was equally convinced that there was a general plot to keep the poor in their place, Daudet's explanation came as a ray of light. Just as bacteria and viruses caused infection in the body, so Jews acted as carriers of the kind of disease that produced the intolerable society so powerfully described in his books. As it was, Daudet and Céline got it exactly the wrong way around: it was the vicious intolerance, the small-minded prejudice both were expressing that was pathogenic. Of course, in the process of rejecting society as it was, Céline might have turned to the revolutionary Left, but any temptation he might have had to look there, instead of to the Right, was ended when, in 1936, he went on a trip to the Soviet Union.

The ostensible reason for the trip was that royalties on *Voyage* had accumulated there and could not be transferred out; so he went to spend the money. Because Céline was at bottom a libertarian, there is every reason to think he would have hated Nazi Germany, had he spent time there, just as much as the Soviet Union; but it was Stalinism at work he saw, and he was, quite rightly, revolted.

The result was *Mea Culpa,* a short (about forty pages) pamphlet, burning with rage and indignation. There is nothing fictional about it; it is a description and denunciation of life in the Soviet Union. But the epigraph hints at something else: "I still lack a few hatreds. I am sure they exist."[7] That is just an amplification of the beginning of *Mort à crédit;* and, in fact, what Céline was discovering was an early form of the nonfiction novel. The hatred he felt, with every reason, for the Stalinist system enabled him further to refine his style. The incantatory prose, the obsessional, visionary quality of the later novels, the biting irony sustained by the telling detail, all that appears first in *Mea Culpa.* Today still, this long-forgotten pamphlet makes wonderful reading.

"You want wit, you want joy, in Russia, you get a machine. What a providential discovery! The true Promised Land! [. . .] Better than the Resurrection! . . . Machines, they're infection itself. The supreme defeat! [. . .] The best designed machine never freed anyone. It stupidifies Man more cruelly, that's all!"[8] Given the fact that the liberation of mankind from toil thanks to the use of beneficent machinery was one of the great myths of the period, that was enough to make a lot of people uncomfortable; but what came next was even sharper. One of Stalin's most frequently used propaganda themes was that it was worth it to suffer in order to build the Communist state, which would bring with it true happiness for the working classes. It did not take Céline long to see through that. "The great desire for happiness, there is the real lie! It complicates everything in life! Makes people so venomous, crooked, sickening! Ain't no happiness in life, only lesser or greater unhappiness."[9]

As for the true state of affairs in the proletarian paradise, that, too, roused Céline. "He's carefully locked away, the new hero of the renewed society . . . He's protected, Prolovitch, behind a hundred thousand barbed wires, the darling of the new system! [. . .] It's him, Prolovitch, that has to cough up for the most numerous, the most suspicious, the most vindictive, the most sadistic police on this earth!"[10] And the book ends with another sharp observation: "In brief, three things, three things only are doing well among the Soviets: army, police, propaganda."[11]

Céline was not the only writer horrified by Russia under Stalin. André Gide, that model of intellectual balance, also went and also wrote an attack on the system when he returned; but for Gide, it went no further. For Céline, the experience confirmed what he had already begun to be-

lieve: only his friends on the extreme Right were at all close to understanding the real nature of the world.

In Paris, though, the regime that the Right so loathed was doing
nicely. When, on February 7, with Daladier's resignation, the Republic
had seemed endangered, its President had demonstrated his total inca-
pacity. "I was a part of the delegation [of right-wing parties] who went
to see President Lebrun," Paul Reynaud remembered. "We urged him to
call on Doumergue for lack of a better solution, upon which the good
man said to us, with a very sad face: 'It is now two-thirty and I have not
yet had my lunch.'" [12] Faced with so grave a trial as a late lunch, no wonder Lebrun dithered; but he was prevailed upon to call Doumergue at his
house in the south of France. The former President agreed to serve, and
everyone — except the Socialists — breathed a sigh of relief.

For the Right, the Doumergue government provided revenge against
the Radicals and a return to power, but it also served the Radicals. In
February 1934 the party as a whole seemed compromised by Stavisky.
There was Garat, of course, the Deputy and mayor of Bayonne, who had
authorized the opening of the *Crédit municipal;* Dalimier, who as minister of commerce had endorsed Stavisky and Dalimier's predecessor, Julien
Durand; Pressard, the Paris attorney general, who had failed to prosecute,
and by extension so had his brother-in-law, Chautemps. Three of the
Radicals' most influential Deputies, including René Renoult, the honor-
ary president of the party, had been Stavisky's lawyers. Dubarry, the editor of *La Volonté* and a man deep into the Radicals' councils, had been the
crook's right-hand man: all in all, it did not look good. That most of these
men were eventually proved innocent made no difference at this point.

There was only one way for the Radicals to escape the taint: by being
a part of the new cabinet they demonstrated conclusively that Doumergue, the savior of the hour, did not think them guilty. Not that
Doumergue had much choice. Crisis or no, he still needed a majority in
the Chamber of Deputies and could not find one that did not include the
Radicals. Those he picked were not, however, just any Radicals: they
embodied the triumph of Herriot over Daladier. Herriot himself became
one of the two ministers of state, Tardieu being the other; and this provided Doumergue with the perfect excuse for pretending that his was a
government above party.

From June 1932 to February 1934, the Radicals had proved abundantly
they were incapable of governing. Now they remained part of the cabinet
but could blame Doumergue for whatever went wrong; and, just as important, the ineffable Albert Sarraut remained minister of the interior, the

post the party had long felt it must have if it was to do well at election time. Altogether, there were five Radical ministers — an obvious minority in a cabinet of eighteen that included Flandin, Laval, and other conservatives. As for Herriot, he had at last found the perfect position: as minister of state and the chief Radical in the cabinet, he had prestige and the capacity to block actions of which he really disapproved, but was spared from actually having to govern. Just as important, he was now again the undisputed leader of his party, the man who had defeated Daladier and could decide which of his colleagues would be ministers.

Thus there were few people left to oppose the new government. The Right backed its own; the Radicals knew better than to attack it; and the very age of many of its members also helped to reassure the French: Doumergue was seventy-one; Jean-Louis Barthou, the foreign minister, was seventy-two; and the new war minister, Marshal Pétain, was seventy-eight. These, apparently, were wise and experienced men, who could be counted on to bring back normality.

There were people, however, who thought that this gerontocracy left something to be desired: *Le Canard enchaîné*, a satirical weekly, put it succinctly in a front-page headline: "Why is France governed by seventy-five-year-old men? Because the eighty-year-olds are dead."[13] At least, it was clear that the Premier, who promptly announced that he would ask the Senate and Chamber to amend the constitution to give the executive greater power, was not a potential dictator. His very nickname, Gastounet, short for Gaston, seemed reassuring. Had there been polls, the Doumergue government would certainly have received a high rating of approval.

Whatever his other qualities — and they were few — Doumergue himself emanated a kind of understanding benevolence mixed with paternal sternness, and he understood just how to communicate this. Radio was becoming widespread; and it was the new Premier who, for the first time, made it his policy to address the country at regular intervals over the air. Never before had the French actually heard the voice of the man who governed them; never before had they been told so directly what was being done and why it was being done. Of course, this was nothing more than an adaptation of FDR's fireside chats; but it was new and it worked.

As is so often the case, however, the highly reassuring Premier was also highly incompetent. Doumergue had seldom before been part of a cabinet; he understood neither the major problem facing him in internal affairs, the Depression, nor the major enemy facing him abroad, Hitler; and so, throughout the spring and summer, the government blundered on. It knew that unemployment was spreading rapidly, and that industrial production was falling month by month; but its only remedy was, yet again, to raise taxes and balance the budget. Clearly these were not men ready to learn from experience.

Just how blind to reality they could be emerges in a telling anecdote. In March 1934 Adrien Marquet, the minister of labor, came as a witness before the Chamber's committee on finances. Marquet himself was not stupid. Starting out as a Socialist, he had become mayor of Bordeaux as well as a Deputy; then he had broken with the Socialists in order to lead a semi-Fascist (and fully authoritarian) group that never gathered more than a few Deputies. Still, in spite of his bizarre ideas, he was not inexperienced. He had, after all, been administering the fourth largest city in France and had done a good job of it; but when he attempted to solve a double problem, unemployment and the lack of modern roads, he came up with an astounding solution. Paul Reynaud, who was a member of the committee, remembered it well.

"Marquet . . . explained to us that, in this country where there were no superhighways, he had given the order that only the least efficient, least modern machines were to be used in road building so as to better fight unemployment by using the greatest possible number of workers for the same job," Reynaud recorded. "You would do better, I told him, to have the work done by the most modern means and to pay the unemployed workers to do calisthenics in the fields by the side of the road."[14]

At a time when the New Deal was building highways, bridges, and parks, Marquet's policy seems remarkably stupid; but it never occurred to him or, indeed, to any of the other ministers, that it might pay to look outside France for solutions. As for Herriot and the Radicals, they were now in what they considered to be an enviable position: the finance minister continued to deflate, but they themselves were not directly responsible.

What was becoming clear even to the cabinet, however, was that, ever since the devaluations of the pound and the dollar, French prices, calculated in gold, were far higher than those in the rest of the developed world; and that, in turn, deepened the Depression. With the dramatic fall in French exports, more unemployment was created, bankruptcies multiplied, and industrial production shrank even further. The government's only solution for this was to legislate lower prices. Doumergue requested, and was granted, the right to issue "decree-laws," decrees that without parliamentary approval had the force of law. Then at the end of six months the Chamber could either confirm or invalidate the decree-laws as a block. By then, of course, they had usually done their work and the point was moot.

In this crowd of the blind, however, there was one single man who began to have glimmerings of understanding. Paul Reynaud was ferociously ambitious, vain, and singularly lacking in depth; he was easily led, both by his political entourage and by his mistress, Mme de Portes; but he was also highly intelligent. Just as important, he spoke and read English, so that he was able to find out what Keynes was thinking and what FDR was doing. He also prized modernity. Early in 1934 Reynaud, in a display of apparent eccentricity, announced that deflation was not the way out of the Depression.

At first, he did so carefully; he was, after all, challenging a sacred dogma. After advocating a lowering of French prices in a speech to the Chamber in February, he concluded: "If it should prove impossible to deflate retail prices . . . , then we will have to resort . . . to a devaluation."[15] Since he seemed to be advocating deflation as the main, the preferable remedy, the speech caused no great stir. It was only at the end of June that he finally explained what he really meant.

"The capitalist countries . . . are divided in two groups: those who are getting better and those who are getting worse," he told the Chamber. "Those who are getting better are . . . the thirty-five nations who have devalued their currencies. . . . A hundred kilos [220 pounds] of wheat are worth 44 francs in Winnipeg and 130 francs in Paris. A kilo of meat costs 1 franc in the United States and 2 to 4 francs in France, an automobile 8,000 francs in the United States, 35,000 francs in France. . . . The only thing the government cannot do is to persevere in the contradictions of its current policy."

"That evening," Reynaud adds in his memoirs, "at a party given by [the well-known journalist] Mme Louise Weiss, M. Tannery [the head of the Bank of France] announced: 'If we had a government worth the name, M. Paul Reynaud would be arrested tonight.'"[16] It is no wonder Tannery was so upset. Reynaud, a former finance minister and a member of the Right, had just spoken the unspeakable, insulted the most sacred dogma. Ever since 1926, Tardieu and his supporters had jeered at the Radicals and the Socialists for allowing the franc to lose so much of its value, thereby devaluing the widow's mite and ruining the orphan (as well as seriously inconveniencing the many wealthy men, part of whose capital was in government bonds). Now Reynaud was suggesting that the franc be devalued again. As it happened, he was right, but that was not allowed to make any difference. For the next two years, he fought a valiant but

In that attempt, no one was better suited to lead the way than the Faucigny-Lucinges. They were, after all, the most elegant young couple in Paris, happily blending an illustrious birth — his — and the great D'Erlanger family fortune — hers. They even looked like what they were. He was tall, athletic, handsome, and dressed as only someone with a good English tailor could; she was dark, pretty, amusing, and had a great flair for clothes. Their friends ranged from the most austere of duchesses to Marie-Laure de Noailles and on to Cocteau. They were seen everywhere; their own parties were eagerly attended; and when invitations went out to the various events connected to the wedding of the Duke of Kent and Princess Marina of Greece, it was found that the Faucigny-Lucinges met the British court's highest standards. Throughout France, only nineteen invitations were received; only four couples were invited to the private view of the wedding gifts at St. James's Palace, the ceremony at Westminster Abbey, and the ball at Buckingham Palace: the Faucigny-Lucinges; the comte and comtesse des Isnards and the comte and comtesse de Castéja, both ladies being the daughters of Daisy Fellowes; and the immensely successful playwright Francis de Croisset, whose wife (it was her second marriage) was none other than Marie-Laure de Noailles's mother.

If Daisy Fellowes herself was not on that short and glamorous list, it was because her husband had been dropped many years before, and George V's notions were still wholly Victorian. That, however, did not prevent her from being the best dressed woman in Paris, a title for which there was much competition and which she achieved with Schiaparelli's help, or from giving spectacular parties in the garden of her house in Neuilly. In June 1935, for instance, she made a fantasy of stability the theme of a ball: colonies were, for the most part, still duly obedient to their European masters and were a link to a time when the world seemed safer and more stable; and so the evening was announced as a ball at Government House, in Africa or in India.

Of course, many women wore more or less literal versions of a sari or an ihram, the jeweled cloak, or robe, that Schiap had rediscovered. Mrs. Fellowes herself was in white satin with purple orchids. The marquis de Robien came in a turban-topped hussar's uniform and was accompanied by two veiled odalisques. There was a Chinese empress, naturally, followed by several Japanese beauties; but Elsa Maxwell probably topped them all when she appeared as a janissary sporting an immense white turban decorated with a huge pair of embroidered scissors. As for the men, they wore white spencers or tails liberally sprinkled with stars and crosses, some true, some invented, the best of these being the row of silver spoons that adorned the writer Paul Morand's breast. Naturally, Lady Mendl was there, probably feeling that the ball was a little tame. It was she, after all, who had given a Circus ball in which she appeared to her guests riding a white elephant; it was also she who, famous as she was for the neutral tones she used in the houses she had decorated, had, when first seeing the golden stones of the Parthenon, murmured happily: "My beige."[20] Still, the decor was quite reasonably spectacular, even by Lady Mendl's standards; there were white stucco palm trees in the ballroom, a huge Buddha was placed at the center of the brilliantly lit garden, and the guests danced all night.

For all its glamour, the Tout-Paris was not very large. Some of its members, people like the Faucigny-Lucinges or the Noailles, belonged to several worlds at once: the old aristocracy, to whom they were related; the intellectuals, from Cocteau to the brilliant, short-lived Surrealist poet René Crevel; and the Tout-Paris proper, with whom they attended important first nights at the theater and certain parties. Others of those seen at the right places at the right time were successful journalists, like Pierre Lazareff, or tycoons, or even politicians, Paul Reynaud first and foremost; but one cannot help suspecting that conversation must have flagged occasionally among people who met evening after evening.

The remedy to that was frantic activity. The more events you attended, the more you had to say to your neighbor at dinner (or lunch or supper). It helped, for instance, if you went to the performance, by the Concerts Colonne, of Ravel's songs, *Don Quichotte à Dulcinée,* not a major work, certainly, but a very pleasing one. The yearly concert at which Stravinsky's new piece was played was another such event; and then there were always the several tiny theaters specializing in political satire.

Of course, the various members of the Tout-Paris also had various political opinions. The *gratin* tended to be firmly reactionary, and so did the Rothschilds and the great industrial families like the Wendels. It was typical, for instance, that the amiable and tolerant Prince Jean-Louis de Faucigny-Lucinge (Baba's husband) should have been a member of the *Croix de Feu.* This was a political organization that had begun as a group of veterans who had been in actual combat during the war; but, more recently, as led by Colonel de La Roque, it had denounced parliamentary democracy and participated in the Sixth of February riots, so that it was considered by many to be proto-Fascist, an accusation Faucigny-Lucinge, for one, refused to believe. For him and others like him the idea was to save the country from the corrupt and ineffective politicians who ruled it. That this entailed a nondemocratic replacement never seemed to bother him. As it turned out, La Roque was a monument of indecisiveness. His verbal attacks on the regime were rarely followed by action, and the movement finally petered out.

Other members of the Tout-Paris belonged to specific parties, usually on the Right: Reynaud was the perfect example of that. Others were closer to the Radicals. All, whatever their opinions, went to hear the newest political satire. And as always when there was something new and quintessentially Parisian going on, Genêt was there. The comedians offer, she wrote, "political wisecracks, ballads and skits on parliamentarians and swindlers to a public that might as well laugh since neither blood nor tears has made anything change. The liveliest has been the Théâtre A.B.C. with a revue called *X.Y.Z.* in which every dishonest Deputy in the alphabet was lampooned until their program was deleted — at the request of a lot of Deputies probably all named Monsieur X. One of the suppressed skit hits dealt with the Three Little Pigs (Doumergue, Tardieu, Herriot), with the increasingly bloodthirsty Average French Citizen as the Big Bad Wolf, so fed up he was ready to gobble them all."[21]

It took a particularly sophisticated American (and one who spoke perfect French) to enjoy these revues; for most foreigners, only the more glittering aspects of Paris mattered. That Flanner should have thought it worth her while to go to the Théâtre A.B.C. said something about the changing times, though. As a critic and reporter, she could have spent those evenings at any theater, any concert hall, any number of parties; but that carefree spirit which survived even the onset of the Depression was no longer easy to find. Even someone who, at heart, thought politics dull and unimportant could no longer ignore them. It wasn't just that, on the Sixth of February, Paris had experienced a semi-revolution; now the future was dangerous and uncertain, the present mostly hard and unpleasant. Politics mattered terribly: no one knew where the antics of Doumergue and company would take the country, but all the chances were that it would not be somewhere pleasant. Even more worrying, 1935 was the year in which a plebiscite was to determine whether the French-occupied Saarland was to return to Germany. With Hitler in power and the French Right claiming the Saar as French, it seemed likely France would do what it must to keep that industrial powerhouse; there was no doubt at all that Hitler would demand its union with the Reich. Sixteen years after the end of the War to End All Wars, in fact, war looked like a distinct possibility. It was thus with a feeling of welcome relief that Genêt sent off her 1934 year-end Paris letter.

"Even if toasted in humble wine rather than the customary festal champagne," she wrote, "and drunk to in the midst of a frightening financial depression, January 1st, 1935, will rank here as the first day of a wonderfully happy New Year. For the fear of war has momentarily passed. With international troops politely policing the plebiscite in the Saar, France and Germany need not come to blows."[22] She was right, of course; no blows were exchanged (between those two countries, at least) within the next year; but for the first time a fear that grew stronger with every year had to be acknowledged. What mattered now was whether, or when, the next war would start. It is no wonder that the Tout-Paris grew giddier, or the masses more disillusioned. On January 1, 1930, France had been on top of the world. On January 1, 1935, racked by the economic crisis, looking fearfully across the Rhine, it had every reason to dread the future.

# CHAPTER
# SEVEN

# THE FAILURE OF THE RIGHT

FEAR, briefly dispelled on occasion but ever returning, is not a pleasant emotion, but it was one with which the French found themselves living from 1935 onward. It took many forms: apprehension about the referendum in the Saar, for instance, was only one of its manifestations. It was also irrational: Germany was in no condition to start a war with France; but the very fact that the French worried so much was a symptom. In a world gone wrong, they had begun to expect the worse.

They were often right to do so. The Depression was getting deeper and more painful month by month, and neither the very moderate Left, during the successive Radical cabinets, nor the rather less moderate Right, under Doumergue, had been able to do anything about it. There were other fears as well: for much of the bourgeoisie, communism was a most effective ogre. More reasonably, the Left thought France might go the way of Italy and Germany. No matter where people looked, in fact, they had reason to be apprehensive; and Hitler's ceaseless attacks on the Treaty of Versailles did nothing to reassure them.

The Left had good reason to worry; the Sixth of February had proved that abundantly. The Right, back in power, should have been triumphant, but it was deeply divided and very conscious that the Doumergue experiment had been a failure, both politically and economically. That would not have mattered so much — the sufferings of the working class did not really worry Tardieu or his friends — except for one major fact: the elections due in May 1936 might offer a repeat of the 1932 results or, worse yet, see a marked progression of the Socialists and the Communists.

Still, in a country whose population felt increasingly alienated from the government, and whose elites seemed intent mostly on having fun, the Right had one hope left. While Tardieu was now firmly rejecting the current parliamentary system and thus rapidly making himself irrelevant, there was one bright, comparatively young man whose coolness and efficiency might, it was hoped, solve the economic and financial problems. This was Pierre-Etienne Flandin.

Flandin, often a minister and, in November 1934 poised to become the new Premier, was tall, cool, aristocratic looking, and superbly dressed. Even better, he *looked* competent. His views were moderately modern — he believed in technology — and in a world of tired politicians he seemed the very image of youthful vigor. He could make a speech that convinced his listeners that he had seen the future and that it would work. Most important of all, he was reassuring: presenting himself as a technocrat, he invariably chose the practical solution to any problem, while his rivals stuck to traditional political ideas — or so he claimed.

In fact, Flandin, who became Premier on November 9, 1934, was that novelty in France, a politician who was all surface. Once you got past the appealing exterior, there was a void. He understood little, signally lacked judgment, and for all his apparent modernity, was essentially a last remnant of the 1840s, that time when the solid middle of the solid middle class ran the country by not making waves. Where Paul Reynaud offered shocking new solutions, Flandin tried to make a few minor adjustments. He was everything Herriot liked in a conservative, and it was largely as a result of Herriot's sponsorship that he became Premier.

For the same reasons Reynaud detested him, and when he described Flandin in his memoirs, the acid flowed freely. "Pierre-Etienne Flandin was handsome, and his excessive tallness gave him prestige but made him shy," the tiny, froglike Reynaud wrote.

> Hence his coolness and his preference for a British style. . . . I asked Georges Mandel [one of Flandin's ministers] one day: "How can you

explain that an intelligent, cultivated man who makes such brilliant speeches should be wrong on every major question?"

"It is simply because he supports the opposite of everything you advocate," Mandel answered cuttingly.

Flandin relied on supposedly competent men to advise him about devaluing, or about the military problem. . . . He had only given the possibility of a devaluation the most cursory study and in foreign policy he thought that appeasing the Hitlerian ogre would sate his appetite.[1]

Reynaud was right: Flandin was the first of the appeasers. It was a fundamental trait. He appeased not just Hitler and Mussolini but his own colleagues as well, Herriot first and foremost. It was typical of him that he chose Pierre Laval, whom he loathed, as his foreign minister; better, he felt, to coopt than to confront. In the end, of course, he got confrontation anyway. Laval ceaselessly intrigued against him and finally replaced him in June 1935.

As it was, Flandin, for the seven months of his government, was the perfect expression of a system that was rapidly running down; and although, as Premier, he gathered his share of headlines, he really interested very few people. As Genêt aptly noted, "No one has the slightest faith [in the new Flandin cabinet] except Flandin."[2] The French themselves, who were increasingly dissatisfied, had given up on the current crop of Deputies and the governments they supported. As for the people who made Paris what it was, they ignored politics even more steadfastly than before. Thus, when Flanner triumphantly announced, "The future of France is safe once more," she was not predicting the end of the Depression or the fall of Hitler. She was merely (and, to be sure, ironically) referring to the new show at the Folies-Bergère, which, she wrote, "has opened with a bang, no leading lady, the best visual entertainment the house has shown in four years and box-office magnetism. The production was mounted by Jean Le Seyeux, a young man who knows his feathers; the big flowers scene is called "Mimosas" and features — in a small electrical way, of course — the rain of comets Paris recently enjoyed; the big laugh is the [Chamber of Deputies] political number, with actors wearing masks in the likeness of half the Parliament; and the Girls have turned into Les Vingt Bluebell's Beautiful Ladies."[3]

Certainly, the Folies-Bergère mattered much more to visiting Americans than the actions (or lack of same) of the Flandin government. As for the elegant French, firmly turning their backs, not just on the future, but on the present as well, they flocked into that nostalgic survival of a lush, prewar world, Maxim's.

By 1935, it had become far more chic than it had ever been. In its earlier, prewar, phase, its stars had belonged to the demimonde; now it was the Tout-Paris who met there to dine and dance. The most fashionable women, in the latest designs, showed off their backs, which, this season, were often bared to well below the waist. The cuisine was once again superb, and in that decor of red velvet, Art Nouveau *boiseries,* and curlicued brass, it was possible to believe that, after all, the world had not changed.

A newer kind of exoticism also had its appeal. After a grand tour of Europe, Josephine Baker was back, as popular as ever; only this time she could be seen in the darkness of movie houses. Aware that many music-hall stars had faded and vanished, she embarked on a new career: films, she thought, would bring her an even wider public. It was not an easy proposition. Although she found financing easily enough — the funds were provided mostly by a Tunisian casino owner and in part, probably, by herself — subjects were harder to come by. In an era when being black meant that she could not play any of the usual roles of the repertoire, or, indeed, any part except that of an exotic femme fatale, it was not easy to find the right story. As it turned out, her first film, *Zou-Zou,* was particularly idiotic, but it showed her off in, surprise, surprise, a music-hall turn, and it had as her costar the young and already dazzling Jean Gabin.

The plot of *Zou-Zou* is as predictable as it is silly: starting out as an impoverished seamstress, Zou-Zou becomes a music-hall star so as to earn the money to save her lover, who loves someone else anyway. But the music-hall scenes, along with Gabin's performance, give the film real interest. To see Josephine young and beautiful, dancing and singing for us, her lithe body twisting sexily, her voice twittering like that of an especially melodic bird, is as great a pleasure today as it ever was; and so the audiences thought in 1934. As for the star herself, she loved it all. "It all seems so real, so true," she said, "that I sometimes think it's my own life being played out on the sets."[4]

It was once again her talents as a singer and dancer that were showcased in her next film, *Princess Tam-Tam.* This time, the scene was frankly exotic: the film took place in Tunisia (but it might as well have been Zanzibar or Tahiti), where a novelist transforms a goat girl into an exotic princess, all to make his wife jealous. The plot is even more hackneyed than that of *Zou-Zou;* Baker is just as enchanting in the musical numbers; but the public could be forgiven if it felt it had seen it all before. Unable to break out of the stale exoticism that alone seemed appropriate for a black woman, Josephine, it became clear, had taken her film career as far as it could go.

It was equally clear that she was as enchanting as ever on the stage. Late in 1934, she revealed a whole new side of herself when she starred, and triumphed, in an Offenbach operetta, *La Créole*. The part was ideal for her: she played a Jamaican girl who is seduced, then abandoned, by a French sailor, but follows him back to France and a happy ending. Albert Willemetz, whose idea it was to cast Josephine as the heroine, was an immensely successful author of musical comedy books and lyrics. He rearranged Offenbach to make him seem more modern; some liberties were taken with the music — "*ça ne jazze pas,*" Josephine had complained[5] — and Paris fell in love all over again. For months, a seat in the Théâtre Marigny was one of the hottest tickets in town.

The paradox was that Josephine, whose appeal had always been quintessentially exotic, had now become thoroughly Parisian. *La Créole,* after all, was a French operetta, sung in French, and the rest of the cast was French. Even the star's blend of sexiness and humor had precisely the right appeal for Parisian audiences. Back in her native United States, she was only, as she soon found out, just another misunderstood black performer.

This became evident when she returned to star in the Ziegfeld *Follies* of 1936. Fannie Brice got all the applause and the critics complained that Baker was not another Ethel Waters. That, together with the racial discrimination she encountered at every step, was too much for her; by the end of the year she was back in France, preparing for yet another triumph at the Folies-Bergère. Whatever her origins, Josephine belonged in Paris.

If, indeed, the future of France was still to be judged by the success of the Folies-Bergère revues, then in December 1936 it was particularly bright. Faithful to her post, Genêt told her readers all about it. "With clothed chorines instead of nudes, and a silken-clad Josephine Baker as the star, the Folies has just mounted the best and most popular show it has offered Paris in the past three years."[6]

Josephine Baker was not the only black American performer to do well in Paris. Marian Anderson, whom the Daughters of the American Revolution thought unfit to tread their stage, earned enormous acclaim every time she performed in Paris. Her concerts in November 1934 were packed by enthusiastic audiences who were well aware that they were hearing one of the century's great voices. Two years later, the great singer, who had been praised by Toscanini and had triumphed in a Brahms recital in

Salzburg, filled not just the hall, but the stage where the overflow crowd was seated. By 1936, in fact, the two most popular Americans in Paris were Franklin Delano Roosevelt and Marian Anderson.

America as a whole was a hot topic in 1935. It wasn't just that its performers were so popular, live and on film, or that, with the Depression beginning to end, American tourists were once again appearing in significant numbers, or even that, with international tensions growing, many people hoped that the United States might help to keep the peace: the most flamboyant product of French technology and savoir-faire was a new ocean liner that crossed the Atlantic and became so fashionable itself that visiting New York was suddenly the thing to do.

The ship in question, the huge and splendid *Normandie,* was a triumph of speed, decor, and service, everyone on both sides of the Atlantic agreed. It is no wonder that it was so popular. At a time of economic failure and political anomie, here at last was a French triumph. That was in part because its owners had been willing to try a unique technological advance. Until then, the prows of great passenger ships had been absolutely straight, blades cutting through the water. The *Normandie,* on the other hand, had, below the flotation level, a bulbous prow that looked distinctly odd but significantly reduced the drag of the water and, together with engines of unmatched power, won it the Blue Ribband for the speediest crossing of the Atlantic.

All this was important, of course. It proved that France was still a major industrial power; it provided splendid publicity when the *Normandie* won the Blue Ribband; and it gave everyone something cheerful to talk about. What mattered far more to most people, though, was how the ship looked, from its canted funnels, which made it seem as if it were speeding even when it was tied up in port, to its sumptuous Art Deco interiors.

The sheer size of the ship was amazing. If put down in Paris, it would have stretched from the center of the Place de la Concorde all the way to the Madeleine — rather more than a football field. Although its crew of sailors numbered a mere three hundred, it carried two hundred cooks and seven hundred stewards to serve the twenty-two hundred passengers. Its bakers were expected to produce over fifteen hundred pounds of bread a day — and that did not include croissants or the pastry on the menus of the three dining rooms, one for each class. It was expected that, on every crossing, the kitchens would go through seventy thousand eggs, seven thousand fowls, nearly twenty-five thousand pounds of meat, twenty-four thousand bottles of vin ordinaire, and seven thousand bottles of estate-bottled wines.

Everything aboard ship was on a vast scale. The *Normandie* boasted the very first floating theater (it had four hundred seats). The first-class dining room, with its entrance down a grand staircase that allowed the ladies to show off their gowns and jewels, was 240 feet long: as the press immediately pointed out, that was twenty-one feet more than the Hall of Mirrors at Versailles. There were also eight first-class suites with private dining rooms of their own, and private decks. Indeed, the largest suite on the ship had an entrance hall, a salon, a dining room, three cabins, each with its own bathroom, and, of course, its own deck. For the first time ever, first-class cabins were not just luxurious and spacious, but also practical: they had closets where you could hang floor-length evening gowns, the most modern of bathrooms, and indirect lighting.

More than just size, though, it was sophistication that mattered. The ship was to show everyone that when it came to a blend of splendor and good taste, no one could match the French — and it succeeded. Today, elements from the *Normandie*'s decor sell for vast prices at auction. Then, it offered not just unmatched luxury, but a compendium of what modern designers could do. Until then, liners had followed the imitative trends of prewar decor: they had Renaissance saloons and Louis XV dining rooms; but the *Normandie* was a showcase for the best and most up-to-date the French could offer.

Typically, the decorators used sumptuous materials but simple, streamlined forms. In the first-class reception hall, the walls were made of Algerian onyx set in green copper mounts; in the dining room, Lalique designed a sleek and luxurious decor of molded, engraved glass panels — "a grandiose, solemn sight," Genêt said;[7] in the first-class bar, it was Dunand who etched, then lacquered, then gold-leafed, then charcoal-rubbed more than a thousand copper panels to cover the walls.

Greenery had always been important on the great liners, but until now it had often consisted of a few drooping palms. The *Normandie* had a vast winter garden complete with pergolas, spouting fountains, lawns, and aviaries lushly stocked with exotic birds. Exercise mattered also; but while the passengers could certainly conform to old custom and walk the decks — they were, after all, the longest ever — they also had for the very first time a pool and an exercise room. If, on the other hand, you were lazy, there were enough elevators to ensure you would never have to puff up a staircase. If you brought your children but preferred not to have them underfoot, there were nurseries. If you could not travel without your dog (or your cat), there were kennels and a special deck section where the pets could get their own exercise. And with all that, in first class the *Normandie* also offered food that was delicious even by French standards: the ship was, in fact, one of the very best of French restaurants. Of course, third class was not so luxurious; but even there the amenities were superior to the norm and the meals, though simple, were eminently palatable.

What was specifically French about the ship was not so much that it was spectacular — earlier liners had also reached for splendor — but that the *Normandie,* for all its grandeur, eschewed noisy luxury. Taste was the key notion: the decor was to look the very opposite of flashy. The grandest suite on board was a case in point: it was a perfect example of a quiet, modern, almost aristocratic interior. The salon, for instance, was paneled with light-colored eye of birch into which ochre and green Aubusson tapestries were set; the seats and tables were also made of the same wood in simple, comfortable forms; the upholstery was golden brown velvet and the carpet a neutral beige, while everywhere there was recessed, indirect lighting. At one end, the salon opened into the circular dining room from which it could be separated by sliding doors. Here, in contrast, the colors were much darker. The furniture was veneered in Japanese lacquer — black and gold — and so were the panels in back of the serving credenza, while the curtains and upholstery were bright green. And there were Lalique vases and Dunand cigarette boxes.

Naturally, Jean-Michel Frank was among the decorators who were asked for designs. Never, indeed, had he been more fashionable, but, even so, early in 1935, he took a step toward making himself more available to the public: he actually opened a shop in the Faubourg Saint-Honoré. There you could buy the very latest in chic objects: the display ranged from screens and vases painted by Bébé Bérard in his pleasantly theatrical neo-Baroque style to Giacometti plaster masks that were used as wall lamps. There were low, natural-wood cocktail tables — part of Frank's famous pale look — but also tables made of brass wire whose curlicues and Victorian shapes represented the very apex of chic. It was now thought deliciously daring to mix contemporary furniture with antiques (or faux antiques, in this case), and the late nineteenth century, considered as the epitome of dowdiness until just recently, was beginning its comeback. By the winter of 1938, no one could any longer doubt that this was the leading trend when Schiaparelli, ever alert to change, brought back the bustle.

Indeed, the return to a safer age was gathering speed: had the *Normandie* been planned, rather than completed, in 1935, it would no doubt have been far less modern looking. As it was, the stark look invented by Frank in the late twenties was giving way to an increasingly elaborate decor. In the illustrated magazines, photos of the latest Paris interiors showed a predominance of antiques, and a pared-down Louis XVI look suddenly seemed desirable.

The comte Robert de Rougemont's new interior was typical. The dining room, done up in Louis XVI style (but using mostly imitations rather than real Louis XVI pieces) had wall paintings by the justly forgotten Beloborodoff. Agreeably pale blue and gray, to fit the decorative scheme, they were pastiches of Piranese and Hubert Robert. In the salon, it was that immensely successful mediocrity José-María Sert who took over with a composition of trompe-l'oeil curtains and neo-Goya Spanish fetes; and these singularly uninspired scenes were set in faux Régence paneling of bleached oak with gilded baguettes.

This return to the past was fast becoming universal. It was perhaps no surprise that Lady Mendl's salon boasted Louis XIII paneling from the château de Courcelles; after all, antiques are a decorator's stock in trade; but everywhere objects and furniture created a link with the past, even as certain habits changed.

It was no longer considered quite right to display rare porcelains or antique silver in your dining room, for instance; but antique furniture was just the thing. At Mme Boutet de Monvel's — her husband was a hugely successful illustrator and totally untalented painter — the octagonal dining room centered on an octagonal table made of eight mirrored panels; but the chairs around this eminently modern piece were (imitation) Directoire in black-painted wood and white upholstery; and then, as if to make up for this, all the table accoutrements were made of glass or crystal, except, of course, for the silver cutlery.

Because of its simplicity, the Directoire style was very much in vogue. It was the perfect compromise between the new affection for the past and the lingering domination of Art Deco. It was typical, for instance, that one hostess, Mme Paul Bizos, contrived a thoroughgoing pastiche in a modern setting. Her dining room had plain golden beige walls and a darker beige stone floor with a stone console made of a plain top on two Ionic columns: all very stark and new, except, of course, for the columns. Then, on the console, she placed two Japanese porcelain vases and an Egyptian carved head of the Saite period. There was a zebra rug under the table — the stripes were fashionably geometric — but the mahogany chairs were Directoire with emerald green upholstery while the curtains were raw silk of the same color. On the dark green gold-embroidered tablecloth, the hostess had placed gold porcelain plates — a novelty — and glass horses and fruit from Murano, a hint at the eighteenth century.

Clearly, the sumptuous look was back. It was no wonder, really; the world outside the walls of Mme Bizos's dining room was beginning to take on a dreadful shape. Between the Communists on the Left and the Fascists on the Right, the future looked uncertain, bleak, and violent.

The Sixth of February had been a foretaste of what might happen. Since then the *ligues* on the Right and the Communist and Socialist defense groups on the Left had clashed repeatedly. It looked, many German refugees warned, just like the last days of the Weimar Republic. The very people who had seemed above the political fray, men like André Gide, for instance, that apostle of civilization and sensuality, were now taking a political stance. In Gide's case it was, as always, reasonable; but an expanding group of intellectuals felt very differently.

On the Left, men like Louis Aragon, a former Surrealist, now identified completely with the Communist party and all its vagaries. On the extreme Right, a whole new ideology was rapidly winning ardent converts. Altogether opposed to the conservative, antichange traditional Right, these men, too, wanted what they saw as a revolution — only it was a revolution in which ultranationalism and racism would be the key elements. Fascism, they thought, would regenerate a country led by the craven and exhausted bourgeoisie.

Those ideas went far. A young, successful, fashionable writer, Robert Brasillach, was the most vocal of the group and he did not mince words. "We have seen . . . the birth of a new human type as specific, as surprising as the Cartesian hero . . . , as the Jacobin patriot, we have seen the birth of Fascist man," he wrote. "For he exists . . . as in other times did the Christian knight leaning on the cross and the sword. . . .

"The several nationalist movements, whether in power or still trying to achieve it . . . have strengthened the notion of a universal revolution. . . . The universe is aflame, the universe is full of song and coming together."[8] That was the great justification; an exhausted world would be rejuvenated by the new ideal. Of course, people like Brasillach had a serious problem. The very essence of fascism is faith in the superhuman qualities of a messianic leader, and France had no prospective Hitler or Mussolini in sight; so, in the meantime, Brasillach celebrated the men and the doctrine.

"The young Fascist, supported by his race and by his nation, proud of

Glamour in many forms:

Mistinguett shows her legs

Josephine Baker reveals her lithe elegance

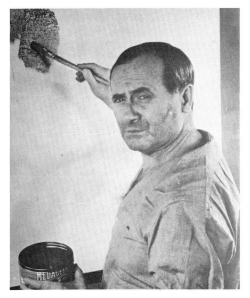

Miró paints

Picasso, as usual, stares hypnotically

Politicians were also stars:

Chautemps, then finance minister, defends the budget of 1933

Premier Flandin (second from right) and Foreign Minister Laval (on his right) meet with Austrian Chancellor Schuschnigg (on his left)

Herriot steps forth decisively (while, no doubt, thinking about how to back up again)

Premiers Ramsay MacDonald (of England), Heinrich Brüning (of Germany), and André Tardieu (left to right) shake hands

Writers came in every shape and opinion:

Malraux, always tense,
always smoking,
stares ahead

Léon Daudet, the editorialist
of *L'Action française*, wears a
characteristically unpleasant
expression

Cocteau looks ethereal and
poetic

Paris in the thirties was also the center of elegance:

Daisy Fellowes (left) confers with Schiaparelli, whose creation she wears

Elsa Maxwell, here with Gloria Swanson (left) and soprano Lily Pons (right), is dressed up as the impresario she really was

King George VI (on the Queen's left) and Queen Elizabeth, on their 1938 visit, were at the center of the social whirl

Scandal, riot, and blood:

Stavisky, the crook who
changed France

His beautiful wife, Arlette

The riot on February 6, 1934,
which was caused by the
Stavisky affair

The best of the new:

Art Deco flourished throughout the thirties

The *Normandie* was the first
ship with a modern interior

The style was everywhere at
the 1937 World's Fair

The view from the Eiffel
Tower: on the left, the Soviet
pavilion; opposite, on the
right, the Nazi pavilion,
designed by Albert Speer

Leaders and mistresses:

Edouard Daladier (center) with Georges Bonnet, his foreign minister (left), and General Gamelin (right), the wholly incompetent chief of the General Staff

*Below left*: Mme de Crussol, Daladier's mistress, at whose salon Daladier reigned

Paul Reynaud, small, dapper and self-satisfied

Mme de Portes, whose plotting helped Reynaud to become Premier in April 1940

1936 and after:

Daladier returns from Munich and is surrounded by a cheering crowd

Léon Blum, eyes shining with intelligence, holds a press conference

Bonnet and Ribbentrop (left), the Nazi foreign minister, sign a friendship treaty in December 1938

About to declare war, Daladier confers with Vice-Premier Camille Chautemps (right); the ineffably mediocre Albert Sarraut is just behind

Note: All photos courtesy of UPI/Bettman, 902 Broadway, New York, NY 10010

his strong body, of his lucid mind, contemptuous of the weighty riches of this world . . . , the young Fascist who sings, marches, works, and dreams is first of all a joyful being," he explained. "Fascism is not for us just a political . . . or economic doctrine. . . . Fascism is a spirit . . . , anti-conformist, antibourgeois before anything else. . . . It is the very spirit of friendship."[9]

There have, of course, always been deluded intellectuals who were ready to believe in the qualities of pure and muscular young men. More surprisingly, Brasillach and his friends were joined by the leaders of the classic Right. The reasoning was simple: since anything was better than communism or socialism or even a fairly strong dose of democratic re-form, it made sense to support the Left's most rabid enemies. Still, a justification was required. It was provided by Pierre Gaxotte, an eminent historian (even if his work consisted mostly of repeating earlier, and con-veniently forgotten, books). In *Je Suis Partout,* one of the weeklies that in 1934 had veered from extreme conservatism to fascism, he explained it all: "[The choice is] either Parliament, with its *incurable* defects, its *incorri-gible* intrigues, its *necessary* waste, its *fundamental* anarchy — or a na-tional dictatorship."[10]

That was a very large step toward endorsing fascism. The *ligues* aimed at being the French equivalent of Mussolini's Black Shirts or Hitler's S.A., a group of violent armed men who would impose a dictator on the rest of the French. By the spring of 1936, in fact, Maurras, that fervent mon-archist, had become eager for precisely this process. "The word 'fascism,'" he editorialized in *L'Action française,* "means union, a militant and even military union of all the national forces, even of the social forces. . . . The revolutionary plots [of the Popular Front] may soon bring about a situa-tion such that the Fascist solution may be essential to preserve order and save the country."[11] If even the royalist Maurras announced that he was in favor of a Fascist takeover, things had already gone very far. There was a major hitch, though; France still lacked a convincing candidate dictator.

Just how badly the Fascists yearned for their very own homegrown Führer becomes clear when we read Brasillach's description of Hitler. In 1937 he was invited to attend the yearly Nazi *Parteitag,* and the result was a text from which all reason has been banished. "When one sees the man with the distant eyes who is a god for his countrymen, how can one not remember that on a June dawn he descended from heaven, like an arch-angel of death, to kill, out of duty, some of his oldest companions. . . . One cannot judge Hitler as one would an ordinary head of state. . . . He is called to a mission he believes to be divinely inspired, and his eyes tell us he bears its terrible weight."[12] Hitler as the redeemer of mankind: for a normally skeptical French intellectual, it was quite an image.

Not all would-be Fascists were so devotedly pro-Hitlerian. After all, the Nazis believed that their race was meant to rule the world. The French, on the other hand, as represented by Maurras and his cohorts, were convinced that it was their compatriots who were superior to the Germans, not the other way around. Being a follower of Hitler also contradicted the ultranationalism invariably associated with fascism; you could not at the same time be super-French and the devotee of a foreign leader. That, indeed, was the position taken by Maurras and Gaxotte. They thought that fascism was just fine (and they preferred Mussolini to Hitler); anti-Semites themselves, they wholeheartedly supported Hitler's persecution of the Jews, and yearned for a French equivalent of the Nuremberg Laws,* which had made the German Jews outcasts in their own country; but they could never fully admire Hitler because the Führer, after all, was German, and Germany was, now as ever, the enemy. As for Céline, who was becoming obsessed with so-called racial purity, he simply considered Hitler to be a grotesque madman whose one good idea, anti-Semitism, was not a sufficient counterweight to his other, insane, beliefs.

For Brasillach, Maurras, and all their friends, the Republic and parliamentary democracy were the most immediate enemies. At the other end of the political spectrum, the Communists also despised the regime and called for a dictatorship, that of the proletariat as incarnate in Stalin. The Communists naturally had their intellectuals: Aragon was the best known of them. A writer of considerable talent and the author of several successful novels, he could be counted on to toe the party line. Now and again, on specific issues, the Communists could also rely on the support of other, more independent-minded writers: André Gide, for instance, who went to Berlin to try to save Dimitrov after the Reichstag fire. A true democrat, Gide did not approve of Stalin or his works, but he felt sorry for the German Communists who were being persecuted and he was always willing to help the oppressed and the unjustly condemned, a category that did not lack for members in the Third Reich. When Gide went to Berlin, though, and met with Joseph Goebbels, he was accompanied by a fellow intellectual of a very different kind.

André Malraux was a living paradox. In a country where education mattered greatly, he had left school at fifteen, and made a living by finding

*They got it from the Pétain-Laval government in 1940 and 1941.

rare books and reselling them. After writing occasional articles for little magazines, he had gone off to Cambodia with his wife, Clara (he was then just twenty-two), with the avowed purpose of stealing carvings from the ruins of a temple and reselling them for a vast sum in the United States. He failed; having hacked the carvings away from the wall of which they were part and shipped them to Saigon, he was arrested by the French authorities, held (but not jailed), tried and found guilty. He then appealed, got off on a technicality, and returned to France.

Amazingly, when the news of Malraux's arrest got back to Paris, a bevy of intellectuals, which included Gide, promptly announced that he should be neither tried nor convicted because he was so talented — quite a startling assertion in view of the fact that Malraux had unquestionably committed a criminal act, and that he had yet to write anything more than a few articles. That belief sprang from Malraux's extraordinary eloquence. Conversation had long been an art in Paris, and, before he went off to Cambodia, Malraux had been shining particularly brightly in a milieu where talking well was a major requirement.

Once back in Paris, he made up for the fallow years before his trip. From 1926 to 1935, he wrote four novels, of uneven merit, which brought him worldwide fame.

There was something fascinating — or, for some, repulsive — in his very appearance: he was quite tall, very thin, with a beaky nose and intense dark eyes. His face was made even more disquieting by the constant twitching that his friends learned to disregard. He appealed to women, though, and after a few years of an idyllically happy marriage he proceeded to be frequently unfaithful to his wife — just as she was, less frequently, to him. His attraction owed a good deal to his extraordinary eloquence. In a city of talkers, Malraux was famous for the brilliance and uninterruptible abundance of his conversation.

Even so, he struck many people as strange. "He could not look you in the eyes," the novelist Jean Prévost noted. "His eyes were always following an invisible bee in every direction. His shoulders contracted as if a dagger was tickling him in the back. His cigarette-stained fingers trembled, tried to free themselves. The moment someone approached, the haggard face seemed to grow more anxious. A punished child, a youthful rebel who as yet had embraced only death — that was Malraux back from Asia." [13]

Death was, in fact, one of Malraux's constant preoccupations: how people faced it, what they thought of it, was for him a devouring question and one that informed his novels. The distance from ordinary people that resulted from this obsession was unquestionably genuine, but many of the writer's other attitudes were nothing more than poses. Acutely aware of the way people saw him, determined to fascinate and be seen as a tormented genius, Malraux usually succeeded in making the impression he wanted. Even Maurice Sachs, the least gullible of men, saw what he was meant to see: "Malraux," he wrote, "produces the most vivid impression. In his gaze there is something of an adventurer, something melancholy and at the same time resolute; the handsome profile of an Italian Renaissance man, yet a very French appearance. He talks very fast, very well, seems to know everything, fascinates you and leaves you with the impression you've met the century's most intelligent man."[14]

That impression was not fully justified. Malraux knew how to dazzle; but behind the torrent of glittering words, the thought was often simplistic or plain silly — his later books on art offer abundant proof of that. As it was, he was one of the heroes of the Left because it was widely believed he had fought with the Chinese Communists in the twenties. In fact, he had done no such thing; but when asked outright, he always managed to fog the issue.

Like Céline's, his works presented themselves virtually as nonfiction novels, and they were often reviewed as such; indeed, in *Les Conquérants* (The Conquerors), the book that catapulted him to fame, one of the main characters, Borodine, was an actual Soviet envoy, and the subject was the struggle between the Kuomintang and the fledgling Chinese Communist party. The difference was that while Céline drew on his own experiences, Malraux, who had never been to China, deliberately misled his reader. That, of course, is the privilege of a novelist; but it is perhaps more honest to let fiction remain fiction and not pretend that it is the glamorous truth.

With all that, however, Malraux's heart was unquestionably in the right place. He was willing to see that people were suffering, instead of looking elsewhere at more pleasant subjects; and, within limits, he was willing to do something about it. While waiting for his second trial in Indochina, for instance, he had edited (and largely written) a newspaper attacking the cruelties of the colonial administration. Once back in France, he mostly forgot about politics, only to become interested again after the advent of Hitler. After accompanying Gide (who liked him) in the attempt to obtain Dimitrov's liberation, both he and his German-speaking wife returned several times to Germany and tried to help victims of the regime who either chose or were forced to remain in the country (that was when Goebbels explained to him the difference between justice and German justice). Naturally, the Malraux failed in their efforts, but they were far more effective in arranging for threatened persons to emigrate.

Malraux's novels fit right into that pattern of political involvement. After *Les Conquérants,* his next novel, *La Voie royale* (The Royal Way) was both less successful and less political; but in 1933 he returned to an earlier theme. *La Condition humaine* (translated for the English edition as *Man's Fate*) told the story of the 1927 Communist uprising in Shanghai and of its defeat, with Russian concurrence, by Chiang Kai-shek's troops. It was a huge success: the reviews were dazzling, the book received that most eminent of French literary prizes, the Goncourt, and the author, who already had a name in Paris, became universally known.

Like so much of Malraux's work, *La Condition humaine* is something other than what it appears to be. At first glance, it is a political novel. We are shown the sufferings of the poor in Shanghai and sympathize with them; we rejoice when their uprising succeeds and mourn its suppression by Chiang. That was enough to place its author firmly among left-wing intellectuals, a place in which he himself felt entirely comfortable. At the same time, the events in Shanghai are only a backdrop, even if a fully realized one; the real theme of the book is mankind's attempt at coming to terms with its position in the world (the English-language title is a mistranslation). The characters in the book try to give meaning to their life through their actions. In a world where there is no God and no redemption, and where the only thing that counts is how you feel about yourself, you can either earn your own respect by fighting oppression and injustice, or try to fill the hiatus before death as best as possible by looking for any sort of shallow comfort available.

Two of the main characters, a father and his son, represent these two possibilities. Gisors, the father, is French, a former professor who has given up all illusions and taken refuge in opium. "We must always escape reality," he says. "This country has opium, Islam has hashish, and the West has women. . . . Love is probably the way Westerners free themselves from the human situation."[15] For Gisors, therefore, action itself is futile: all we can hope for is alleviation, not improvement. That Malraux, via Gisors, should rank women with opium as an escape from reality says a good deal about his feelings for them.

Kyo, the half-Japanese son, comes close to being the hero of the novel. Unlike his father, he believes in action. He is revolted by oppression, and active in the revolutionary movement that briefly takes over Shanghai. Human dignity, he thinks, is the freedom not to be demeaned. "He did not worry. His life had a meaning, and he was aware of it: to give each one of those men whom hunger, at this very moment, was killing like a slow plague, the possession of his own dignity."[16]

All through the novel, it is quite clear that the author's sympathy is with the revolutionaries; but, even so, *La Condition humaine* is in no way akin either to "Socialist realism" or to the old French tradition of books meant to bring about a transformation of the society. As a deep-laid pessimist, one to whom death is almost more important than life, Malraux was the very opposite of a propagandist. Sure enough, the book ends badly: as the uprising is put down, Kyo is captured and ultimately dies; but he also triumphs because his death is his own choice, the result of his refusing to betray his friends. At that point, his imminent death becomes the justification, as well as the logical outcome, of his life. Here he is, in the prison which he knows he will not leave alive:

> Lying on his back, his arms crossed on his chest, Kyo closed his eyes: it was precisely the position of the dead. He imagined himself, lying down, motionless, his eyes closed, on his face the peaceful expression which death eventually gives to almost all corpses, as if it had to express the dignity of even the most miserable. He had seen many people die and, thanks to his Japanese education, he had always thought that it is a fine thing to die of one's *own* death, of a death which is akin to one's life. And dying is passivity, but to kill oneself is action.[17]

It is, according to Malraux, only through braving death, through choosing to die rather than to live a life of compromise, that mankind can find the ultimate freedom. "The meaning of life," one of the characters says, is "the complete possession of oneself."[18]

For all its qualities, *La Condition humaine* is a far more limited achievement than either of Céline's great novels. Written in an effectively broken-up style that reminds one of the fade-ins and fade-outs of movies, occasionally descriptive, sometimes impassioned, the novel remains fairly conventional. There is nothing here like the new language, the new feeling for time and movement, devised by Céline.

For all his pessimism, however, Malraux is less passive than Céline. While to Céline the world is a dreadful place that can only be suffered, Malraux advocates doing something about it: he was, in fact, the first of the *engagé* writers. Not only does the content of his work reflect real-life issues, Malraux, in his own life, put himself on the political line, and did so with a great deal of courage. This was particularly clear in his relationship with the Communists.

Although by the summer of 1934 the Popular Front was beginning to come together, and the Communists, therefore, were becoming allies of other left-wing forces, most liberal writers were fully aware of the party's rigid intolerance. They knew that in the Soviet Union a period of freedom and experimentation in the arts had been brought to an end, and that in the name of "Socialist realism" the most closed-minded orthodoxy prevailed. Writers were not yet being sent to concentration camps — that only started to happen the following year — but already it was made clear that the arts existed only to serve the regime. It thus took a good deal of courage for the determinedly non-Communist Malraux to attend the All-Soviet Writers Congress that took place in Moscow in August 1934.

As it turned out, he was the only non-Communist writer there. Thomas Mann, who had been expected to attend, sent his son; Theodore Dreiser, whose presence had been announced, never came. It was just as well: the congress predictably reaffirmed the virtues of Stalinism, with Andrey Zhdanov explaining that Soviet literature was heroic because it depicted the virtues of the working class and Maksim Gorky attacking his Western colleagues for concentrating on unsavory and even criminal characters. There were violent speeches that denounced those archetypical "decadent" authors, Proust and Joyce, and rejected formalistic innovation of every kind.

In that atmosphere, it took real courage to dissent; but that is just what Malraux did. "Art," he said, "is not an act of submission but a conquest. A conquest of what? Nearly always of the unconscious and quite often of logic. Your classic writers give a richer and more complex picture of the inner life than the Soviet novelists."[19] Naturally, Soviet officials promptly rose to rebuke him, but the point had been made.

Writers' congresses are perhaps a contradiction in terms, writers being usually individualists. In the Soviet Union, of course, they had a clear purpose, that of praising the regime. With liberty disappearing from a growing list of countries, however, Malraux and a group of French intellectuals decided it was time to call together an International Writers Congress to reaffirm the humanistic tradition of the West. It met in Paris in the summer of 1935 and was, Genêt explained, "the most important literary event of the year, though literature, for once in France, was not mentioned. Assembled as an anti-Fascist protest against the worldwide increasing loss of intellectual liberties, the congressionalists, who came from ten different lands, included André Gide and André Malraux as leaders; E. M. Forster, Aldous Huxley, and John Strachey from England; Waldo Frank from America; and [Aleksey] Tolstoi, [Henri] Barbusse, Louis Aragon, Luc Durtain, [Tristan] Tzara, Paul Eluard, Lion Feuchtwanger, Heinrich Mann, etc., etc. All, including the etceteras, made speeches."[20]

Genêt was right: there were many speeches. Most of them were dull, some of them — the ones given by Communist writers — were pure propaganda. Even so, the frequent reaffirmation that a writer's first duty is to himself, that propaganda of any sort is a denial of his purpose in life, greatly annoyed those who spoke for the totalitarian states. Indeed, in his closing speech Malraux addressed this very question.

"By the anger it has provoked," he said, "we know our conference exists. We have permitted some people who had been gagged to speak and we have allowed a joint responsibility to exist. It is in the nature of fascism to be narrowly nationalistic; it is in our nature to belong to the entire world."[21] In the face of claims by the dictatorships that the purpose of art was to praise them, these were things that needed to be said.

They were being said loud and often, that summer, in Paris. Just as the traditional and Fascist Right came together, so did the Communist and non-Communist Left. The hour, many people felt, was late; either the dictators would be stopped soon, or they would triumph. There was, however, one rather awkward contradiction. The Communists were welcome to the rest of the anti-Fascist forces because they, too, denounced Hitler, Mussolini, and their followers; but these very anti-Fascists, once they started looking at the Soviet Union closely, were entitled to wonder why the Communists were being so loud in the defense of liberty. This, after all, was the summer of the Moscow trials, in which many of the Russian leaders were falsely accused, falsely convicted, and promptly executed on Stalin's order.

Thus it hardly made sense for the liberals to accept the Communists as allies. Still, the danger from Hitler, Mussolini, and their imitators was so great that all helpers were welcome. The congress had been a temporary proof that the spirit of humanism survived; there was also a permanent Association of Intellectuals Against Fascism, which, indeed, was felt to be so important that it became one of the components of the Popular Front along with traditional political parties.

All this political activity seeped into Malraux's next book. *Le Temps du mépris* (The Time of Contempt) is a straight-out piece of propaganda; and while its goal is laudable, it reads more like a pamphlet than like the long short story (about 170 pages) it is. The book tells the story of Kassner, a Communist organizer arrested by the Nazi police. Malraux describes his interrogation, imprisonment, escape, flight, and reunion with his wife in Prague. The characters are two-dimensional, the Communists all virtuous, the Nazis all stupid brutes; the plot is predictable; the end, in which Kassner decides to go back clandestinely to Germany, is scarcely believable. All in all, this is a completely third-rate work, as Malraux himself came to realize; but it does have one immense merit: it is the first book whose subject is the terror inflicted by the Nazis on their own people.

Malraux and his friends on one side, Brasillach and his cohorts on the other, shared at least one thing: they all thought it necessary to pay attention to what was going on, in and out of France, and they wanted to have a hand in shaping it. That did not prevent Malraux from making good on another of his ambitions, however. First, he had made a place for himself among the intellectuals. Now, for all his left-wing views, he yearned to become a member of the Tout-Paris. Given the success of his books, this was easily achieved. The result was yet another split in his persona: it is not easy to be an ardent revolutionary and a chic man-about-town at the same time.

In one way, though, society agreed with Malraux: the world was, it felt, a nasty place. But instead of trying to reform it, the Tout-Paris chose instead to ignore it. Distractions were essential precisely so that current events would seem unimportant. Sometimes, however, that nasty feeling of impending doom which was likely to result from an interest in current events could be assuaged by a double dose of the poison. If you convinced yourself that you knew far more about what was going on than the common people, that you were thoroughly familiar with those who, in spite of all appearances, actually controlled events, then you could make yourself believe that all would end well after all. This extraordinary way of using information specifically to defuse its content and make it less alarming was characteristic, for instance, of the salon whose star was none other than that firm anti-Fascist Alexis Léger.

Its hostess, the comtesse de Fels, understood just what made a salon successful, and was bold enough to say so on her invitation cards, which read, after the date and time: "A little tea, a little conversation."[22] Having one major literary star was an old tradition of Paris salons. At the duchesse de La Rochefoucauld's, it was Paul Valéry who reigned; but Valéry, that great and recondite poet, was not involved in the affairs of the day. Léger, on the other hand, a major poet (as St. John Perse), was also the most important civil servant in the foreign ministry. Ministers came and went, Léger stayed, and, on occasion, ran France's foreign policy, partly because he was far more competent than some of the politicians he was supposed to serve.

Although invariably discreet, Léger was not above relaying the latest news or analyzing the latest crisis, thus giving Marthe de Fels's salon that essential attraction, first-rate information. Her visitors could hear about the newest diplomatic events and listen to explanations of longer-term trends. These were not, on the whole, reassuring, but it hardly seemed to matter. Because Mme de Fels's guests felt so much more knowledgeable than most of the French, they could also maintain the illusion that they were, somehow, above it all, invulnerable to what might happen. It was, in fact, a salient characteristic of Paris society that it felt thoroughly alienated from the rest of France: it was, in its own eyes, an elite group whom no event could touch.

Just because Léger played so important a role in Mme de Fels's salon did not mean that he went nowhere else. International politics were important, but, like most of Mme de Fels's friends, Léger had other interests as well. He loved music, and so, very naturally, he was often seen at the comtesse Jean de Polignac's — where, indeed, he found some of the same people he had just seen in Marthe de Fels's salon. It was one of those curious coincidences that Marie-Blanche de Polignac, the comtesse Jean, who loved music passionately, should be the niece by marriage of another passionate music lover, the princesse Edmond de Polignac. The daughter of Jeanne Lanvin, the great fashion designer, Marie-Blanche had every advantage. Her mother adored her; she had one of the happiest marriages in Paris and was very rich to boot; she was beautiful, with the elegant, slightly mannered look of an eighteenth-century duchess, and knew just how to flirt — all very safely since she remained absolutely faithful to her husband.

She was also a talented singer, something the princesse Edmond and her friend Nadia Boulanger noticed immediately; and if you came to see the comtesse at her house on the rue Barbet-de-Jouy on Sunday night, in the large, simple upstairs salon with its organ and two pianos, you would not only hear her perform, but also be present for a kind of informal concert in which Francis Poulenc, Georges Auric, or Henri Sauguet was likely to take a hand; and it was expected that when Rubinstein or Horowitz came through Paris, they, too, would stop in and play. The range of acceptable music was wide; from Mozart to Ravel and Offenbach, many pieces were played on the spur of the moment and the guests were invited only if they really liked music. On occasion, there would be more formal parties; and then Mme de Polignac received in the gallery hung with the Renoirs and Vuillards bought by Jeanne Lanvin and given to her daughter, with the guests eventually having supper in the dining room which the ever-fashionable Bébé Bérard had frescoed "in the style of Raphael."

It was virtually impossible to make fun of Marie-Blanche de Polignac. It was quite easy to mock another lady whose receptions were sumptuous and well-attended, but whose vanity was literally on display. Elizabeth Drexel was a rich American who had married an English peer, Lord De-cizes, because she wanted a title, and then moved to Paris, which she preferred to London, and which had the great advantage of being a place where her husband did not live. All the same, no one was ever allowed to forget her status; she kept dropping "accidental" references to her presentation at the British court, or to the balls she had attended at Buckingham Palace. Soon she was able to do even better. "She would show proudly," André de Fouquières recorded, "a wax figure of herself wearing the crimson court cloak lined with ermine and bearing a peeress's coronet on its head . . . sitting on the chair that she had used at Westminster Abbey during George VI's coronation, and that she had insisted on buying afterward."[23] Because she came from an excellent family, had a great deal of money, and gave sumptuous parties, the Tout-Paris came; but, of course, it laughed behind her back.

It was no kinder about Pierre-Etienne Flandin once he became Premier; and in truth he was not a hard man to mock. He managed to combine a pretentious smugness with great sensitivity to criticism, always an irresistible combination; and people took full advantage of it. It was typical of him, for instance, that while putting together the most hackneyed of cabinets, he claimed he was engaged in carrying out fundamental reforms.

To a significant extent, the new government was what Herriot wanted it to be. Tardieu was gone, replaced by an honorable and rather dim right-winger, Louis Marin, and Herriot himself remained minister of state. The ministry of the interior was given, naturally, to a Radical, Marcel Régnier, who could be counted on to obey Herriot's every request. The ministry of war, where Pétain refused to continue serving, went to a particularly dense officer, General Maurin. Laval was rewarded with the foreign ministry in the hope this might keep him from intriguing against Flandin (it didn't); and in a triumph of obtuseness, the key finance ministry was given to the grossly incompetent Germain-Martin, the very same man who had failed several times before to solve the financial and economic crisis, most recently in the 1932 Herriot cabinet.

Given Flandin's wish to look like an intelligent, if moderate, reformer, this was a positively comic government. The Premier himself went on at great length about the changes he was making. Instead of taking on a ministry, like all his predecessors, he announced that he would set up an office that would allow him more control over the cabinet and devote all his time to being an in-charge Premier. This was meant to remind the public that the still-popular Doumergue had thought France needed a powerful prime minister, and to make it believe that Flandin himself was really going to run the show.

That was all very well; unfortunately, it was all window dressing. Flandin's economic policy consisted in further deflation and a completely useless tinkering with the markets. His foreign policy was what Laval made it. Nothing could be done without Herriot's approval; and, finally, the level of intelligence and competence of the ministers reached something very like an all-time low.

Germain-Martin, for one, could always be counted on to reveal the vast extent of his ignorance. In May 1935, for instance, at a time when unemployment was soaring and the economy grinding to a halt, he cheerfully explained to the Chamber: "The general condition of our finances, of our credit and of our banks, is all perfectly healthy. The current difficulties [the budget was, as usual, way out of balance] are due to a sudden and violent assault by speculators. France's monetary situation is, in spite of this, worthy of envy."[24] The Deputies who heard this extraordinary evaluation were stunned. Clearly, Germain-Martin had mistaken reality for a Marx Brothers film.

Flandin himself was no better. Since neither Herriot nor Germain-Martin would have allowed him to devaluate the franc, he announced that he was refusing that dangerous expedient because "a devaluation would have significantly perturbed the world economy, which was barely convalescing."[25] That one sentence was worth its weight in overvalued francs: while the American and British economies were, in fact, beginning to recover, France was sinking rapidly. Refusing to devalue in order not to upset the world economy, therefore, was the equivalent of saying that the sun is highest in the sky at midnight.

The results of this fudging were predictable. Because short-term government notes were less visible than long-term bonds, Flandin used them to finance the deficit while, Micawber-like, hoping that something would turn up. What did happen was not an improvement of the economy but a scathing denunciation from Paul Reynaud. In order to deflate further, in May 1935 Flandin asked to be allowed to use decree-laws. That is when Reynaud, who was still pleading for the desperately needed devaluation, decided that enough was enough. Rising in the Chamber, he denounced the cabinet in terms that proved to be fully effective:

> The finance minister, who is responsible through his inaction for the catastrophe he had predicted, asks us to give him yet again, extended powers. "The way I used them the first time," he tells us, "will surely reassure you. And when the country learns you have renewed them, it will feel such a psychological boost that the economic problems will be solved." He is telling us, in other words: I have made a mistake, now trust me. . . .
>
> The government announced that prices would sink no further; they did. It predicted that interest rates would go down: they went up; that bonds would go up: they went down. It announced that the franc was in danger, but did nothing to save it. This is indeed the first time that a government argues that a situation created by its own incompetence requires that it be given greater powers.[26]

It was a scathing denunciation, and an effective one: the next day the government fell.

Three things were now clear. Since the beginning of the legislature, not a single government had in any way improved the economic situation; the Right, as represented by Doumergue and Flandin, was no more capable of governing effectively than the Radicals had been earlier; and the next government would be what Herriot wanted it to be.

By the time the Flandin government fell on May 31, 1935, though, Herriot's position was becoming uncomfortable within his own party. Daladier, whom he had so pitilessly disposed of after the Sixth of February, was once again on the rise. Faced with the vast unpopularity of the government, and with the strong possibility that the Communist-Socialist alliance would crush their own party, the Radicals developed second thoughts about the course being pursued by their leader.

Already in May, the Radicals had done badly in the countrywide municipal elections. Early in July, the party decided to be present at the unity parade (including Communists, Socialists, and several anti-Fascist organizations) to take place on July 14. Once again, Herriot was losing control, and he reacted in the usual way. First, when Flandin fell, he backed a government under the amiable but incompetent Fernand Bouisson, a Radical who was Speaker of the Chamber. The idea was, of course, that Bouisson would do what Herriot wanted, but take on the responsibility for the many predictable failures of such a cabinet — which, with the exception of the Premier, was exactly the same as the previous cabinet. Many of the Radical Deputies had had their fill of deflation, though; so, on June 4, the party split: when Bouisson asked for the same extended powers that Flandin had failed to receive, his five-day-old government promptly fell. Sixty-five Radical Deputies had voted against him, 30 had abstained.

At that, Lebrun tried Laval, who declined because the Radicals would not give him those same extended powers. Next, the President turned to Herriot, who refused on the grounds that by voting against Flandin, many Radical Deputies had shown they were not yet ready to follow him. Still there was no government. Lebrun then chose a young and energetic Radical, Yvon Delbos, in the evident hope that he would be the next Daladier, but Delbos declined; so it was the turn of Pietri, a right-winger who had just been minister of the navy. That day, Pietri told the journalist Louise Weiss, "Albert Lebrun asked me to lead a new government . . . [but] he told me he hoped I would not succeed. He wanted to use a series of spectacular failures to bring Laval to power. Laval himself clearly yearned for this and, thanks to his use of the foreign ministry's *fonds secrets,* he had bought himself the backing of much of the press."[27]

Pietri did not have a chance. Laval's intrigues were much too effective; so he gave up, just as he was meant to do. The way was now open for Lebrun's favorite, but the whole process had looked very much like a breakdown. Lebrun might think that the system was working satisfactorily, but the rest of the country did not; all too clearly, these games were wholly unrelated to France's real problems. Worse, the whole regime seemed to be in question: these parliamentary sports dramatically increased the already prevalent feeling of alienation; and Léon Blum summarized it all quite neatly: "The truth is that . . . the Chamber is ravaged by jealousy and resentments, by the rivalries of many small clans, by the clash of wild, impatient and mindless ambitions. The head of the government can no longer count on anyone, and less on his friends than on the others.

"Tardieu's dislike of Flandin creates chaos in the Center and the Right. The Daladier-Herriot duel is tearing the Left apart. . . . Tardieu put an end to the Flandin cabinet because he can't bear him; Flandin plots against Bouisson because Reynaud and Herriot support him."[28] In this poisoned atmosphere, Laval, with his talent for intrigue and his willingness to bargain, had every chance of success. Besides, it was clear that the country would not put up with this game much longer. As Chautemps remarked: "We have reached the Fifth of February; it is time to end this."[29] And, indeed, on June 7 the new Laval government came into being, with the Premier retaining the foreign ministry. Naturally, Herriot continued to be minister of state; Flandin was given the same office; and, as usual, there were five Radicals in the spending ministries: interior, finance, commerce, pensions, and education. This time, more than half the Radicals balked: while 72 voted for the new cabinet, another 72 abstained (so as not to embarrass Herriot by voting against), and 7 openly voted no.

For the professionals, all was well: the new cabinet, although markedly more conservative than its predecessor, was expected to last until the May 1936 elections, if only because Laval was a master at conciliating his supporters. In the real world, however, France had just been given exactly the wrong government, and the country watched the process and its conclusion with disgust. It had good reason to feel that way. While the politicians played their games, the French were suffering and the country drifting. The Fascist and proto-Fascist *ligues* were growing every day more violent, Hitler was becoming more menacing, and it looked as if the economy was entering its final collapse.

By the time Laval took office, almost everyone in France was affected by the Depression. According to a new index of economic activity, lack of demand had caused the price of wheat, for instance, to fall from a level of 100 in 1929 to 51, wine to 49, and meat to 45, thus ruining the vast majority of the population since France was still an agricultural country. As for the falling prices at the consumer level, they quite failed to help the unemployed (over 800,000 of them) or the far more numerous underemployed. Real income had come down just as drastically, from 100 in 1929 to 41 for the farmers and 54 for workers and small retailers. With 4 million of the still employed earning less than 9,600 francs a year ($1,200 of the period, about $10,000 in 1993 value), even having a job meant severe deprivation.

It was this situation that Laval proceeded to make significantly worse. On the advice of the so-called experts, one of whom, Jacques Rueff, continued to enjoy the same position into the 1960s, the Premier, with the full concurrence of his Radical finance minister, proceeded to deflate even more brutally than before. On July 16, a series of twenty-nine decree-laws began the job: all Treasury payments were cut by 10 percent. This applied to the salaries paid by the state to its employees, from schoolteachers to civil servants to street cleaners; to all civil service pensions; to the interest paid on Treasury bonds (a crucial source of income for many members of the lower middle class); and to all public service subsidies, including those to the railroads. And as usual, those people who were already barely eking out a living were most adversely affected.

Because this reduced demand yet further, gross and retail prices fell some more. In theory, since French goods were far more expensive than those produced in the other advanced countries, this should have helped exports. Wheat fell some 50 percent that summer; but that was still not enough to compensate for the gross overvaluation of the franc, and so the Depression deepened dramatically. For the year 1935, tax revenues shrank to 39.4 billion; in 1930, they had been 65 billion. And, predictably, the deficit still soared, now to nearly 10.5 billion.

That Laval should have remained in power in a parliamentary democracy seems incredible. The Deputies, after all, knew how badly their constituents were hurt; but, in fact, the system was no longer functioning properly. In the first place, the power to promulgate decree-laws meant that Laval could legislate single-handedly, without the concurrence of either Chamber or Senate; then, in an unprecedented action, the parliamentary holiday, which normally lasted for some six weeks or two months, was vastly expanded and lasted nearly five months, from June 30 to November 28. There were two good reasons for this. Herriot, anxious to show that deflation was the only possible policy, had decided to give Laval every chance; and even those Radicals who disapproved of Laval realized there was no hope of a government of the Left before the elections. It was best, therefore, to give Laval all the rope he needed, and then run against him.

Of course, the conservatives were delighted. "The Laval government can now act," *Le Temps* crowed on June 9; "substantial cuts in spending . . . will create a sufficient psychological effect. . . . Deflation is in the interest of every citizen."[30] That was bad enough: not only was the vast majority of the French suffering, the slowdown of industrial activity meant that while Germany was busy rearming, the French industrial plant, already antiquated, was growing more inadequate still. To take just one striking example, by June 1936 the country was able to produce only six war planes a month, while Germany was building over a hundred of a newer and more effective model.

While Laval was entirely willing to see his compatriots suffer, he felt the tenderest sympathy for the dictators and was determined to do whatever would please Mussolini in order to gain his alliance. Of course, there was a rationale: because he was so good at bargaining in the back rooms of the Chamber, Laval felt quite sure he could outnegotiate anyone and get the best of any accord. What he had yet to discover was that international relations can be a hard and dangerous game. As it was, he was brimming with confidence when he received the eminent journalist Geneviève Tabouis.

"In the majestic and simple setting of the foreign minister's office, how disconcerting is the aspect of the new minister, Pierre Laval!" she noted. "Small, very dark, almost Armenian looking, the eyes evasive and moving constantly, he spoke in the purest slang. . . . 'Well, look,' said Laval, 'when you live in a house and you are quarreling a little with all the tenants, it is with your closest neighbors you begin to make peace. . . . I myself have common sense, so I know that we must begin by settling with Germany and Italy."[31] There can be no doubt that he really meant it.

When on March 16, 1935, Hitler had announced that he would no longer be bound by the clauses of the Versailles Treaty that forbade Germany to rearm, Flandin had sent Laval, his foreign minister, to Moscow. The reasoning was simple: since Hitler was as great a threat to the Soviet Union as he was to France, the two countries should cooperate militarily, just as they had in the time of the czars. Stalin, at that point, was willing. He promptly declared that he understood and fully approved the French national defense policy; treaty negotiations were soon completed; but rather than upset Germany, Laval simply held back from presenting the draft treaty to Parliament — something Stalin would remember four years later.

As for Mussolini, Laval was convinced he could outsmart him every time, and that he had done so when he visited him in Rome that summer. Indeed, he frequently boasted of it. Pierre Lazareff of *Paris-Soir*, the most widely read of the Paris papers, knew all about that:

> Pierre Laval told me: "I said to Mussolini: 'My dear friend, we are here because we can reach an agreement. Unfortunately, I am not nearly as free as you are. You can make decisions by yourself; but the Council of Ministers, which authorized me to come, has put a limit to the concessions I can make. And I have here, in my pocket, a little piece of paper which does not allow me to offer you much. If I were to do more, my government would disavow me." Since Mussolini wanted an agreement, he was forced to give in to me, believing as he did that I could not do more. But in fact . . . my colleagues had given me full freedom to decide. You must admit that the story of the little piece of paper, which I had actually scribbled myself in the train, was quite a find!"[32]

It certainly makes for a good story; but in fact, Laval had invented the whole thing in order to make himself look good; and it was Mussolini, not Laval, to whom the key concession was made.

Lazareff, who had his own excellent sources, knew it. What had really happened was that when Mussolini asked the French Premier: "If Italy were to do to Ethiopia what France did to Morocco, what would you do?" (Morocco was then a French protectorate), Laval answered: "I will see to it that we watch silently or put forth a purely formal protest. We are not going to quarrel about that."[33] There are other versions of the same conversation in which Laval is represented as shrugging eloquently; at any rate, what is certain is that he made it clear that France was perfectly willing to let the Duce invade Ethiopia.

When the Italian invasion of Ethiopia actually began on October 3, Laval was understandably not surprised, and even less indignant. That one member of the League of Nations should, without provocation, invade another bothered him not at all. What did annoy him was that neither his colleagues in the cabinet nor French public opinion would allow him openly to support Mussolini. Instead, he did exactly what he had said he would do: he protested weakly and opposed the imposition of sanctions against Italy.

That was going too far: the League, with eventual French concurrence, voted to impose sanctions, but they were too weak to be effective, and a petroleum embargo, which would have brought the Italian war machine to a halt, was carefully avoided. Even so, the French Right, ever in love with Mussolini, was outraged. In *Je Suis Partout,* Gaxotte denounced "the aggression of the League against Italy [*sic*]" and "the tyranny of international [read Jewish] finance."[34] For Maurras, things were even simpler. He announced that those who backed the imposition of sanctions "must have their heads chopped off. Since ordinary good citizens do not have the use of the guillotine . . . we must tell them: you must have somewhere a gun, a revolver, or even a kitchen knife. That weapon, whatever it may be, must be used against the murderers of peace whose names you know."[35]

This was no figure of speech: Maurras really hoped that the men he hated, Blum first and foremost, would be assassinated — and, as noted in Chapter One, Blum very nearly was. Still, *L'Action française,* the Fascists, and the rest of the Right needed a rationale: after all, they stood for ultranationalism, which was hard to conciliate with a series of surrenders to the dictators; so they played on the widespread horror of war and explained that they were merely trying to save the peace while the Left, on the other hand, was composed of murderous "bellicists" who wanted to declare war on Hitler and Mussolini for purely political party reasons. It was an ingenious twist, and it deceived quite a few people. Their real reason, however, was not quite so altruistic: they hoped that fascism would prove contagious, and that strong and successful dictatorships abroad would make it easier for them to create a similar regime in France itself.

In the real world, Laval was busy trying to help Mussolini. As it happened, the British, who cared far more about Ethiopia than the French, had a foreign secretary, Sir Samuel Hoare, whose moral standards were on a par with Laval's; and when, on December 7, the two men came up with a peace plan, it not surprisingly gave Italy most of what it wanted. The sanctions were to be lifted; Italy was to be given two-thirds of the Ethiopian territory and allowed to send colonizers into the remaining third; and to make it look better, Haile Selassie was to continue ruling the rump of his empire.

This was too much for the British Parliament. When the accord became known, Hoare was forced to resign and George V, not a notably witty monarch, made the best *mot* of his life: "No more coals to Newcastle," he said, "no more Hoares to Paris!" The plan itself was rejected by both Italy and Ethiopia; but even so, Laval's foreign policy was debated in the Chamber on December 27, and the attack against him was led by Yvon Delbos, the brilliant young left-wing Radical, who unhesitatingly went to the root of the matter.

"By not discouraging Mr. Mussolini, you were encouraging him," he told Laval in a speech in the Chamber, "and you encouraged him further by allowing him to hope that the sanctions would be virtually nonexistent. . . . You did not even get the results you wanted from Italy; all Mr. Mussolini saw in your project was a sign of weakness which made him more intransigent still. . . . You have displeased everyone without even pleasing Italy."[36]

Delbos was right, of course: by kowtowing to Mussolini, Laval had gained nothing. It was left to Léon Blum, that same day, to draw the moral lesson. "Sir Samuel Hoare," he said, "has resigned. He has been replaced as foreign secretary by the man who had most determinedly opposed your accord, by Mr. Eden. As for the disgust of international opinion . . . it is Sir Samuel Hoare who has expressed it the most forcefully: 'Our proposals,' he told the Commons, 'have the whole world against them.'

"We separated [for the Christmas recess] ten days ago. We meet again. And of all that existed still ten days ago, there is nothing left but dust and ruin. No, I am wrong: you are left."[37] The next day Blum was more devastating still because he was more personal. "You have proceeded in the great affairs of the world as we have seen you proceed in your own little business. You have tried to give and keep back. You have canceled your words by your actions and your actions by your words. You have corrupted everything by combinations, intrigues and second-rate cleverness. You have brought everything down to the scale of your own small talents."[38] It was a strong but entirely justified indictment.

Surprisingly, Laval survived the debate by 296 to 276 votes; but it was clear that his authority had been badly shaken. As for his future, it hardly looked encouraging: 93 Radicals had voted against him and only 37, led by a personal friend, Chichery, for. Even more important, Herriot was beginning to have serious doubts.

Herriot's misgivings were genuine. For all his shortcomings, he was, in his idiosyncratic way, a patriot — especially when he realized that the policy he opposed was rejected by most of his fellow Radicals. There, in fact, lay the nub of the problem. For Herriot personally, the post-February governments had been ideal: as minister of state, he had had power without responsibility; he was comfortable with the conservative policies of Doumergue, Flandin, and Laval; and he thoroughly approved of the deflation they practiced, if only to prove that he had been right to proceed that way himself. The Radicals, however, were moving in a completely different direction.

By July, they had agreed to join the unity demonstration. All through the fall, they were negotiating with the Socialists and Communists so as to become part of the Popular Front. For many Radicals it was a matter of conviction and conscience. As Daladier told the Radical convention in October: "Some believe there is a Fascist peril, others don't. For myself, I believe there is. We are witnessing the methodical preparation for a civil war. The *ligues* must be dissolved."[39] Of course, Daladier, who had always stood for an alliance with the Socialists, knew that this time it would bring him back to the presidency of the party. In October Herriot's prestige still prevailed and he was reelected; in December the government's policies were so hated by most of the party that he felt compelled to resign. And to no one's surprise, Daladier was his successor. That happened on January 20, 1936. Four days later, Herriot, who realized that he was about to be rejected by his own party, resigned from the cabinet, taking the other Radical ministers with him.

It was more than Laval could survive. The government fell, and was replaced by a Radical-led successor under the ineffable Albert Sarraut. This was the cabinet whose only job, it thought, was to prepare for the

May elections. It turned out to be the cabinet that watched passively as Hitler remilitarized the Rhineland.

Throughout the country, there was a sense that France itself was out of whack, that, somehow, it had ceased functioning. Perhaps a song told it all.

The hit of the season, it was hummed by dukes and porters alike; it was played constantly on the radio and trilled in every night club. "*Tout va très bien, Madame la Marquise*" (All is just fine, Madame la Marquise) began, innoculously, with a call to the marquise from her factotum in the country: All is just fine, the good man explains, except that a cow has died — but otherwise all is just fine, just fine, just fine. Well, he goes on, the cow has died because the stable has had a little accident; but all is just fine. And as the song progresses, the incident turns out to be a fire, which was caused, it finally turns out, by the fire that leveled the castle itself; but all is just fine, Madame la Marquise. In a Europe soon to be ravaged by its own fire, in a country where the do-nothing Sarraut government sold the future for a moment of peace, it was an appropriate song. It was also one people remembered in the years to come.

# THE PEOPLE'S TRIUMPH

THE PARISIANS in May 1936 had good reason to wonder. Their usually busy city was both amazingly quiet — almost everyone was on strike — and amazingly animated — many of the strikers were camping out on the streets. Even more unusual, the widespread strikes were a sign of jubilation. The Popular Front had won the legislative elections, change had become possible, and the working class was making sure it would not be cheated at the last moment.

This extraordinary spectacle, in which exultation and the demand for reforms came together, marked a radical change of mood for the Parisians and, indeed, for the rest of the French. Just a few weeks before, it seemed as if the political system had stopped working; the reinstallation of right-wing governments after the Sixth of February and their instability had proved it clearly. As for the Radicals, who were the traditional alternative to the Right, they, too, from 1932 to 1934, had shown their inability to govern. Few men were more generally loathed than

Laval; but the voters were not about to give Herriot another go at the premiership.

Together with this political collapse went the steady deepening of the Depression. The country, which had been so prosperous in 1930, had now sunk to an almost unbearable level of misery. Unemployment, already so widespread, was growing; more businesses were closing every month; and even those workers who still had (sometimes part-time) jobs were so underpaid as to have trouble surviving.

Then, as if that were not all bad enough, there was the state of Europe. Hitler had just remilitarized the Rhineland and was making ever more hostile speeches. Mussolini, still trying to swallow Ethiopia, was an open enemy. Fascism, it seemed, might well be the way of the future, and might even take over in France. Even if the Sixth of February had failed, who could tell how the next attempt might turn out?

Given all these failures, the electorate might well have lost interest. Instead, as the legislative elections neared, a new mood swept the country. A compound of hope, pride, and fierce resentment, it was visible everywhere: in Paris, too, there were Popular Front rallies and marches. The intellectuals (at least those who belonged to the Left) were mobilized, and so was a vast array of well-known figures from painters to scientists, from politicians to union leaders. Even women took part in many of the rallies, and, for the first time in memory, the entire Left — Communists, Socialists, together with several smaller parties and even the Radicals, now led by Daladier — had come together. In a Europe that was rapidly becoming a congeries of dictatorships, France would lead the way to an economic and democratic revival. And so, amazingly, instead of being sullen and depressed, many of the French, many Parisians, were exultant.

Naturally, that went together with a good deal of hostility targeted not just at the Fascists but also at the traditional Right. There was, in fact, something like a prerevolutionary mood. It seemed just remotely possible that the elections might result not merely in a new majority in the Chamber of Deputies but in reforms so radical that they would change the face of society.

That was more than enough to alarm many members of the Tout-Paris, but while the right-wing press and politicians ceaselessly denounced the coming upheaval and urged the French to vote for permanence and the status quo, society felt it was more elegant to ignore the situation. The result was that the spring parties were as numerous and as lavish as ever — all on the now well-established principle that if you ignored the current unpleasantnesses long enough, they would go away. Thus, it seemed perfectly normal that the marquise Casati decided to give a splendid ball, and her elegant guests all flocked to her house in the accustomed manner.

The marquise Casati had, in her time, been a great beauty; that was before and just after the war. In 1936 she was still a great eccentric. She had always worn strange, spectacular dresses, and was given to collecting dangerous pets — leopards were among her favorites. Her habits were no less unconventional: half-recluse, half-socialite, she had always given spectacular parties that had contributed to the shrinking of her fortune. Now she decided it was time for a costume ball; the theme was famous couples; the Tout-Paris was invited; and although they wondered how she would pay for it, everyone came.

The venue of the party was as peculiar as the hostess herself. The marquise had rented the pink marble pavilion built at the turn of the century by Robert de Montesquiou; only, since then, the suburb he had chosen, Le Vésinet, had become lower middle and working class; and the ball was to take place just after the elections in which the Popular Front triumphed, not the best time at which to give a spectacular and lavish party in that particular place.

Naturally, the Faucigny-Lucinges were there.

From the very beginning [the prince remembered] everything went wrong. Neither the hostess nor the orchestra seemed to be present. The guests wandered through the garden, watched by a mocking and hostile crowd perched on the property's low walls (and, worse luck, the adjoining road was heavily trafficked). Having decided to behave as if all were normal, we ambled about, waiting for God knows what, and, suddenly, there was an incident. Servants came, in a panic, with accounts of a new Varennes: in her eighteenth-century carriage, Marie Antoinette (Daisy de Segonzac), accompanied by the comte d'Artois (the handsome Meyer, the revue star), had missed the gate because her horse had turned too sharply. Our brightly costumed little group rushed forward to bring in the "Queen" and her "brother-in-law" under the jeers of the local sans-culottes. It was all getting to be a little too realistic.

In the meantime, the marquise, furious that the musicians [who were no doubt on strike] had not come, worried by the noises from the outside, displeased with her costume (she was to receive as "Eve escorted by Adam and the Snake"), had locked herself in her bedroom.

Obviously, there would be no ball. But how were we to retreat with dignity? We had to go back to our cars and that meant facing the *demos* on the road wearing absurd and anachronistic costumes. At that moment there was a miracle: the rain, which had been a drizzle, became a deluge. . . . Thus ended the last party given by the marquise Casati; the next morning, the bailiffs sent by her creditors took over.[1]

Coming just after the triumph of the Popular Front, the marquise's ball was all too emblematic, down to the incident in which "Marie Antoinette" had been hissed. It seemed as if this might, indeed, be the beginning of a new revolution — not a pleasant prospect for people whose major preoccupation was the costume they would wear at the next ball. Still, even if the evening had been spoiled, no one was hurt. Distractions were needed as always, and so the fun continued.

There was, for instance, a competition for the most beautiful Amazon, in which ladies rode sidesaddle. That took place as usual on the polo field at Bagatelle; and elsewhere, in the Bois de Boulogne, there were the usual displays of automobile elegance, to which that year was added a new competition for the best-dressed woman with the best-bred dog. As for fashion itself, it was as important as ever. In 1935, the seasonal flood of Americans had already resumed, greatly to the benefit of the couture; and in 1936, the emphasis was once again on really dressy outfits — for the evening in Paris, aboard ship, at a resort, at a château. As usual, Schiaparelli led the way — all the more easily since she was alone among the couture houses in not having a strike; the personnel, of whom she had taken such good care, who had been paid the highest wages, whose medical care was largely free, felt they had no reason to complain. All through the turmoil in May and June the seamstresses were as busy as ever.

What they made was, of course, also as chic as ever. There was the long dress for the country, for instance, embroidered in white and yellow squares on pink organdy, with short puffy sleeves, a lozenge-shaped decolletage, and a striped green, pink, and white leather belt — not something you would wear when bringing in the crops. As always, Schiap also designed dresses for very specific occasions, so there was a gown for an evening at the Casino that was made of pink striped muslin, with wide sleeves, an almost crinolinelike skirt, and a train of pink tulle; and it came with a bolero for when its wearer chose to be less decolleté. All that was perhaps normal, if very stylish; but this was also the time when Schiap began to work with Dalí. By then the Surrealist painter already had his eye firmly fixed on fortune and success, and designing for Schiap struck him as a move highly likely to advance his career. Altogether, it was a happy collaboration: Schiap got the touch of wild fantasy she liked, and Dalí came up with a number of amusing ideas. In 1936 he and Schiap designed a black suit whose lines were very simple, but whose many pockets were trompe-l'oeil drawers with handles in black bone.

Current events, in fact, were simply not allowed to interfere with the glittering life of the Tout-Paris, at least until the widespread strikes of the early summer; but before that, the remilitarization of the Rhineland and France's failure to stand up to Hitler apparently made no difference at all. Writing at the end of May, Genêt described a serenely unchanged atmosphere. "The first weeks of the 1936 Season's Grandes Fêtes de Paris were auspicious; sun and sport were fun and fine," she reported.[2]

If you read Genêt's reports selectively that year, you might have thought that nothing really unusual was happening. Of course, in July she noted that the July Fourteenth celebrations were "going to be reinforced by monster Communist and Socialist meetings in favor of the League of Nations and application of sanctions against Italy, which seemed to be the proletariat's idea of a special good time," but then she went on in a far more normal vein: "At the théâtre du Chatelet, ten free performances of Romain Rolland's revolutionary piece, *Quatorze Juillet,* will start, with décors by Picasso and music by Darius Milhaud and Albert Roussel of the Opéra," and continued: "A great new modern theater trio has suddenly appeared at the Athénée in the form of Louis Jouvet, Christian Bérard, and Jean-Baptiste Molière. *L'Ecole des femmes* is the best Molière we've seen. Jouvet's silent, equine laughter, his coarse agony make a man, not a monkey of the character of Arnolphe. Bérard's costumes play not only a visual but almost an audible role on the stage; his set, with its tower, arcade, and mechanical garden lodge, whose walls open (to music by Rieti) to form a rose garden and, above all, his red velvet candelabra, suspended like a parlor constellation, set a new date in French stage decoration."[3]

Nothing much happened during August — it never did in Paris — and in September, the life of the city was proceeding along its usual lines. Still, in Genêt's report, there were hints that something unusual had happened in May and June. "Paris is having its spring and summer season in September," she wrote, but having thus reminded her readers that June and July had not been quite normal, she went on blithely: "Luncheon tables at Maxim's and the Ritz are as crowded as they should have been last May. Also there is a new Rue de la Paix champagne bar, called the Bar Edward VIII, which seems a mistake since that monarch is one for whiskey. Otherwise, the place and idea are the height of logic. Here, daily, five different brands, chosen by rotation from among the twenty best known ones, are obtainable by the glass, for from five francs per, on up to eight, for a beaker of heavy sparkling Krug."[4]

That was in September. Obviously, there had been no revolution; but, beginning in late May, Paris had for nearly two months offered a very unusual spectacle: not only were most of its workers on strike, they filled the streets and behaved with a kind of good humor that took nothing away from the force of their demands. In May, the Popular Front won the elections and the working class wanted to make sure it would enjoy the fruits of its victory.

Depending on your point of view, you could either be struck by the cheerfulness that was so visible a feature of the situation, or, especially if you belonged to the group of reactionary industrialists against whom the exercise was directed, you could be convinced that ruin was awaiting you. Panic, in fact, was characteristic of precisely those people who had, all their lives, shown the most withering contempt for those less rich than themselves. Genêt, on the other hand, was a foreigner and very far from rich. She also had no ax to grind, and her account of the events — or, at any rate what she saw of them — is worth reading.

The strikes to which she refers began spontaneously when the election results were published; they continued until the new government headed by Léon Blum — as leader of the largest group in the new Chamber — took office; they persisted while the new Premier negotiated an accord between the unions and the employers that ended some of the worst injustices from which the workers had suffered; and they were over, for the most part, well before the end of June. As for what they were trying to achieve, it was simple enough. The workers wanted decent working hours (forty a week), a week's paid holiday in the summer, decent working conditions, and wages such that they could rise above absolute poverty.

It was not that the workers mistrusted Léon Blum, the Premier-designate; but even with a Popular Front majority in the Chamber, they did not believe that the employers would give in; so they decided to strengthen the new government by showing the employers that even the lowest of their employees was no longer powerless. Unlike other widespread strikes, in fact, these were not really political: the workers made practical demands, they did not try to change the system.

Even so, the period was a watershed: the working class realized it need not forever be at the mercy of the most reactionary industrialists in Europe. The industrialists thought they saw the shadow of the guillotine, and, in their terror, begged Blum to save them. As for Janet Flanner, she just went for a walk in the streets of Paris, and what she saw was anything but frightening:

If the French Government had been as well run in the last seventeen years as the strikes in the past seventeen days were, there probably wouldn't have been any strikes. . . . For months Paris has existed clamorously on little business; for a week it has lived quietly on none. A connoisseur of strikes now, the city discovered which it liked least — that of the journal-deliverers. Apparently what nourishes a famished populace most is news. Especially if the populace has laid in a stock of noodles, lentils, sardines, rice, potatoes, sugar, flour, and cheese first, as Parisians had. During the two days on which no papers appeared . . . the only news was that given hourly over the government radio station, PTT. Blum's noon speech calling on the country to be legal where it could, and where it couldn't, to be calm, was repeated by a gramophone record over the air at intervals until midnight. It was on these two days that Paris was nervous, that many foreigners and numerous rich French left France. Those who stayed in town saw odd sights: the Renault automobile factory . . . with thirty thousand strikers and their red flags parading behind the great locked gates; the babies brought by *mamans* to the barricaded doors of the Printemps department store to throw kisses to Papas who had been sleeping for a week on the bargain tables; the salesgirls in the sunny doorways of the Monoprix, embroidering themselves pretty new underwear. Strikers everywhere wisely organized amateur theatricals, dances, and games. Striking musicians gave the Galeries Lafayette strikers an orchestral concert in the glove department. . . . The most publicized of the strikers . . . were the cement workers of the Carrousel Bridge [opposite the Louvre] who had their stay-in strike out of doors on the *quai* where they slept, cooked, and gave a vaudeville show from breakfast to midnight to audiences lined up on the bridge. The strikers installed a stage with a spotlight, a fox terrier, a radio, one black-and-white plaid parasol, one broken opera hat, and one skillet of flour for their clown, placarded as Tonio, the funniest striker in Paris."[5]

Less than a revolution, more than just a labor incident, the strikes were both the expression of long-endured frustrations and the spontaneous empowerment of a hitherto powerless working class. There was no question of taking over the government: that had already been done, in the most legal way possible, by the elections, which took place, in two rounds as usual, on April 26 and May 3. The result was a sea change in the membership of the Chamber of Deputies.

Overall, the Center and Right received 43.85 percent of the vote to the Left's 56.14 — a very large majority in terms of the usual percentages, and one made larger still by the Popular Front alliances in the second round. That, in fact, was the second major innovation. The Radicals, led now by Daladier, had joined the Socialists and the Communists. On July 14, 1935, the heads of the three parties, Blum, Maurice Thorez, and Daladier, led a march of several hundred thousand men and women; upon which, together with ten thousand delegates gathered in the Buffalo Stadium, they took a great oath to remain united and carry through the needed reforms.

It was a noble undertaking. Ten months later, it bore electoral fruit that changed the face of French politics. For the first time ever, the Socialists received more votes than the Radicals — 20.68 versus 20.25 percent. The Communists passed the 10 percent limit, rising to 15.21 percent. And in the Chamber, the Popular Front could rely on the widest, most solid majority of the century. Starting on the Left, the Communists elected 72 Deputies, a gain of 60. The Socialists now had 147 (instead of 129), while the Radicals, saved by their joining the Front, but still unpopular because of their role in the 1932 legislature, emerged with 106 seats (down from 157). Added to the three major parties were 51 members of the left-leaning Union socialiste républicaine and of the Socialistes indépendants, for a total of 376 Deputies. The Center and Right parties, taken together, were left with only 222 seats, which gave the Popular Front a majority of 154.

The horror with which the Right greeted these results is indescribable. For Maurras and the Fascist Right, their defeat was made all the more stinging by the fact that Blum was Jewish. On April 9, Maurras, who saw what was coming, had written in *L'Action française:* "Blum, that German Jew, naturalized or son of a naturalized immigrant [the Blum family had been French for centuries], must not be treated like a normal person. He is a monster produced by the democratic Republic, human garbage and must be treated as such. . . . He should be shot, but in the back."[6] It was a sentiment with which people like Brasillach and Céline wholeheartedly concurred.

On June 1, five days before Blum took office, but at a time when it was already known that he would, *L'Action française* took anti-Semitism yet a step further, and in doing so reflected the opinion of a significant proportion of the Right: "Thanks to Blum," Daudet wrote, "the Talmud will be the law of the new Chamber. . . . All its reflexes will be specifically Semitic, from that of hatred to that of fear,"[7] while four days later Maurras simply claimed that the government born of the recent and free elections was un-French: "The Jewish cabinet is in office . . . and it poses the question of the nation. This is a debate between those who belong to the nation and those who are against it. . . . All resistance and counterattacks, now so necessary, will be effective only if we dare to attack the Jews."[8] It was, of course, easier to rely on anti-Semitism, especially when Hitler was doing the same, than to blame the millions who had voted for the Popular Front.

All this bigotry and all this venom were surprisingly effective among the upper middle classes and some sections of society; they were, however, rightly seen as sick and grotesque by most of the population. As for Blum himself, he had nothing but contempt for Maurras and the other anti-Semites. More, he seemed practically made to measure to reassure those who felt some apprehension at the idea of that unprecedented occurrence in French history, a Socialist government.

From the day the election results were known, Blum made it plain, in any event, that it would be a Socialist-led coalition cabinet that would assume power a month later, not a Socialist government. "There is no proletarian majority," he told a Socialist convention on May 31, "there is a Popular Front majority with a specific [and very moderate] program. We will be in power, but we have not conquered it, and we will not have it alone."[9] As it turned out, the Communists, refusing to enter the cabinet, gave Blum a taste of that "support without participation" which he had so often inflicted on Radical governments; so he was left with the Radicals and the smaller left-wing parties.

Still, although this was not a purely Socialist government, there could be no doubt in June 1936 that Blum was its dominating personality, the man whom the working classes trusted and to whom the propertied classes turned in the — justified — hope that he would save them. It was, in fact, a situation not unlike that of Franklin Roosevelt in March and April 1933: it was, it seemed, either him or bloody chaos.

Blum was, of course, a well-known figure. Still, all manner of people now looked at him with new interest, and most were enormously impressed by what they saw, unless, of course, they were either reactionaries or anti-Semites. This was in part because to a degree almost too great for a public man, Blum was so transparently honest. In a milieu where self-praise was the norm, the Socialist leader, while claiming the premiership as the head of the largest group in the Chamber, also promptly announced he was not sure he could do the job. "In these new circumstances, a new man [within myself] must come forth," he told the party's National Committee. "I do not know whether I have the qualities needed by the leader of so difficult a struggle. . . . It is a test. . . . I must impose on myself. But I will never lack resolution, courage, and faithfulness."[10]

He was, as so often, quite right. Together with a dazzling intelligence, courage, moral and physical, was one of his chief characteristics, as was his utter lack of personal resentment at attacks that might have driven other men mad. All this was a subject of frequent description. Blum, in fact, was the main topic of the day; and the comments were extraordinarily favorable. Even so disinterested an observer as Genêt immediately took to him. Blum, she wrote, "was author of a book on Goethe, and another on Stendhal, which infuriated Beylists; can recite Victor Hugo's verse by heart, also good kitchen recipes; loves Ravel's music; buys modern paintings; and adores cats, flowers, and fine *objets d'art,* with all three of which his beautiful apartment in a beautiful eighteenth-century mansion on the Quai Bourbon is always full. He has an odd gait, since he turns his toes far out; he wears spats and thick spectacles, is myopic and absent-minded. . . . His mind is subtle and dialectic; his speeches are lucid, fluid, and delivered in a flutelike tone."[11] Perhaps because she was so impressed by the man, Genêt overpraises the apartment. A cooler-headed observer described it more accurately: "Blum," wrote Pierre Lazareff, "lives in an old building on the Left Bank opposite Notre Dame and from his windows there is a superb view of the Ile de la Cité. . . . The appartment is tastefully, but not luxuriously furnished, it is comfortable, very pretty but small. There is nothing formal. . . . There are some fine books on his shelves . . . others, which have just been read, are scattered on his desk."[12] It was, in fact, the residence of an intellectual, but not that of a rich man.

There were very few leading politicians who were capable of not using their office to make a good deal of money — Herriot was one, but he and Blum were almost alone. There were even fewer with Blum's intelligence or his culture; but that did not make him feel superior. Different as he was from men like Chautemps and Daladier, he felt nothing for them but friendship. There were very few of his colleagues whom he despised — although Laval was one — and so he was quite ready to work with the Radical members of the government. More than anything, though, he was reasonable: while firmly intent on carrying out his promises to the voters, he understood that the circumstances limited his possibilities; at the same time he believed so deeply in the supremacy of reason, and in the ability of even the most uneducated to respond to it, that he refused ever to talk down to his audiences. People noticed with amazement that he addressed workers as if they had been members of Parliament or intellectuals. More amazingly still, the workers listened and understood.

They also trusted him. Unlike most politicians, Blum actually did what he had said he would do. It therefore should have surprised no one that, as soon as he was in office, he brought the Chamber bills he had promised his electors. Within a few days the amazed Genêt commented: "Ten minutes after he took office as Premier, he began fulfilling his election promises; in an hour, he had fulfilled the major four. His statements have been clear. When he told his Socialist striking friends to get back on the job, he was just as precise as when he told the opposition to get down to brass tacks. In debate, he corrected ex-Finance Minister Reynaud for attributing to La Rochefoucauld a literary citation which belonged to La Bruyère."[13]

It is no wonder that Blum and Reynaud were friends although they belonged to opposite ends of the political spectrum. That, of course, never prevented Reynaud from attacking Blum's positions or vice versa. Sometimes, the criticism was what might be expected as between the Right and the Left. At other times, Reynaud understood the situation more clearly than Blum. When it came to disarmament, for instance, Reynaud saw right through the illusions that Blum, who remained basically a pacifist, mistook for reality.

It had always been a dogma of the Socialist party that war was wrong: one of the verses of the "Internationale" spoke of "turning our guns on our own generals"; but, in 1914, the Socialists had promptly joined the rest of the French in standing united against German aggression. Once the war was over, though, they returned to their earlier stance and made universal disarmament one of their key demands. In the twenties, this could be held to make sense. After Hitler became Chancellor and started to rearm, it was a different proposition. Even then, Blum refused to admit that disarmament was a lost cause because Hitler would give up neither his army nor his plans for a greater Germany.

Today, that seems like willful blindness. We know just what Hitler had in mind, we remember what he proceeded to do; but in 1935 it was still possible to assume that Hitler was not as monstrous as he turned out to be. It was not that Blum thought that he should be appeased at the expense of smaller nations: simply, he could not bring himself to believe that there were people to whom war was an object of yearning, to whom violence was desirable. Hitler, he thought, would, if properly treated, turn out to be reasonable after all. He could not have been more wrong, of course, and Paul Reynaud, who understood the Nazis, pointed this out in the course of repeated speeches in the Chamber.

So, paradoxically, did the Communists. After fifteen years during which they attacked the army as a tool of the capitalists and kept demanding that France disarm unilaterally, they received new instructions from Moscow and changed their position. *L'Humanité,* the party's morning daily paper, made the reasons for this transformation entirely clear: the USSR was in danger, and it was up to France to help save it. Obviously Blum did not have the same reasons for supporting a French military expansion.

Nor did he understand how incredibly old-fashioned the French army had become. His notion, which always remained vague, was that if one day France were threatened by an aggressor, the country would rise en masse and defend itself; but also that if French policy were sufficiently enlightened, there would never be an aggressor. So it was that this brilliantly intelligent man utterly failed to see that the theories propounded by Paul Reynaud were, in fact, right, that Hitler was very likely to start a war, and that what was needed was an army abundantly provided with the newest weapons and led by officers who understood their use. By 1936, in fact, enthusiasm and mere numbers had become irrelevant.

Reynaud himself counted Major de Gaulle among his advisers. He had read the young man's book, *Vers l'armée de métier* (Toward the Professional Army), in which he argued that modern armament was qualitatively different from what had come before, that tanks made a new form of warfare possible, and that only tank corps would prove effective. De Gaulle went even further: he explained just how a tank corps could defeat an army that either lacked tanks or dispersed them. The book was read with much admiration in Germany by General Guderian, the founder of the *Panzer-Divisionen,* and by Hitler. In France, it was mocked by the General Staff and rejected by virtually everyone except Reynaud.

Blum, in particular, thought the idea appalling, not for reasons of military strategy, but because he saw the creation of elite forces as the first step toward a military coup. Writing about the selection necessary to choose the officers of a professional armored corps, he asked what seemed to him the key question: "Is it imprudent to expect that such a choice would include only a very small quantity of republican officers?"[14]

Throughout 1934 and 1935 the debate continued, and Reynaud earned himself a solid reputation as an eccentric: first, he had backed a devaluation, now he demanded an armored corps. "The German shock troops can engage in a lightning offensive," he warned the Chamber. "Are we so armed as to stop it? . . . If the attacked does not have reflexes as quick as those of the attacker, all is lost."[15] Reynaud was right: the collapse of the French army in 1940 proved it; but, in the meantime, he was derided by his fellow politicians and the military alike. Answering Reynaud's speech, General Maurin, the minister of war and one of the most incompetent men of his time, asked the Chamber: "How could anyone think that we might be considering an offensive when we have spent billions on a fortified barrier [the Maginot Line]? Or that we would be mad enough to go beyond our barrier to God knows what adventure?"[16] That the Maginot Line stopped at the Belgian border, that it failed to cover the Ardennes forest, General Maurin did not think worth mentioning. The official doctrine, warmly defended by Marshal Pétain, was that the Ardennes forest's terrain was such that no major army corps could get through it and therefore there was no need to prolong the Maginot Line all the way to the sea. And when Reynaud offered an amendment to the military budget creating a corps of six heavy armored divisions and one light armored division, the amendment was easily defeated.

Blum was no admirer of General Maurin, but, for his own reasons, he, too, opposed the creation of these elite divisions. Thus when he came into office, he found an army whose armaments had been allowed to become largely obsolete, the Maginot Line being the perennial answer to all problems. At the same time, Germany, whose armed forces were being rapidly rebuilt, displayed increasingly aggressive intentions. That, together with the widespread strikes, would have been enough to daunt any man. Instead, the inexperienced and untried premier set to his task as if he were the most seasoned — and most energetic — of statesmen.

The crisis Blum inherited was the result of four years of incompetent governments. The social explosion he faced when he came into office, on the other hand, was due to a peculiar feature of the French constitution: although a new Chamber had been elected, the outgoing Chamber sat for another month. Obviously, the old Chamber would not support a Socialist-led government; so for a month the increasingly terrified Albert Sarraut continued to dither as he watched events that he did not understand.

It is a measure of the fear felt by the conservatives that President Lebrun himself, that scrupulously constitutional head of state, tried his best to stop Blum from coming into office. Jules Moch, one of Blum's close aides, heard all about it. He wrote:

Albert Lebrun sent for Léon Blum . . . and told him: "I must call on you [to become Premier]. I will do so. But don't you think it would be best if you gave up being the head of the government? There have never been any Socialists in the cabinet.* Don't you think it will cause some strikes?"

Léon Blum, who told me about this soon afterward, added, smiling: "The President reminded me of a hen that has just hatched a duck's egg. I remained firm, and he gave up his idea."[17]

Where Lebrun and the rest of the Right made their mistake was in taking Blum for Lenin. No one, in fact, could have more scrupulously obeyed the law; no one was more anxious to reestablish order; but the difference between Blum and the Right was that Blum would not shoot workers down. And while, certainly, the strikers felt empowered because they knew that a Popular Front government would soon take office, there was nothing revolutionary about their strikes: they just wanted to be paid a little less poorly and treated a little better. It is characteristic of their attitude that although they most often occupied their factories, the strikers, far from damaging anything, usually cleaned and oiled the machines.

Still, by June 4, the last day of the Sarraut government, 4 million workers were on strike, and the leaders of the Socialists' left wing, who were not nearly as moderate as Blum, thought that perhaps they were on the edge of a revolution. "What millions of men and women demand," Marceau Pivert wrote in *Le Populaire,* "is a radical change of the political and economic situation, carried out in a brief period of time. . . . The masses are far more advanced than most people think. . . . All is possible, now, at top speed."[18]

Blum knew better than that. The voters had indeed demanded change, and Blum was determined to provide it; but there was no question of ending capitalism and private property, or even of amending the constitution. The changes had to remain within the framework of the established system. Thus it is typical that Blum's very first act when he took office was to list the improvements he planned to make and ask everyone to remain calm. That he did so on June 4, the very day the Sarraut government finally resigned, shows just how urgent the situation had come to seem.

Normally, there was a two- or three-day hiatus between cabinets, but Blum this time came to see Lebrun the moment Sarraut resigned, and he already had the list of his ministers in his pocket. The President then made

*In fact, two Socialists had joined the cabinet in August 1914.

him Premier, but the custom was that the new head of government would take no action until he had been voted in by the Chamber. In 1936 it all happened very differently.

After Blum had formally appointed his ministers of interior and labor, he wrote:

> M. Albert Lebrun asked me to remain with him and said to me: "The situation is terrible. When do you expect to go before the Chamber?"
>
> I answered, "On the day after tomorrow, Saturday; I do not see how I could do it any sooner."
>
> He then asked me: "You're going to wait until Saturday? Don't you see what is happening?"
>
> "How could I go any faster," I replied. "I still have to write the *déclaration ministérielle* [the speech in which a new Premier outlined his program], and I must then call a cabinet council [the ministers attended but not the President] and then a Council of Ministers [chaired by the President] to approve it. In any event, it would be physically impossible to call the Chamber into session tomorrow."
>
> M. Lebrun then answered: "The workers trust you. . . . Please talk to them by radio tomorrow. Tell them that the Parliament will be meeting, that you will ask it to vote quickly and without delay the laws they are asking for at the same time as a raise in salary. They will believe you, they trust you, and then this [strike] movement may stop."
>
> I did what the President asked me to do.[19]

It was unheard of. Ever since Doumergue's debacle, the succeeding premiers had known better than to address the country on the radio; but now it was the President himself who was begging; and so the French, many of them for the first time, heard those flutelike tones Genêt had described, and all, even the Right, agreed that it was a masterful performance. Indeed, in paralyzed Paris, where, under the warm June sun, people were strolling and talking to one another as they had not done in a very long time, the speech was the topic of the day, and the approval was universal.

"The government will meet the Chamber and the Senate tomorrow," Blum told the French. "Its program is that of the Popular Front. Among the bills which it will promptly bring before the Parliament . . . are: the forty-hour week; collective bargaining; yearly paid holidays, that is, the main reforms demanded by the workers.

"The government's action must, if it is to have effect, take place in an atmosphere of calm and safety. . . . Any panic, any confusion would merely serve the purposes of the enemies of the Popular Front. . . . The government therefore asks the workers to rely on the law . . . and the employers to look at the workers's demands in a spirit of large-minded fairness." [20]

In his appeal for calm and reason, Blum had the full support of his coalition partners. That might have been expected of the Radicals, who were quite apprehensive themselves. Far more surprising, the Communists also supported him because they were determined that the new government should succeed. Stalin, after all, was anxious to see anti-Fascist Popular Fronts established in as many European countries as possible, so the French Communists declined to use the strikes in an effort to overthrow the government. Already on June 4 they were calling for an end to the strikes. By June 11, Maurice Thorez, one of the party's leaders, was making speeches to the striking metal workers in which he harshly reproached them for disrupting the government's efforts, told them it was time for compromise, and added that one must know how to end a strike. Coming from a self-defined revolutionary party, this was little short of apostasy.

The Communists' moderation reassured no one on the Right, though: like a troop of bleating sheep, they rushed at Blum and begged him to save them. "At that moment," Blum remembered, "among the bourgeoisie and especially among employers, I was considered . . . a savior." [21]

It is easy to see why the employers were so terrified. In the area in and around Paris — by far the most visible, as always in France — the strike was virtually total. The strikers occupied the factories, which they could easily have destroyed had they chosen to do so; and no one knew whether they would demand the owners' expropriation. The normal method, bloody repression, was clearly no longer appropriate: there were simply too many strikers, and the industrialists themselves had begged Sarraut not to use force. No one, of course, thought that Blum would do so. Instead, the representatives of the Confédération Nationale du Patronat Français, the cross-industry association of owners, asked Blum to chair negotiations with the unions: the employers would raise the salaries across the board, the workers would then evacuate the factories.

That is just what happened. On June 7, Blum convened a conference at his official residence, the Hôtel Matignon. It included four representatives of the employers and six delegates from the unions, and, after Blum's opening speech, it was chaired by two of his ministers. This was the first meeting ever between the delegates of the owners and those of the Confédération Générale du Travail, the French equivalent of the AFL-CIO, and agreement was not easy. Soon, however, an accord was reached. The employers agreed to the immediate conclusion of collective bargaining contracts; they guaranteed the right of workers to belong to a union; they promised to end the policy of dismissal of employees in retaliation for union membership. That left salaries as the sticking point, and Blum was finally required to arbitrate: the increases were to range from 15 percent for the most underpaid to 7 percent for those that were relatively better off. At 12:30 A.M. on June 8 the accord was signed; and although the strikes did not end completely before the end of the month, by the twenty-sixth there were only 165,000 strikers left in the whole of France.

It was a remarkable achievement. It was also carried out in a remarkably short time. In his ministerial declaration to the Chamber, on June 6, Blum had announced that he would convene the conference; thirty-six hours later, it had met, done its work, and disbanded. Indeed, as Genêt noticed, speed and efficacy were two of the new government's principal characteristics. It all began with the way in which Blum modified the structure of his own office. Instead of taking on a ministry along with the premiership, as was normally done, he remained unburdened by departmental responsibility. He set up an Office of the Premier, which allowed him to oversee his ministers and govern effectively; and because the military needed modernizing so desperately, he created a brand-new ministry of national defense, regrouping the former ministries of the army, the navy, and the air force. The idea, of course, was that henceforth the procurement and strategic policies of the three services would be integrated so as to provide the country with a more effective defense.

Even so, Blum could do nothing without the Chamber and the Senate: the two houses had to pass all laws. It is a measure both of the urgency felt by the Deputies and Senators and of Blum's own ability to present them with fully worked-out bills that, within five days, three key measures were already on the statute book: the first legalized and enforced collective bargaining; the second reversed Laval's deflationary decree-laws; and the third, which gave every working man and woman two weeks' paid holiday a year, led to an explosion of joy throughout France. "I did not often leave my office while I was Premier," Blum recorded, "but when I did leave it, when I went through the Paris suburbs and I saw the roads full of jalopies, of motorcycles, of tandems, with working-class couples wearing matching sweaters which showed that the notion of free time gave birth, even for them, to a sort of natural and simple elegance, then I had the feeling . . . that I had, after all, brought a little blue sky . . . into their hard and obscure lives."[22] Blum was right. Beginning that summer of 1936, and continuing every year until the war, a brand-new phenomenon was seen in the countryside, in the mountains, on the beaches. Workers who had never before left their grimy industrial suburbs now were able to go away for two weeks and see what it was like to enjoy nature. Just as important, the government established a program through which wage-earners could get a 40 percent discount on train tickets — 60 percent if they took special slower trains — so that within the first three months over half a million such tickets had been sold. It made a huge, visible difference. Until then, holidays had been reserved for the bourgeoisie; now the lower classes were entitled to the same privilege. It was something no member of that generation ever forgot.

The new law was passed and promulgated on June 11. Two days later, another key bill became law: it limited the work week to forty hours and mandated higher pay (usually time and a quarter) for overtime. This had been one of the most basic of working-class demands. It was greeted by employers with rage. Sarcastically dubbed "the week of the two Sundays" by Paul Reynaud, the new work week aroused what can only be seen as irrational opposition, especially since, in spite of their outcry, the employers were not ruined by the new working schedules.

Blum had been in office only a week when the law was passed. Before the end of the month, he had changed the structure of the Bank of France so that it was no longer controlled by its two hundred largest shareholders, and was, within limits, responsible to the government; the last remaining *ligues* had been dissolved; children, who until then were required to attend school only until the age of twelve, were given another two years of compulsory education. By the middle of August, the trade in wheat, which had allowed for unrestrained speculation, was regulated; most armament factories were nationalized; a form of workmen's compensation came into being and a series of large-scale public works was ordered on which 20 billion francs were to be spent over three years as a way of fighting the Depression.

For the working class, and indeed, for much of the country, these achievements meant that hope had returned, that the people were once again in control of their government. For the upper classes, they were an unforgiveable injury to which was added the insult of actually seeing workers on the beaches from which they had heretofore been excluded. Simone Weil, a brilliant and selfless social critic, understood it well: "As for the young bourgeois," she wrote, "no harm had been done them, but they had been afraid, they had been humiliated by those they considered their inferiors and that, to them, was an unpardonable crime."[23]

Both emotions, the gratitude and the resentment, were clear to all. Another sharp-eyed observer, Pierre Mendès-France, who became Premier himself eighteen years later, saw them too. "The workers," he wrote, "have retained a moving and luminous memory of the Popular Front: for them, it marked the beginning of an emancipation, of a new life. For others, it was, perhaps, the time of a great fear, which led some of them to say then, 'Rather Hitler than Blum,'"; [24] and General Gamelin, soon to become chief of the General Staff and commander in time of war, noticed the same thing: "The crisis of May–June 1936 terrorized a great segment of the French bourgeoisie," he noted. "It made many of us lose sight of the dangers of Hitlerism and fascism." [25] When, in 1940, the French army collapsed before the Nazi onslaught, the Right was prompt to accuse the Popular Front government of unpreparedness; in fact, its own outrage at seeing a few of its privileges diminished was a far more significant cause of the debacle.

As if the Right had not already been furious enough, there was the all-important fact that Blum was Jewish. Of course, men like Paul Reynaud thought of anti-Semitism as a loathsome aberration, but there were many others, and the attacks on Blum as a Jew were ceaseless during his premiership. In the debate that followed Blum's ministerial declaration, it was a right-wing Deputy, Xavier Vallat, who said: "This old Gallo-Roman country will, for the first time, be governed by a Jew. . . . To govern France it is better to have someone whose origins, however modest, are tied to the bowels of our soil than a subtle student of the Talmud." [26] As for *L'Action française,* in the course of May and June, it averred that Blum's real name was Karfulkenstein (pure invention); that he had been born in Bessarabia (a lie; he was born in Paris); that he was a slave of Moscow; and it went on to refer to the hateful yid, to the man from the ghetto, to the idiot-Talmud cabinet, and so on ad nauseam. Sadly, many people in Paris read the paper, and they loved every word of it.

For the moment, though, they were a minority, and the government enjoyed an approval all the more widespread since the ever-reassuring Radicals were an important part of it, having slightly less than half of the ministries. The new ministers were not, however, the Radicals whose presence in conservative governments had been such a prominent feature of the last two years. Herriot himself, who knew when he was beaten, refused all Blum's offers and was elected to the essentially nonpolitical speakership of the Chamber. It was an ideal office for him: he lived in an eighteenth-century palace, was treated with all the respect due his function, and was spared those uncomfortable decisions he so disliked.

Daladier, on the other hand, enjoyed his hour of triumph. Head of the party, Vice-Premier, and minister of defense, he was the second most important man in the government. There were three Radical ministers of state — Chautemps was one: Blum liked and trusted him. And the foreign minister, Yvon Delbos, was a Radical as well, also a friend of Blum's, but chosen most probably because this charming and cultivated man, who had led the attack on the Hoare-Laval agreement, had very little independence: through him, Blum could count on controlling the ministry.

There were other young, reform-minded Radicals in the cabinet, though, and they were hard-working and effective. Jean Zay, who was charged with implementing the changes resulting from the change of the school-leaving age, was open-minded and brilliant; Pierre Cot, the air minister, under Daladier's oversight began the rebirth of his long-neglected force; and Marc Rucart, the justice minister, showed himself a man of principle and integrity.

Counterbalancing this, Blum had given the economic ministries mostly to fellow Socialists. Finance went to Vincent Auriol, who became President of the Republic eleven years later; a newly created ministry of the national economy, whose task was to fight the Depression, went to Charles Spinasse; public works was given to Jean Monnet, who after the war became the creator of the European Community. These were all honest, well-meaning men who understood, at least, that the only way to balance the budget was to bring back prosperity. Unfortunately, with the possible exception of Monnet, they had no idea how this should be done, nor did they have any grounding in modern economic principles; and so economics soon proved to be the government's greatest weakness.

All these appointments were routine, except for the presence of the Socialists and the new emphasis on the economy as opposed to the budget; but four other newly created secretaryships of state — a secretary of state was one grade below a minister — enraged the conservatives. The first was the secretaryship for leisure, which was entrusted to the Socialist Léo Lagrange. Now that the workers had annual holidays, it was important to create the appropriate structures — hotels, well-kept beaches, and the like — and Lagrange, who did a superb job in a brand-new field, became deservedly popular. To the Right, that was merely encouraging laziness, but the innovation was so successful that no amount of criticism made any difference.

Just as shocking in a country, unlike the United States and Great Britain, where women did not have the right to vote, was the appointment of three women as secretaries of state for education, scientific research (this was Irène Joliot-Curie, Marie Curie's daughter), and the protection of children. The Right greeted these appointments with hoots of derision and a spray of often obscene jokes: women, as everyone knew, were incapable of doing serious work. These gibes utterly failed to deter Blum, who was a firm believer in the equality of men and women.

With the sixty-four-year-old Premier fully in charge, with a solid majority backing him in the Chamber, the government inaugurated a new political era; the do-nothing Radical cabinets and their retrograde successors suddenly belonged to the dead past. Or so it seemed. Obviously, the cabinet depended on both Communist and Radical support in the Chamber. The first was assured unless orders to the contrary came from Moscow; the latter seemed equally firm for the moment; but there were soon indications that some Radicals thought that reform was an excellent thing only in relatively small doses. And at the defense ministry, there was the ever-ambitious Daladier.

For the moment at least, the new president of the Radical party was satisfied. He had thoroughly trounced Herriot and was running the party; he was given his favorite ministry and shown the greatest respect by Blum; but he had also once been Premier himself, and it seemed clear that he would want the job again one day. More, his ministry gave him enormous power as well as virtual immunity from political attack. By the summer of 1936, the danger from Germany was clear and present. As for the deplorable state of the French armed forces, although it was, of course, a state secret, it was well known to all competent people, among them the ad hoc parliamentary committees. As the man who was building up the country's defenses, therefore, Daladier could do no wrong; and the truth is that he worked hard and earnestly at his job. There was much to do: the General Staff (the French equivalent of our Joint Chiefs of Staff) asked for an additional credit of 9 billion francs to be spent exclusively on rearming. Daladier, with Blum's support, decided to raise that amount still further, to 14 billion, which in September was voted by the Chamber. This, obviously, was a huge amount in an overall budget of a little over 50 billion. As it turned out, it was, for the moment at least, too much: the armament factories were so few and so antiquated that it proved impossible to spend the full sum.

That Daladier perceived the need to rearm so as to resist future Nazi attacks is thus certain; in that sense, France was doing far better than

Great Britain. Unfortunately, the advantage of this early start was canceled by the massive imbecility of the French General Staff. Convinced that tanks were virtually useless, unable to believe that the air force could play a major role, fondly attached to obsolete concepts and weapons, its generals saw to it that the money was wasted — or rather, Daladier saw to it on their behalf. In a classic demonstration of what can happen to an ignorant but well-meaning minister faced by so-called professionals, Daladier made it his goal simply to implement the General Staff's requests. In 1933, when he was war minister, Lazareff had been rightly appalled by Daladier's lack of knowledge and understanding. And when Daladier became minister of defense on June 5, 1936, an office he retained until 1940, he knew nothing more. His job, he thought, was simply to give the generals what they wanted. That the generals might be wrong, that their notions might be out of date, if only because so many of them were in their late sixties or seventies, never once occurred to him. Of course, he had to answer, on a number of occasions, the much better-informed Paul Reynaud's attacks; he invariably did so by claiming that the professionals knew best, and that Reynaud was wrong because the generals said he was wrong. Of course, Reynaud himself was advised by a military man, Major de Gaulle: but what was a major compared to a whole bevy of generals?

All this in July and August 1936 was still hidden by the euphoria that had seized the country. By the time the Parisians — all of them — were getting ready to leave for their holidays, it seemed clear that the new government was a spectacular success. The national holiday on July 14, which Genêt described, took the form of nationwide rejoicings. Even so, Blum made it plain that peace, the peace which had for so long been one of his chief objects, was by no means assured. He hinted at this strongly in the speech he made that day.

Still, most everyone hoped for the best. Hitler might, after all, prove to be reasonable, peace might, in spite of everything, be maintained; and so the Popular Front's many supporters rejoiced in its success. As Blum pointed out in mid-August, the government had already fulfilled every one of the pledges made in the ministerial declaration nine weeks earlier. In a mere seventy-three days, 133 laws had been passed, and almost the entire electoral platform of the allied parties had become a reality. Moreover, Blum himself, who had so candidly expressed doubts about his capacity to lead, had dispelled them all.

His close collaborators, who until then had been accustomed to his unwavering good temper, were struck by the authority he had begun to radiate. "For all his tremendous willpower and his great tenacity," André

Blumel, his chief executive assistant, remembered, "he was not a man who made noise. He did not bang his fist on the table, he didn't need to. . . . When he had once taken a decision, no influence could change it."[27] This was confirmed by another one of his aides, who never knew, he said, a more immovable man once he had made up his mind. "He never would agree to do anything which went against the law or against his own rectitude," Charles-André Julien noted. "Léon Blum's scruples were such that I remember once when I was insisting on [the ardently right-wing governor of Tunisia] Peyrouton's recall," he answered typically: "I wrote a very strongly worded article against Peyrouton six months ago and I wonder to what extent I am unprejudiced.'"[28]

Both Blumel and Julien knew Blum from close up. Many of the French, who had merely seen his photo in the papers and heard his voice on the radio, understood that here, indeed, was a man of exceptional caliber; but then, that was because they paid attention to reality. The right-wing press, however, was wholly free as ever from that exacting standard, so it had no difficulty attacking Blum and the government. In June, it was Pierre Gaxotte who announced in *Je Suis Partout:* "M. Léon Blum is not governing. The result: the people despise him,"[29] upon which he went on to hope that France would follow the Italian and German examples. As for *Le Temps,* that voice of the great industrialists, it bemoaned repeatedly the "dictatorship of the proletariat,"[30] under which, it said, France was writhing. Clearly, it had mistaken France for the Soviet Union.

For much of the Tout-Paris *Le Temps* was right: for all it knew, servants would soon expect a full day off every week. The Tout-Paris was a small minority, though; for most Parisians, particularly those who lived in the poorer suburbs, the summer of 1936 was a sunny and glorious moment. Real holidays, the government's great reforms, the sense that the years of alienation were over, all combined to make people feel that after the years of despair, hope, motivated hope, was back. The voters had, after all, made a difference. They had elected a government that carried out its promises. Of course, the Depression was not over, but it surely soon would be. Without a revolution, without any serious conflict, the people had won democratically. Now they could relax; their future was in good hands.

# NINE

# A DISTANT DOOM

THE TRIUMPH at the polls of the Popular Front in May 1936 had kindled a great hope. Without wasting a moment, the Blum government had made good on it; and even if many problems remained urgent, they were less conspicuous than the ones that had been solved. Few people (Reynaud was an exception) in Paris understood just why it was a bad mistake not to devalue the franc in June, for instance; even fewer knew just how backward, how slow, how inefficient the armament and aircraft factories had become. What everyone except the hard Right acknowledged, though, was that in June Blum had spared France grave civil disorders while greatly improving the lot of the working class. Of course, the Depression was not over — but some of its effects were masked by the crowds going off on their first summer holidays ever. Hitler still loomed menacingly across the Rhine — but many people hoped that Blum's transparent decency and sincerity combined with his love of peace would convince even the Führer to come to some sort of agreement. For a moment, in fact, even the prospect of a future, unavoidable war seemed to recede.

It was in this cheerful atmosphere that in mid-July the news came from Spain: fascism, spreading across the Mediterranean, was at work again in the form of a military pronunciamento led by Francisco Franco, a little-known general. In very short order it became clear that Franco was backed by Hitler and Mussolini. The Soviet Union, inefficiently at first, tried to help the Republican side. The question was now whether France, ruled by a Popular Front cabinet, would come to the help of the legitimate, Popular Front government of Spain. And both during the original suspense, and much more when Blum announced that France would remain neutral, it became clear that very little had changed: a future war was even more probable than before. The great burst of joy of the early summer had lasted a bare two months. Now it was back to the daily expectation of bad news.

That, however, served only to intensify the search for pleasure that all visitors to Paris noticed. As political tensions grew, as Germany began its relentless expansion, thinking about the exaggerations of the latest fashion provided a welcome relief. In a world that feared its approaching end, life was being made as brilliant as possible — partly, of course, as a distraction but also, more profoundly, as part of that instinct great civilizations seem to carry within themselves: often, they are never more dazzling than when they see they are in the gravest danger. For the Tout-Paris during these years the inventive costumes to be seen at a wide variety of entertainments were proof that France remained what it had long been, the center of elegance.

Paris itself could cope with anything. In June the strikes, while certainly slowing the city down, had turned it into a street festival. The July 14 celebrations had shown, not just that the people could enjoy themselves, but that the victory of the Popular Front had brought reform, not revolution. By September, with life back to normal, the season, which had been markedly shortened by the political events, was back in full swing. The theaters were full, the really elegant restaurants had to turn people away, and fashion resumed its sway.

Actually, it had never been fully eclipsed. Schiaparelli, not an easily frightened woman, was moved by the victory of the Left to design a hat that looked like a Phrygian cap, the headgear worn by the revolutionaries in the 1790s and by the figure of the Republic since then. The records do not show whether this inspired piece of frivolity proved a popular item; we may surmise, however, that the leading ladies of the Tout-Paris decided to give it a miss for fear of gravely shocking their anything but liberal husbands.

Political connotations aside, though, the shape of the Phrygian cap was just that of Schiap's new coiffures and hats. Her look for 1936 included tall coiffures covered or sometimes crowned by upswept hats, or, for the evenings, combs made of mother-of-pearl, jeweled crystal, or tortoiseshell. These were not just decorative; when it was a question of holding a multitude of little curls in place, they came in quite handy. As for the hats themselves, there were no limits to Schiap's inventiveness. After the Television hat (it celebrated the invention of that instrument and bore a replica of a screen), which looked to the future, there was the Botticelli Pageboy hat, a felt cylinder straight out of the master's work, which looked back to the past, and the Lobster Basket hat, which looked at nothing except that always picturesque shellfish. All this was mere preparation for greater eccentricity, though: in 1937, Schiap's clients were offered the Upside-down Shoe hat, with its heel sticking up at the back (it was not popular, but the designer wore it proudly), and the Mutton-Chop hat complete with white frill.

There was a lot to be said for all these startling new designs. In a world where anything was better than being forced to face reality, it was clearly a help if the *élégantes* had their attention distracted by the amusingly improbable. Always true to her taste for the modern, Schiap's silhouette in 1936 was inspired by planes and their accessories. She showed (and sold) wing-shaped collars, sleeves made to look like parachutes with their rows of cording, billowing skirts cut in panels and sometimes worn over bright-colored shorts.

There were many ways of attracting, or distracting, people's attention. It was, not surprisingly, Daisy Fellowes who wore, to a concert of the Orchestre de Paris, Schiap's evening suit accessorized with multicolored bracelets that clanked loudly whenever she moved and thus neatly, if annoyingly, advertised her arrival in mid-program. For a gala performance at the Opéra, Mrs. Fellowes gave up her bracelets but attracted just as much attention by wearing a dress with a demure navy blue front and a deeply scooped satanic red back.

That seemed quite normal, though, compared with some of the motifs with which Schiap adorned her dresses. There was the map of Normandy surrounded by gamboling pigs on a midnight blue crepe dinner suit, for instance; next to that, the two birds holding a love letter in their beaks seemed almost prosaic. In case you forgot just how much attention the designer received, there was a fabric printed with a collage of her reviews. If you liked music, there was the dark blue satin dress embroidered in gold below the waist with a violin, a French horn, a tuba, and a harp; if you preferred flowers there was the black dress whose ornate pink appliqué bosses were decorated with a gold-edged ruby sequin abstract pattern and tiny white china roses.

No theme was too improbable. In 1938, a year in which the future did not look bright, comfort might be proffered by a helpful astrologer, and so there was a dark blue velvet coat dusted with silver and gold stars, the planets, comets, and the signs of the Zodiac. And in case the past seemed more reassuring, there was another evening gown with a back embroidered with sequins, bugle beads, and bullion, representing the Fountain of Neptune in the park of Versailles.

It wasn't just embroidery, either. On her suits Schiap put buttons shaped like acrobats, horses, or ballerinas; and to that was added the jewelry Jean Schlumberger designed for her: cufflinks shaped like jeweled bagpipes, ostriches, horses, roller skates, plumed hats, starfishes, all made into precious pins. There were necklaces made of golden fish, or strings of hands and wrists, a choker of gilded water lily leaves on which sat little frogs, earrings in the shape of tiny cupids.

All these fantasies, charming as they were, also had a more serious connotation: they were part of the defense against the anxieties of life. What made Schiaparelli particularly interesting was that her designs echoed other, more important, achievements. Chanel, Vionnet, Molyneux made beautiful clothes; Schiap brought into hers an echo of Surrealism, the movement that transformed literature and the arts. Dali, when he drew his lobster designs for her, was still a worthwhile artist who owed everything to Surrealism — and because Surrealism focused on the unconscious, it, too, was becoming a way to escape the dreadful reality of everyday life. In their way, Schiap's own eccentric motifs were an echo of that movement: what André Breton and his friends had done was to discard conventional limits in favor of the endless riches of the unconscious. That, throughout the thirties, is what they continued to do, in spite of many factional battles; and as a result, everything in the world, from the way one thought to the look of advertisements, was transformed.

Of course, many great artists and writers were responsible for this. It is possible to argue that Miró or Max Ernst would have been what they were even if Surrealism had not existed, or that Eluard would still have written great poetry; but certainly the specific content of their work owed much to the movement, and to one man of peculiar genius and massive personality. André Breton was not, in his own person, all of Surrealism, but Surrealism could not have existed without André Breton. More than a poet, a critic, and a writer, he was a great inventor of definitions, a great discoverer of new paths. A handsome man with a Roman profile and an imperious expression, Breton gave an impression of absolute solidity. He spoke commandingly, was a master of polemics, and never hesitated to define an issue or excommunicate those who disagreed with him. He would be forgotten today, though, if, under that regal manner, there had not been imagination, sensitivity, and the ability to understand the masterpieces of contemporary painters and so-called primitive civilizations.

Just how receptive Breton could be is described by Valentine Hugo, with whom he had a brief, passionate affair that turned into an enduring friendship. "André Breton," she wrote, "when faced with grasses, flowers, trees, an object, or an animal . . . was both a highly enthusiastic and very young man, and a severe old judge. It seems to me that during those years when we were traveling together with Paul Eluard and other friends, André Breton from one day to the next could go through many moods and expressions as inspired by the secret spirit of the moment. That mood could go from the most cheerful to the most unbearable only to turn into one more cheerful still."[1]

Unlike Schiap's dresses, Surrealism was not meant to be a distraction from unpleasant facts. From the very beginning, Breton and his friends had firmly rejected not just the literary and artistic conventions promulgated by the bourgeoisie, but its political-economic system as well. Firmly defending the proletariat, revolted by the greed of the great corporations, the Surrealists made it plain that their goal was revolution across the board. In 1926, when the Soviet Union still seemed to offer a great hope for fairness and renewal, Breton joined the Communist party; by the time he finally left it in 1934, he had denounced all the horrors with which we are now so familiar — Stalin's police tyranny, the deadly conformism of "Socialist realism," the utter lack of any sort of liberty. Breton, in fact, could no more be taken in by Soviet propaganda than by bourgeois conformity, and that did not make his position easier.

This also made for a number of violent quarrels that helped split the movement: Louis Aragon, who to the end of his life remained a stalwart member of the Communist party, broke with Breton because his friend had clearer eyes and a more demanding conscience. Throughout the thirties, in fact, various members of the group left, and sometimes returned, for a variety of frequently silly political reasons; but then, that, too, was characteristic of the Surrealists. The movement was nothing if not contentious.

Much as Breton cared about politics, though, it was in the end a very minor part of what mattered about him. His great contribution was as a poet, a novelist, and most of all as a man who could make others feel, think, and see as they had not thought possible before. Imagination, Breton thought, was what mattered the most: "the imaginary," he explained, "is what tends to become real."[2] He was right, of course: we create what we imagine. At the same time, the imagination must be cultivated, conquered almost, through an awareness of the unconscious from which it springs. One of the ways in which this could be done was through what Breton called "automatic writing" in which the words that came up to the surface of the mind were written down whether or not they appeared to make sense. The images thus produced were often bold, shocking in that they answered to none of the conventional parameters: one of Breton's books of poems, for instance, was entitled *Le Revolver à cheveux blancs* (The White-Haired Revolver).

With a little effort, this deliberate attempt to bring to consciousness at least a part of the unconscious could produce results that were beautiful, haunting, and invariably true: the method excluded all pretense. It also sometimes produced startling results. In 1930, Breton and Eluard wrote a book together that they titled *L'Immaculée Conception* (The Immaculate Conception). Inspired by the title placed at the top of the page on which they were working, the two men almost became one as they worked, sometimes writing not just a paragraph, but even a sentence together, a word by Breton preceding or following a word by Eluard. One of the texts they produced, *Les possessions,* simulates the results of certain mental disorders in a way which psychiatrists have found entirely convincing. That, too, made perfect sense: it was Breton who first offered the notion that the so-called insane are capable of being important artists.

This reliance on the unconscious, and on chance, naturally owed something to Freud; but the father of psychoanalysis himself never understood Surrealism, perhaps because he saw the unconscious more as a source of neurosis than as a treasure to be explored at leisure. For Breton and his friends, it was an inexhaustible mine; and because each person's unconscious is individual and specific, but also, in some respects, universal, each product of the Surrealists' oeuvre was at the same time highly individual — a Max Ernst looks very unlike a Miró — and yet related since it was based on a similar mental and psychological process.

This attitude carried with it a willingness to look, and not infrequently admire, what had been rejected as simply strange. The dreamlike "Ideal Palace" of the mailman Cheval, at Hauterive in the south of France, is a case in point. Over many years, using mostly shards of glass and porcelain, Cheval had built himself a strange, towered structure inspired in part by dreams of the Orient. The result is as unexpected as it is original and beautiful. Until Breton saw it, it had interested no one, because it seemed the work of a madman. Today, tourists in the thousands visit it.

Breton applied this same ability to see what had until then been rejected when he discovered the art of the Eskimos, the American Indians, the pre-Columbian peoples. And, of course, he collected the works of the Surrealist painters in spite of a chronic shortage of money. In 1938, he owned paintings by Chirico, Ernst, Magritte, Miró, Man Ray, and Tanguy among others, and any visitor to the Surrealist Exhibition of February 1938 could see them, along with his *poèmes-objets,* in which apparently unrelated objects were put together so as to create a psychological resonance.

The exhibition, which was held at Georges Wildenstein's Galerie des Beaux-Arts, was an immense success, the great hit of the season, in fact. Following another Surrealist Exhibition organized by Roland Penrose in London the previous year, it proved once and for all that Surrealism was international, and that it expressed better than any other movement the creative spirit of the time.

Staged — the word is not too strong — by Marcel Duchamp, the exhibition appropriately began with the shock of the unexpected: the gallery's big window was masked by twelve hundred coal bags. Inside, mannequins dressed in strange and inappropriate ways stood around Dalí's "rainy taxi" — it rained *inside* the taxi. Breton's own collection and other works by the movement's artists, which were on display, could be guessed at: absolutely devoid of light, the whole space had to be explored with the help of the flashlights you picked up at the door.

That in itself could be interpreted in a number of ways: the darkness was perhaps a metaphor for sleep, and the objects revealed by the flashlight's beam the dreams that inhabited it. The visit to the exhibition could be seen as a voyage of discovery in which revelation came out of the night. Even more to the point, perhaps, the darkness, the window masked with coal bags, the flashes of great art lost in the prevailing darkness, even the taxi that so signally failed to shelter its passengers, could be read as a metaphor for the political climate. The Surrealist Exhibition opened six months before France and Great Britain betrayed their ally, Czechoslovakia, at Munich, and a year and a half before the war, which was already clearly looming. As an image of the years to come, it could hardly have been more to the point.

Just as important to Breton, the exhibition fulfilled the task he assigned Surrealism, the double need to change the world radically and to interpret

it as completely as possible. The only difference between this imperative
and its actual effect was that the exhibition was limited to art and literature. Still, it was a major achievement, and the crowds that came in daily
proved it. By 1938, in fact, Surrealism, which had begun as a radical rejection of much that had preceded it, had itself become almost an institution; and that was due, not just to its preference for shocking, but to the
talent of its participants. Breton himself, who could seem so coldly doc-
trinaire, was capable of writing the most tender love poetry. In 1934 he
married a young woman, Jacqueline Lamba, whom he met as the result
of a series of coincidences: having glimpsed her once in a cafe, he ran into
her again elsewhere and became almost obsessed by her. There is nothing
hermetic about the verses his new love caused him to write:

> *Il y a*
> *qu'à me pencher sur le précipice*
> *de la fusion sans espoir de ta présence et de ton absence*
> *j'ai trouvé le secret*
> *de t'aimer*
> *toujours pour la première fois . . .*
> (It is/ that as I bend over the precipice/ of the fusion with-
> out hope of your presence and your absence/ I have found
> the secret/ of loving you / always for the first time.)[3]

Nor was there anything recondite about his artistic position: for himself, nothing less than first-rate writing would do; for the others, nothing
less than genius, and when it came to that, he did not limit himself to just
the Surrealists proper. It was typical of him that he should write a long
and admiring article on Picasso. And Picasso himself, although he was
never a Surrealist, was fascinated by the movement as well as by its leader.

Of course, Breton remained closer to the members of his own group.
Dali, Miró, Ernst, Magritte, Tanguy, Man Ray, all then living in Paris,
were its greatest artists; and they, too, found that they could neither ignore the world around them nor change it. Some, of course, were more
directly involved. The Nazis had promptly put Max Ernst on their black
list of decadent artists, and he could no longer go back to Germany, and
Miró, a Spaniard and a Republican, watched, from the summer of 1936,
the civil war that ravaged his country and ended with the victory of
Franco and his Fascists.

Spain had been a republic since 1931. At that time, Alfonso XIII had
left the country in deference to the antimonarchist majority manifested in

the municipal elections. Since then, the new governments had had to contend with fierce opposition from the conservative and neo-Fascist Right as well as from the extreme Left; but, on a continent where democracies were growing fewer every year, the fact that Spain was unquestionably free meant a very great deal, to all democrats and to Miró in particular.

Both Miró and Ernst were reduced to transmuting their feelings into their work. Because there was no organized anti-Hitler movement in France, Ernst could do so only in painting. Miró at least could make his feelings clear; there was, for instance, the poster he designed in 1937. *Aidez l'Espagne* (Help Spain), it begged, and against a brightly colored ground, it showed the heroic figure of a peasant with an enormous clenched fist, while the price of the poster — one franc — was a prominent part of the design: the money raised from the sale of the poster went to help the Republican cause.

Even more eloquent, though, are two works he painted that same year. One, *The Reaper,* was commissioned by the Spanish government and placed in the Spanish pavilion at the 1937 Paris World's Fair near Picasso's contribution, *Guernica.* Moving away, to a degree, from the abstraction he had practiced earlier, Miró shows a Catalan peasant who has been reduced to a great, misshapen head seen in profile, a long stem growing directly out of the soil, and two tendril-like arms, one of which holds a scythe. The head itself, set against a stormy ground full of explosive stars and splotches, seems to shout defiance; and it is topped with a crumpled Phrygian cap, that international emblem of the Republic.

Nothing could have been more appropriate. Unlike the church-ridden south of Spain, Catalonia — the area around Barcelona — was firmly Republican, and its peasants, who fought long and bravely, paid a huge toll during the war and the bloody massacres that followed it. Miró himself was a fiercely patriotic Catalan and, of course, strongly anti-Fascist; thus the civil war was a devastating blow for him as he watched the triumph of fascism and the ruin of his fatherland. That is entirely clear from another emblematic painting in which he reached back, for just that one time, to a representational style close to that which he had developed in the early twenties.

The *Still Life with an Old Shoe* uses as its elements objects of everyday life: bread, wine, an apple, and an old shoe; but they are set on a black ground while a great conflagration takes place within them and in the sky above. The colors are lurid: acid yellow and green, purple, flame red; the objects themselves are lit from within and distorted as if they had been caught in the middle of an explosion, while the light they emit is projected into the stormy clouds above. The shoe, clearly, is unwearable; the bread is as hard as stone; a huge fork is planted aggressively into the apple and looks more like some murderous medieval weapon than a table instrument; the bottle, glowing eerily, is grotesquely misshapen and obviously no longer holds wine. Nothing, in other words, will sustain life.

Miró's deliberate return to representation was not a momentary whim. He worked long and hard on the painting in a little room lent him by his dealer, Pierre Loeb. Having uttered that cry of anger and despair, however, he returned to his current style; and while the expression of his anguish was less direct, it remained nonetheless visible in works like his 1938 *Woman's Head*. Set against a brilliantly blue sky, a huge black head is linked by a tiny pivotlike neck to a black torso. The arms are thrown up in a movement of fierce ecstasy; the bloodshot eye (this is a profile) set in a yellow circle, the wickedly pointed teeth, some white, some black, some blood red, the sparse, bristling hair all give an impression of primeval evil accentuated by the birdlike character of the head; and the drooping red breasts with their sharply pointed yellow and green nipples reinforce the feeling that this is a primitive and devouring deity.

This expression of Miró's inner anguish obviously relates to the Spanish civil war. Unlike Picasso, whose relationships with women were often stormy, Miró was a devoted and loving husband married to an equally loving and devoted wife. *Woman's Head* clearly has very little to do, therefore, with his personal feelings about women. What we see, instead, is a terrifying, bloodthirsty goddess, a Kali or a primitive Demeter who destroys before she creates, a symbol of the catastrophe even then taking place in Spain.

Of course, there were also works in which the artist's evolution continued regardless of exterior disaster. Miró, in 1938, went right on using words as both pictorial elements and poetic carriers of symbols: that is the case of *A Star Caresses the Breast of a Negress*, in which the words form a garland across the canvas and are framed by brilliantly colored and almost completely abstract forms. Even more poetic, the series of four successive Portraits blends blues, yellows, and reds with carefully balanced forms, references to parts of the body, and the signs — stars, abstract fishes — that are used as a second language. The feeling here is almost tender, dreamy, and yet profound: more than a specific woman, the Portraits show us the unconscious feelings connected with femininity; and the result is an accumulation of masterpieces.

Tormented as he was by his country's disasters, Miró, who lived in Paris, was able to go on working. Léon Blum, who experienced an equal degree of anguish, continued to govern France; but every day, he felt torn by his two conflicting desires, the first to preserve the European peace, the second to help the Spanish Republicans.

Blum himself was on friendly terms with several members of the Spanish government who, like him, were Socialists. At the same time, he was committed to keeping France at peace; indeed, he said so repeatedly on coming to power and offered to negotiate all pending issues with Germany so as to avoid any possibility of armed conflict. Given the Nazis' attitude to the Jews, that in itself was no mean proof of Blum's willingness to disregard his private feelings in order to ensure the welfare of France.

Countenancing a Fascist attack on Spain, however, was another matter. Quite aside from his own friendships, Blum knew, not just how greatly the Spaniards would suffer from a civil war, but also that it was not at all in France's interest to have an ally of Hitler and Mussolini across yet another border. He was thus legitimately appalled when he heard that on July 18, 1936, part of the military — mostly troops stationed in the Canaries — had risen under the command of General Francisco Franco.

The question was what to do next. Blum, whose own government had been in place for only six weeks, had already abundantly proved his willingness to make an effort to defuse tensions. Much against his previous convictions, he had agreed to lift the League of Nations sanctions against Italy, merely refusing to appoint a new ambassador to Rome because his letters of accreditation would have had to be addressed to the King of Italy and Emperor of Ethiopia, Victor Emmanuel III's new title. He also allowed French athletes to participate in the Berlin Olympics, which opened on August 1. The foreign minister, the Radical Yvon Delbos, was not a man given to bold and dangerous gestures. Still, the fact remained: a legitimate, freely elected government was being attacked by rebel officers. If that government were to ask for help in the shape of planes, guns, and other weapons, it seemed obvious that France would grant its request. Indeed, when within days a Spanish delegation arrived in Paris for just that purpose, Blum's first reaction was to give them just what they needed.

From a purely legal point of view, Blum's decision was entirely justified; he was dealing with the legitimate, recently elected government of the Spanish republic. Politically, it also made sense: by the summer of 1936, it was not a moment too soon to stop the spread of fascism. Finally, there was Blum's own anguish: the struggle between freedom — the legitimate government — and the worst sort of tyranny — Franco's cohorts — meant a great deal to him personally, and it was made all the more poignant by the fact that Spain had only recently become free.

Unfortunately, Blum and his Socialist friends were not alone in the government. The Radicals should also have wanted to defend democracy on the other side of the Pyrenees: in France they stood for the separation of church and state and a parliamentary system. There were, however, many conservative Radicals who loathed the Socialists far more than any conceivable reactionary regime, and that made the more progressive Radicals hesitant to back any cause not crucial to them. Worse still, as the result in part of their repeated failures between 1932 and 1936, many Radicals had now become so scared that anything seemed better than risking a fight. Thus, even those who felt sympathy for the Spanish government were convinced that it would, in the end, be beaten and that therefore the strictest neutrality must be kept.

The two most important Radicals in the cabinet were Daladier, the defense minister, and Chautemps, minister of state; and Chautemps was both conservative and scared. A master at avoiding responsibility and the attacks that come with it, he tried to please everyone by flattering all of them. Well aware that his future might entail alliances with the Right, he did not want to be seen as supporting a policy — aid to the Spanish government — that the Right would abominate. More, as the most radical of Radicals, he had made it an absolute custom to be always on the same side as the party's leaders, and the still-influential Herriot was firmly opposed to intervention. Thus, at the very heart of the Blum cabinet, Chautemps was prepared to do whatever was necessary to block the Premier's policy.

He was also in a position of great power. Blum, misled by his charm and intelligence, had failed to note his lack of backbone. The two men had become friends. Worse, Chautemps was the Radical whom Blum trusted most; and that gave him even more power.

Just before the Council of Ministers that was to decide the French position in regard to Spain, "Chautemps took to one side the young ministers," one of Blum's aides noticed, "and walking up and down with them on the rue de Varenne [outside the Premier's office] . . . , lectured them vigorously, pointing out that the military insurrection would be victorious in a few weeks and that the Republican government would collapse like a house of cards."[4] This position was shared by Daladier and Yvon Delbos, the Radical foreign minister; ironically, this colorless man, whom

Blum had put in that particular place because he intended to run France's foreign policy himself, now prevented him from defending a cause about which he cared so greatly.

The Radicals were not alone. The Right, of course, was delighted by Franco's pronunciamento, and so was President Lebrun: here, in fact, was the beginning of his revenge. He had been forced by the electorate to nominate Blum as Premier even though he loathed everything he stood for. Now he could help change one of the government's key policies by encouraging those in the cabinet who were hostile to it.

Thus, without preparation, the Premier found himself facing a powerful coalition ready to defend nonintervention by almost any means. And thanks to Blum himself, we know just how it happened:

> As I arrived from London at Le Bourget airport [on July 24], I found . . . Camille Chautemps waiting for me. I said, "Oh, you came to meet me?"
>
> "Yes," he answered, "It is because I want to fill you in on what is happening in Paris. The situation is serious. . . . While you were in London, you probably were not told that Kérillis [a right-wing Deputy and journalist] had started a violent campaign in *L'Echo de Paris*, that all the dispositions that have been taken [to help the Spanish government] have been made public. . . . The feeling, especially in the Parliament, is running very high."[5]

As it turned out, Blum's intentions had been leaked to the fiercely right-wing *L'Echo de Paris* by the Spanish military attaché, whose loyalty was to Franco; thus the paper's information was, for once, accurate. Whether it was fitting for the government to change its policy because it was attacked by a fiercely partisan paper whose circulation was well under a hundred thousand was perhaps another question. It was, obviously, not one Chautemps was willing to ask.

What Blum now quickly discovered was that all the mandarins of the regime shared Chautemps's position. The Radicals' reasoning was simple: since Hitler had been allowed, under the Radical Albert Sarraut, to remilitarize the Rhineland, then nothing else was worth fighting for. The place might be Spain; the subject was appeasement; and the Radicals, without whom nothing could be done, were in favor of giving in every time. Nor was this all. French foreign policy had, for some while, been based on the understanding that British support was indispensable. Great Britain, under Baldwin and later Chamberlain, was even more appeasement-minded than the Radicals themselves. It was thus easy for

Chautemps to point out that any resistance to the dictators would cause an unacceptable split with England.

Conveniently, the British government looked on Franco's attempt with ill-concealed favor; there could be no doubt that if a European war resulted from France's help to the Spanish republic, Britain would not fight. It was a powerful argument: were the two democracies to risk disunion for the sake of saving the Spanish Republicans? To this the Radicals added another: given the nature of the German and Italian regimes, war would be sure to follow any major French support of the Spanish government.

Actually, neither Hitler nor Mussolini was prepared for a war with France. Both were aware that if hostilities actually broke out, they were not unlikely to lose: in 1936, German rearmament had just begun. Italy, all boasting to the contrary notwithstanding, was not a serious military factor. There is thus every reason to believe that a firm attitude on the part of France would have frightened the dictators; but having once tasted appeasement and cravenness, the Radicals had come to think that no other policy was possible.

In fact, when it came to being weak, the Radicals could display amazing firmness. Their leaders told Delbos just what was expected of him, and the foreign minister did as he was told. At the cabinet meeting on July 25, Blum found all the Radicals, Delbos chief among them, absolutely opposed to helping Spain. That day, the cabinet decided that it would remain strictly neutral and let the Spanish fight out their war among themselves. Given Blum's intelligence, as well as his highly developed ethical sense, it seems like an extraordinary surrender. Indeed, it caused him the greatest suffering, but he really had no choice. At the end of July, his government was barely two months old. It had only begun to implement the reforms promised by the program of the Popular Front. If Blum left office he would betray the millions of voters who had backed him. Torn between his feeling of what was right and his duty to his compatriots, the Premier, in the end, chose his duty. It is a choice that still today cannot be blamed. What can, however, be criticized is the way in which that choice was implemented.

In the course of three agitated cabinet meetings, it was decided to follow a policy of nonintervention that would then be urged on the other powers. The rationale, which Blum explained on August 1, was that, in any event, Germany and Italy were likely to give Franco far greater quantities of weapons than France could offer the Spanish government since France itself was grievously short of planes and modern firearms. Great

Britain, clearly, was not about to help the Loyalists; the United States refused to be involved. If, therefore, the dictators could be convinced to join a nonintervention treaty, the Loyalists would, in the end, have a better chance than if France actually intervened.[6]

Nonintervention all around was also the solution put forward by Alexis Léger and the foreign ministry, all the more urgently because on July 30 an Italian warplane had crashed in North Africa, thus providing proof that Italy in fact was arming Franco. Stopping the flood of Italian supplies therefore seemed like a good idea. Unfortunately, this rational argument had two fatal flaws. The first was that, while France made its offer and promptly stopped its deliveries, Italy and Germany waited several weeks before agreeing and in the meantime shipped even more armaments. The second was that, while France and Great Britain were likely to honor their commitments, Hitler and Mussolini were not. Thus, as in fact happened, they were likely to supply Franco secretly while no one (except the Soviet Union) helped the Loyalists. As for the few weapons that Blum and Pierre Cot, his air minister, did manage to send through Mexico, they, sadly, amounted to very little.

This was torture for Blum because he felt himself to be morally in the wrong. In the first few days of August, torn between his duty to France and his understanding of the support deserved by the Spanish government, he decided to resign and was convinced to stay in office only by the Spanish envoy, Fernando de los Ríos. Obviously Blum, although he was committed to a policy of neutrality, was still likely to prove a better friend than whoever might succeed him. Still, as the Premier had feared, nonintervention ensured Franco's victory. That it took the immensely better equipped Fascist forces three years to beat the Republicans says something about the strength of democratic feeling in Spain.

For Blum himself, the Spanish civil war was a tragedy. It was not just that he felt so personally concerned: it caused a first and dangerous rift in his government; it provided the Right with a rallying cry shared by its entire spectrum, from mild conservatives to outright Fascists; and it gave yet another convincing proof that France was prepared to give in to the dictators. Just as bad, it threatened to alienate the masses from the government. For the working classes, there was no doubt: France should be supporting the legally elected government of Spain with all its might.

It was not Blum's least difficult task to explain his policy to his supporters. With characteristic courage, he did so at a huge rally on September 6, and while his argument first met with boos, he finally convinced his audience — largely, perhaps, because his tone was anything but defeatist. Indeed, he started with an attack: "If there is something that is a thorough scandal," he told the crowd, "it is that France's obvious interest [in having a legal, friendly government in Spain] should have been denied by a criminally and treacherously partisan press." And then, he went on: "Ask yourselves: who through the concentration of all power in a single man, and the ability to act in secret, through the intense rearmament effort under way, through that country's industrial potential, will gain the advantage [if both sides are sending arms to Spain]?

"The solution, which may save Spain and the peace, is an international nonintervention agreement."[7] It is one of the tragedies of these increasingly tragic years that Blum, who more than half believed his own argument, should have proved so wrong. Even so, he would not have settled for nonintervention if he had not cared so deeply about preserving the peace. Like all those who had seen the massacres of the First World War, indeed, like the rest of the French, Blum felt that France would not survive a second European war. The potency of this feeling was evident everywhere in the democracies; and it was typical that the once-bellicose Right should be denouncing the Left as "bellicist": no accusation was more likely to cause dread and rejection.

This was something of which William Bullitt, the new United States ambassador to France, was well aware, just as he understood the Radicals' fears: "Delbos is terrified with regard to the possibility of a general European war emerging from the conflict in Spain," he reported in a private letter to FDR in December.[8] Bullitt knew just what he was saying: seldom in the history of diplomacy has an ambassador been so close to the government to which he was accredited. Harold Ickes, the secretary of the interior, and a man known for his pungent language, put it best: "Bullitt," he noted in his diary, "practically sleeps with the French Cabinet."[9]

There were a number of good reasons for this. First, of course, was Bullitt himself. A lifelong Francophile, but also an experienced ambassador — he had just come from Moscow — he had been raised in France and spoke perfect French. He could, when he chose, exert immense charm, and his considerable, if quirky, intelligence was of just the sort that appeals to the French. By the time he arrived, in fact, he already had many friends, some of whom were in the government, some of whom, like Thorez, Duclos, and Cachin, the Communist leaders, supported it, and others of whom, like Reynaud, Laval, and Flandin, opposed it.

Equally important, the French were just then turning to the United States as a potential last resort: perhaps, if the worst came to the worst, the United States would once again join France in defeating Germany. That, in turn, was felt to depend entirely on the President. Virtually no one in Paris realized that isolationism was still a major force in the country at large and in the Congress, and that the very notion that the United States might once again be involved in a European conflict was anathema to most voters. Since it was well known that Bullitt and Roosevelt were very close friends, Blum and his colleagues hoped that trusting Bullitt and letting him in on most government secrets would bring about a thorough understanding with the United States. This was all the more easily done since most of the ministers felt the liveliest admiration for Roosevelt.

As a result, the President's reelection that November was much applauded. As long as FDR remained in the White House, the French government felt it had a friend. "The wave of enthusiasm in France which greeted your election was really phenomenal," Bullitt reported. "Blum came personally to express his congratulations. This is unheard of. . . . He entered the door, flung his broad-brimmed black hat to the butler, his coat to a footman, leaped the three steps to the point where I was standing, seized me and kissed me violently! I staggered slightly; but having been kissed by Stalin, I am now immune to any form of osculation. . . .

"The French regard you as a national leader who has succeeded in giving the lower classes a greater proportion of the national income without disturbing any of the ancient liberties."[10]

Bullitt was right: Blum felt the greatest admiration for FDR. But there was more to this exchange than the ambassador was willing to acknowledge. Blum and his colleagues hoped that the United States, now that it was led by Roosevelt, would give up the stultified isolationism that had prevailed under Harding, Coolidge, and Hoover. The time for that had not yet come, however. Bullitt had been given firm instructions by the President not to hold out the hope of any American involvement in a possible conflict. All through his tenure, Bullitt made it very clear that the United States, although willing to participate in negotiations, absolutely declined to enter into an alliance.

The relationship between Roosevelt and Bullitt, moreover, was more like that of monarch and courtier: Bullitt's letters to FDR are invariably sweetened by what today looks very like flattery. They were also deliberately written to amuse as well as convey the most serious information. Most important, because the President and the ambassador both distrusted the hidebound State Department, the official reports from the Paris embassy contained only the most routine matters. Bullitt's letters to

FDR — "Secret and Personal," the envelopes said — conveyed the real information, and they went straight to the Oval Office.

Happily, Bullitt had a sharp eye and an equally vivid style, and his letters are just as entertaining as he meant them to be. On October 24, for instance, he sent FDR a long report after lunching with Blum at the house of a mutual friend. The ambassador wrote:

> He looks exactly like the caricatures of him and has the sort of quick-silver intelligence and the fluttery gestures of the hyper-intellectual[s]. . . . He seemed to be . . . honestly delighted when I said to him that you felt his task in France was like the task that had faced you in America. He has taken the position that if the Communists refuse to support him [because of their opposition to his Spanish policy], he will not attempt to deal with the Right but will ask the dissolution of the Chamber of Deputies and new elections. The Communists know at the present time that new elections would mean an immense reduction in their vote and unless they get orders from Moscow to raise hell (orders based on Russian interests, not French), they will, I think continue to support him . . . for some time.
>
> The aristocracy and upper bourgeoisie are just as dumb here as their opposite numbers in the United States. They show no sign of appreciating the fact that Blum is as conservative as anyone who can hold the situation together. If Blum were in for a four-year term as you were in 1933, I have no doubt that he could do a highly constructive job. . . . But as he has to maneuver to maintain his position . . . he is not exactly a rock of Gibraltar. . . .
>
> There is no one on the Right. . . . Tardieu is utterly discredited. . . . Chautemps is considered a jellyfish with lots of common sense. Herriot's health has been failing and his position with it. Daladier is completely distrusted by everyone except Daladier. . . .
>
> I have talked with Paul Reynaud and [Georges] Mandel [another leader of the moderate Right]. They believe that they will be able to upset Blum and make a series of political deals which will produce the sort of government under which France has suffered for the last ten years.[11]

Bullitt was well informed — the plan outlined by Reynaud was eventually put into operation — but in the meantime, as he noted, Blum was firmly in place. As the months passed, however, he faced growing opposition. First, on the Left, the Communists were growing more critical every day as a matter of policy because they hoped to push Blum into more radical reforms than those he was willing to carry out, and because they wanted France to help the Spanish government. Then the Radicals, firmly opposed to intervention, and loath to see any more change now that the strikes were over, acted as a drag within the cabinet, while never forgetting the old practice according to which they could at one and the same time be part of a ministry and fight it. As for the Right proper, it was recovering from its scare of May and June, and attacked Blum with unbridled rage.

Two events, one at the end of September, the other from July through November, seemed ideally designed for just this sort of assault. The first was a devaluation, the second one of the most vicious libels in French history.

When Blum had come to power at the beginning of June, he had refused to devalue the overpriced franc; economics was not his strong point, and he was convinced that the new government's policies, by creating jobs, would also raise the tax yield and thus bolster the value of the currency. He could not have been more wrong. By September, although unemployment was in fact declining, speculators were betting heavily against the franc. With the reserves rapidly falling, Blum found that he had no choice: on September 25, the franc lost about 30 percent of its value in relationship to the pound and the dollar, with the value of the latter rising from 15.19 francs to 21.47 francs.

This was, on balance, a positive move, but it was not bold enough: in August 1931, the dollar had been worth 25 francs. Thus, even after the devaluation, the franc still cost more than it had five years earlier and French products, although less overpriced, were still expensive in terms of the dollar and the pound. As it was, no one would have dared to complain if Blum had devalued on taking office, but he was now violently attacked for doing so after he had promised to maintain the value of the franc. Once again, the Right claimed, the Left had proved it was incapable of running the country; and this silly argument gained a wide audience partly because the French did not understand that a devaluation is not necessarily followed by an inflationary burst, partly because the now obsolete value of the franc had been set by Poincaré in 1928, and Poincaré was all the more admired since he was safely dead. Finally, many people had still not recovered from their memories of the postwar inflation; that had gone together with a dramatic fall of the franc in the foreign exchange markets; and they assumed that the devaluation meant a return of this unpleasant process.

The second event that seriously wounded the cabinet was the attack on its interior minister, Roger Salengro. It all started on July 14, when *L'Action Française,* with its usual shameless disregard for the truth, announced that during the war Salengro had been a deserter. This was an absolute lie. Salengro, who had volunteered for a dangerous mission, had, in fact, been taken prisoner by the Germans in No-Man's-Land. He was, indeed, immediately after this accused of being a deserter, but the truth soon became evident, and by the time he was liberated, he had been fully exonerated and, indeed, commended for his bravery.

By 1936, Salengro had become mayor of Lille, the great industrial city in the north of France, a Deputy, and interior minister in the Blum cabinet. It was Salengro who had conducted the negotiations that led to the Matignon accord between the employers and the labor unions in early June, and he was responsible for many of the social and industrial reforms that had recently become law. He was thus an essential member of the government.

The attacks against him that began in July continued uninterruptedly through the summer and fall, with both *L'Action française* and another right-wing sheet, *Gringoire,* harping on the fact that a "traitor" was a key minister in a cabinet led by a Jew. Not surprisingly, *L'Echo de Paris,* Kérillis's paper, which, at the same time, was attacking Blum for supporting the Spanish Loyalists, picked this up under the hypocritical guise of reporting on the press. Had these papers had any regard at all for the truth, the campaign would soon have come to a halt; all the appropriate documents exonerating and commending Salengro were duly produced and laid before the Chamber. The attacks were wholly unrelated to reality, however, and they continued — on the grounds, no doubt, that if you just keep libeling people, some mud is bound to stick. This was possible and easy: France, in 1936, had no libel laws.

These constant attacks soon proved more than Salengro could bear. Already depressed by the death of his wife, exhausted by overwork, he committed suicide on November 17. This time, the scandal was so great that even the Catholic Church sided with the victim. At the funeral, which was attended by Blum, the ministers, and an immense crowd, Cardinal Liénart told the mourners: "A press which specializes in libel is not Christian."[12]

There was no reason to be surprised at the behavior of the editors of *L'Action française.* What is far more shocking is that the more moderate Right, while expressing regret at Salengro's death, carefully abstained from blaming the two papers which had caused it. *Le Temps,* in its mealy-mouthed tribute, was absolutely typical. "Let us bow to the memory of a man who was exhausted and discouraged by the political wars and their element of unfairness and even sometimes of cruelty," it editorialized,[13] carefully smudging the difference between legitimate politics and shameless libel.

Cardinal Liénart, however, was not alone in blaming *L'Action française*. Blum himself made an eloquent speech at Salengro's funeral in which he denounced the "bandits and mercenaries who sully [the French people]'s honor,"[14] and soon put a bill to punish libel before the Chamber. Sadly, it had not passed when his cabinet fell and never became law. The extremist press, therefore, remained entirely free to print whatever lies it chose; and it did so abundantly.

In spite of all this, Blum continued his attempts at reaching an agreement with Germany; he was almost alone in thinking he might succeed, though. In November 1936 Bullitt wrote FDR: "I have never encountered such complete hopelessness. There is no feeling of crisis because no one believes that war is imminent; but there is a universal belief that Europe is drifting toward war,"[15] and a few days later, he added: "Everyone is convinced that war will come by the spring or summer of 1938. . . . Czechoslovakia, clearly, is the next item on Hitler's list." And then, in a strikingly accurate piece of forecasting, Bullitt went on: "If Hitler should send forces into Czechoslovakia the position of France, as well as Czechoslovakia, would become tragic. . . . The French would have to decide whether or not to carry out the obligations of their treaty of alliance with Czechoslovakia. . . . I am inclined to believe that the greater part of the country would be dead set against carrying them out."[16] Bullitt could not have been more right. The crisis came in the summer of 1938 with exactly the results he predicted.

Within France itself, another kind of crisis was becoming more likely every day, and it did much to end the great hope that had arisen with the Popular Front's victory. That Blum represented the incarnation of that hope was obvious; but without the full support of the Communists on his left and the Radicals on his right the Premier could do nothing; and the support was waning fast.

The Communists, in fact, were merely appropriating Blum's own tactic of support with eclipses. While in theory they backed the government, they did not hesitate to attack its foreign policy, which they found much too conciliatory; and they did so with tremendous violence. The Radicals, on the other hand, saw this as a perfect pretext for breaking up the coalition and returning to the sort of alliance with the center Right they usually favored. At their congress late in October 1936, speaker after speaker denounced the May-June strikes and demanded the end of the alliance with the Socialists. Daladier did actually fight back, but weakly; and at the end of November, he made it entirely clear that it was no longer a question of whether but of when the Popular Front would break up: "The party," he said, "has signed a program. It will support the realization of this program, but not of anything more. . . . We accept all the reforms, but only when peace and order are preserved."[17] Here was the perfect pretext: henceforth, the Radicals could leave the government whenever they chose.

That, and the growing economic difficulties, singularly complicated Blum's task. Because no one really understood how the new laws about the eight-hour day and the five-day week were to be applied, productivity began to drop, and the economic indexes, which had risen for a while, went down. It looked very much as if the Depression were deepening again; and on February 13, 1937, Blum felt compelled to call for a "pause" in the reforms. Although the cabinet survived for another four months, everyone knew that it was doomed. With the familiar maneuvers in the corridors of the Chamber of Deputies resuming, with the daily growth in the dictators' power, it became clear that the Popular Front had been no revolution — merely a brief enthusiastic burst of reform; and the collapse of the great hope it had carried took with it much of the spirit of France.

Something about the condition of the country, in fact, was not unlike that of the noble family described by Genêt a few years earlier. "Since his arrival in France," she reported,

[Prince Felix Yussupoff] has already been identified with a losing lawsuit over some Rembrandts, with the bankruptcy of a dressmaking shop, with the murder of Rasputin, and with a subsequent small scandal that threatened deportation. He is now up to his ears again, but this time it is poison. It seems that his valet encouraged another valet to put scopolamine in the tea of the latter's masters [who were cousins of Yussupoff's] and their guests, of whom the poor Yussupoff was occasionally one. . . . In interviews to the press, read by a delighted, incredulous countryside, [Yussupov's relative] explains the state of gagaism which scopolamine produced on her noble family and all their tea-drinking friends — a state of complete stupidity which none of these aristocrats found strange. Memory vanished, general conversation lagged, the two children dropped behind in their studies and became unable to add two and two without exciting comment from their proud parents. Casual guests popping in for *le five-o'clock* were led back to their limousines in a state of complete imbecility; and an aunt, the Duchesse de Luynes ("born d'Uzès," the Comtesse interpolated for the benefit of a democratic public), fell flat on her face after having sipped a cup of weak Orange Pekoe ("which was abnormal for Her Grace").[18]

It was, obviously, an irresistibly funny picture, much funnier, in fact, than the current condition of the country. Unfortunately France itself in 1937, was beginning to look as if it, too, was suffering from an overdose of scopolamine. It had not quite fallen on its face yet, but it was as befuddled, as vague, as cut off from reality, as if it had been a victim of drug poisoning. For a few months, Blum had given the country a feeling of returning health; now, its knees buckling, it seemed ready to collapse.

CHAPTER

# TEN

# THE DAZZLE OF THE EXPO

THE SPANISH CIVIL WAR, by 1937, had long ceased being a mainly Spanish event. For Hitler and Mussolini it offered a double opportunity, that of ensuring the triumph of fascism in yet another country, and that of testing their newest weapons while training their soldiers and aviators. For the French it provided the final divide. Before 1936, the increasingly alienated population had come to see the politicians and great industrialists as its chief enemies; briefly, in the summer of 1936, a wave of concord and progress had seemed to sweep away many evils. Now, as 1937 began, the alienation was back, and it took an even more destructive form than before.

Blighted expectations looked very much like the theme for the year. At home, the Blum government had proved more fallible and more fragile than any of its supporters could have imagined. There was the Spanish mess; the budget deficit was growing alarmingly; a "pause" in the reforms had to be proclaimed. It was, Blum explained, not a "retreat . . . but a phase of prudent consolidation,"[1] but everyone understood that it was, actually, an end; and the Radicals were preparing for the kill. The Blum government did not fall until mid-June, but already in February the Radical carpings and the extreme Right's violent onslaughts showed that progress had been merely transitory. More and more, left-wing voters distrusted a regime that was rejecting reform in order to indulge in its ingrown political games. As for the Right, a growing section of it looked, not to the traditional French conservatives, but to the new proto-Fascist fringe.

Neither section felt represented by the cabinets that came and went; neither section liked what was happening, either within France or outside; most important of all, each section bitterly hated the other. Before 1936, there had been a deep divide between the well-to-do and everyone else. Now the rift split the French so completely that they no longer felt that they belonged to the same country. Just as, across the Rhine, the German masses were, apparently, united in slavish devotion to their Führer, in France a growing number of people felt that catastrophe was not too great a price to pay in order to eliminate the enemy within.

Still, life had to go on, and there were palliatives. For the Tout-Paris, the resumed dance of the ministries provided an ever-renewed fount of gossip; and Paris itself, at the beginning of 1937, was livelier than it had been in a while. There were amusements to which it very much looked forward, the World's Fair — it was actually called L'Exposition Internationale des Arts et Techniques — first and foremost. It was, in fact, a favorite topic: not only were the future pavilions, rides, and fireworks eagerly discussed, but so was the fact that it was most unlikely to open, as planned, in May. By January 1937 the Communists, though still supposedly supporting the Blum government, were doing their best to undermine it. That took the form not only of violent criticism in their newspapers and at the Chamber, but also of endless strikes by Communist unions whose members were building the pavilions of the Exposition. As a result, the Expo offered every enticement as a subject. If you were on the Left, you explained at length why it would, after all, open on time. If you were on the Right, you cited it as the perfect example of Blum-induced inefficiency. What was quite certain, though, was that it would attract a great many people to the city, and everyone agreed that this would be unquestionably a bonus: the provincials and foreigners would bring their money and spend it. After years during which the Depression had reduced tourism to a trickle, Paris once again looked forward to being the center of the universe, and so, of course, did the owners of its many shops, hotels, and restaurants.

That, however, would not start happening until May, and in the meantime, there were other topics to discuss. "Right now . . . what makes French news is what is happening in Spain," Genêt noted.

> After all the months of assertion by Italy, Germany, England, Russia, and France that nonintervention in Spain was being officially observed, the unofficial nonobservance of nonintervention has suddenly become overwhelmingly revealed. All is known now: the thousands of German male "tourists" touring Spain in Nazi boots; the thousands of Italian "trippers" who landed in Cadiz; the five hundred to a thousand English volunteers; the Russian-paid Red French flying corps, known as the Escadrille España, and supposedly organized by the author of *La Condition Humaine,* André Malraux; and the White French flying corps which the Fascist *Le Jour* brightly says is killing its opponents in Spain "*en bons sportifs*" [in a sportsman-like spirit].[2]

In fact, all too predictably, Germany and Italy were doing far more than the democracies. France itself inaugurated a policy of "loose nonintervention" through which it sold a few arms to the republic; the British volunteers, though brave and dedicated, were too few to make much difference; and the Soviet Union, although eager to help, was so far away that its aid was spasmodic. Not even the bravery of men like Malraux could counterbalance the steady supply of Fascist and Nazi troops and armaments. For all those who believed in democracy and saw Spain, accurately, as the testing ground for the future European war, the news was bleak.

Indeed, it was hard to know where hope might be found. For many, whether or not they belonged to the Communist party, the Soviet Union had long been the place where a more just, more efficient society was being created; and not least among those was André Gide. Ever scrupulous, ever fair, Gide had visited the Soviet Union in the twenties and concluded that a noble experiment was taking place. He had a point. The horrors of the civil war were over, those of Stalin had yet to happen. Certainly liberty was in rather short supply, but it seemed possible, even likely, that as the new regime settled in it would prove more tolerant year by year.

That, sadly, is not what he found on a return trip in 1936. Although his *Retour de l'U.R.S.S.* (Return from the USSR) bends over backward to praise where it is possible — the modern schools, the well-tended parks — the ultimate conclusion was inescapable. After reviewing what he had seen and heard, Gide wrote: "Today, it is obedience and conformity which [the state] demands. All those who do not declare themselves satisfied are considered to be 'Trotskyites.' Thus one begins to wonder whether Lenin himself, if he were to come back . . .*

"We were promised a dictatorship of the proletariat. We have been cheated. Yes, of course, there is a dictatorship, but that of a single man. . . . It is precisely this we did not want."[3] With Stalin, a great hope had died; with Hitler, a vast threat loomed larger every day. For those who believed in freedom and democracy, Europe was becoming a very uncomfortable place.

Naturally, Blum fought back. In January, for instance, he sent off Georges Bonnet to be French ambassador in Washington as a way to cut off his intrigues in Paris. Coming from someone who prized his relationship with Roosevelt and the United States, it was a desperate act. It was also a wise one. Bonnet was not only mad with ambition, he was utterly devoid of scruples, fundamentally reactionary (like many of his fellow Radicals), and as craven, when it came to opposing the dictators, as he was brave in plotting against Blum. Even his face, with its sharp profile and its snakelike expression, was unappealing; and his wife was as socially ambitious (and anti-Semitic) as her husband was politically hungry. Bullitt, who knew him well enough, wrote FDR: "You will, I think, dislike Bonnet. He is highly intelligent and well-versed in financial and economic matters but he is not a man of character. . . . He now pretends to be a great friend but he has a shifty eye."[4]

Bonnet, in fact, was just the kind of Radical who had prospered in the previous legislature. Now he and his friends were eager to get rid of Blum so as to form a Radical government firmly weighted to the Right; and the conservatives, naturally, were happy to help. Sometimes, the result was comical. In February, for instance, Pierre-Etienne Flandin, whose own tenure as Premier in 1935 had been so disastrous, told Blum in the Chamber: "You are not here to carry out the will of the masses with their sordid materialism."[5] To call the demands of people who did not make enough money to eat properly "sordid materialism" would be funny if it were not so revolting, and the tag stuck to Flandin. Still, it was clear enough that the cabinet was in grave danger.

On February 11 Daladier, in a speech, announced that he intended to defend the middle classes, a clear criticism of the Popular Front. In April the Radical Youths organized a widely attended meeting in Carcassone that set the party on a new path: it was becoming not just conservative — many Radicals had always been that — but actually proto-Fascist. It was

*Ellipsis is in the original.

perhaps not very surprising: the petty bourgeoisie, from which the party drew many of its votes, was precisely the socioeconomic stratum that in Germany had supported Hitler in his quest for power.

As for the cabinet, it looked hapless even to itself. Buffeted by the Radicals — and nearly half the ministers belonged to the party — unable to evolve a coherent foreign policy, it sat and watched scenes like the one described by Jean Zay: "[In the course of a Council at the Elysée], the foreign minister had just described the situation. . . : Germany was becoming more menacing. England refused to support us. The United States was completely isolationist. Italy turned its back on us and the Spanish imbroglio was worsening. . . . An appalled silence greeted the minister's report. The latter, in order to end it, continued, with forced cheerfulness: 'I would have liked to give the Council less worrying news' . . . upon which the president . . . answered: 'But, that's all right, my dear Minister, everyone knows you have nothing to do with any of this.'"[6] For once, Lebrun was right: the hapless Yvon Delbos was indeed out of the game.

Even the major rearmament effort undertaken by Blum failed to reach its goals. The funds voted by the Chamber could not be spent because the factories were so antiquated they could produce neither planes nor weapons at the required rate. As for the country's military leaders, they had turned defeatist. Whether they scorned Czechoslovakia's military potential or predicted, as did General Vuillemin, the air force chief of staff, that in a war with Germany, France would lose every one of its planes within a fortnight,[7] their views were always the same: anything was better than fighting. That was also the Radical position; not by chance were General Vuillemin and Georges Bonnet close friends.

The last nail in the government's coffin was hammered in on March 16, when a Fascist provocation in Clichy, a working-class suburb, led to riots that resulted in seven dead and three hundred wounded. It was now just a question of when the Radicals would bring the cabinet down. Even the supposedly loyal Chautemps, on April 30, made a major speech on a law and order theme, while Daladier carefully positioned himself to succeed Blum as Premier. Only a pretext was needed. It was found when Blum asked for extended powers to deal with the financial and economic crisis. *Le Temps,* always faithful to its owners, denounced this as "the first step toward a dictatorship."[8] On June 21, Blum told the Senate "the majority of the members here is not in favor of the Popular Front."[9] That was, to say the least, an understatement, and that body promptly passed a no-confidence motion. Within the hour, the Premier brought his resignation to the Elysée.

It had, as so often in the previous legislature, been the Radical senators who had thus dispatched the cabinet, and they knew that in doing so they were only following the secret wishes of their colleagues in the Chamber. Still, it would have looked bad for the party to turn its coat so soon. In a masterpiece of political hypocrisy, therefore, the Radical Deputies had voted in favor of the cabinet, safe in the knowledge that the Senate would bring it down.

The question was now who should become the next Premier. Blum, in his resignation meeting with the President, recommended Chautemps rather than Daladier, because he "preferred the diplomatic suppleness and the moderation of the former to the explosions followed by surrenders of the latter."[10] In fact, Lebrun did not yet have a choice. Although Daladier, who had made a startling comeback from his unpopularity of 1934, was fast becoming the leader of the Radicals' center and right wing, he was also the man who had backed and signed the Popular Front accord. Having him succeed Blum would have made the betrayal too obvious. From that point of view as well, Chautemps was much to be preferred, especially since he promptly announced that the Popular Front was continuing, only this time with a Radical-led cabinet.

At first glance, it looked as if the new government was not all that different from the old. Chautemps was Premier, but Blum was Vice-Premier. Many of the ministers remained in place, Daladier at war first and foremost, and Delbos at the foreign ministry; but there was a major change. Georges Bonnet was brought back from Washington and given the finance ministry. It was back to the deflationist policies of the previous legislature, and, indeed, taxes were soon raised while outlays were cut. Because, however, not even Bonnet, that rabid defender of appeasement, could seriously cut the defense budget (and the deficit it caused), his policies, while harmful, were not as disastrous as they would otherwise have been. They were further defanged by the government's decision to let the franc float. It seemed the only way to discourage speculators who expected a further devaluation; but by allowing the currency to find its real value, it helped to stimulate exports. Thus the dollar, which had bought only 15 francs in January 1936 and 21.4 francs in October, was now worth 26 francs.

For all those who understood the game, it was clear that Chautemps had become Premier because he knew just how to conciliate the two wings of his party. For everyone else, the new government was rather startling. "That Chautemps, who was execrated in the Stavisky scandal, should be Blum's successor makes one believe the rumors that Chautemps's successor will be Daladier, who was execrated for the February 6th deaths, and that his successor, in turn, will be Laval," Genêt noted.[11] As it turned out, she was a good prophet, but what she failed to see was the meaning of it all. Chautemps was now solidly backed by the Right because, under the cover of a Popular Front government, he was willing to resume the bankrupt economic policies of the previous legislature; and Daladier was equally popular with the same people because he had shifted from the Left to the Right of his party and represented anti-Socialist authoritarian tendencies. Still, he now had a new rival: Bonnet began to be seen as the future Premier who would head a Radical-conservative coalition.

His position was all the stronger in that, in foreign policy as well as in finance, he embraced the Right's position; no one was willing to go further in appeasing the dictators than Bonnet. That the occasion would come to do so was scarcely in doubt. Already in May, Bullitt had written FDR: "Delbos and Blum are more or less in despair with regard to the possibility of keeping Austria and Czechoslovakia out of the hands of Germany. . . . I do not expect an immediate crash; but before next October we ought to be ready for anything."[12] No one had ever expected Chautemps to resist anything; Bonnet could be counted on to give in; and Delbos was just as weak.

High officials like Delbos and diplomats like Bullitt were not alone in realizing that Hitler's demands were growing with every month. War loomed large on everyone's horizon, and for many Parisians it was both dreadful and incomprehensible. That less than twenty years after the armistice the great massacres should be a probability once again was more than they could accept; so they tried to think of other things. The city's amusements that summer had a brittle, slightly hysterical quality; but then, that seemed to fit right in with the spirit of the World's Fair.

Nothing had been spared to make the Expo a success. There was its location: right in the center of the city, it spread on the banks of the Seine, from the Concorde bridge all the way to the Ile des Cygnes, and from the top of the Trocadéro hill to the Invalides and the Eiffel Tower. There were great new permanent structures: the old and shabby Palace of the Trocadéro, which had been built for the 1889 World's Fair, was replaced by a vast modern building that was to house several museums. Farther down the hill, between the Place d'Iéna and the river, another huge building was to house the two museums of modern art, that of the state and that of the city of Paris. Part of the Grand Palais, which had been built for the 1900 World's Fair, was transformed into the Palais de la Découverte, a museum of science. And then there were the many temporary pavilions: those belonging to foreign nations, those put up by the French provinces and colonies, those in which particular industries were represented, from fashion to electricity, from tobacco to decoration. And of course there were scores of restaurants.

All through the winter and spring, though, the only visible sign that there would eventually be an Expo was a sea of mud, and by April it became clear that almost nothing would be ready on time. The scheduled opening date was May 1. That day, Pierre Lazareff noted, "the day of the official inauguration of the fair, which was meant to be a triumph for the Popular Front and the democracies, only three pavilions [were] completed: those of Germany, Russia, and Italy, the three dictatorships."[13] It was no wonder. Breaking the rule according to which all labor must be French, Germany and Italy had imported their own workers, and the Communists had seen to it that no strike was allowed to delay the Soviet pavilion.

It all seemed unfortunately emblematic: the efficient dictatorships facing the democracies in disarray; but even more striking was the siting of the German and Soviet pavilions, which faced each other on either side of the Pont d'Iéna. Both, naturally, tried to make grandiose statements; both reflected the kind of empty bombast typical of totalitarian regimes. On the right as, standing on the Left Bank, you looked across the river, the German pavilion, designed by Albert Speer, the Führer's favorite architect, consisted of a long rectangular building to the front of which was affixed a one-hundred-and-seventy-foot-tall tower with giant stone pilasters framing mosaics set in a vaguely Greek design; and above that a huge golden eagle held the swastika in its claws. As it was, the building made one obvious statement: the Nazi emblem was visible from everywhere. But in its odd blend of meanness and inflated forms, in the awkwardness of its proportions, it was also a typical example of the kitsch that passed as architecture in the Third Reich. Nor was the interior any better: ever-present portraits of the Führer, a little, mostly ugly, modern Dresden porcelain, and models of ideal workers' cities to be built at some time in the future hardly made for an interesting visit.

Just across the street, the Soviet pavilion was scarcely more successful. A low building with broad windows, it rose at one end to a towerlike plinth faced in marble. This was topped with a seventy-five-foot sculpture of a worker and a young woman from a state farm, their bronze draperies streaming in the wind as they held the hammer and sickle aloft. While there was nothing funny about the German swastika, this sculpture, which was promptly dubbed "Hurrying to the Lubyanka" (the Moscow prison), was the cause of a good many ironic smiles. So, in a different way, was the interior decor.

"The fresco which adorns the great hall represents the regime's leading men," Lazareff noted.[14] "But between the time when the fresco was commissioned and the time when the Paris public was able to see it, most of these great men had been arrested on Stalin's orders, charged with treason, . . . convicted and, in most cases, executed. . . . When my photographer arrived, a painter, perched on a ladder, was trying to disguise the victims of the purges by adding, for instance, a beard to Marshal Tukhachevsky's face, sideburns to Radek, hair to Zinoviev, etc. . . . Just as the photographer was about to take a shot of this, two 'comrade guards' threw themselves brutally on him" and prevented him from taking a picture.

Awkward likenesses aside, the Soviet pavilion offered one other surprise: although supposedly representing the land of workers and peasants, it was far and away the most luxurious in the fair. Most other buildings were made of lath and plaster; the German pavilion, which was to be taken apart and reerected in Nuremberg, was faced with stone; but the Soviet pavilion's walls were entirely covered with the rarest marble. And that was only the beginning. Inside was what Genêt rightly described as "the most costly item in the whole grounds — a fabulous, outsize wall map of new, industrial Russia made entirely of gold and precious and semi-precious stones. The capitals of the provinces are marked by great stars of rubies, the petrol lines from Baku are like a long bracelet of topazes . . . , the names of the cities are lifted in rich letters of gold. . . . We saw," Genêt added, "some French peasant women, in crimped white caps, spit toward the gold and jewels, muttering 'Hypocrites!'"[15]

Compared with all this, the group (only life-size) representing the triumph of fascism, which was placed before the Italian pavilion, looked like an afterthought. The Italians had decided to concentrate on tourism rather than on the Duce's achievements and show the country's monuments instead of Mussolini's various postures; of the three totalitarian states, Italy, at the fair as in life, was far and away the least frightful.

There was, in fact, a good deal to be said for the architecture of its pavilion. The work of Piacentini, it was well proportioned and pleasingly modern. A low tower was connected to a lower pavilion, and both were unified by the white grid pattern set in front of the facade and forming balconies. Behind the grid, the tower's only openings were bands of windows placed high in the wall of each story while the pavilion's walls were almost entirely glass, thus creating both a contrast and an echo, and giving both a soberly elegant look.

All this was ready on May 1. By the time the fair finally opened officially, on May 24, progress had been made on the other pavilions, but many were not completed until the end of June. When they were, however, everyone agreed that the spectacle was dazzling, whether it was the view from the Trocadéro or the fountains or the lighting.

"Starting at low ebb because of mechanical difficulties," Genêt reported, "[the fountains] have now been brought to a height of artistic perfection which nightly rivals the occasional fountain displays at Versailles. Fountains arranged like a formal garden on the edge of the Seine, spouting water shaped like trees, curving like hedges, bursting like tinted blossoms, assuming all the outlines of garden perspectives; fountains in the center of the river, playing like geysers of liquid electric color while superb fireworks spiral and bang in the sky overhead — these are now . . . making Paris's nights." [16] The evenings were, in many ways, the best time to visit the fair: the fountains were on, the pavilions, most of which were anything but handsome, looked their best in the flattering illumination, the restaurants, many of them first-rate, provided a welcome reason to sit down. Most of all, though, there was the lighting.

Even though the 1900 World's Fair had been dedicated to the "Fairy Electricity," it was in 1937 that outdoor lighting really came of age. "Light," the guidebook published by the Paris edition of the *New York Herald Tribune* explained, "is queen of the Exposition. . . . All the buildings are furnished with indirect lighting. A new process has transformed fountains and pools into gold and silver. The multicolored shimmering of the Seine at night is produced by the play of searchlights on a thin layer of oil sprinkled with gold dust. The Eiffel Tower is the pivot of this lighting." [17] The scene must indeed have been magical: the golden river, the tall, multicolored fountains springing from its edges and its very midst, the brilliantly lit pavilions on both banks.

Unquestionably, the Expo of 1937 was a success, and attendance proved it. By the time it closed in November, it had sold well over two hundred million entrance tickets. It was no wonder: aside from all the displays, the restaurants, and the art shows, there were the many novelties of life at the fair. After paying the six-franc entrance fee (about $1.50 in 1993 values), the visitors had many choices of transportation. There were small electric buses that ran, smoothly and silently, on standard routes, at two francs a ride; electric taxis, which cost five francs plus fifty centimes per minute; and launches that went up and down the river, stopping at the Place de la Concorde, the bottom of the Trocadéro hill, the Ile des Cygnes, and the Champ de Mars. If the visitors wanted their own guides, they could hire one for ten francs an hour; if they were foreigners, interpreters were available for the same fee. And throughout the vast grounds, booths were scattered where information could be had along with relief of a different kind since all had clean and modern toilet facilities.

Of course, there were also special events: orchestras and ballet companies came from all over the world to give concerts and recitals; special music was written by Honegger, Florent Schmitt, and others as an accompaniment to the nightly light and water shows. Art, in fact, was an important part of the fair. There were the new, permanent museum buildings; there was art, of varying merit, in many of the pavilions; and there was the great Masterpieces of French Art show in which paintings, tapestries, sculptures, miniatures, silver, drawings, and engravings from the fourteenth to the nineteenth century showed the very best France had done. Much of this had been borrowed from museums abroad; some came from French public and private collections; and it turned out to be the first of the blockbusters. Never before had an exhibition with so ambitious a theme, so great a number of displays, or so many borrowed objects been put together. Never before had so many people visited a single show, and the example it set proved to be lasting — not at the time, the war came too soon for that, but in our own era. The masterpieces of French art were also a comfort to many of the Parisians who saw them: that long series of major works seemed to say that France, which had had such a glorious past, must have an equally brilliant future. After so many reverses, political and otherwise, here was a sign that France was still a great nation.

There was more, of course — a show of Gallo-Roman bronzes, a van Gogh retrospective, and collections of the works of foreign artists in their countries' pavilions. Of these, however, none even came close to what Spain had to offer. It is reassuring to note that not one of the great Spanish artists then working sided with Franco and his crew. As a result, the republic's offerings were nothing short of dazzling, for, besides the Mirós mentioned earlier, there was what may well turn out to be Picasso's masterpiece, *Guernica*.

Picasso was not only the greatest Spanish artist alive, he was also a devoted supporter of the Republican cause and had given the Spanish

Aid Fund over 400,000 francs (about 200,000 1993 dollars). Before that, however, he had been asked by the organizers of the Spanish pavilion to paint a huge mural — it ended up being eleven feet five and a half inches by twenty-five feet five and three-quarter inches. This was so large that he had to rent a new space, in a seventeenth-century building on the Left-Bank rue des Grands Augustins; but once there, the artist stopped working because he had, as yet, no idea what he wanted to do.

That indecisiveness was brutally ended on April 27, 1937. That day, an air fleet given to Franco by Hitler, and made up of Junker and Heinkel bombers protected by Heinkel fighters, attacked the little Basque town of Guernica. By the time the raid was over, the town, an ancient center of Basque tradition, which was holding its weekly market, had been leveled, and many of its people had been killed. As soon as Picasso heard this — the news reached Paris and London the very next day — he began work in a powerful surge of indignation; but as always, he kept careful track of what he was doing. The many preliminary drawings are precisely dated so that today the visitor to the Reina Sofía Museum in Madrid, where both painting and drawings are displayed, can follow the development of one of this century's key images.

Because it was meant to make visible the horrors inflicted by the Fascists on the Spanish population, it disappointed the officials who first saw it and found it insufficiently realistic. It quickly became obvious, however, that they were utterly mistaken: in its vivid depiction of the horrors of war, *Guernica* has ensured that at least one of Franco's crimes will be remembered forever.

Painted in an almost monochromatic palette — black, gray, white — *Guernica* looks simple: on the left, a woman clutches a dead child; her mouth is wide open in a shout of pain, her tongue rigid and pointed; above her the front of a bull emerges from the darkness, while below, forming a base to the painting, lies a figure holding a broken sword. In the center of the canvas, below a glaring light, a disemboweled, agonized horse is straining. On the right three figures, one rushing in, her elongated arm and hand holding a kerosene lamp, the other dragging a broken leg, the third her arms raised in horror as she falls from a burning building, add to the sense of catastrophe. The figures are larger than life-size; the movement violent and compelling.

As is often the case with a masterpiece, *Guernica* is not nearly as simple as it looks. Of course, all of Picasso's artistic experience had gone into it: the terrified, shrieking women, the tortured horse had all appeared, separately, in earlier works. Just as important, though, the preparatory drawings show us the care, thought, and detailed planning that went into the painting. The first sketches define the horse, the bull, and the woman with the lamp who illuminates the sudden calamity; the other figures came later, but the horse was, from the beginning, the central element of the composition. It went through a number of transformations; but as the painting reached its final shape in early June, the horse's head was made to reach upward. "The open mouth," Roland Penrose noted, "spits defiance like the last salvo of a fortress that will not surrender, a gesture which echoes the cries of the defenders of Madrid: "'They shall not pass.'"[18] Even more moving, the four women (and the dead child) express grief, fear, terrified astonishment as their world collapses in flames. Their bodies and faces are distorted, but those very distortions emphasize the painting's terrible message, and are extremely easy to read: simplicity, reached through extreme sophistication, is everything here. Herbert Read saw it well: "His symbols are banal, like the symbols of Homer, Dante, Cervantes. For it is only when the widest commonplace is inspired with the intensest passion that a great work of art, transcending all schools and categories, is born; and being born lives immortally."[19]

Although Picasso went on painting very different subjects, *Guernica* is as true a summary of his artistic achievement as it is of the horrors of a bombed city. Through Cubism and its adaptations in the twenties, the artist had developed a style in which strict reality was subjected to the distortion imposed on it by emotion so as to reach a higher truth. That is unquestionably what happens here; and it is also why *Guernica* remains both one of the key images and one of the transcendent artworks of this century.

There were also other works by Picasso in the pavilion — two large sculptures and the series of etchings entitled *Sueño y mentira de Franco* (Dream and Lie of Franco) in which the story of the misery and violence inflicted on Spain by the dictator is made both tangible and savagely funny. Just as important, the building itself was, architecturally, one of the best at the fair — another proof that talent was on the side of the republic. Its architect, José-María Sert, who eventually became head of the Harvard School of Architecture, designed a simple, square pavilion with wide windows and walls made of metal panels on which texts praising democracy were etched. The forms were simple and harmonious, the materials eminently modern, and the setting perfectly suited to the masterpiece inside. As a result, aside from the Masterpieces of French Art exhibition, the Spanish pavilion was unquestionably the most artistically significant part of the fair, a fact that, at first, not many people realized.

And even if in their bombast, the German and Soviet pavilions seemed grander and more powerful, the Spanish pavilion illustrated an essential truth: it is only in the democracies that the human spirit flourishes.

Unfortunately, the permanent museums that were built as part of the fair left much to be desired as architecture. Both still exist; neither adds much to the beauty of Paris. Perhaps it was because there was something a little mean about the spirit that had inspired the architects. "The facades are *functional*," the official guidebook underlined. "Large plain areas have been kept so that the sculpture . . . is reserved for the essential spots. Everywhere, complex decorations have been avoided, the richer effects being better achieved by the contrast of closed and open, the opposition of vertical and horizontal."[20]

That certainly sounds good; unfortunately, the architects who were chosen to implement these guidelines were competent but utterly uninspired. At the Musée du Trocadéro, Carlu, Boileau, and Azéma designed two great curving buildings set on either side of an open plaza. The site is dramatic: from the top of the hill, gardens stretch down to the Seine while across the river the Eiffel Tower, which was built for the 1889 World's Fair, closes the vista. Unfortunately, the buildings themselves are bland and bloated; the plain facades with their tall, narrow windows look both forbidding and mean; the end pavilions, which are meant to anchor the buildings, are too shallow; and the general effect is of a thin decor pasted on as an afterthought to an otherwise featureless and graceless building. Near the Place d'Iéna, the twin Musées d'Art Moderne look even worse: the central open peristyle linking the two wings and the wings themselves have tall, thin columns as their main ornament. The proportions are bad, and the look, instead of bloated, is feebly anemic.

There was, however, some good architecture at the Fair. Alfred Mallet-Stevens, much in vogue for the past twenty years, gave several of the temporary buildings both dash and drama. At the Pavilion of Light and Electricity, for instance, the sweep of the curved facade was enlivened by the movement forward and back of layered elements, one of which, coming out boldly, served as the entrance. All this was plain wall, with a single oval window placed high on the right, but there was nothing dour about it; and the whole pavilion was anchored by the great multilayered tower that jutted from its midst.

Among the foreign pavilions, the best, after the Spanish one, was that of Finland, designed by Alvar Aalto. Its lower floor was faced with glass, while the simple wood facade above added a feeling of solidity; the forms were simple, clearly influenced by the Bauhaus, and wholly successful.

That was more than could be said for the pavilion of the United States, however. Designed by Paul Wiener, it consisted of a cubelike structure. At the bottom, the white wall was adorned with red stripes, then came a windowless wall, painted dark blue, with three rows of gold stars. At the side, an awkwardly shaped rectangular tower with a semicircular glass protrusion on the front was decorated with totemlike symbols strongly reminiscent of those to be found on the hoods of contemporary cars. In its blend of awkwardness, half-hearted modernism, and vulgar decoration, the building left much to be desired. Inside, at least, there were some exhibits of interest. First-rate Steuben glass, paintings by Bellows, Luks, and other modern artists, photos of some of the TVA's dams, images of early American objects, all brought in the crowds; but perhaps the most successful American contribution was the temporary loan of the Rockettes, whose precise legwork dazzled the Parisians.

Still, there was one pavilion that was not like any other — because it had been designed by an innovative and sometimes eccentric genius. Unlike his officially accepted colleagues, Le Corbusier received no commissions; but, undaunted, he set up his own Pavilion of the New Era. He did not have much money to spend; on the other hand, he was rich in invention, so he designed a simple framework of steel pylons, which came in standardized shapes and were therefore cheap; and instead of masonry walls, he simply used waterproof cloth. The main hall, for instance, had a gold ceiling, one green, one blue, one purple, and one dark gray wall, while the ground was covered with natural ochre-colored gravel. The total effect was thrillingly sumptuous, and cost very little.

The exhibits inside consisted of designs, texts, and maquettes of new buildings belonging to the *ville radieuse* (radiant city). They look already very much like the splendid Cité Radieuse that Corbu designed for Marseilles in the 1950s and offer a strikingly clean, modern, pleasing look: here, in fact, was the great architecture of the future. Naturally, there were also exhortations of all kinds; the great man was nothing if not didactic. Thus, at the entrance a panel said: "Visitors, here is the severe science of urbanism. Urbanism, the bearer of the unhappiness of cities and countryside, or the bearer — soon — of essential joys. Urbanism, that total manifestation of an era's lyricism."[21] Here, more than anywhere else at the fair, the future was in fact being born.

There were glimpses of it elsewhere, though. Air transport was finally coming of age. Once you had seen the fair, you could fly off on visits to the other European capitals. By the spring of 1937 there were five flights a day between Paris and London on Air France, and six on Imperial Airways. The earliest of these left Le Bourget airport at eight A.M. and arrived at Croydon ninety minutes later. Rome, which was farther away, could be reached in a little over six and a half hours, with a stopover at Marseille, but it took only four and a half hours to get to Berlin via Frankfurt. That, certainly, was progress.

What also pointed to the future and was anything but positive was the overall political atmosphere. It surprised no one that Italy, in December, should leave the League of Nations; but it marked the end of the postwar era. Ever since 1920, the security of Europe had been predicated on a strong League, capable of deterring aggression. That this was a mere fantasy had been proved abundantly when Italy invaded Ethiopia; now, even the fantasy was gone.

Just as ominous, on one side of the great divide that split the French, was the rise of Fascist and anti-Semitic publications. For several years already, a few papers and periodicals had been spouting their venom. Now they were joined by a man whose horror of war and resentment of capitalism fused to produce an irrational, indeed demented, hatred of the Jews. That Céline should have fallen into that dark and dreadful trap was a tragedy. It also denoted the perversion of an important part of the French intellectual tradition. Now the country had to face not just a menace from outside, but an inner subversion of its greatest traditions.

Because, in spite of all this, he remained a very great writer — he proved it abundantly after the war — Céline's anti-Semitic books reached a wide public: *Bagatelles pour un massacre,* for instance, sold over eighty-six thousand copies. It is, however, difficult to say which is the harder, understanding how anyone could believe the nonsense he spouted, or actually reading through hundreds of pages of monomaniacal and endlessly repetitive hatred. The first of these novel/denunciations was published in 1937. The framework of *Bagatelles pour un massacre* (Bagatelles for a Massacre) is typically Célinian. In real life, he had fallen passionately in love with a ballet dancer who was to become his second wife. In the book, his hero has written the plot of a ballet but it is rejected because the man in charge favors his Jewish friends; so, in the guise of a conversation with a friend, "Ferdinand" begins to rant: "They know all the darkest corners of the public's opinions, those Yids who run the world, they're pulling all the strings. Propaganda, gold, publicity, radio, the press, 'little envelopes' [bribes], the movies. From Hollywood the Jewish to Moscow the Yid, it's all the same deal. . . . Publicity! What do today's crowds want? They want to kneel before their gold and their shit."[22] As if that were not clear enough, Ferdinand then explains himself: "I have become an anti-Semite," he tells his friend, "and not just a little bit for a laugh but ferociously all the way! . . . To blow up all the Yids!"[23] And, as if that were not ferocious enough, he goes on: "They're all vampires! Rotten to the core, better send them all back to Hitler!"[24] Disgusting as this is, it must in fairness be mentioned that no one, not even Hitler and Himmler, had yet thought of the Final Solution. And there was an explanation: since the Jews all hated Hitler (as if they were not thoroughly entitled to do so), they were going to cause a new European war; and so they had to be stopped. "Fighting a war for the bourgeoisie, it was already shitty enough, but now, to fight for the Jews! . . . That's really licking their gangrene, their worst abcesses. I can't imagine a worse humiliation than to get yourself killed for the Yids."[25] What is wrong here (among many other things) is that logic has been turned upside down: it was Hitler who had attacked the Jews, not the other way around; it was Hitler who was preparing for war; it was Hitler whose program, as detailed in *Mein Kampf,* was a series of brutal conquests.

Partly because *Bagatelles* was such a success, partly because he clearly felt he had more to say, Céline reiterated, and aggravated, his attacks in *L'Ecole des cadavres* (The School for Corpses), which was published the next year. Although its content is, if anything, even more offensive than *Bagatelles, L'Ecole* marks a new step forward in the style that had first appeared in the earlier novels: an apparent stream of consciousness, made of elisions and exclamation points, in which slang and obscenities are freely and frequently used and attain, on occasion, an epic grandeur. This is most noticeable in the first chapter of the book, a dialogue with a siren that is a brilliant (and scatological) exchange of insults.

That mythic creature marks an important evolution in Céline's work, the introduction of delirium as the opening of a gate through which all kinds of semiconscious material can come out; it was to be used again in one of his postwar masterpieces, *D'un Château l'autre.* Here, the dialogue is marked, not just by the language used, but by a kind of exuberant and compelling fantasy. Within a few lines, the exchange of insults between the siren and "Ferdinand" has attained its full intensity.

"'Corpse yourself! [she tells him] Whore-loving crumbling old fart! Old failure! [. . .] old skirt-lifter! Ravager of vaginal sores! Shameful! Shameful prostate cripple! Fuck eater!'

"Ah! I tell her, disgusting garbage! Sewer flower! Shit cleaner! I will abolish you."[26]

That exchange is, in fact, the mechanism through which the subject emerges: after a little more dialogue, "Ferdinand" reaches his goal:

"Hand me the ink of [the polluted] Seine . . . You'll see how much I have to say . . . how I dip my cock into vitriol! It's gonna blaze, burn, crackle, my plea! I'll never have fucked them more thoroughly than when they're pissing on my arse [. . .] Bring me some solid turd, right nearby! . . . Some chance Kaminoky! And I'll be dipping my pen on the double."[27] It is one of the many paradoxes in Céline's work that *L'Ecole,* that pro-Fascist, anti-Semitic book, should have been written, at least in part, in a style and tone that none of the dictators would have allowed for a second in their own countries.

Even more than in *Bagatelles,* the theme here is the coming war. "[It's] no dramatization . . . we're already practically at war," the narrator asserts,[28] and he goes on to explain why: "Let's go right to the bottom of things. The Democracies want war. The Democracies will finally have war. Democracies = aryan masses domesticated, robbed, divided, barbarized, stupidified by the ravaging Jews [. . .] lamed and maddened by the infernal yid propaganda [. . .] Jewish conspiracy, Jewish satrapy, Jewish gangrenous tyranny. [. . .] They stop at nothing. Negroid Jews against the Whites."[29] Here, in fact, is another of Céline's obsessions: race and the superiority of peoples with white skin. Within a few more years the Chinese had, for him, replaced the Jews as the oppressors of the ever more fragile Aryans; in the meantime, the Jews were assumed to have black blood as an easy explanation for all their supposed delinquencies.

In *L'Ecole,* though, the main themes remain Jewish domination and the coming war. In his usual inversion of reality, Céline explains it all: "The Fascist states don't want war. They have nothing to gain from a war. Everything to lose. If peace could last another three or four years, all the European countries would simply and spontaneously turn Fascist. Why? Because the Fascist states are carrying out, under our very eyes, as Aryans, without gold or Jews, without freemasons, the famous socialist program which the Communists and the Yids are always nattering about but which they never carry out."[30] That, of course, was the great rationale: instead of exploitation and unemployment, Hitler provides the workers with jobs and the good life. Today, we know better. Even in 1937 and 1938, many people denounced this for the lie it is; many others, however, were just as credulous as Céline.

Hitler, in fact, as seen in *L'Ecole* is simply the genius who is doing to the Jews what they used to do to the Gentiles. "All Hitler has done is take from the Jews their stupendous, dazzling so-called Marxist program [. . .] He even got the better of them on racism [. . .]. Before Hitler, the Jews thought that racism was just fine. They never themselves hesitated about being racist . . . And by the way there is no more a Semitic race than butter in the clouds. Just a freemasonry of hybrids [. . .]. The Jewish religion is a racist religion, or, more accurately an anti-Aryan [. . .] fanaticism."[31] And, of course, all non-Fascist leaders are seen as simply the tools of the Jews. The list makes for unexpected proximities: "George VI, Beneš [the President of Czechoslovakia], Daladier, M. Lebrun, Roosevelt, Pétain, Mrs. Simpson, Baruch, Stalin [. . .] the House of Lords [. . .] Thorez [the French Communist leader]!

"Who are the bosses of all these marionettes? [. . .] The Jewish bankers."[32]

If *Bagatelles* and *L'Ecole* were simply the ravings of a delirious writer, they obviously would not matter much; but Céline, for all the excesses of his arguments, was in fact giving voice to widely held feelings. Anti-Semitism was rife in France in the thirties — as, indeed, it was in the United States. But whereas in the United States it was merely another form of bigotry, in France it mattered very much more because, just across the German border, it was implemented as a state policy. *Kristallnacht,* the destruction of the Jewish-owned stores throughout the Reich, was almost exactly contemporary with *L'Ecole;* and when other anti-Semites, those, for instance, who wrote in *L'Action française* or *Je Suis Partout,* urged the assassination of Blum, they meant it. Just as dangerous, the admiration they felt for Hitler made them a powerful adjunct to the appeasers. There were many people in Paris in 1938 who saw very little wrong with Hitler; many of them were in positions of influence or power; and that, in turn, helped to determine the French reaction to Nazi aggression. Even men like Chautemps or Daladier or Delbos, who were neither anti-Semitic nor pro-Hitlerian, felt the weight of this atmosphere. At the very least, it did not encourage them to resist the dictators.

Of course, there was also the other side: the Communists and the anti-Fascists; and that helped to create the feeling of tension beginning to pervade Paris. While Céline was dishonoring himself in words, others were gaining glory, not just on the written page, but in action. Many intellectuals, for instance, supported the Republican side in the Spanish civil war, and none earlier or with greater dedication than André Malraux.

As it was, Malraux had already spent two weeks in Spain in May 1936, in the course of which he met intellectuals and political men. The moment he heard about the pronunciamento, therefore, he decided to help the legitimate government; four days later, on July 21, he was back in Madrid. There, it became clear that the government's most urgent need was for planes; aviation was the only way to stop the armored columns making their way to the capital. Planes, Malraux decided, it must be. Returning to Paris, he used all his connections, both in securing planes and in seeing that they reached Spain in spite of the policy of nonintervention. In the end, he managed to transfer some forty planes, accompanied them, and organized the España Escadrille, for which the government made him a colonel.

In fact, Malraux was no aviator, but he was brave and had principles. "By fighting with the Spanish Republicans and Communists, we were defending values which we held (and which I hold) to be universal,"[33] he wrote a little later. For seven months, from August 1936 to February 1937, he often exposed himself to great danger while at the same time taking a key position on the current debate among government supporters. That, too, was important; as a famous French writer, as the friend of the leading members of the government, what Malraux said made a difference, and early on he backed a practical line.

Although the Republicans all worked for the same goal — liberty and the defeat of the Fascist forces — the different parties among them differed as to the best way to succeed. Some of them felt that radically modifying the economic structure of the country was as important as fighting the war, and would indeed give the troops an even more compelling incentive; others, the Communists first and foremost, argued that all efforts must, on the contrary, be directed toward the defeat of the Fascists; that nothing, in a word, was more important than winning. It is to this last camp that Malraux added the weight of his influence; and he was unquestionably right. He was also highly visible, and that, too, was important.

"His manner was simple, direct and, once the contact was made, relatively easy," a journalist remembered.

> Wound as tight as a spring, his hair falling over his eyes, a cigarette hanging from his lips, his face constantly moved by tics, dressed in a casual but elegant way, his daily conversation was made of a bouquet of images and of brilliant ideas which literally fascinated the little circle around him. . . .
>
> "Before and after the coming together of his international squadron, Malraux could be seen every day in the late afternoon in the hall of the Florida Hotel. . . . It was the time when the news was analyzed. Everyone told what he had seen at the front or in town. There were the Russians Ehrenburg and Koltzov, the Chilian Pablo Neruda, the American John Dos Passos, the great Spanish poet Rafael Alberti. It

was the most brilliant literary salon of the time. . . . I remember conversations between Malraux and Hemingway during which "Ernie," staring at his glass and having visibly lost track [of Malraux's rapid and complex French] waited peacefully until, Malraux having come to the end of his breathless improvisations, he could in turn take over.[34]

Fighting the Fascists was important; for a writer like Malraux, whose words were widely read, telling about that battle mattered just as much. More than any of his other books, *L'Espoir* (Hope), which came out in November 1937, is close to the reality. While *La Condition humaine* always keeps a certain distance, the immediate, gritty style of *L'Espoir,* and its publication right in the middle of the war, made it a classic example of committed literature; and because it is less inflated than some of Malraux's other works, it is also one of his best.

Although several of its characters express Malraux's own views and feelings, *L'Espoir* is first and foremost a cry of anguish and rage for the sufferings of the Spanish people, almost defenseless before the arms sent to Franco by the dictators. It is also a vivid description of the kind of warfare that was ravaging Spain, of the feelings of the people, and of the foreign volunteers. Now and again, a chapter is preceded by a date. Here is August 14:

> In the general exaltation and the killing heat, six modern planes were moving up the runway. The Moorish troops [i.e., from the Morocco garrisons] who were attacking in Estremadura were marching from Mérida to Medellín. It was a strong, motorized column, probably the elite of the Fascist troops. A phone call from operation command had just informed Sembrano and Magnin that it was led by Franco in person.
>
> Without leaders, without arms, the militias of Estremadura were trying to resist. From Medellín, the harness maker and the owner of the bar, the farm laborers, a few thousand men among the poorest in Spain were marching, armed with their hunting rifles, against the machine guns of the Moorish infantry.
>
> Three Douglas planes and three multiplace fighters with 1913 model machine guns filled half the width of the field. No fighter planes: they were all in the Sierra. . . . The squadron started following a road which led to the enemy lines. . . . The two Douglases which were behind Sembrano's slowed down: the enemy column was nearing.
>
> Darras, who had just turned the plane over to the first pilot, was staring out intensely. . . . During the war, he had only looked for a

German brigade; this time, he was looking for the thing he had been fighting against in so many ways, in his city hall, in the working men's organizations so patiently built . . . : fascism. . . . Here, in Spain, barely had the hope Darras found in the world been given its chance than fascism was present again.[35]

That Malraux should have eloquently expressed the feelings of an anti-Fascist volunteer is not surprising; but this brilliant intellectual, this inexhaustible talker, also knew how to listen to the people. Among the book's most moving pages is the story of Christ as told by one of the peasants who has come to fight Franco.

Christ Jesus [the peasant says] thought things just weren't going right [in Spain]. He said to himself: that's where I'll go. The angel looked for the best woman in the area, and he appeared to her. She answered: "Don't bother: the child would be born premature, seeing as how I won't have enough to eat. In my street, only one of the peasants has eaten meat, these last four months: he ate his cat." . . . The noise of passing trucks was so loud that, for a moment, the two officers no longer heard the words.

. . . forced the landowners to farm out their fields to the peasants.* Those who have oxen yelled that they were being victimized by those who have rats. And they called in the Roman soldiers. . . . So, for the first time ever, men from all the lands, those that were near and those that were far away, those where it was hot, and those where it was freezing, all those who were brave and poor, started marching *with rifles.* . . . And they understood with their hearts that Christ was alive in the community of the poor and the humiliated here. And in long lines, those of every country who knew poverty well enough to die fighting it, with their rifles when they had rifles, and with their hands when they had none, came to lie, one after the other, on the Spanish earth.[36]

Whether Malraux invented this parable or adapted it from a story he had heard doesn't matter. The peasants and the pilots, fighting poverty and tyranny, have become one in *L'Espoir* — as they did in actuality. For Malraux, and many other writers, from Hemingway to Orwell, the war defined a world in which fascism had for too long been allowed to triumph. For the first time in a very long time, war had become a crusade,

---

*Ellipsis at the beginning of the sentence is in the original.

a way for men to defend right and justice. In 1937 it still looked as if it might succeed.

Back in Paris, the book was predictably criticized by the Right and applauded by the Left. Certainly it helped to keep Spain in the forefront of conversations, as did another book on the war, *Les Grands Cimetières sous la lune* (The Vast Graveyards in the Moonlight); this last, however, surprised more people. The work of Georges Bernanos, it marked the conversion of an ardently Catholic conservative moved by his horror at the priests who so cheerfully officiated at—and encouraged—the execution of many thousands of Republicans. Bernanos had been a friend of Charles Maurras and the *Action française* group; but he was also an honest man and added his considerable talent to the great outcry against Franco, Mussolini, and Hitler.

Still, even if in Spain the massacres continued, life in Paris went on, just as frivolously as ever — more so, in fact, as if a frenzy of pleasure-seeking was taking over. There were, naturally, fashionable new bars. At Le Tardets, there was splendid Basque food as well as a decor by Jean-Michel Frank; it was agreed that fashionable women (and men) looked at their best in the setting of pale *faux-bois* walls and indirect lighting; while at Michel et Doucet's the chief attraction was neither the food nor the clientele but Doucet's own entrancing jazz piano.

Fashion, as usual, contributed its note. Chroniclers decided that evening dresses had become stranger, more daring, and they were right. Lucien Lelong, for instance, designed a plain, belted black lace sheath with two enormous black tirelike ruches at the bottom. During the day, the hats took over: from huge turbans to witches' pointed bonnets, the Parisiennes sported increasingly large and eccentric headgear.

Perhaps the oddest social innovation, all in the interest of having a good time, was recorded by Janet Flanner. "Ted Peckham, the boy from Cleveland who launched the Guide Escort Service in New York, through which lorn ladies could rent a guaranteed Harvard, Yale, or Princeton man to squire them around town at night, has just opened his Paris branch," she wrote. "While a diploma from a fashionable alma mater may be enough of a credential for a guide in Manhattan, it is to be noted that a French cavalier has to produce a mother who is in the *Almanach de Gotha*. . . . So far about a hundred sprigs of the French nobility are enrolled — for, of all things, patriotic reasons. They and their elders feel that American ladies have in the past been getting bad notions about France and Frenchmen. . . . The Paris escorts come cheaper than the New York . . . lads. The charge for a Frenchman is only two hundred francs [about $90 in 1993 value] until two A.M., and a hundred francs an hour from then on."37

History does not record whether the scheme succeeded. There was, at any rate, no shortage of presentable men in Paris. Indeed, with the passing of every month, having fun came to seem more important. Of course, that could take many forms. The intrigues directed by Mme de Portes, Reynaud's mistress, at the Chautemps government, and those engineered by Mme de Crussol to propel Daladier into the premiership no doubt struck these two ladies as the very height of a good time. At any rate, even after the World's Fair closed its doors in November, the swirl of activities continued. Paris, at the close of 1937, was determined to have as much fun for as long as possible.

Here, indeed, was yet another divide. While ordinary people might be split between the group that thought Hitler should be resisted and the group that thought he should be appeased, between pro and anti-Fascists, between decency and anti-Semitism, the Tout-Paris, firmly convinced that it was above it all, concentrated on its own little games. Parties, the latest gossip, the most intricate political plot, all activities from which the mass of the population was excluded, mattered enough to become a separate reality. It was a good way to pretend that nothing would ever change, that the privileged would always retain their privileges. It was also a good way to hasten the catastrophe they were so busy ignoring.

CHAPTER
# ELEVEN

# PEACE AT ANY PRICE

THE FRENCH, as 1937 faded into 1938, were so busy hating one another that they paid relatively little attention to what was happening outside the country. At the same time, they found themselves agreeing on one basic idea: anything was better than war. Partly as the result of the dreadful losses of the Great War, partly because the Right's pacifist and anti-Semitic propaganda had had a wide effect, a majority of the electorate felt sure that nothing was worth fighting for. This was based, in part, on a complete misunderstanding of Hitler's goal: at the worse, people thought, he would claim the German populations given by the Treaty of Versailles to other countries. That seemed only mildly alarming; no one cared very much where the Sudetenland (now in Czechoslovakia) ended up. As for the increasingly likely Anschluss between Germany and Austria, well, that hardly seemed worth opposing seriously.

Still, people worried, and the utter feebleness of the Chautemps cabinets — the first having fallen, a second one replaced it — did nothing to reassure them. The world, they realized, was a dangerous place, and a government that did its best not to govern seemed less than adequate. What the French wanted, really, was that oxymoron, a government strong enough to cave in whenever war threatened. They also wanted to be reassured in any way possible. And while it was still possible they wanted to enjoy themselves.

These last two needs came together in a great festival whose pretext was the state visit of the King and Queen of England, and the government understood it perfectly. That Great Britain should still be a close ally seemed highly reassuring. Not even Hitler, surely, would be rash enough to declare war on France *and* the British Empire, and just in case anyone forgot, the press, illustrated magazines first and foremost, kept running articles on the size and might of Britain's overseas possessions. Then the exceptionally sumptuous reception given Their Majesties was gratifying in itself, and reassuring because it proved that France still knew how to do things on a grand scale.

As for the government that really governed, but could be counted on to avoid war at any cost, it, too, came into office: Daladier, whom those in the know described as a reed painted to look like an iron bar, proved very good at putting down the Deputies and even better at giving in to the dictators, and so he earned himself a solid popularity. Thus reassured, however, the French still worried; but they did their best to think about pleasanter things.

Happily for the Parisians, the many distractions available throughout the city made it easy to ignore reality. The quality of these amusements varied, of course. Kirsten Flagstad, appearing in France for the first time and singing Isolde in such a way as to deserve twenty-eight curtain calls, did not belong in quite the same category as that perennial entertainer, Maurice Chevalier. But then Chevalier, too, was triumphant; in what was essentially a straight recital at the Casino de Paris, he crooned, he danced, he jutted his famous lower lip, and, to the delight of his packed audiences, he barked out a German love ballad in the hysterical tones used by Hitler when addressing a mass audience.

That was funny. So, in her way, was another perennial. Mistinguett, in her mid-sixties, had evidently decided that about forty-two was a comfortable age and there she remained, her famous legs as lithe and lovely as ever. "She performed," Genêt reported, "in a good, tough melodrama of the *fortifs* [the raw area at the edge of Paris], in which she was rattled about; the show was smothered under ostrich plumes and *jazz hot;* there was a dog tableau with *Mis et les boys,* all equipped with canines in a *pastiche* sketch of other days. There was indeed everything to make the spectator believe the Casino's management's claim that they spent three million francs on Mistinguett's latest comeback and recovered five hundred thousand francs of it, thanks to her ageless energy, in the first three days."[1]

Anyone could buy a ticket to Mistinguett's show. Only the select few — or, actually, the select many — were invited to Lady Mendl's great ball on July 2, but it was lavishly covered by the press, French and American, and served much the same purpose: whether they watched *la Mis* kick up her heels or the Tout-Paris guzzle champagne, the message of those who reported on these great events was the same: life was going on, after all, and more cheerfully than ever.

"The most beautiful ball Paris has seen in ages" is how, according to *Vogue,* Lady Mendl's fete was described, with guests adding ecstatically, as they watched the lavish goings-on: "It's prewar" or "It's pure Boni de Catellane,"[2] a reference to the spendthrift nobleman whose parties had dazzled Paris at the turn of the century. Indeed, the hostess had gone all out to please. The guests who arrived at her villa in Versailles found themselves in a magical setting. On that warm summer night, there was the illuminated garden, of course, with its fountains, marble statues, and great urns full of cut flowers silhouetted against the shrubbery. The specially built green and white dance pavilion, with its white banquettes, colored plaster trees, and striped draperies, had a floor resting on tiny springs, so that you felt you really were floating on air. You needed to: there were three orchestras, a black American one, a Cuban one, and an all-woman Hungarian waltz band. When dancing (or gossiping) made you thirsty, you could go out to the round champagne bar, which was topped by a large striped umbrella with a treetrunk for a handle. And there were the arrangements within the house itself.

Small supper tables were set around the rooms so as to create a nightclub-like atmosphere. Garlands of red roses, three airplanes full, were made up by Constance Spry and brought over from London. They hung over the doorways, were draped over the mantels, and twined around the candelabra. As for the vast hot and cold buffet, it was served from eleven at night to five in the morning, by which time all the elements of a solid English breakfast were at the ready.

Still, there was more — a circus, in fact, with satin-clad acrobats (a ropewalker was performing as the guests arrived), a pailletted clown, and trained Shetland ponies that Lady Mendl herself took through their paces. But all that was at nothing compared with the glamour of the hostess and her guests. All fashionable Paris was there that night, and the couturiers had been working hard. Elsie Mendl herself, dazzling in a diadem and necklace of aquamarines and diamonds, set the tone by wearing a white organdy dress from Mainbocher. White, indeed, was the keynote of the evening. "Bouffant white dresses floated across the garden," *Vogue* reported. "Madame Paul-Louis Weiler [was] in a white satin pannier dress and diamonds, the comtesse de Montgomery . . . in Chanel's white net dress trimmed with baby-lace bows. . . . Chanel herself had on tiers of white lace, with gardenias in her hair and a great display of her most beautiful jewels. Mlle Eve Curie was at the height of her beautiful neat perfection in pink tucked tulle. Schiaparelli wore a white Directoire gown embroidered in gold with a long fuchsia chiffon scarf and white satin sandals with three-inch soles."[3] It was, everyone agreed, the ball of the season. By the time it was over, the Tout-Paris had every reason to feel sated with splendor, for less than two weeks earlier, the French government had set itself to prove that when it came to receiving a state visitor it was the true successor of the Sun King. Never, perhaps, had an allied monarch been greeted with such display.

That the monarch in question was King George VI had, of course, a political significance. In a world where the dictators were all too clearly in the ascendent, a dazzling reaffirmation of the Entente Cordiale, which had linked France and Great Britain before and during the war, seemed to offer hope. With France and England so closely united, the reasoning went, surely even Hitler would think twice about his next move. Whether a series of lavish fetes was an adequate substitute for the political will to resist the Führer or for a strong army was perhaps questionable, especially since the visit was pure display: no treaty was signed, no new agreement reached. That, however, was a worry everyone was busy avoiding. Instead, the royal visit was treated, not just like the wonderful spectacle it was, but as the visible sign of a political renaissance.

Already in February, Pertinax, one of the most influential journalists in Paris, had written: "The royal trip . . . is the equivalent of a warning to the powers who think our disorders will last and who are behaving in consequence."[4] The visit itself was to last four days, from the nineteenth to the twenty-second of July; and the arrival on French soil of King George and Queen Elizabeth (today the Queen Mother) was greeted with equal joy by virtually all the papers.

"Paris gives a triumphant welcome to the British sovereigns," a huge headline announced on the front page of *L'Oeuvre,*[5] while *Le Petit Parisien,* across its front page, played on happy memories: "1918: Frenchmen, remember the Tommies! 1938: Paris under the sign of the Union Jack!"[6]

and *Paris-Soir* announced: "We have discovered that England always delivers on its promises, and almost always does even more than it has undertaken to do."[7] As for *L'Illustration,* it simply put out a whole special issue on the visit.

Of course, facts occasionally gave way to a more pleasing fiction. General Weygand, recently retired as chief of the General Staff, explained that in its resistance to German aggression Great Britain "gives us an example of determination, of union, of hard work which cannot inspire us too thoroughly."[8] Clearly, the general had failed to notice that Neville Chamberlain, the British prime minister, was determined only to appease Hitler. These, however, were felt to be petty cavils. Parisians wanted to rejoice, to feel secure, and to enjoy the display; and so they did.

It was easy. The French government went all out, spending 24 million francs (about $8 million in 1993) on the organization of the festivities, and that sum did not include the cost of permanent installations: the gold bathtub in the King's bathroom or the silver bathtub in the Queen's, or the complete redecoration of the apartment in the foreign ministry that was to be their home during their stay. As for the program, the events, even the menus, all had been painstakingly planned: a ministerial committee, presided over by Camille Chautemps, saw to every detail.

The visit began the moment the King and Queen stepped onto French soil at Boulogne, with the inauguration of a monument commemorating the Franco-British alliance in the war. That afternoon there was a drive throughout a wildly enthusiastic Paris, followed in the evening by an "artistic soiree" given by President Lebrun at the Elysée Palace. Just how much attention the guests paid to the performers who came on after the dinner remains uncertain, however; any normal human being would have felt a little sleepy after a dinner that, beginning with a consomme with quenelles went on to medallions of lobster à la Marinier, turkey à la Rosemonde, asparagus with chantilly sauce, ortolans (small game birds) with foie gras, Vendôme salad (it had eggs in it), ice cream, and assorted desserts, all washed down with 1923 Château Yquem, 1924 Haut Brion, 1923 Chambertin, 1928 Pommery Champagne, and port.

What struck everyone, in spite of this, was the royal pair's attentiveness, politeness, and charm. The King was immensely conscientious, spoke to everyone, saluted tirelessly, but it was the Queen with whom everyone fell in love. Endlessly smiling, endlessly delighted, she made everyone feel as if she cared about them personally. More amazing still, in the crinolined evening gowns designed by the British couturier Norman Hartnell, she struck the usually critical French as a model of chic; and the dazzling jewels that went with the dresses fascinated everyone. Starting on the nineteenth, her first day, she had seduced the crowds; on the twentieth, it was official and social Paris that fell under her sway. That both her attentiveness and her evident delight should have been so steadily sustained through ceremony after ceremony, everyone agreed, was a major feat.

Once again driving through ecstatic crowds, the royal couple, on that second day of the visit, lay the obligatory wreath on the Tomb of the Unknown Soldier; then, in the afternoon, there was a dance performance at Bagatelle, the eighteenth-century house and more recent rose garden in the Bois de Boulogne; and in the evening a gala performance at the Opéra, where the Tout-Paris, in white tie, orders, and jewels, filled every available seat. Indeed, there had been many a drama when it came to making up the list of invitations. "There were begging letters and telephone tragedies. Those who were not invited felt insulted; those who were given one seat wanted two," Jean Zay, the education minister, remembered.[9] It was no wonder he felt so superior; as a member of the cabinet he automatically rated two seats. Still, those who finally made it to the Opéra that night were thrilled, and ready to show it: "When the King and Queen appeared," the writer André Maurois recorded, "a cheer began, swelled out and became a hymn of love."[10]

By then the royal couple must have been feeling tired and overfed; but the program was relentless. On the morning of the twenty-first, they visited a British hospital, then watched a military parade, after which they lunched at the Palace of Versailles, and watched a specially staged ballet. That, however, cannot have taxed them as heavily as the lunch itself; George VI had a delicate stomach, and it must have taken real heroism to cope with four days of menus that went on and on and on.

First there was caviar; then melon, with sherry to drink; then trout in a crayfish-laden sauce, with 1926 Montrachet; then lamb mignonettes, with 1915 Hospices de Beaune; then stuffed quails, with 1919 Corton-Grancey; then duck with cherries and 1918 Mouton-Rothschild; then a salad; then a sorbet made with 1921 Lanson Champagne; then supremes of chicken, with 1904 Latour; then baked truffles; then an iced mousse with 1921 Yquem; then a further peach dessert with 1911 Pol Roger Champagne. Of course, the French have always been known for the glories of their cuisine, but it is still a daunting list. Nor was it the only huge meal of the day; that evening, Georges Bonnet, the foreign minister, was giving a musical evening to honor the King and Queen.

"As one came into the dining room, which opens out to the garden," the ever-modest Bonnet remembered, "our guests were enchanted by the spectacle that awaited them: on the tablecloth embroidered with leaves and garlands in gold lamé, the wide-facetted Baccarat crystal sparkled along with the gold of the plates and the cutlery, and the light of the candles set in two huge Empire candleholders placed at each end of the table. In the middle, in harmonious order, were set the incomparable pieces from Napoleon's ormolu service — epergnes, soup tureens, center-piece . . . and from all the epergnes filled with grapes there came bunches of pink flowers."[11] And, of course, there was another huge meal.

It was all a triumph: the solidity of the alliance had been demonstrated, France's ability to put on a dazzling show was confirmed. The visit, the *Times* of London commented, "was not an event but an epoch,"[12] and a usually more critical American fully agreed. It was, Genêt wrote, "the biggest and most popular public event since the armistice. . . . [That night] superb synchronized fireworks were shot from the top and bottom of the Tour Eiffel, the multicolored fountains of last year's Exposition were revived to play in the Seine, searchlights at the Grand Palais criss-crossed geometrical patterns in the dark sky. . . . Diplomatically, artisti-cally, even humanly, the royal visit was a roaring success. . . . For four friendly days, republican Paris resounded to the loud singing of 'Godd Saive ze Kinng.'"[13]

Most gratifying of all, perhaps, was the fact that Paris had now proved that it could put on an even more impressive show than the dictators; for a few days at least, the Führer's parades in Nuremberg seemed tacky. Unhappily, it was only for a very short while. In London, Neville Cham-berlain remained firmly committed to giving Hitler whatever he wanted while in Paris, Bonnet, the foreign minister, was an even more ardent appeaser. As for French politics, they were as complex and as self-defeating as ever.

Early in 1938, in fact, it looked as if the economy was beginning to plunge back into depression. Unemployment remained high, businesses were failing again in great numbers, and at the same time the rate of inflation was speeding up. That last phenomenon was actually positive; the prices, which had fallen so catastrophically from 1932 to 1936, needed to go up again; but salaries were not keeping up with the rate of reflation. It was at that point that Chautemps, who had been the Premier for almost seven months, came up with a typically Radical maneuver.

Naturally, it involved a sharp turn to the Right, but the trick was to make it all look like a parliamentary necessity. This was easily done. On January 14, 1938, Chautemps and his highly conservative finance minister,

Bonnet, asked for special decree powers that would be used to raise taxes, cut outlays, and limit the power of the unions. This, obviously, violated the charter of the Popular Front; the Communists could therefore be expected to resist and, indeed, announced that they would abstain in the ensuing vote. The Radicals, however, still did not want to be seen as responsible for a break with the Socialists, which might well shock their electorate. The trick was, therefore, for Chautemps to arrange for the fall of his own government in such a way that he would be called on to succeed himself. In a most unusual departure from his usual careful courtesy, the Premier announced that he was giving the Communist party its liberty, thus neatly but subtly excluding it from the majority supporting the cabinet. It was the end of the Popular Front, and the Socialists promptly resigned. This was just what Chautemps had wanted: now that the Socialists had taken themselves out of the cabinet, Chautemps also resigned, thus bringing down his own government.

So far, his scheme had proceeded exactly according to plan. Avoiding the odium of the break, the fallen Premier could now move on to an alliance with the conservatives: it was, after all, a Radical tradition to get elected on the Left, then move, in mid-legislature, to the Right. Before that could happen, however, the usual rites had to be followed. First, Lebrun called on Herriot, who, as Speaker, could expect to gather a majority. Herriot, however, intended to be a candidate for the presidency of the Republic a year hence, so he declined.

Bonnet, the outgoing finance minister, was then sent for. This was precisely what he had been scheming for and, as a Radical and a cabinet minister, he should have had a good chance. What he forgot, though, was that his party had changed: while there were indeed some Radicals who were as conservative as himself, there was also a solid liberal group who considered him anathema. Still, he came before the Radical Deputies to ask for their support. "He announced," his fellow Radical Jean Zay noted, "that he could count on the support of the Union sociale républicaine [a small party halfway between the Radicals and the Socialists] even though its president had said the reverse, and that the Socialists would display a favorable neutrality. In fact . . . Georges Bonnet had in his pocket a letter from Léon Blum warning him that the Socialists declined to support him, and several of his listeners knew it. . . . During the vote [within the Radical group] Bonnet leaped from his chair in order to count the raised hands himself. On his face, one could see ambition and love of power, the evil genies of this man."[14] Both the dishonesty and the self-seeking that Zay noticed were indeed characteristic of Bonnet, and they made him a dangerous man. That, together with his deflationary economic views, was enough: not even his fellow Radicals would support Bonnet's bid for the premiership.

Next, Lebrun sent for Blum, who announced that he would put together a national union government so as to cope with the looming foreign policy crisis; but the Right refused to cooperate, and Blum withdrew.

That was precisely what Chautemps had expected; and when Lebrun now called on him, he had his new cabinet all ready: it was to be all Radical, with the Socialists going back to their old tactic of support without participation. That there would be actual support was ensured by Bonnet's removal from the finance ministry to the exalted, but largely meaningless, position of minister of state for economic affairs. As it was, Chautemps had every reason to be pleased. His deliberate fall had led, as planned, to a new cabinet over which he still presided; the Socialists were out; but the transition to an alliance with the Right had been so managed as to seem easy and necessary. It was, however, also clear that the new government was just a stop on the way, and thus not likely to endure: there was no majority in the Chamber for a purely Radical cabinet following conservative policies. That hardly mattered to Chautemps, though: the great art of frequent premiers was to fall in just the right way. By easing the transition to the Right, Chautemps knew that he would be a member of the next cabinet and that at some future date he was highly likely to become Premier again.

Bullitt naturally watched it all, and reported to FDR. "You have doubtless followed with amusement the gyrations which resulted in the calling of Monsieur Chautemps to replace Monsieur Chautemps," he wrote on January 20. "The curious thing about the 'crisis' is that no one in France took it seriously. I have never heard so many roars of laughter from the leading politicians as during those days which were supposed to be critical."[15] Of course, Bullitt had failed to perceive that it was all a highly sophisticated, and not unfunny, ploy in which the players knew from the beginning just how it would all end.

Unfortunately, these gyrations proved more than sufficient to absorb Chautemps's attention. That in Central Europe Hitler was preparing to swallow Austria worried him not at all. In any event, given his proverbial lack of backbone, he was not likely to seek a confrontation with the Führer. Bullitt may have on occasion been flummoxed by French politics, but he saw the rest of the situation very clearly indeed: "Austria will fall into the hands of Germany," he went on in the same letter, "and France will do nothing except protest feebly. . . . That will give Germany a control-ling position in Central and Eastern Europe."[16]

And so it happened. With the Anschluss crisis unfolding, France had a government led by a man whose greatest talent was for doing nothing, and whose foreign minister was so peace-loving as to be an appeaser at any price. The result came soon enough. On March 8, Chautemps asked again for special financial powers, knowing this would bring about his fall, and thus free him from responsibility for France's reaction to the Anschluss; on the ninth, the Socialists refused; on the tenth, Chautemps resigned; and on the twelfth, Hitler sent his army marching into Austria. On the day the Anschluss was proclaimed, therefore, France was without a government. Once again, Hitler had won at no cost to himself.

There were, however, a few uncharitable observers who thought that Chautemps had fallen *in order* not to deal with the Anschluss. Chautemps himself always denied it; but, certainly, he knew it was coming; and even if he resigned purely for reasons of internal politics, it remains that he demonstrated a very skewed sense of priorities.

In any event, the facts remained. Hitler had just swallowed Austria and France was without a government. Clearly, something had to be done, but it was still too soon for the right-leaning Daladier cabinet toward which President Lebrun was working. First, the President decided to prove conclusively that the Popular Front was dead. He did so by asking Blum to take power.

Of course, everyone understood that Blum would either fail to form a government, or else would succeed only to fall within a few days. Blum knew it as well, but, unlike many of his colleagues, he had become fully conscious of the German threat and knew there was no more time to be wasted in political games. So he called a meeting of the non–Popular Front Deputies and begged them to enter a government of national unity, but, keeping firmly to politics as usual, most of the conservative Deputies rejected his offer. It was no wonder: many of them hated him far more than they dreaded Hitler.

The new Blum government, therefore, looked very like the first: the immovable Daladier was still at defense, but this time Chautemps was out, and Delbos was replaced at the foreign ministry by the more vigor-ous Paul-Boncour. Another thing remained unchanged: the General Staff's unwillingness to contemplate the possibility of war. At a meeting late in March that brought together Blum, Paul-Boncour, Daladier, and the top generals, the latter "revealed that they had not considered, that they were not considering any plan to defend Czechoslovakia," the foreign minister noted;[17] clearly, if Hitler was to be stopped, the French army would not be doing the stopping.

Nor would Blum; his new government lasted a bare three weeks. On April 7, his financial measures were approved by the Chamber, but with 56 Radical Deputies abstaining; the next day, the Senate, repeating itself, brought down the government. The demonstration engineered by Lebrun and the Radicals was now complete: the Popular Front majority in the Chamber was finally dead. So this time there was no confusion: after Lebrun had ritually sent for Herriot, who ritually declined, and for Bonnet, who failed again to convince his own party that he deserved to be Premier, it was Daladier's turn. No one doubted that he would succeed. As defense minister, he appealed to the Right and was thought to have just the sort of competence needed at a time of crisis; so three of its leading politicians, Paul Reynaud, Georges Mandel, who had been Clemenceau's assistant, and the moderate Auguste Champetier de Ribes became ministers. The Left, remembering that Daladier had led the Radicals into the Popular Front, still believed in him, and the Socialists, who refused to join the new cabinet, agreed to support it. As for the Radicals, both wings of the party were equally represented, with Chautemps, naturally, as minister of state, all according to plan. The new government had something for everyone, as became clear when, to the amazement of all, it was voted in by 576 to 5.

Right at the heart of the new team, however, there was a most dangerous discrepancy: Daladier owed part of his popularity to the assumption that, as defense minister (an office he kept when he became Premier), he could be counted on to resist Hitler. It was an impression that Daladier himself seemed to confirm. "His only passion," a close assistant remembered some years later, "was the defense of the country against the danger from outside."[18] The man he chose as foreign minister, however, was prepared to do anything to avoid resistance to Hitler. Paul-Boncour understood it quickly: as his cabinet was being formed, Daladier asked him to come in to see him. "I would like to keep you [at the foreign ministry]," the Premier-designate told Paul-Boncour, "but let us be frank with each other. Your attitude [of support] for Czechoslovakia is worrying people, and not just in France [a clear allusion to the British]. Germany is telling us: 'Why does M. Paul-Boncour concern himself with Central Europe? It is our domain, France has nothing to do there.'" Against that argument, Paul-Boncour's plea that the security of France was dependent on that of Poland and Czechoslovakia proved useless. "I have thought about all that," Daladier told him. "The policy you are defending is a great policy, it is worthy of France; I do not think we are strong enough to follow it. I am going to take Georges Bonnet instead."[19]

With that, the die was cast. Not only was Bonnet notoriously sympathetic to Hitler and a leader of the appeasement forces, he was also a liar and a cheat. Thus, any time he thought that Daladier was not giving in fast enough or thoroughly enough, he proceeded to do so in his stead, while lying to his colleagues about it. Daladier could not have handed Hitler a better present, in fact, than his choice of foreign minister.

In the meantime, the new Premier proceeded to give a convincing impersonation of a resolute leader. On April 10, when he took office, he addressed the country over the radio and sounded like a very model of firmness. "Today," he announced, "the only problem is to save the country. . . . Let all of us think about what France has given us, in material goods, moral dignity, and freedom."[20] It was an effective propaganda line; henceforth, Daladier presented himself as the only strong leader available, and the people believed him, largely because it seemed reassuring to have someone so firmly taking charge. Within a few days, in fact, Daladier had become a semidictator; after requesting, and getting, special powers from the Chamber and Senate, he prorogued them for the next six weeks. By the end of the year the Parliament, whose sittings in earlier years had been virtually uninterrupted, had met for only six weeks out of nine months.

Even more striking, when it met, it had almost nothing to do; because it authorized the cabinet to rule by decree, its role was reduced to ex post facto approval of decisions in which it had had no share. That, obviously, was a great convenience for Daladier; and to ensure the Chamber's compliance, he played heavily on the already widespread feelings of antiparliamentarism, coupling this with carefully disseminated rumors that a dissolution of the Chamber might follow any attempt by the Deputies to reassert themselves.

That was typical of the new state of things. Without changing the constitution or even announcing a reinforcement of the executive, Daladier was actually beginning to behave very much like a strongman. All the propaganda resources of the state were mobilized in a great campaign that portrayed him as inflexible but just, firm but thoughtful: on the state-owned radio, on the state-financed newsreels, the Premier could be heard or seen, week after week, lower lip jutting out ferociously, as he inspected army or navy groups or made enthusiastically received speeches.

That might have been all very well — certainly the French needed to be reassured — if it had not been for two small facts: first, Daladier's apparent decisiveness was just a mask for his weakness and indecision; second, he was no more the master of his own government than he was of the events themselves. Indeed, he was not at all sure of what he wanted to do, and his economic policy was muddled in the extreme, blending incentives — a program of public works and credits for commerce and industry — with an 8 percent rise in taxes.

By August it had become clear that this policy was a failure, so Daladier tried again. "The strength of a country, which guarantees its independence, is not measured only by the might of its armed forces but at least as much by a daily effort in the factory. . . . We must put France back to work," he explained in a radio speech.[21] When he went on to say that the forty-hour week could no longer be considered sacrosanct, he promptly lost two ministers from the left wing of the cabinet; but now it no longer seemed to matter. It was even arguably a convenience since it allowed him to shift the cabinet further toward the Right: the departing ministers were replaced by two extreme conservatives, one of whom, Anatole de Monzie, was a declared admirer of Mussolini — this four days after the Premier had told Jean Zay: "If there is a man whom I will never have as a minister again, that man is M. de Monzie."[22]

This sort of cave-in was typical. Another, even more noticeable example of it came in November. The economy still had not improved; production still was low. Bullitt, as always well informed, warned FDR that while France was producing only forty-five warplanes a month, the Germans were turning out between three and five hundred — an obviously catastrophic imbalance, and one confirmed by the air minister, who admitted that the Luftwaffe would most probably drive the French air force out of the sky shortly after the opening of a war.[23] Clearly, something was not going right; so the Premier called on the rival he most feared.

Although Paul Reynaud was Daladier's minister of justice, the Premier was well aware that both Reynaud and his mistress, Mme de Portes, were intriguing to replace him. Indeed, the war of the salons had replaced speeches in the Chamber, and the pro-Reynaud faction made sure to blame Daladier's irresolution and incompetence at every opportunity. Still, Reynaud understood the economy, so, on November 1, Daladier shifted him from justice to finance, thus giving great power and greater visibility to the man he most feared.

That the Premier should thus be at a loss about running the country was bad enough. His management of foreign policy was worse yet, in large part because he had very little control over it. "Georges Bonnet is carrying out personal negotiation which he conceals from Daladier and the Council of Ministers," Reynaud complained in August,[24] and he was right: because Reynaud, Zay, and a few other ministers were antiappeasement, Bonnet simply conducted his own foreign policy in a secrecy so deep that it extended even to his chief civil servants. There was no mystery about his position, though; anything was better than war, any sacrifice was justified if it prevented it.

For all his constant scheming and lying, Bonnet made it very clear where he stood: "Let us not be heroic, we are not up to it," he told Pierre Lazareff. "It is all very well to make yourself the policeman of Europe but for that you need something more than water pistols, straw handcuffs, and cardboard prisons."[25] The consequence of this attitude was an eagerness to give in to Hitler's every demand. As for the atmosphere at the foreign ministry and within the government, it was poisonous.

"I was struck and saddened by the fear everyone expressed," a French diplomat noted. "One man would point in confidence to the stagnation of our aviation, another announced that Poland was deserting us, everyone wondered whether our position vis-à-vis Czechoslovakia had not become untenable."[26] This was the daily fare at the foreign ministry. Indeed, by the end of May, Bonnet, in his conversations with foreign ambassadors, was referring to the French commitment to Czechoslovakia as entered into "rightly or wrongly,"[27] leaving no doubt about how he felt. Thus when, in September, Hitler started demanding the Sudetenland, he was well informed about the French willingness to cave in.

Of course, Bonnet was hardly alone. In the Senate, a surprisingly large section of the Chamber, and the upper reaches of the civil service, appeasement was seen as the only possible policy. That the result of giving in time after time to Hitler might, as Churchill was predicting, bring dishonor and then war was not even considered. Soon the "bellicists," as those in favor of resisting Nazi Germany were called, found themselves under general assault. Even the Paris salons were wildly pacifist, not least that of Marie-Laure de Noailles, whose advanced artistic positions and Jewish parentage might have entailed a little more revulsion at Nazi "culture."

This craven attitude went comfortably together with the rapidly rising wave of anti-Semitism. The connection was simple: the Jews wanted to fight Germany because Hitler was putting them in their place; any

attempt at resisting German expansion was thus just one more manifestation of the Jewish plot. It was a line that was tirelessly repeated in all the
extreme-Right publications, *L'Action française, Gringoire, Je Suis Partout,*
and a number of others. The "bellicists" were either Jewish — Mandel,
Zay, Blum — or bought by the Jews — Reynaud first and foremost, the
argument ran. It was also a line favored by Bonnet's own wife, Odette,
and she was known to influence him; and when the Académie française
elected Maurras in June, it, too, was sending the same message.

Daladier's position was very much less clear. In July, for instance, he
said firmly that "France's solemn pledge to Czechoslovakia [was] unbreakable and sacred,"[28] even as his foreign minister was doing his best
to see that no alliance was concluded with the Soviet Union so as to
"avoid upsetting Hitler";[29] but France needed that alliance in order to
check the expansion of Germany. Nor were Daladier and Bonnet willing
to put pressure on Poland — which was wholly dependent on France for
its military supplies — to allow the passage of the Red Army in case of
war; and without that permission, there could be no hope of Soviet help.
At the same time, the Premier was genuinely trying to rearm, and half
trying to conduct a foreign policy different from Bonnet's, going so far
as to tell an American visitor that fall: "Bonnet is very difficult and I
cannot have full confidence in him."[30] Still, there could be no question of
his firing Bonnet: the foreign minister's following in the Chamber was
just enough to worry the Premier.

What was striking to all well-informed observers was the general feeling of hopelessness within the cabinet, and the lack of discretion when it
came to vital information. Orville Bullitt, William's cousin, was a visitor
that fall.

> One evening when my wife and I were staying [at his house in] Chan-
> tilly, Bill invited Léon Blum, Paul Reynaud, Minister of Finance at that
> time, and Yvon Delbos to dine" [he noted]. These men all had brilliant
> minds. We were particularly struck by the reasoning and philosophical
> approach to problems by Blum and the quick, keen, analytical insight
> of Reynaud. What shocked us in the conversation, which was very
> frank and open, was the freedom with which they discussed France's
> unpreparedness for war. Three men were serving dinner and there was
> always one in the room. Figures were given as to the number of French
> planes and anti-aircraft artillery and I remember the statement by one
> of them that the Germans would be able to bomb Paris at will. After
> they were gone, I told Bill of my surprise that they should talk so

openly with others present. His reply was that the servants were carefully passed upon by the French Secret Service and could be depended on, and that there was nothing he could do about it.

I still feel that within twenty-four hours the Germans were in full possession of all the figures that passed across the dinner table.[31]

Orville Bullitt was right, of course, the German Archives prove it, but then indiscretion was general: similar discussions took place, even more carelessly, across other, nondiplomatic, Parisian dinner tables.

When, on September 12, therefore, Hitler demanded the cession of much of Czechoslovakia, not only was no one surprised, there was really very little doubt as to what the outcome would be. That Hitler's demands were humiliating for France and Great Britain, however, was all too plain; and, for a few days, Paris waited in anguish to find out whether war could still be avoided. Had the average Parisian been able to read the note send by Lord Halifax, the British foreign secretary, to Georges Bonnet, he could have relaxed. "While His Majesty's government," it said, "would never allow the security of France to be threatened, they are unable to make precise statements of the character of their future action, or the time at which it would be taken, in circumstances they cannot at present foresee."[32] That was all Bonnet needed. It was, in fact, Chamberlain who flew to Germany and gave in to Hitler's demands, but the French foreign minister concurred heartily in the betrayal of his country's ally.

This was not only dishonorable but foolish. Czechoslovakia had built a highly effective fortified line on its border with Germany; its Skoda armaments factories were among the most modern in Europe. Left intact, therefore, it could have provided real help against Germany. Once its industrial heartland (and the fortified line) were turned over to the Nazis, however, it became defenseless and was thus of no further help to France. Bonnet's position, however, was both clear and well known: "Bonnet considers . . . that a European war in the present circumstances would be absurd and must be avoided at any cost. . . . The Czechs will have to accept any proposition guaranteeing peace," the Polish ambassador reported.[33] With British Prime Minister Neville Chamberlain equally eager to sell out the Czechs, the result of the crisis was a foregone conclusion — at least for those in the know. For most of the Parisians, though, there were several days of considerable anguish. War, which had been approaching steadily, now seemed very close indeed.

That was because Daladier kept saying that he was prepared to defend the integrity of Czechoslovakia. In fact, he was ready to do no such thing. After hearing from Chamberlain that Great Britain would consider intervening only if France itself was invaded,[34] he told the cabinet on September 19: "No Frenchman can take the risk of throwing his country against Germany and Italy without being sure of English help."[35]

Naturally, the right-wing press clamored against any support to Czechoslovakia. "Not a widow, not an orphan for the Czechs," *Je Suis Partout* headlined on September 16,[36] while *L'Action française* simply repeated, day after day, in huge type: "No! No war!"[37] As for Bonnet, he was less noisy, but far more effective. In the night of September 20–21, he decided to warn Czechoslovakia that France would not honor the treaty under which it was obligated to defend its ally. This was obviously a grave decision, and Bonnet was warned by a subordinate that it was not one he could take without the cabinet's agreement. Without a moment's hesitation, however, he called the French ambassador in Prague and repeated his warning.[38] This, from his point of view, had three advantages: he had warned the Czechs; he had informed the Germans as well since, as he well knew, the phone lines were tapped as they crossed Germany; and he had left no paper trail that could eventually be used against him.

The result is well known. At Munich, on September 29, France and Great Britain agreed to the dismemberment of Czechoslovakia; but while Chamberlain thought he had bought a permanent peace, Daladier knew better. "Have no illusions," he told one of his aides, "this is just a respite and if we do not make good use of it we will all be shot."[39] As it was, he thought he might well be lynched. Pierre Lazareff met him as he returned from Munich. "When Daladier stepped out of the plane and saw the huge crowd awaiting him at the airport, he stepped back for a moment. Guy La Chambre, one of the few ministers who had come to greet him, admitted later to me that Daladier had told him: 'I thought this crowd was here to do me in.' He then saw with amazement that, on the contrary, it was there to cheer him and exclaimed: 'The idiots, they don't know what they're applauding!'"[40]

Daladier was right; but the crowds, throughout that day, kept gathering in front of his office and cheering him wildly. The Premier himself, try as he might, never managed to look pleased: in the newsreels, his expression of surprise and embarrassment is plain to see. As for the press, it was virtually unanimous. From right to left, it praised Daladier's wise and enlightened policy, as if, indeed, France had not just abandoned a key ally to Hitler's tender mercies. Some went further: Flandin sent Hitler a telegram of congratulations (which struck many of his compatriots as going a little far), *Le Temps* talked about the gratitude owed Daladier and

Bonnet,[41] and the Left-Radical *L'Oeuvre* celebrated the "poignant and admirable day . . . which has renewed our taste for peace."[42] Only Léon Blum, more clear-eyed than most, wrote about his "cowardly relief."[43] The relief was widely shared: one of the very first opinion polls ever carried out in France showed that 57 percent of those questioned were in favor of the Munich agreements, with 37 percent against and 6 percent undecided.

Daladier knew that he had just purchased a very short respite at a very high cost. The Parisians remained entirely unaware of this — more, for the moment at least, because they did not want to know than because the future was hard to predict. In the salons, all the pacifists rejoiced and felt sure that war had been averted for good. After all if, as all well-informed people supposed, Poland was next, why should France fight for Poland any more than it had for Czechoslovakia? And the country itself was safe behind the Maginot Line, so the military leaders had been saying for years. There was really nothing to worry about.

Still, the rejoicings on September 30, and the ever-faster pace of Parisian life after that took on an increasingly fevered quality. Just like the refusal to believe that war was possible, it was a way of dealing with fear and uncertainty. In every respect, Paris was shining so brightly as, apparently, to deny the possibility that it might one day go dark. There was no end to the possible amusements. Panama Al Brown, for instance, after regaining his title as world bantamweight champion, moved right over to the Cirque Médrano, where, to Cocteau's great pleasure, he could be seen to skip rope, tapdance, sing, and lead a black jazz band — with, however, rather less talent than he had displayed in the ring. Of course, there were popular shows at the Casino de Paris, with Mistinguett, Maurice Chevalier, or the perennial Josephine Baker; but serious music concerts in 1938 also offered richer programs than ever. Naturally, there was a Stravinsky evening, complete with a new work — his Concerto for chamber orchestra, conducted by the composer. A new mass by Poulenc, which was heard on a different occasion, showed him at his elegant best. Almost forgotten compositions by the likes of Palestrina and Buxtehude were revived. The Opéra put on one of its best seasons, a highlight of which was that glorious performance of Flagstad as Isolde. And for those whose preoccupations were less artistic, there was always the new Schiaparelli look: short kimono sleeves, a little drapery around the high waistline, and tight, knee-high skirts were well worth discussing at length.

There was also the development of a new phenomenon. For the first time since the Great War, local films had become as popular as the American imports. "French films used to be films which the French rarely went to see," Genêt reported with a little pardonable exaggeration. "Celluloid has been changing lately. The movie that French fans are now queuing up for is . . . *Un Carnet de bal,* which is . . . one of the grandest films Hollywood never made."[44] It was no wonder the Parisians were flocking to see French films. They were, at long last, technically equal to those produced in Hollywood; their directors were immensely talented; and the new stars, from Jean Gabin to Danielle Darrieux, contrived to look as striking as their American counterparts while not infrequently turning out better performances.

The plot of *Un Carnet de bal,* the hit mentioned by Genêt, is simple enough. A rich widow looks over the *carnet de bal* (the little book in which, at turn-of-the-century dances, ladies would write the names of the men who had asked them for one of the dances yet to come). There her partners of an evening many years ago are listed; and then the public sees what has become of the different young men. What made the film was that the young men in question were played by extraordinary actors — Louis Jouvet as a nightclub owner, Harry Baur as a musical monk, Raimu as the mayor of a small Provence town, Fernandel as a barber with a passion for card tricks. There was also Françoise Rosay, an actress of great and enduring talent, playing the crazed widow of one of the dancers; Marie Bell, as beautiful as she was talented, was Christine, the central character, and the part launched her on a dazzling career; finally, the direction of Julien Duvivier kept the action moving fast, while the images were beautiful and striking.

There was, for instance, the beginning of the film, which set the right tone of mystery. The opening shot is of a lake surrounded by mountains; then, through the arch of a bridge, we see a boat coming near; in it are two caped and hooded figures. Soon, the boat reaches the bank; the two unknown figures climb out and walk to a castle nearby. It is only once they are inside that we realize that we have been looking at Christine and a friend, returning from her husband's funeral. After that, all the flashbacks seem entirely natural. There are many surprises; several of the episodes are as funny as others are tragic; and there is always just the right amount of melancholy under it all.

Just as important, the French could, at long last, produce films that were technically sound. Until 1935, the French movie industry, although it could boast of very considerable acting and directorial talent, had been turning out films that were hard to see — the images tended to be dark and blurry — and to hear — the sound was scratchy, fluctuating, and sometimes virtually inaudible. Thus, a 1932 comic masterpiece like *Boudu sauvé des eaux* (Boudu Saved from the Waters) found only a small public. Even so, the extraordinary performance by Michel Simon as an anarchic, sexy tramp, and the send-up of the staid French bourgeoisie had delighted many of those who saw it and shocked the rest. Now, at last, French films were not only brilliant but technically acceptable to a wide public, and the box-office receipts showed it: between 1934 and 1938, they went up over 60 percent.

Many of these new films were highly representative of their time in that they showed a world that had lost confidence in itself and the future. One of the best of these, *La Grande Illusion,* was directed by Jean Renoir and starred Jean Gabin, the picture-book–handsome Pierre Fresnay, and Erich von Stroheim. The story of three French war prisoners bent on escaping, *Grand Illusion* mercilessly punctures all the clichés about the brotherhood of man, the selfless bravery of the troops, and the generally glorious character of the French army. The characters, each with his narrow life disrupted by the war and to a degree resumed in the prison camp, are coolly and exactly depicted. Even better, the images are stark and powerful, and the acting absolutely first-rate, a fact recognized when the film won the 1937 New York Film Critics Award.

Two years later, in 1939, Jean Renoir went still a step further, so far, in fact, that his new film *La Règle du jeu* (*Rules of the Game*) was promptly banned as antisocial. In its merciless depiction of the behavior of members of the upper classes, it seemed to undermine not only their preeminence but also the rules by which many of the French still conducted their lives. For once, the censors had got it right: after *Grand Illusion,* patriotism and human goodness were seen as hoaxes; after *Rules of the Game,* it was society itself that was pictured as a corrupt and decadent structure teetering on the brink of self-destruction. "An exact description of the bourgeoisie of our time," as Renoir called it,[45] *Rules of the Game* portrays a post-Munich society whose privileges and prejudices are as spectacular as they are fragile, through characters whose lives, though still luxurious, are in utter disarray. And more than just an accurate picture of a particular social grouping, the film also offered a perfect simile for the situation of France in 1939.

The film takes place in a country château to which the characters have been invited for a shooting party; nothing could be more conventional; but as we soon discover, everything has gone wrong. The owner of the castle, the marquis de la Chesnaye, played by Marcel Dalio, has a Jewish grandmother, and is thus considered a "dirty foreigner" (*métèque*) by his gamekeeper. The marquis tries to seduce his wife's maid, and so does a tramp trying to take the job held by the maid's husband; the marquise is having an affair with a glamorous pilot who, in the course of the intrigue, is killed, but the marquis passes off the murder as an accident; so the party goes on, a kind of dance of death in which all, from master to servant to poacher, are equally corrupt and corrupting. Only one character is really appealing, that of Octave (played by Jean Renoir himself), and then only because he is too withdrawn to be a part of the goings-on; but he makes up for that by his deep cynicism. Deception, he tells Christine, the unfaithful wife, is what keeps society functioning: "Listen, Christine, that, too, is a thing which belongs to our era! We live in an era where everybody lies: pharmaceutical advertisements, governments, the radio, the movies, the newspapers."[46]

*Rules of the Game* was so strong that it met first with violent protest, then with an outright ban; but it was only repeating, better and more vividly, what had already been said on the screen before. In Yves Mirande's *Derrière la façade* (Behind the Facade), for instance, we are shown the interior of an apartment building in which a murder has just taken place. Here too everyone cheats, lies, and steals; the victim is an old lady who owned the building and pimped on the side; the murderer is her long-exploited concierge; one of the most striking characters, played with enormous strength by Erich von Stroheim, is a German gambler, who wins a fortune by cheating at cards, and who treats the police with "typically German" arrogance, thus allowing the film to display the xenophobia that was rapidly becoming a national trait. Here too the unsavory side of France serves as a symbol of its appalling position at the eve of the war.

Indeed, although *Un Carnet de bal* had its funny moments, and so did Pagnol's *La Femme du boulanger* (The Baker's Wife), most of the great films produced in the immediate prewar years were singularly grim. They were also often masterpieces. *Rules of the Game* today is just as powerful as it was in 1939; so are two of Marcel Carné's films, *Quai des brumes* (Quay of the Mists) and *Le Jour se lève* (The Day at Dawn). The first is the story of a deserter hiding from the police in a desperately poor section of the city; the other that of a man who has committed a murder and goes over it in his mind, again and again and again. In both movies, the setting is deeply gloomy, the prospects more depressing still; the world they show us has gone bad; there are no happy memories, no hopes for a better future. All in all, that was right enough: Paris, in that last year before the war, could try hard to fool itself, but no matter how bright the glitter, its people knew that they were living at the end of an era. In September 1938 the war had been avoided. It might still be put off another time, but, in the end, it was bound to come.

That, at least, was a feeling shared by most Parisians. The euphoria following Munich was as brief as it was intense. It was not just that it left a bad taste. The French knew, finally, that they had weakened themselves by betraying an ally. Far worse, it was becoming clear that it had bought only a little time. By 1939, no one doubted that Hitler would simply keep swallowing country after country until, at last, it was France's turn. Even so, the Parisians were determined to enjoy themselves — at least, while they still could. But it said a great deal about how they felt that the way they tried to forget the real world was by seeing deeply depressing films.

# CHAPTER
# TWELVE

# THE END OF THE BALL

IT WAS ONLY a short time, a bare three months, but already
the Parisians who after Munich thought that they could stop
worrying knew that they had been mistaken. Hitler had not been
bought off, not for any length of time; another confrontation
would surely come, and with it the final conflict. This could be
felt rather than seen in the tension that pervaded every activity,
every conversation. The city had not lost its glitter; its amusements were as numerous as ever; only, it is hard to be carefree
when a sword is suspended above your head by a fraying cord.
That this was the case no one, save the extreme Right and
Georges Bonnet, doubted. War must come, war would come, and
probably sooner than later. It was bound to have catastrophic
effects, culturally and economically; but it could no longer be
avoided, and having been duly warned by a variety of officials,
the city expected that its onset would be marked by heavy aerial
bombing. No wonder the director Marcel Carné said later that
his *Le Jour se lève* was his blackest film: "Everyone," he explained,
"lived in despair."[1]

"Parisians go to their offices but their minds aren't on their work; they go to nightclubs, cafés, movies, or they even go home, but their minds aren't on their pleasure," Genêt reported in July.[2] Suddenly, long-term planning was almost impossible: who knew what would happen in six months or a year? Even deciding where to go for the summer holidays was a problem. Wars, traditionally, started in August. Did it make any sense to go away if the men had to return to join their regiments?

At the same time, a new, more deleterious atmosphere was spreading. There was, for instance, the new nonaggression treaty Bonnet had negotiated with Germany. In December, he invited Ribbentrop, the Nazi foreign minister, to come and sign it in Paris, an invitation that made many members of the cabinet very uncomfortable. Others, however, rejoiced. "We were beginning to hope [that France would align itself with Germany]," the pro-Nazi Brasillach wrote. "The non-Aryan ministers were not invited to the official banquet [given by Bonnet for Ribbentrop]."[3] He was right about that: Jean Zay, for instance, found himself left out; and while Bonnet later explained that it was only because Zay was minister of education, not because he was Jewish, he convinced no one, especially since his wife was often heard to express openly anti-Semitic feelings. Just as bad, even among those who had no doubt that fighting was the only way to stop Hitler, there was a gnawing suspicion that the French army was not everything it should be.

Daladier himself, Bullitt reported, "realizes fully that the meeting in Munich was an immense diplomatic defeat."[4] Even worse, he was thoroughly convinced that if the war came soon, France would lose. That estimate was based in part on the gross insufficiency of the air force. In 1938, Germany built sixty-six hundred war planes, France five hundred; but the complacency of General Gamelin, the head of the General Staff, was hardly reassuring either. When he and his subordinates explained that the French army already had too many tanks and did not need special motorized divisions, Daladier believed them, even if he ordered that the making of tanks be continued; but he must have wondered about Gamelin's strategy. This was predicted entirely on the defensive qualities of the Maginot Line; but at the same time the general expected the Germans to attack (as they did) through Holland and Belgium, and it was his plan to march into these countries (both of which were neutral) to meet them. What use the Maginot Line was to be in this case, he did not say.

All that was bad enough, but it was known only to the unhappy few. Something else worried a much greater number of people: the new economic and social policies of the government. Good Radical though he was, Daladier differed from premiers like Herriot, Sarraut, and Chautemps in one major respect: he could see that the reactionary financial policy practiced by Marchandeau, the minister in charge, was a failure; and on November 1, 1938, he actually decided to change it. This took the form of an exchange within the cabinet: Paul Reynaud moved from justice to finance, Marchandeau from finance to justice. In many ways this was a wise move: Reynaud, at least, had read Keynes and understood the causes of the lingering Depression. Unfortunately, he was, in every other respect, a classic conservative, and thought it advisable, therefore, to break the unions with all possible speed.

To do this, Reynaud simply took, by decree, just the kind of measures that were most likely to provoke a general strike. He fired forty thousand employees from the national railroads and ended the program of public works, at the same time cutting the rate of income tax for the upper brackets. Even more important, he ended the forty-hour week and the two-day weekend, those most prized of all the Popular Front laws. The result was just what Reynaud had expected; the unions called for a strike; but, as he also expected, the high rate of unemployment ensured the strike's failure.

That Reynaud should thus have needlessly affronted, then defeated, the working class was most unfortunate; now a significant part of the population was disaffected. It was also unnecessary. Other measures, which mattered far more, had the happiest effect. By freeing the markets and raising the salaries of all civil servants, Reynaud allowed the economy to make a forward leap; and if only overtime for blue-collar workers had been presented as an opportunity for making money instead of being imposed as a punishment, then the working class would have supported the new dispensation. As it was, by June 1939 the index of industrial production had climbed from 83 to 100 (the same level as in 1929): that of steel went up 40 percent while the prices rose only 2 percent and unemployment decreased by 10 percent. It is only fair to add, however, that the vast sums spent on rearmament were an essential component of this improvement; and that, of course, would have occurred even without Reynaud.

There were other causes of the general malaise. In Paris itself, some of the most influential people around drew what seemed to them the obvious conclusion. Early in April 1939, for instance, Pierre Lazareff was present at a luncheon in the course of which he listened as Hélène de Portes, Reynaud's mistress, leaned over to Anatole de Monzie, himself a member of the cabinet and a pacifist. "She told him: 'It is high time these bellicist campaigns were silenced. Since Hitler is the strongest, the best thing to do is to give in to him, and that's all.'

"'What would Paul Reynaud say if he heard you say that?' Monzie exclaimed.

"'Pff!' Mme de Portes answered, 'I tell him that every day. I'll surely convince him in the end.'"5 As it turned out, she never did; but she was very far from alone in expressing these feelings; and she had her way in many other things, largely because Reynaud cared so deeply about being a part of society and looking young and chic. At sixty-two, he was still carefully keeping himself tanned and lithe, dying his hair, and behaving as if he were thirty years younger. Mme de Portes, who was herself an essential part of this image, knew just how to take advantage of it.

Neither she nor Mme de Crussol, her arch-rival, ever behaved as if all were not going well; but for the rest of Paris, many new events added to the widespread sense of unease, not least among these the increasingly barbaric policies of the Nazis. In November 1938, *Kristallnacht,* that attack on Jews and Jewish stores, followed the assassination of a German diplomat by a German Jew who was a refugee in Paris. It was now becoming increasingly clear that, in fact, Hitler was about as reliable as Attila the Hun; and any remaining doubts vanished on March 15, 1939. That day, the German army marched into the remains of Czechoslovakia, and Hitler announced that henceforth that unhappy country would be considered a German protectorate. This was a violation of the solemn guarantee given by Germany at Munich only six months earlier.

For Daladier, it was the gloomy confirmation of what he already knew about the Nazis, and the final proof that Bonnet was not to be trusted. On March 18, Bullitt reported that the Premier had told him that "he had no confidence whatsoever"6 in his foreign minister. It still was not enough to unseat Bonnet, though. Although Daladier now involved himself far more closely in the formulation and application of the country's foreign policy, he allowed the chief appeaser to retain his office.

The Nazi takeover of Czechoslovakia did, however, prove to many of the pacifists that they had been wrong. Even the strongly pro-Munich *Le Temps* talked about "feelings of pity [for the Czechs] and horror."7 For a while, in fact, a feeling of numbness was widespread. Bullitt reported that the fall of Czechoslovakia "convinced every Frenchman and every Frenchwoman that no promise of the dictators was to be relied on, that words were useless, and that Hitler could be stopped by nothing but force," but he misread the prevalent mood as one of "curious *serenity.*"8 He was wrong; it was silent despair. As for Daladier and Reynaud, they now saw eye to eye: both were convinced that Germany would precipitate a general war by the middle of May.[9] Indeed, on March 23, Daladier told Juliusz Lukasiewicz, the Polish ambassador, that "the occupation of Prague had made absolute and determined opposition to further German expansion indispensable, even if this opposition were to result in armed resistance."[10]

In spite of this view, great care was still taken not to annoy the Nazis. At the Council of Ministers on March 17, a proposal that France forward a solemn protest to Germany was defeated. "President Lebrun said that we must be very careful. Recalling our ambassador, given Hitler's character, could be a pretext [for him to start the war]," Jean Zay noted.[11] Naturally, Bonnet supported Lebrun, and no solemn protest was sent. It was, in fact, not against the Nazis the cabinet decided to act, but against the Chamber of Deputies. On March 18, Daladier requested, and received, new, extended powers that allowed him to govern without parliamentary control, thus stilling any protest from the Deputies who thought that appeasement should stop. Then in April, to avoid the election of a competitor, he backed a draft-Lebrun movement; on the fifth, the President was duly reelected, thus removing any possible counterpoise to Daladier himself. In June, finally, the long-prorogued Chamber was recalled to vote a reform of the electoral law and a postponement of the elections from 1940 to 1942, all in the name of strengthening the nation, upon which it was prorogued again.

The only victim of Daladier's new firmness, clearly, was French democracy. By the beginning of July, he was exercising dictatorial powers and the widespread atony was such that very few people even bothered to protest. Almost alone, Blum dissented. "Until now your behavior has been fundamentally weak and changing," he told Daladier in the course of a debate in the Chamber. "You think that you can leap, almost without transition, to an extreme tension of all the nation's energies, to a kind of state of siege. . . . You are mistaken yet again."[12] As so often, Blum, though right, was ignored.

It was all the more difficult to mobilize the nation's energies now that people began to think that what France did no longer mattered. Still, for the moment at least, all the pleasures of peace were still available; hence no doubt the huge success enjoyed by one of Cocteau's most unoriginal plays, *Les Parents terribles* (The Awful Parents).

This play is as unreal as it is unpoetic, but it had just what was needed to please both the highly chic first-night audience and the more general public: a touch of scandal that titillated without being really disturbing.

There is a son who is in love with his mother, although he does not know it; he has a fiancée, too, and loves her, but she is none other than his father's mistress. As for the father, as selfish and in his way infantile as the mother, he is passionately loved by his wife's sister, who exerts every effort and every wile to conquer him. Because the sister was played by Gabrielle Dorziat, an actress of extraordinary talent, she turned out to be the star of the play and added greatly to its popularity. As it was, *Les Parents terribles* had to leave the posh Théâtre des Ambassadeurs because of the scandal it caused. When, within the week, it reopened at a less puritanical venue, its success grew even greater.

The other triumph of the season was altogether less risqué, but it was, if anything, even more spectacular: Walt Disney's *Snow White*. One of the very first color films to be seen on Parisian screens, this charming and familiar story, retold in cartoon form, full of slightly saccharine whimsy, enchanted the crowds who lined up to see it. It is no wonder: not only is *Snow White* highly pleasing, it also takes place in the safest of worlds where everything ends well, the wicked are punished, and the good prosper. That alone made it an alluring substitute for the current, and very different, reality.

There were other ways to make yourself feel good, if you were a Parisian, and that was to get back to basics, which in this case meant the superb food for which the city was so justly famous. Restaurants offering a three-hundred franc (about a hundred 1993 dollars) New Year's Eve dinner (wine not included) were packed; sales of champagne, foie gras, oysters, and lobsters soared. Not even Munich could dim the luster of French cuisine, but a war, with its attendant shortages, surely would; and so the Parisians were determined to enjoy themselves while they still could.

Distractions, to be fully effective, had to be increasingly recherché, though. Naturally, the great couture houses made their own contributions, and Schiaparelli was, as usual, firmly in the forefront. There was her May 1939 collection, for instance, at which music tinkled from unexpected places. Sometimes it was reasonably clear that the little tune came from a music box placed in the model's handbag, but when the music box was hidden in a suit pocket, or in the feathers on a hat, the effect, a commentator noted, was "downright spooky."[13]

That note had perhaps already been sounded in the August 1938 Zodiac collection. By 1939, though, fantasy reached new heights: one dress was decorated with trompe-l'oeil French windows whose green shutters were fastened shut—a preview of what was soon to happen in reality.

All this was new and amusing, but Schiap also reacted to the unsettled times by retreating headlong into the past. In her last collection before the war, evening dresses sported large, complicated bustles and were often made of particularly sumptuous materials. This was the case, for instance, of the floor-length dark red velvet dress with white buttons down the front and a multilevel bustle. The main theme of this collection, Vertés's Gay Nineties prints, emphasized the return to the past even more. Vertés himself was a thoroughly mediocre painter who achieved a measure of notoriety for his vapid landscapes and empty-eyed, long-necked women; but he was also a competent illustrator and designed fabrics on which men in top hats, with handlebar mustaches, bowlers, beards, monocles, and canes, mingled with women wearing the fashions of the 1890s — all in bright yellows, reds, pinks, and blues on white.

That Schiap should have chosen Vertés instead of Dalí or Cocteau said a good deal about her infallible instincts. People wanted to be soothed, not challenged, and brought back to a world that, in retrospect, seemed a model of safety and stability. She had, in fact, already felt this two years earlier when she moved from her Boulevard Saint-Germain apartment to a house at 22, rue de Berri. With its courtyard in front and deep, lush garden in the back, the house itself was an oasis of peace, a retreat from the world. Inside, too, it was meant to comfort. Gone was the modern look of the apartment. Instead, there was a pleasingly unorthodox appearance that recalled the comfortable past — lots of large, well-upholstered pieces of furniture, lots of objects: a crystal chandelier from Schönbrunn, Boucher Chinoiserie tapestries, carved leopards, silver birds and shells, Chinese porcelain figures and bronzes, elephant tusks mounted in silver that looked like Brancusis, and everywhere ashtrays, lighters, casually opened rare books, leopard skins. There was not a bare surface anywhere.

Comfort was important, too. The library, for instance, had an elongated S-shaped sofa so that Schiap and her guest could recline with trays in their laps instead of having to sit up in the dining room. There was even a bistrolike basement, where the pipes had been deliberately left on view, to which only the chosen few were invited for supper on Sundays. There was a proper bar, complete with sink, wood tables, gilt chairs, and nineties vaudeville posters; here, too, the real world was far away. Even the entrance hall was meant to take the guests away from everyday life: Schiap had adorned it with life-size wooden statues of Mr. and Mrs. Satan, the latter lavishly hung with necklaces, bracelets, and rings. More and more the remark made by Helen in Giraudoux's *La Guerre de Troie n'aura pas lieu* seemed to come true. "Misfortune and ugliness," she said, "are mirrors that people cannot stand." Upper-class Parisians from 1937 on not only refused to see the misfortune and ugliness that increasingly surrounded them; they tried to forget that they might even exist. That was easier than it might seem. They had done their best to ignore the Depression in the first half of the decade; they saw no reason why they could not ignore the Nazi menace now.

Naturally, the social life of the city was as busy as ever. Mme de Crussol's salon had as its chief asset the frequent presence of the Premier himself; and even if Daladier tended to be rather dour, still, that salon remained a center of power and a source of information. So, to only a very slightly lesser degree, did the rival establishment run by Mme de Portes, where the always loquacious Reynaud habitually shone. It was well understood that Mme de Portes and her friends were busy plotting to have Reynaud succeed Daladier, a fact that did not endear the finance minister to the Premier. It was an uphill battle, however, as Daladier well knew. Reynaud, who was given to mocking remarks, had offended many Deputies, and he also was thought too erratic, too frivolous, for the office.

Information, the very latest and deepest secrets, was a currency of both salons and was easily available at Mme de Montgomery's as well; the level of indiscretion reached by ministers and their friends in these years seems, in retrospect, not merely staggering, but positively criminal. No matter how grave the circumstances — from the remilitarization of the Rhineland to the invasion of Poland and the actual battle in France in 1940 — nothing remained a secret for even half a day, an enormous convenience for Hitler, who actually needed no spies to tell him what the French government was up to. The conversation that had so surprised Bullitt's cousin was bad enough; at least the people at the table were reliable, even if the servants were not; but, far worse, ministers made it a practice to come straight from the council and tell all to social groups among whom there were friends of the Nazis. Everything could therefore be expected to reach Berlin within twenty-four hours.

This was so well-established a habit that it continued during the war. An anecdote told by Pierre Lazareff is entirely characteristic. In mid-April 1940, he was giving a lunch party at which several ministers were present. One of them, arriving a little late, announced as he sat down: "'If you promise not to repeat it, I will tell you about what happened at the secret session of the Chamber this morning.'

"A huge burst of laughter greeted the minister's offer. . . . He was already the third member of the cabinet to make this offer . . . and was ready to give the most precise information on national defense."[14] Oddly enough, this flow of information was a part of the flight from reality. Although the news was usually anything but good, the mere fact of having access to it when most everyone else remained in the dark conferred a privileged status; and that, in turn seemed a guarantee of invulnerabilty.

For those who had no reason at all to feel invulnerable, there were other distractions. It was typical of the current mood that the award for the best recorded (pop) song was given, in December 1938, to Charles Trenet for a cheerful, if nonsensical, number entitled *Boum,* the first line of which was "There's joy all over." Like Snow White, the characters in Trenet's songs lived in an ideal world: there the sun was always shining, the girls pretty, the lovers happy. Tall, loose-limbed, lithe, fair-haired, Trenet had a cherubic face and round blue eyes that fitted his songs perfectly. That he was their composer and lyricist as well as performer added to his fame. By the spring of 1939, he was the idol of the young and half the population besides; and because he stressed his own eccentricity, he was promptly dubbed *le fou chantant,* the singing madman. It helped that he had a good tenor voice and a sophisticated sense of rhythm; but what made him an unrivaled star was that he sang about a world of sunny fields and green meadows in which carefree lovers romped, a world in which flowers whispered, brooks babbled, and Charles Trenet himself repeatedly burst into melodic song.

Even so, there were many young people for whom Trenet was a little too sweet: their idols came from across the Atlantic. "Paris is conducting itself on the theory that until there is bloody belligerence everybody had better go about his business or pleasure while either is left," Genêt reported in April. "Close to three thousand young *jazz-hot* fans recently gathered in the modernist Palais de Chaillot . . . to hear Duke Ellington and his orchestra."[15] Ellington and his players knew what jazz was all about, and his fans were delighted. It wasn't just that they liked his music; it brought a kind of enthusiastic liveliness very different from the jaded atmosphere of Paris. It also spoke of a world where, to be sure, gangsters might roam the streets, but where the kind of menace with which the French were living was canceled by the breadth of the Atlantic Ocean.

*Le jazz-hot,* by and large, was for the young. There was also a sophisticated public for the new classical music, and it filled the Salle Gaveau for the first performance of Béla Bartók's Sonata for Two Pianos and Percussion, in which the composer and his wife played the pianos. The kettledrum had been given new pedals, which allowed it to be played faster and more often, and the music was new, sober, and rich. Leaving standard melody behind, as, indeed, Stravinsky was also doing, Bartók gave the public music that seemed difficult at first hearing but was still immediately perceived as a masterpiece. That was a good deal more than could be said for the recent works of more readily accessible composers like Milhaud and Poulenc.

Like music, the visual arts were a privileged means of escape. The Galerie Rosenberg put on an exhibition of thirty-five Cézannes, mostly late works, and the Parisians flocked in, as they did to see the still lifes exhibited by Frida Kahlo. Another kind of visual feast, although not of the same quality, also proved popular: the sets and costumes designed by the Russian emigré Pavel Tchelitchew for Giraudoux's new play, *Ondine*. The play itself was rapturously received, although it was remarkably unlike the author's earlier work. Giraudoux's strength had always been his irony, his disillusioned distance from the official view of the world and its history. When, until now, he had made use of historical or mythical figures, it was always to bring them down to earth. With *Ondine,* however, he brought forth a misty, romantic work about the wicked daughter of a poor fisherman who is brought up as a princess and a medieval German knight who falls in love with a water sprite, the Ondine of the title. It is, on the whole, not a very good play; but it was helped by Jouvet's stellar performance and, most of all, by its theme. Audiences found it awfully pleasant, in June 1939, to spend an evening safely ensconced in a medieval romance.

They needed to. By early July, a poll showed that by 45 to 34 percent people thought that war was now unavoidable, and that it would come before the end of the year; quite a change in the nine months since Munich. Amazingly, although Daladier had, at the time, been given credit for ensuring the peace at Munich, this quite failed to lessen his popularity. After having been seen, the previous October, as the man who would do anything to save the peace, by the end of January he had become the emblem of resistance to aggression. For this, Mussolini was in large part responsible. He announced that Italy demanded the cession of Tunisia, then a French protectorate; Corsica, which had been French since the middle of the eighteenth century; and Nice and Savoy, which had French populations and had been given to France in 1857 as a reward for helping the Italians defeat Austria.

That was too much even for Daladier. Having firmly rejected the Duce's claims, he embarked on a well-publicized trip to Corsica and Tunisia, reviewing the troops and units of the fleet and making speeches at the monuments to the dead of the Great War. It was in one of these that he announced: "Our country is peaceful and quiet because it knows that it is strong, and able to face all attacks."[16] Of course, Mussolini and his comic-opera army hardly represented the same sort of threat as Hitler; but since it was assumed (wrongly) that the two dictators were in full accord, the Duce's speeches and the belligerence of the controlled Italian press caused much alarm. Daladier's firmness thus seemed reassuring: at last, France was drawing a line in the sand.

That made Daladier seem almost heroic, especially compared with Bonnet. In mid-January, in one of its rare sittings, the Chamber debated foreign policy, and Flandin — who had been finance minister, foreign minister, and Premier — paid homage to "the constructive work of fascism and National Socialism" and went on to demand a "meeting" of Germany and France "on the road to peace and not in the inferno of war."[17] He was not alone in doing so. Within the cabinet Bonnet, Chautemps, and Monzie were the leaders of this tendency; outside the government, the same point of view was frequently and vociferously pushed by the extreme Right and its press organs. In contrast, Daladier seemed to be almost a new Clemenceau, and many of the French trusted him to do the right thing.

That was, sadly, a wildly exaggerated view. There was, for one thing, the little matter of the foreign minister. Although Daladier now thoroughly distrusted Bonnet,[18] he allowed this appeaser-in-chief to keep his office, and that made well-informed people think that when the next crisis came the Premier would cave in yet again.

That view was made even more probable by Daladier's deep and general pessimism. "Daladier lunched with me alone today," Bullitt wrote Cordell Hull, the U.S. secretary of state, on February 6. "[He said] that he considered Chamberlain a desiccated stick; the King a moron; and the Queen an excessively ambitious woman who would be ready to sacrifice every other country in order that she might remain Queen of England. He added that he considered [the antiappeasement Anthony] Eden a young idiot and . . . did not know one single Englishman for whose intellectual equipment and character he had respect. He felt that England had become so feeble and senile that the British would give away every possession of their friends rather than stand up to Germany and Italy."[19]

Obviously, these scathing comments sprang from a thoroughly defeatist view of the situation, but they were also startlingly off the mark. Although it was true that Chamberlain was not exactly forthcoming, and that intelligence was not George VI's chief characteristic, Daladier was grotesquely wrong about the Queen and Eden, and wrong as well about the evolution of British policy. Less than two months later, Chamberlain (and Daladier) concluded a guarantee treaty with Poland that committed Great Britain to declare war on whoever would attack that country.

France itself had long had a binding alliance with Poland — but then, it had had the same ties to Czechoslovakia — and it seemed an open question, in March, whether it would honor its commitment. In the meantime, the French attitude toward Italy remained the great test. At the Council of Ministers on March 27, for instance, Bonnet told the cabinet: "Public opinion in Italy favors a reconciliation with France. If we disappoint the Italians, we will allow Mussolini to regroup them symbolically for war," upon which, Jean Zay recorded, "Bonnet announced that he wanted to begin negotiations. . . . A very lively discussion followed. With slight differences, Bonnet, Monzie, Chautemps, Marchandeau are for beginning talks immediately."[20] As usual, Bonnet eventually had his way, but to no avail; Mussolini, at this point, was simply not interested.

Except for the guests of a few Paris salons, none of the French knew about all this. What they did hear was Daladier explaining in a radio speech at the end of March: "France hopes that peace can be preserved because it hates war. But if war is forced on us, or if it became the only alternative to disgrace and dishonor, she would rise unanimously to defend her liberty."[21] Far more significantly, he told the cabinet, after Mussolini's invasion of Albania in early April: "The time has come for a more virile policy. . . . The country is fed up and will sweep away a weak or hesitating government."[22] That was all very well; but Chautemps remained Vice-Premier and Bonnet foreign minister. It looked, in fact, very much as if Daladier's statements were simply what a satirical weekly called "verbal words."

This mattered all the more because by now French politics had been transformed. While even a former pacifist like Léon Blum could write "An appeal to force is, today, a way to peace,"[23] there was now a significant group who were prepared to endure any humiliation, make every sacrifice, in order to avert war. In an odd and contradictory shift, the pacifist Left came together with the pro-Fascist Right to denounce war, any war, and even resistance to aggression. Blum's fellow Socialist Paul Faure, for instance, advised his readers that any cession of French territory was preferable to "the death of a single wine-grower from the Mâconnais."[24] Of course, no one wanted to see a repetition of the slaughter of 1914–1918; and pacifism had indeed been the hallmark of the progressives in the twenties; but now, unable to see that the world had changed, they stuck to their slogans and lost their souls. It was an odd reordering of French politics; suddenly ardent left-wingers like Paul Faure found themselves defending the same positions as extreme right-wingers and actual Fascists.

Perhaps the most spectacular example of this regrouping occurred at the beginning of May. Having swallowed the rump of Czechoslovakia, Hitler was now demanding Danzig and its corridor, a strip of land that crossed German East Prussia and connected Poland to its only port, now a free city ruled by its own senate. That Danzig was only a beginning was obvious enough, hence the Franco-British guarantee to Poland. The question that would soon have to be answered was whether Danzig and Poland were to be carved up at some future international conference that would be a second Munich, or whether France and Great Britain were prepared to fight for the integrity of Poland.

For the appeasers, the answer was not in doubt, and it came in an article that marked a watershed. Published in *L'Oeuvre*, a liberal daily, written by Marcel Déat, a neo-Socialist who had become a Fascist (and was to collaborate enthusiastically with the Nazi occupiers between 1940 and 1944), it was entitled "To Die for Danzig?" and went on: "If, today, the master of all the Germanies decides he wants to grab Danzig, who will stop him! To start a European war because of Danzig would be a little too much and the French farmers have no desire to die for the Polacks. . . . We will not die for Danzig!"[25]

It was a catchy headline and an almost convincing article — not to mention a line of reasoning nearly identical to that of Neville Chamberlain in September 1938, when he had told his radio listeners that it was incredible to expect the English to die for a faraway people (the Czechs) of whom they knew nothing. The fallacy, in both cases, was that Hitler, once having swallowed Poland after Czechoslovakia and Austria, was not likely to stop; but that was a piece of reality Faure, Déat, and their friends were not prepared to acknowledge.

That so vocal a group should trumpet these beliefs was the clearest indication that the war, when it came, would find France sharply divided. On the other side, there was a group whose pronouncements were almost as noxious: their theme was that it was useless to worry because France was so much the stronger. That group included conservative political and military leaders who saw that it would be necessary to fight but thought it was far more important to reassure the edgy population than to tell it the truth — what one might call the anti-Churchill approach. For Tardieu, it was simple: the only possible way the war might start would be if the Germans thought the French were panicking; but, he pointed out, the French had no reason to panic. As soon as the first shots rang out,

Hitler would be assassinated by one of the Nazi chiefs and that would end the war.[26]

Even if Hitler should survive for a little while longer, however, there was still nothing to worry about. So said General Weygand, the now retired chief of the General Staff and the most prestigious officer in France. "The French army," he announced in the course of a speech in Lille at the beginning of July, "is stronger than ever before in its history. It has first-rate armaments, first-rate fortifications, excellent morale, and an outstanding high command. No one wants war, but I assure you that if we are forced to win a new victory, win it we will."[27] As for Gamelin, the current head of the General Staff, who would automatically become generalissimo in wartime, he had no doubts at all. "The day war is declared against Germany," he told the Chamber on August 23, "Hitler will collapse. Instead of defending the borders of the Reich, the German army will have to march on Berlin in order to repress the risings there. We will then cut through Germany like a knife through butter."[28] It would have been difficult to be more completely wrong, and the problem was that people felt it. In spite of the now constant propaganda barrage aimed at reassuring the public — the chief slogan as of September was: "We will win because we are the strongest" — the general malaise was palpable. Of course, those who realized that war could no longer be avoided dreaded it. No one, except a few officials, thought it was likely to be less than harrowing.

One of the best informed men in France agreed with this dire forecast. Early in April, Bullitt had written Roosevelt: "In considering the question of the defense of the United States and the Americas, it would be extremely unwise to eliminate from consideration the possibility that Germany, Italy and Japan may win a comparatively speedy victory over France and England."[29] Bullitt was right, of course. He knew just what Daladier's failings were; he was familiar with the imbecility of the top French generals; he was fully aware of the air force's inferiority; and he understood, finally, the depth of reluctance with which the French were approaching the conflict.

Daladier himself was not unaware of all this, although he still believed that the high command was the best available in the circumstances; but he also saw clearly that the population might, if it learned the truth, become severely discouraged. In an unprecedented act, therefore, he decreed the establishment of a wartime press censorship even though France was still at peace. A commissioner of information was appointed; it perhaps said something about the government's general lack of realism that the man appointed was none other than Giraudoux, a convincing poet, an admirably skilled playwright, but the very last person to manage the censorship. As for the radio, which was rapidly becoming the primary source of information, it was put directly under the Premier's control.

That the charming, sophisticated, and witty Giraudoux should be made the chief censor struck the Tout-Paris as yet another proof that the real world would not be allowed to intrude into its diversions. Indeed, the season of 1939, those six weeks in June and July when the grandest balls, the most elegant parties, were given, was exceptionally brilliant. Nothing, it seemed, could stop the festivities, not even the unusually cold and rainy weather that prevented many hosts from using the gardens of their mansions.

"There have been magnificent costume balls and parties with dancers footing it till early breakfast," Genêt reported, "formal dinner parties in stately houses . . . alfresco fetes held in the *salon* because of the sunspot storms . . . garden parties that couldn't be held in the garden but were not dampened in spirit by the rain."[30]

Some of these festivities were relatively simple, like the white-tie dance given by Bullitt for the visiting Yale Glee Club, at which the Tout-Paris mingled happily with the college students and watched them, in the early hours, doing the new American dances. Others were thoroughly sophisticated. The most literary ball of the season was given, naturally, by Etienne de Beaumont to celebrate the three hundredth anniversary of the death of Racine, the great French playwright. All the guests were asked to come dressed either as characters from his plays or as his contemporaries. So there was Marie-Louise Bousquet, whose political-literary salon was just then prospering, dressed as Mme de la Vallière, Louis XIV's mistress, and wearing a chiffon mask painted to look like that seventeenth-century beauty. Racine redivivus was there courtesy of M. de Beaumont. There was a lavishly Oriental *entrée* designed by Bébé Bérard for three Parisian beauties — the court of the Sun King had been partial to a mythical East. Schiaparelli made astonishingly sumptuous costumes for a "Persian Embassy," reminiscent of the one who came to Versailles in 1715, which included her own daughter, Eve Curie, and the famously beautiful princesse Poniatowska. Brenda Balfour appeared as Louis XIV and Daisy de Cabrol, her cousin, as his Queen; Chanel was Watteau's *Indifférent,* all androgyne dress and pastel silks. The young Balenciaga, who had just begun to work in Paris, contributed a ruby-red velvet Velázquez costume that was thought to be both the most handsome and, amazingly, the most wearable of all. Unquestionably the most spectacular of the guests was the baron Maurice de Rothschild. Dressed as the Turkish sultan Bajazet, one of Racine's heroes, he was covered with his mother's famous diamonds as well as his even more spectacular collection of Benvenuto Cellini jewels.

There had always been a number of balls in June and July, but in 1939 party giving became frantic: night after night, every night, new fetes were held, each more splendid than the last. So there was a charity ball at the Eiffel Tower where a group of fashionable young women dressed by Schiaparelli in bustles and plumed headdresses danced a quadrille; and a Louis-Philippe ball in which the guests dressed in the fashions of the 1830s and waltzed in the garden (it was not raining that night); and a blue and white ball for Princess Alexandra of Greece, the Greek flag being blue and white; and a Diadems and Decorations ball given by a rich American, Mrs. Louise Macy, which took place in the Hôtel Salé, now the Picasso Museum, but then a deserted and semiruined building, done up for the night, complete with running water and bathrooms.

Of course, Lady Mendl had no intention of doing less than her friends, so she, too, gave a ball; and, just like the year before, the garden of the Villa Trianon was lavishly decorated — rather a waste since the cold weather mostly kept people indoors. The question was, of course, what she could do to top the circus and ponies of the previous year. The answer, the guests realized as they arrived, was obvious: elephants, three of them, which were not ridden — the Maharani of Kapurthala gave it a try — but which were certainly spectacular, though no more so than the buffet. One of the pleasures of the evening was the presence of many English visitors, seldom seen in Paris and specially invited by the hostess. That made her ball international; so the baronne Philippe de Rothschild gave a ball that was quintessentially Parisian; she invited only the most elegant people in the city and no foreign guests to speak of. And then there was the ball which ended the season.

It was given by Juliusz Lukasiewicz, the Polish ambassador, and everyone was there, from Bullitt to the German ambassador, from Daladier (and Mme de Crussol) to a bevy of duchesses. The house and garden were splendidly decorated; many of the guests had come from Poland for the occasion and proved that the famously beautiful Polish women had lost none of their attractions, that the famously elegant Polish officers danced as beautifully as ever. There were waltzes and mazurkas; there was a splendid supper; then, around three in the morning, "the Poles came together for a wild quadrille; the Ambassador was leading the dancers; fireworks exploded at the end of the garden, and the dancers stopped."[31] Soon, more than just the dancers stopped, and more than just fireworks exploded. Less than two months after the end of this Paris season, the most brilliant anyone remembered, the war began.

All through that last brilliant moment, in fact, the war had come visibly closer, day by day. If the Tout-Paris danced so often, so frantically, it was because they knew that soon they would not dance at all. As for the government, it drifted along, going from bad surprise to bad surprise. When, on August 21, Pierre Lazareff, the editor in chief of *Paris-Soir,* heard that Stalin and Hitler had just concluded a nonaggression pact, he telephoned Bonnet. "'I have heard nothing of this,' the Minister said, 'wait a minute.' At the other end of the phone there was a silence. I heard a rustle of paper, then again Georges Bonnet's voice, now sounding highly distressed: 'Havas [the news agency] has just given me the same information. I think it must be true. If you hear anything more, I would appreciate your telling me.' . . . The next day . . . , I learned that Daladier, on the other hand, had lost no sleep over the news. Georges Bonnet had called him immediately to tell him about the pact, but he had answered: 'It is a false rumor, my dear Bonnet. It's just an idiocy, completely improbable.'"[32] Indeed, three days later, the Premier told his cabinet that he thought it was still possible to reach a mutual defense agreement with the Soviet Union; and, at the last, his only reaction was to forbid the publication of the Communist newspapers.

After that, it seemed obvious to almost everyone that the war would come within days. Not to Georges Bonnet, though. The foreign minister, having sold out one ally already, was now preparing to give Poland the same treatment. At that same cabinet meeting of August 24, Reynaud denounced him for having called Warsaw (once again using lines tapped by the Germans) to ask the Poles to do nothing irreparable should Hitler seize Danzig. At that, Daladier reprimanded Bonnet; but it would have taken more than that to change the foreign minister's policy.

By the twenty-seventh, however, Daladier had finally learned his lesson. In order to stop Bonnet from secretly betraying Poland, he called in Lukasiewicz and told him: "I definitely ask you to communicate with me directly on any matter you consider important."[33] At least, that seemed to guarantee that French policy, whatever it might be, would not be in Bonnet's hands. Still, the foreign minister made one last effort. On August 31, Mussolini, in a reedition of Munich, offered France and Great Britain the holding of a conference on September 5. At the Council that considered this, Bonnet naturally pleaded for acceptance; and even at this late date he might still have had his way had it not been for a letter from

François Coulondre, the French ambassador in Berlin. "I have learned from the best sources that Hitler is hesitating, that the party is undecided and that [police] reports note an increasing popular dissatisfaction," Coulondre wrote.[34] He could not have been more thoroughly mistaken; but his letter at least convinced Daladier, and with him a majority of the cabinet, not to accept the Italian proposal. More, the Premier pointed out, Munich had made it clear that Hitler's word was not to be trusted: it was thus senseless to reach an agreement with him over Danzig. That, however, still did not mean that France was prepared to reject the Italian proposal outright; it merely decided to wait for the outcome of the current German-Polish talks.

Naturally, these failed to produce a solution. The Poles refused to cave in; Hitler would not modify his demands. On September 1, the Wehrmacht entered Poland and the French army was mobilized, despite Bonnet's arguments for a further wait. Even then, Daladier was unwilling to declare war. He asked the hastily recalled Chamber to vote emergency credits to cover outlays resulting from the international situation. The next day, with the British pressure intensifying, Daladier turned down Bonnet's plea to do nothing for three more days; and on September 3, the Franco-British ultimatum to Germany having expired, France and Great Britain found themselves at war with the Third Reich.

Finally, after all those fears and all those betrayals, the war had come. Dreaded by all alike, it had proved unstoppable. Now, when it actually began, the government, and with it the rest of the French, felt as if they were living the kind of nightmare in which you try to run in order to escape a terrifying monster, but can go no faster than the slowest walk. In many ways, people tried to pretend that nothing had happened. The constitution notwithstanding, Daladier never asked the Chamber and Senate to declare war on Germany: he merely requested supplementary credits; and after that, he was careful never to order an attack.

So month after month passed. In Paris, the theaters and cinemas remained open, as did the salons. The ministers still went to lunch parties where they repeated all the secret information they had sworn to keep to themselves. Mme de Portes's intrigues continued, more frantically than ever, until she finally triumphed: Daladier fell on March 20, 1940, and was succeeded by Paul Reynaud, who came into office by a plurality of just one vote. It seemed almost reassuring: if the old cabinet could fall, and the new one totter just like in the old days, perhaps the war did not matter so much after all. Rumors abounded, which said that a compromise peace was in the making: Hitler would be allowed to keep Poland,

and all else would be as before. Neither Daladier nor Reynaud were fool-ish enough to entertain that thought, but much of the Tout-Paris clung to it as the ultimate hope. As for the millions of mobilized Frenchmen, many of them were sitting in the bunkers of the Maginot Line, and they were just plain bored.

For years, Paris had lived in fear of the war; now it had come, but it did not seem to matter. Certainly, except for the men who had been mo-bilized, it did not alter the life of the city. Still, the oppressive feeling that a disaster loomed grew stronger every day. Having failed to maintain the peace, France seemed unwilling — unable, some said — to fight the war. Clearly, something needed to be done; and it was Hitler who did it. On May 10, 1940, the Wehrmacht invaded Holland, Belgium, and Luxem-bourg; on May 15, Holland capitulated, and Queen Wilhelmina, accom-panied by the government, fled to London; on May 21, Amiens and Arras, in northern France, fell to the enemy; on May 28, the King of Belgium capitulated; on June 6, the front was broken at the Somme; on June 14, the German army occupied a virtually deserted Paris.

For the city, after so much brilliance, after so many efforts at ignoring reality, it was the end. Under its new masters, the capital was just another Nazi victim. It had to bear a final insult, though. When Marshal Pétain set up his government, it was in Vichy, and, to that extent, that old-fashioned spa replaced Paris as the capital of France; but even when, in the summer of 1944, the Liberation came, it was not the same. After so many years during which it had, in many ways, been the center of the universe, Paris had become a capital like most others, livelier than Brus-sels, less important than Washington. It was just as well, after all, that it had been shining so brightly throughout the thirties. Those fireworks, artistic, intellectual, social, did not outlast the decade, but while they roared, full of color and dazzle, across the darkening skies, they thrilled all who saw them.

# EPILOGUE

THE WAR changed not just the regime but almost everyone's life. Parliament was suspended by the new regime of Marshal Pétain. The former commander in chief, now in his eighties, became Premier, then dictator. He surrounded himself with reactionaries who welcomed the defeat because it enabled them to impose their policies on France, promulgated anti-Semitic laws, and collaborated with the Nazis. Then, at the Liberation it was General de Gaulle who governed France. Before the war, he had been a mere major best known for being Paul Reynaud's military adviser. As for Pétain, he was tried in 1945, found guilty of treason, and condemned to die; de Gaulle commuted his sentence, and he finally died, well into his nineties, in a prison cell.

The politicians of the Third Republic fared better. Herriot, out of a job, spent most of the war hiding in a comfortably appointed lunatic asylum; and when he emerged, it was to become Speaker of the National Assembly under the Fourth Republic. Neither Daladier nor Reynaud did as well: after being imprisoned by the Pétain government, they, too, reentered politics, but they could not regain their former power. Daladier was elected a Deputy from his old constituency, but never again entered a government; Reynaud was once finance minister for just two days. Tardieu died during the war. Flandin was briefly foreign minister under Pétain; he was arrested after the Liberation, found not guilty of collaborating, but never reentered politics. Chautemps thought it prudent to remove himself; he spent most of the rest of his life abroad. Bonnet crossed over to Switzerland and remained there after the Liberation, writing wholly distorted, self-justifying memoirs. He died in the late forties.

That leaves two extreme cases. Blum was arrested on Pétain's orders, charged with responsibility for the defeat of France, and condemned to life imprisonment without being convicted. Eventually, the Nazis seized him from his French jail and transferred him to one of their concentration camps, where he was treated better than most because it was thought he might eventually be exchanged for German prisoners. He was freed in 1945 and returned to France with a martyr's aura, to become the grand old man of French politics. He was Premier again for the thirty days between the end of the temporary regime and the start of the new constitutional order, then happily retired to his house outside Paris.

Laval, seeing 1940 as a revenge for 1936, became Pétain's prime minister. He willfully and happily collaborated with the Nazis. "I wish for a German victory," he told the French in 1942 — and fled to Germany when France was liberated. As Germany itself was overrun by the allied armies, he sought refuge in Franco's Spain but was turned over to the French government. He was tried, very properly convicted of treason, and shot.

For the writers of the thirties, too, the war brought great changes. Malraux, true to his ideals, fought with the Resistance, turned into an ardent Gaullist, and eventually became minister of culture in 1959. He was responsible for the law stipulating that the facades of Parisian buildings must be cleaned every ten years, so that we once again look at a white city.

Gide, who moved to the south of France in 1940, survived the Occupation and went on, after the war, to become the patriarch of French letters. Giraudoux died just before the Liberation in 1944. Maurras's *L'Action française* went right on denouncing the Jews throughout the Occupation; even worse, it often listed specific hiding places, thus facilitating many arrests. At the Liberation, Maurras was arrested, tried, and convicted. Because of his age — he was seventy-six — he was not executed. He died in jail, as did Pétain, who was spared for the same reason.

Céline greeted the defeat of France with a mixture of glee — he had been right, after all — and sorrow. A star of the official circles in Nazi-occupied Paris, a frequent guest at the German embassy, he turned out to be no more respectful of Hitler than of anyone else and thus proved rather an embarrassment to his new masters. Prudently, however, he left with them in 1944, then found refuge in Denmark, where he was preventively kept in jail for several years. In 1951, after the French National Assembly voted a general amnesty, he returned to France. He then lived long enough to write three masterpieces, *D'un Château l'autre, Nord,* and *Rigodon.* Today still, he is considered to be in the very first rank of French writers.

Stravinsky moved to the United States, where he spent much of the rest of his long life. So, for the duration of the war, did André Breton, who discovered the art of the Northwest Indians in the course of his visits to New York's American Museum of Natural History. Max Ernst, who, as a German refugee, was in danger of his life, was rescued by Peggy Guggenheim, who married him and got him to the United States. The couple soon separated. Ernst met a beautiful and talented American painter, Dorothea Tanning; together they moved to Arizona, a state whose landscapes, so Ernst-like in themselves, soon found a place in his work. Miró retreated to Barcelona, then to Palma de Mallorca, and continued to paint masterpieces until his death in 1982.

Others moved to the United States as well. Jean-Michel Frank, who settled in New York, found he could not live away from Paris; he committed suicide in 1942. The *Normandie* burned and sank at her pier in the Hudson. Josephine Baker, on the other hand, stayed, joined the Resistance, and received a bevy of medals after the Liberation. She was still singing and dancing in the sixties. Mistinguett, who was her senior by many years, retired and died soon after the war. The Casino de Paris and the Folies-Bergère never stopped prospering.

For the Parisians, the war was a fearful time. As the years passed, the shortages of everything, from food to electricity to medicine, grew more acute. The Gestapo was present everywhere, and so were German soldiers. Still, a number of people showed no sign of minding this. There were out-and-out collaborationists, of course, who lived lushly and prospered greatly; but also people like Cocteau, who made many new German friends, and lent his name and prestige to a number of German-sponsored cultural events. They were not collaborationists in the strictest sense, since their activities were limited to attending parties given by the Germans; they denounced no one and, strictly speaking, committed no crime.

Whether their behavior was honorable, or even minimally decent, is another question. Amazingly, Marie-Laure de Noailles, whose father had been Jewish, continued to give parties throughout the Occupation; many of her guests were now German. Then, with minimal awkwardness at the Liberation, as if what she had done somehow did not count (it helped that some of her husband's family were prominent in the Resistance), she resumed her social position in postwar Paris, and gave balls to which invitations were as eagerly sought as ever. Janet Flanner, who returned to the United States in 1940, followed the American troops back to France and lived on to write many more "Letters from Paris." Schiaparelli, who closed her couture house in 1940, reopened it after the war; eventually, Chanel did the same.

Of all the great figures of the thirties, though, none remained so unalterably himself, so absolutely impervious to the convulsions of war and politics as Picasso. All through the Occupation, bravely, he stayed in Paris, unscathed although he never pretended to approve of either Pétain or the Nazis. As before, his work came first. Eventually, in the fifties, he moved to the south of France; and until his death remained the greatest painter of the age.

As for the thirties themselves, seen in retrospect, they quickly took on the form of a nightmare. The Depression, the Sixth of February, 1934, the many incompetent governments, the rise of Hitler, the final collapse in 1940, gave the decade a bad name. Eventually, Art Deco, long despised, became fashionable once more: today the great furniture of the thirties sells for huge prices. Fairly soon, too, Blum and the Popular Front came to be seen as the one bright interval in ten years of gloom and decadence.

Of course, the works and lives of the artists, writers, composers, architects, and designers who worked during the decade have all been studied since then; but that last brilliant moment for Paris as a world capital, the thirties themselves, has been largely ignored. It is time, once again, for us to know that before the end the City of Light glowed as brightly as ever before in its dazzling history. The thirties, laden as they were with justified gloom, were also a time of extraordinary achievement, a time when in a final and poignant burst of genius, the Parisians, from Picasso to Schiaparelli's seamstresses, from Giraudoux to Etienne de Beaumont, proved that they were still able to tell the world just what civilization should be.

# NOTES

## CHAPTER ONE

1. *Le Figaro,* 2 March 1936.
2. Eluard, *Poèmes,* 104.
3. Penrose, *Picasso,* 282.
4. *Cahiers d'Art,* 7 October 1935.
5. *The New Yorker,* 2 February 1936.
6. Ibid., 29 February 1936.
7. *Le Figaro Illustré,* January 1936.
8. Ibid.
9. Ibid., February 1936.
10. Ibid., 4 March 1936.
11. *The New Yorker,* 28 March 1936.
12. Ibid., 26 May 1936.
13. *L'Illustration,* 22 January 1936.
14. Fouquières, 186.
15. *L'Illustration,* 25 January 1936.
16. *Le Figaro,* 7 March 1936.
17. *L'Illustration,* 4 April 1936.
18. *The New Yorker,* 14 March 1936.
19. Gide, *Journal,* 1245.
20. Colette, *Mes Apprentissages,* 107–108.
21. *Le Figaro,* 29 February 1936.
22. *L'Illustration,* 4 April 1936.
23. *The New Yorker,* 11 April 1936.
24. *Le Temps,* 18 January 1936.
25. Soulié, 474.
26. *L'Oeuvre,* 21 January 1936.
27. Ibid., 22 January 1936.
28. *Le Temps,* 10 January 1936.
29. *Gringoire,* 10 January 1936.
30. Zay, *Souvenirs,* 196.
31. *Le Populaire,* 22 January 1936.
32. Tabouis, 284.
33. *L'Action française,* 19 February 1936.
34. Lazareff, 301.

35. *Le Populaire,* 9 October 1935.
36. *Le Temps,* 9 March 1936.
37. Zay, *Souvenirs,* 66.
38. Lazareff, 303.
39. Bonnefous, V, 386.
40. Lazareff, 303 ff.
41. Reynaud, II, 58.
42. *L'Oeuvre,* 9 March 1936.
43. *Le Temps,* 9 March 1936.
44. *Je Suis Partout,* 14 March 1936.
45. Ibid., 28 March 1936.
46. Ibid., 11 April 1936.
47. *L'Oeuvre,* 22 March 1936.

## CHAPTER TWO

1. Wineapple, 116.
2. Bonnefous, V, 160.
3. *Le Temps,* 1 January 1930.
4. *Le Figaro,* 1 January 1930.
5. *The New Yorker,* 31 May 1930.
6. *Le Figaro Illustré,* January 1930.
7. White, 89.
8. *Le Figaro,* 31 January 1930.
9. *Le Figaro Illustré,* June 1930.
10. Ibid., February 1930.
11. Ibid., May 1930.
12. Maxwell, 158–159.
13. *The New Yorker,* 26 July 1930.
14. Smith, 247.
15. *L'Illustration,* 4 October 1930.
16. Ibid., 13 December 1930.
17. Colloque Blum, 28.
18. Lapie, 10–12.
19. Coulondre, 14.
20. Aubert, 43.
21. Rupied, 112.
22. Weiss, *Mémoires,* II, 290.

## CHAPTER THREE

1. Faucigny-Lucinge, 98.
2. Ibid., 99.

3. Martin du Gard, 206 ff.
4. Rose, 146.
5. Ibid., 147.
6. *The New Yorker,* 1 November 1930.
7. *L'Action française,* 1 January 1932.
8. Ibid., 3 January 1932.
9. *Le Temps,* 19 April 1932.
10. Allain, 426.
11. *L'Action française,* 17 April 1932.
12. Zay, *Carnets secrets,* 153.
13. Maxwell, 155.
14. Fouquières, 181.
15. Smith, 248 ff.
16. White, 92.
17. Chanaux, 9.
18. *Le Figaro Illustré,* October 1932.
19. Ibid., April 1932.
20. Ibid., November 1932.
21. Herriot, II, 280.
22. Ibid., 308.
23. Céline, *Voyage,* I, 489.

## CHAPTER FOUR

1. *The New Yorker,* 22 October 1932.
2. Paris-Couture-Années-Trente, 228.
3. Fouquières, 247–248.
4. Delperrié de Bayac, 74.
5. Bonnefous, V, 139.
6. Paul-Boncour, II, 342.
7. *Mantes-Républicain,* 8 February 1933.
8. Berstein, II, 226.
9. Pertinax, I, 105.
10. Soulié, 437.
11. Lazareff, 188.
12. Jeanneney, 484.
13. Lazareff, 293–295.
14. *The New Yorker,* 5 December 1931.
15. Ibid., 5 November 1932.
16. Ibid., 21 January 1933.
17. Russell, 108.
18. Penrose, *Picasso,* 244.

CHAPTER FIVE

1. *The New Yorker*, 17 February 1934.
2. Kessel, 7 ff.
3. Charlier and Montarron, 182.
4. *Le Canard enchaîné*, 12 January 1934.
5. *Le Temps*, 7 January 1934.
6. *L'Action française*, 7 January 1934.
7. Ibid., 9 January 1934.
8. Ibid., 10 January 1934.
9. Ibid., 13 January 1934.
10. Ibid., 22 January 1934.
11. *The New Yorker*, 3 February 1934.
12. Berstein, II, 119.
13. Herriot, II, 375.
14. Ibid., 377–378.
15. *The New Yorker*, 20 January 1934.
16. Faucigny-Lucinge, 132–134.
17. Steegmuller, 407–408.
18. *The New Yorker*, 12 May 1934.
19. White, 101.
20. *Le Figaro Illustré*, July 1934.
21. Ibid., November 1934.
22. *The New Yorker*, 26 May 1934.
23. Ibid., 25 November 1934.
24. Charlier and Montarron, 258.
25. *The New Yorker*, 17 March 1934.
26. Crouy-Chanel, 197.

CHAPTER SIX

1. *The New Yorker*, 1 September 1934.
2. Céline, *Mort*, 2.
3. *Cahiers de l'Herne*, 3:31.
4. Ibid., 5:28.
5. Ibid., 5:36–37.
6. *L'Action française*, 25 January 1934.
7. Céline, *Mea Culpa*, 1.
8. Ibid., 14–15.
9. Ibid., 18.
10. Ibid., 25.
11. Ibid., 38.

12. Reynaud, I, 368.
13. Delperrié de Bayac, 84.
14. Reynaud, I, 370.
15. Ibid., 369.
16. Ibid., 370 ff.
17. Ibid., 439.
18. *Le Bourbonnais républicain*, 5 October 1934.
19. *Le Figaro Illustré*, January 1935.
20. Faucigny-Lucinge, 87.
21. *The New Yorker*, 22 December 1934.
22. Ibid., 5 January 1935.

CHAPTER SEVEN

1. Reynaud, I, 382.
2. *The New Yorker*, 8 December 1934.
3. Ibid., 22 December 1934.
4. Rose, 163.
5. *The New Yorker*, 8 December 1934.
6. Ibid., 5 December 1936.
7. Ibid., 25 May 1935.
8. Brasillach, 235–236.
9. Ibid., 282–283.
10. *Je Suis Partout*, 10 November 1934.
11. *L'Action française*, 29 April 1936.
12. Brasillach, 275–276.
13. Cited by Madsen, 100.
14. Ibid.
15. Malraux, *Le Condition humaine*, 271.
16. Ibid., 80.
17. Ibid., 360.
18. Ibid., 221.
19. Cited by Madsen, 160.
20. *The New Yorker*, 20 July 1935.
21. Cited by Madsen, 172.
22. Faucigny-Lucinge, 103.
23. Fouquières, 214.
24. Reynaud, I, 385.
25. Flandin, *Discours*, 26.
26. Bonnefous, V, 336.

27. Weiss, *Ce que femme veut,* 142.
28. *Le Populaire,* 7 June 1935.
29. Herriot, II, 551.
30. *Le Temps,* 9 June 1935.
31. Tabouis, 216.
32. Lazareff, 257.
33. Ibid.
34. *Je Suis Partout,* 7 December 1935.
35. *L'Action française,* 13 October 1935.
36. Bonnefous, V, 365.
37. Blum, *Oeuvres,* IV, Part 1, 132.
38. *Le Populaire,* 28 December 1935.
39. Delperrié de Bayac, 144.

### CHAPTER EIGHT

1. Faucigny-Lucinge, 115–116.
2. *The New Yorker,* 6 June 1936.
3. Ibid., 4 July 1936.
4. Ibid., 26 September 1936.
5. Ibid., 20 June 1936.
6. *L'Action française,* 9 April 1936.
7. Ibid., 1 June 1936.
8. Ibid., 5 June 1936.
9. *Le Populaire,* 1 June 1936.
10. Ibid., 11 May 1936.
11. *The New Yorker,* 6 June 1936.
12. Lazareff, 326.
13. *The New Yorker,* 20 June 1936.
14. *Le Populaire,* 28 November 1934.
15. Reynaud, I, 429.
16. Ibid., 434.
17. Moch, *Le Front populaire,* 125–126.
18. *Le Populaire,* 27 May 1936.
19. Blum, *Oeuvres,* V, 259.
20. *Le Temps,* 6 June 1936.
21. Blum, *L'Exercice,* 47.
22. Blum, *Oeuvres,* IV, Part 1, 270–271.
23. Delperrié de Bayac, 273.
24. Mendès-France, 172.
25. Gamelin, II, 219.
26. Colloque Blum, 154.

27. Ibid., 38.
28. Ibid., 40.
29. *Je Suis Partout,* 13 June 1936.
30. *Le Temps,* 9 June and 1 July 1936.

### CHAPTER NINE

1. Béhar, 261.
2. Ibid., 234.
3. *Minotaure,* December 1934.
4. Zay, *Souvenirs,* 244.
5. Blum, *Oeuvres,* IV, Part 2, 374 ff.
6. Moch, *Entretiens,* 195.
7. Blum, *Exercice du pouvoir,* 178 ff.
8. Bullitt, 198.
9. Ickes, III, 124.
10. Bullitt, 178–179.
11. Ibid., 173 ff.
12. *Le Populaire,* 23 November 1936.
13. *Le Temps,* 20 November 1936.
14. *Le Populaire,* 23 November 1936.
15. Bullitt, 179.
16. Ibid., 185–186.
17. Berstein, II, 486.
18. Flanner, 51.

### CHAPTER TEN

1. *Le Populaire,* 14 February 1937.
2. *The New Yorker,* 23 January 1937.
3. Gide, *Retour,* 76.
4. Bullitt, 206.
5. Delperrié de Bayac, 347.
6. Zay, *Souvenirs,* 156.
7. Colloque Blum, 35.
8. *Le Temps,* 17 June 1937.
9. Blum, *Oeuvres,* IV, Part 2, 27.
10. Moch, *Entretiens,* 236.
11. *The New Yorker,* 14 August 1937.
12. Bullitt, 213.
13. Lazareff, 400.
14. Ibid., 401.
15. *The New Yorker,* 19 June 1937.

16. Ibid., 28 August 1937.
17. *New York Herald Tribune, Guide,* 22.
18. Penrose, *Picasso,* 305.
19. Read, "*Guernica.*"
20. *New York Herald Tribune, Guide,* 25.
21. Le Corbusier, 3.
22. Céline, *Bagatelles,* 53–54.
23. Ibid., 56.
24. Ibid., 65.
25. Ibid., 86.
26. Céline, *L'Ecole,* 12.
27. Ibid., 15.
28. Ibid., 20.
29. Ibid., 25.
30. Ibid., 100.
31. Ibid., 114.
32. Ibid., 163.
33. Lacouture, 230.
34. Ibid., 232.
35. Malraux, *L'Espoir,* 104–106.
36. Ibid., 185–186.
37. *The New Yorker,* 30 January 1937.

CHAPTER ELEVEN

1. *The New Yorker,* 15 January 1938.
2. *Vogue,* 15 August 1938.
3. Ibid.
4. *L'Echo de Paris,* 10 February 1938.
4. *L'Oeuvre,* 20 July 1938.
6. *Le Petit Parisien,* 18 July 1938.
7. *Paris-Soir,* 18 July 1938.
8. *Le Journal,* 19 July 1938.
9. Zay, *Souvenirs,* 412.
10. *Paris-Soir,* 22 July 1938.
11. Bonnet, I, 173.
12. The *Times* of London, 23 July 1938.
13. *The New Yorker,* 30 July 1938.
14. Zay, *Souvenirs,* 429.
15. Bullitt, 251.
16. Ibid., 252.
17. Paul-Boncour, III, 86.
18. Colloque Daladier, 75.

19. Paul-Boncour, III, 96 ff.
20. *L'Oeuvre,* 11 April 1938.
21. *Le Temps,* 22 August 1938.
22. Zay, *Souvenirs,* 122.
23. Bullitt, 256–257.
24. Lazareff, 57.
25. Ibid., 32.
26. Coulondre, 148–149.
27. Lukasiewicz, 100.
28. Lazareff, 55.
29. Coulondre, 145.
30. Bullitt, 282.
31. Ibid., 281.
32. Bonnet, I, 360–361.
33. Lukasiewicz, 125.
34. Zay, *Carnets secrets,* 3–4.
35. Ibid., 5.
36. *Je Suis Partout,* 16 September 1938.
37. *L'Action française,* 18, 27, 28 September 1938.
38. Bonnefous, VI, 426–427.
39. Raphael-Leygues, 199.
40. Lazareff, 71.
41. *Le Temps,* 1 October 1938.
42. *L'Oeuvre,* 1 October 1938.
43. *Le Populaire,* 1 October 1938.
44. *The New Yorker,* 2 October 1937.
45. Sadoul, 215.
46. Ibid.

CHAPTER TWELVE

1. Interview on TF1, 7 April 1975.
2. *The New Yorker,* 15 July 1939.
3. Brasillach, 304.
4. Bullitt, 287.
5. Lazareff, 113.
6. Bullitt, 324.
7. *Le Temps,* 17 March 1939.
8. Bullitt, 332.
9. Ibid., 335.
10. Lukasiewicz, 177.
11. Zay, *Souvenirs,* 46–47.

12. Blum, *Oeuvres,* IV, Part 2, 236–237.
13. *Vogue,* 20 May 1939.
14. Lazareff, 227.
15. *The New Yorker,* 29 April 1939.
16. *L'Oeuvre,* 4 January 1939.
17. *Flandin interpelle,* 9.
18. Bullitt, 313.
19. Ibid., 309–310.
20. Zay, *Souvenirs,* 51.
21. Bonnefous, VII, 42.
22. Zay, *Souvenirs,* 56.

23. *Le Populaire,* 16 April 1939.
24. *Le Pays socialiste,* 7 April 1939.
25. *L'Oeuvre,* 4 May 1939.
26. *Le Journal,* 30 June 1939.
27. Bonnefous, VII, 87.
28. Ibid., 97.
29. Bullitt, 338.
30. *The New Yorker,* 22 July 1939.
31. Fabre-Luce, 29.
32. Lazareff, 153.
33. Lukasiewicz, 263.
34. Bonnefous. VII, 103.

# BIBLIOGRAPHY

PERIODICALS

*L'Action française*
*Arts and Decoration*
*Le Bourbonnais républicain*
*Cahiers d'Art*
*Cahiers de l'Herne*
*Le Canard enchaîné*
*L'Echo de Paris*
*Le Figaro*
*Le Figaro Illustré*
*Gringoire*
*L'Illustration*
*Je Suis Partout*
*Le Journal*
*Mantes-Républicain*
*Minotaure*
*The New Yorker*
*L'Oeuvre*

*Paris-Soir*
*Le Pays socialiste*
*Le Petit Parisien*
*Le Populaire*
*Le Temps*
*The Times* (London)
*Vogue*

BOOKS AND OTHER
PUBLICATIONS

Allain, Jean-Claude. *Joseph Caillaux:
    L'Oracle*. Paris, 1981.
Aubert, Martin. *André Tardieu*. Paris,
    1957.
Béhar, Henri. *André Breton: Le grand
    indésirable*. Paris, 1990.
Berstein, Serge. *Histoire du parti radical*.
    Paris, 1980.

Blum, Léon. *Oeuvres.* Paris, 1948.
———. *L'Exercice du pouvoir.* Paris, 1938.
Bonnefous, Edouard. *Histoire politique de la Troisième République.* Paris, 1962.
Bonnet, Georges. *De Washington au Quai d'Orsay.* Geneva, 1946.
Brasillach, Robert. *Notre Avant-Guerre.* Paris, 1941.
Bullitt, Orville H. *For the President: Correspondence between F.D.R. and William C. Bullitt.* Boston, 1972.
Céline, Louis-Ferdinand. *Voyage au bout de la nuit.* Paris, 1933.
———. *Mort à crédit.* Paris, 1935.
———. *Mea Culpa.* Paris, 1936.
———. *Bagatelles pour un massacre.* Paris, 1937.
———. *L'Ecole des cadavres.* Paris, 1938.
Chanaux, Adolphe. *Jean-Michel Frank.* Paris, 1980.
Charlier, Jean-Michel, and Marcel Montarron. *Stavisky, Les secrets du scandale.* Paris, 1974.
Colette. *Mes Apprentissages.* Paris, 1936.
Colloque Blum. Fondation nationale des sciences politiques. *Colloque Léon Blum, chef de gouvernement 1936–1937.* Paris, 1967.
Colloque Daladier. René Rémond and Jeannine Bourdin, eds. *Colloque Edouard Daladier, chef de gouvernement.* Paris, 1975.
*Commission d'Enquête chargée de rechercher toutes les responsabilités politiques et administratives encourues depuis l'origine des affaires Stavisky.* Paris, Imprimerie de la Chambre des Députés, 1935.
Coulondre, François. *De Staline à Hitler.* Paris, 1950.
Crouy-Chanel, Etienne de. *Alexis Léger.* Paris, 1989.

Delperrié de Bayac, Jacques. *Histoire du Front populaire.* Paris, 1972.
Eluard, Paul. *Poèmes,* in *Poètes d'aujourd'hui.* Paris, 1958.
———. *Avenir de la poésie.* Paris, 1937.
Exposition Internationale Arts et Techniques. *Guide Officiel.* Paris, 1937.
Fabre-Luce, Alfred. *Journal de la France.* Paris, 1942.
Faucigny-Lucinge, Jean-Louis de. *Un gentilhomme cosmopolite.* Paris, 1990.
Fisch, Eberhard. *"Guernica" by Picasso.* New York, 1988.
Flandin, Pierre-Etienne. *Discours: Le Ministère Flandin.* Paris, 1935.
———. *Flandin interpelle le gouvernement sur la politique extérieure.* Paris, 1939.
Flanner, Janet. *Paris Was Yesterday.* New York, 1972.
Fondation nationale des sciences politiques. See *Colloque Blum.*
Fouquières, André de. *Cinquante ans de Panache.* Paris, 1951.
Gamelin, Général Maurice. *Servir.* Paris, 1947.
Gide, André. *Journal.* Paris, 1948.
———. *Retour de l'U.R.S.S.* Paris, 1936.
Halèvy, Daniel. *Une Année d'histoire.* Paris, 1938.
Herriot, Edouard. *Jadis.* Paris, 1952.
Ickes, Harold L. *The Secret Diary of Harold L. Ickes.* New York, 1953–54.
Jeanneney, Jean-Noël. *François de Wendel en République: L'Argent et le pouvoir 1914–1940.* Paris, 1976.
Kessel, Joseph. *Stavisky: L'Homme que j'ai connu.* Paris, 1974.
Lacouture, Jean. *André Malraux: Une Vie dans le siècle.* Paris, 1973.
Lapie, Pierre-Olivier. *De Léon Blum à de Gaulle.* Paris, 1971.

Lazareff, Pierre. *Dernière Edition*. New York, n.d. [1941].

Lebrun, Albert. *Témoignage*. Paris, 1946.

Le Corbusier [Charles Jeanneret-Gris]. *Des Canons, des munitions? Merci! Des logis, S.V.P.* Paris, 1937.

Lukasiewicz, Juliusz. *Diplomat in Paris 1936–1939*. New York, 1970.

Madsen, Axel. *Malraux: A Biography*. New York, 1976.

Malraux, André. *La Tentation de l'Occident*. Paris, 1926.

———. *Les Conquérants*. Paris, 1928.

———. *La Voie royale*. Paris, 1930.

———. *La Condition humaine*. Paris, 1933.

———. *Le Temps du mépris*. Paris, 1935.

———. *L'Espoir*. Paris, 1937.

Martin du Gard, Maurice. *Soirées de Paris*. Paris, 1932.

Maxwell, Elsa. *RSVP: Elsa Maxwell's Own Story*. Boston, 1954.

Mendès-France, Pierre. *La Vérité guidait leur pas*. Paris, 1970.

Moch, Jules. *Entretiens avec Léon Blum*. Paris, 1970.

———. *Le Front populaire, grande espérance*. Paris, 1971.

*New York Herald Tribune,* Paris Edition. *American Guide to Paris*. Paris, 1937.

*Paris-Couture-Années-Trente. Catalogue of the Exhibition at the Musée de la Mode et du Costume, Palais Galliéra*. Paris, 1987.

Paul-Boncour, Joseph. *Entre deux Guerres: Souvenirs sur la IIIème République*. Paris, 1945.

Penrose, Roland. *Picasso: His Life and Work*. Berkeley: University of California Press, 1981.

———. *Miró*. New York, 1969.

Pertinax. *Les Fossoyeurs*. Paris, 1946.

Raphael-Leygues, Jacques. *Chronique des années incertaines*. Paris, 1977.

Read, Herbert. "*Guernica*" in *London Bulletin,* October 1938.

Rémond, René, and Jeannine Bourdin. See *Colloque Daladier*.

Reynaud, Paul. *Mémoires*. Paris, 1960–1963.

Rose, Phyllis. *Jazz Cleopatra: Josephine Baker and Her Time*. New York, 1989.

Rupied, Jean. *Elysée 28–34*. Paris, 1952.

Russell, John. *Max Ernst: His Life and His Work*. New York, 1967.

Sadoul, Georges. *Dictionnaire des films*. Paris, 1974.

Sevran, Pascal. *Le Music-Hall français*. Paris, 1978.

Soulié, Michel. *La Vie politique d'Edouard Herriot*. Paris, 1962.

Smith, Jane S. *Elsie de Wolfe: A Life in the High Style*. New York, 1982.

Steegmuller, Francis. *Cocteau*. Boston, 1970.

Tabouis, Geneviève. *Vingt Ans de suspense diplomatique*. Paris, 1958.

Tardieu, André. *Sur la Pente*. Paris, 1935.

Waldberg, Patrick. *Max Ernst*. Paris, 1958.

Weber, Eugen. *Action française*. Stanford, CA, 1962.

Weber, Yves. *Les Idées politiques d'André Tardieu*. Nancy, 1967.

Weiss, Louise. *Mémoires d'une Européene*. Paris, 1969.

———. *Ce que femme veut*. Paris, 1954.

White, Palmer. *Elsa Schiaparelli: Empress of Paris Fashion*. New York, 1986.

Wineapple, Brenda. *Genêt: A Biography of Janet Flanner*. New York, 1989.

Zay, Jean. *Carnets secrets*. Paris, 1942.

———. *Souvenirs et solitude*. Paris, 1945.

# INDEX